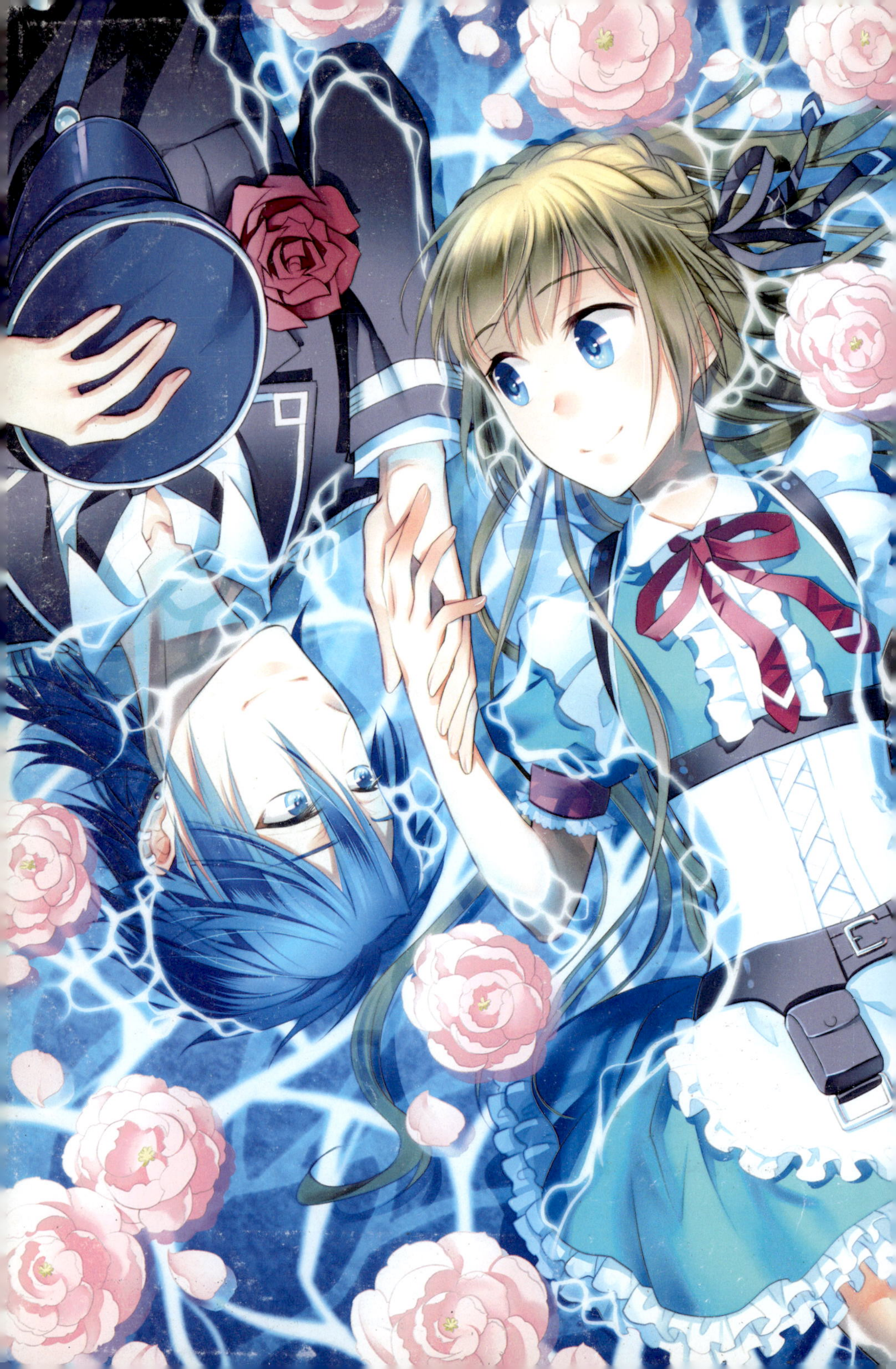

I AM ALICE

ALICE

The girl who is now in Makoto's body. Strong, likeable, and obsessed with weapons.

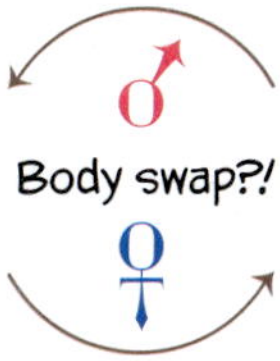

♂
Body swap?!
♀

MAKOTO

The protagonist, dragged into Wonderland--and into a girl's body. Essentially good-natured.

THE WHITE RABBIT

Captain in the King of Hearts' army. A responsible, brotherly type, he keeps the more chaotic elements in line.

THE HATTER

Soldier in the King of Hearts' army. Sharp-tongued and sadistic, he shouldn't be trusted too far.

THE CHESHIRE CAT

Palace cat who gradually transformed into a human boy. A playboy with a heart of gold.

THE DORMOUSE

A beautiful gentleman who left the army to indulge his love of naps. Far more dangerous than he appears.

DUM (TWEEDLEDUM)

Formerly under the direct supervision of the king, he is now the leader of the rebel army. Taciturn and serious.

Access BLobby from right here to play the social game *I Am Alice: Box x Boy!!*

The new *I Am Alice* game!! Get your original body back-- by winning a fashion contest?!

Click on the Login/ Registration button. Price: Free! Note: Charges may apply for some items.

http://gadget.blby.jp/6

THE KING OF HEARTS

The ruler of Wonderland. A ruthless, ambitious leader for whom the ends may very well justify any means...

THE KING OF HEART'S VALET

Loyal retainer trusted completely by the king.

The Story So Far

Makoto, all-around average high school student, is abruptly sucked into a mysterious library book and finds himself in the world of Wonderland--and body-swapped with Alice!! Makoto and Alice need to get back to their own worlds (and bodies/), so they head for a magical gate in the palace of the King of Hearts, along with the White Rabbit, the Hatter, the Dormouse, Cheshire, and Dum. After many adventures, they make it to the King of Hearts' palace, but at the sight of Makoto's (or rather, Alice's) face, the king becomes enraged and sends Makoto and the Hatter deep into the woods!

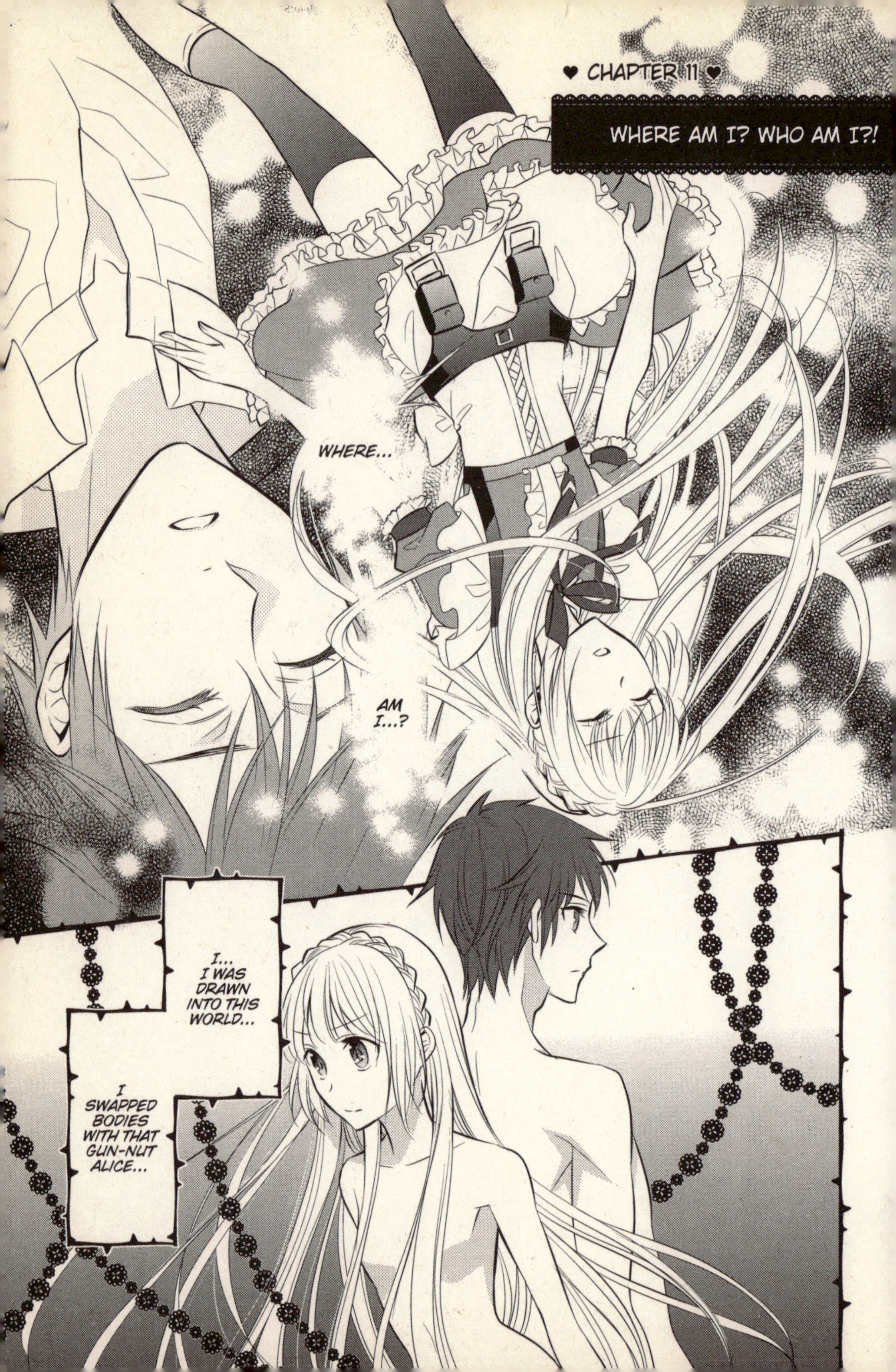
CHAPTER 11
WHERE AM I? WHO AM I?!
WHERE...
AM I...?
I... I WAS DRAWN INTO THIS WORLD...
I SWAPPED BODIES WITH THAT GUN-NUT ALICE...

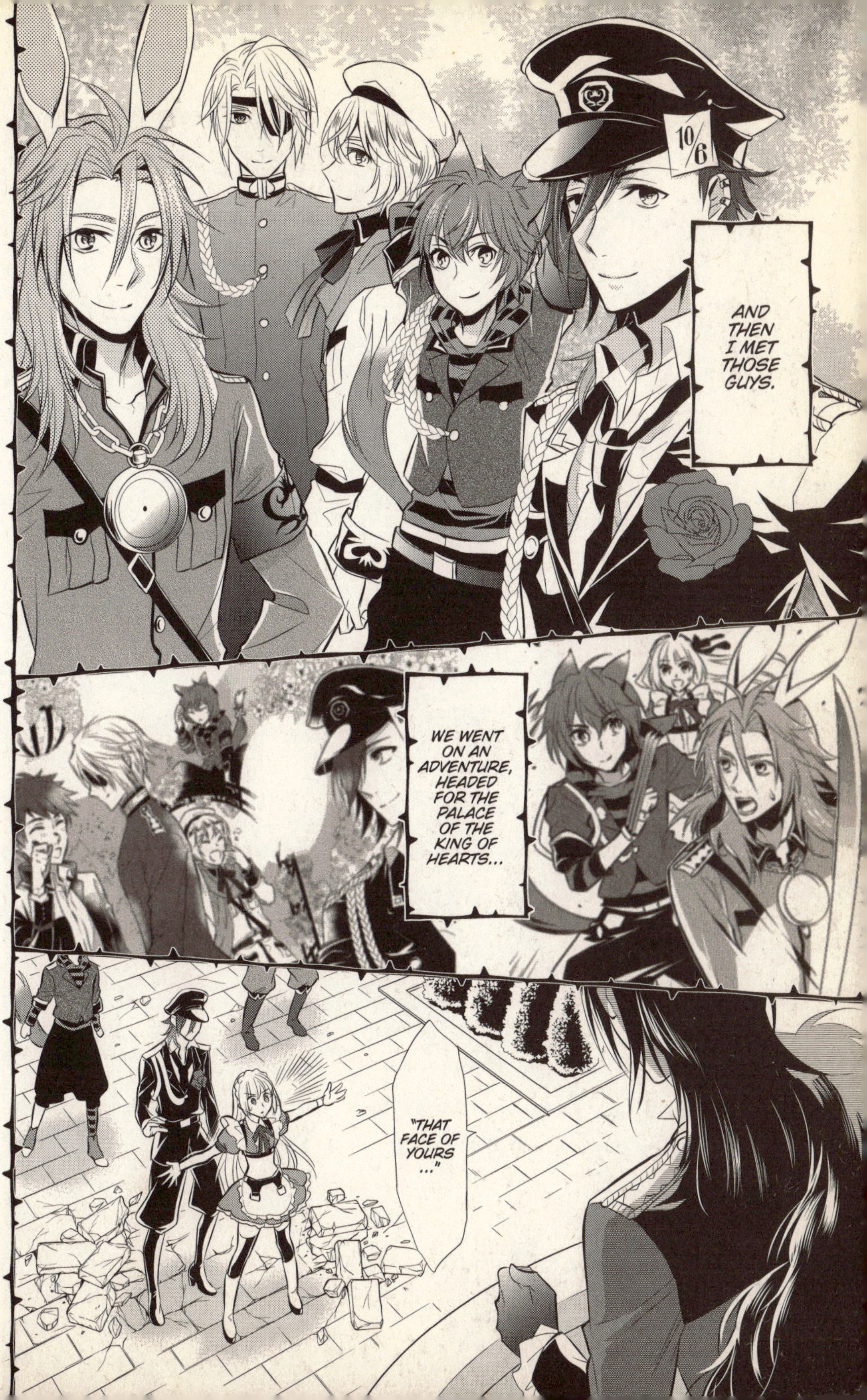
10/6
AND THEN I MET THOSE GUYS.
WE WENT ON AN ADVENTURE, HEADED FOR THE PALACE OF THE KING OF HEARTS...
"THAT FACE OF YOURS ..."

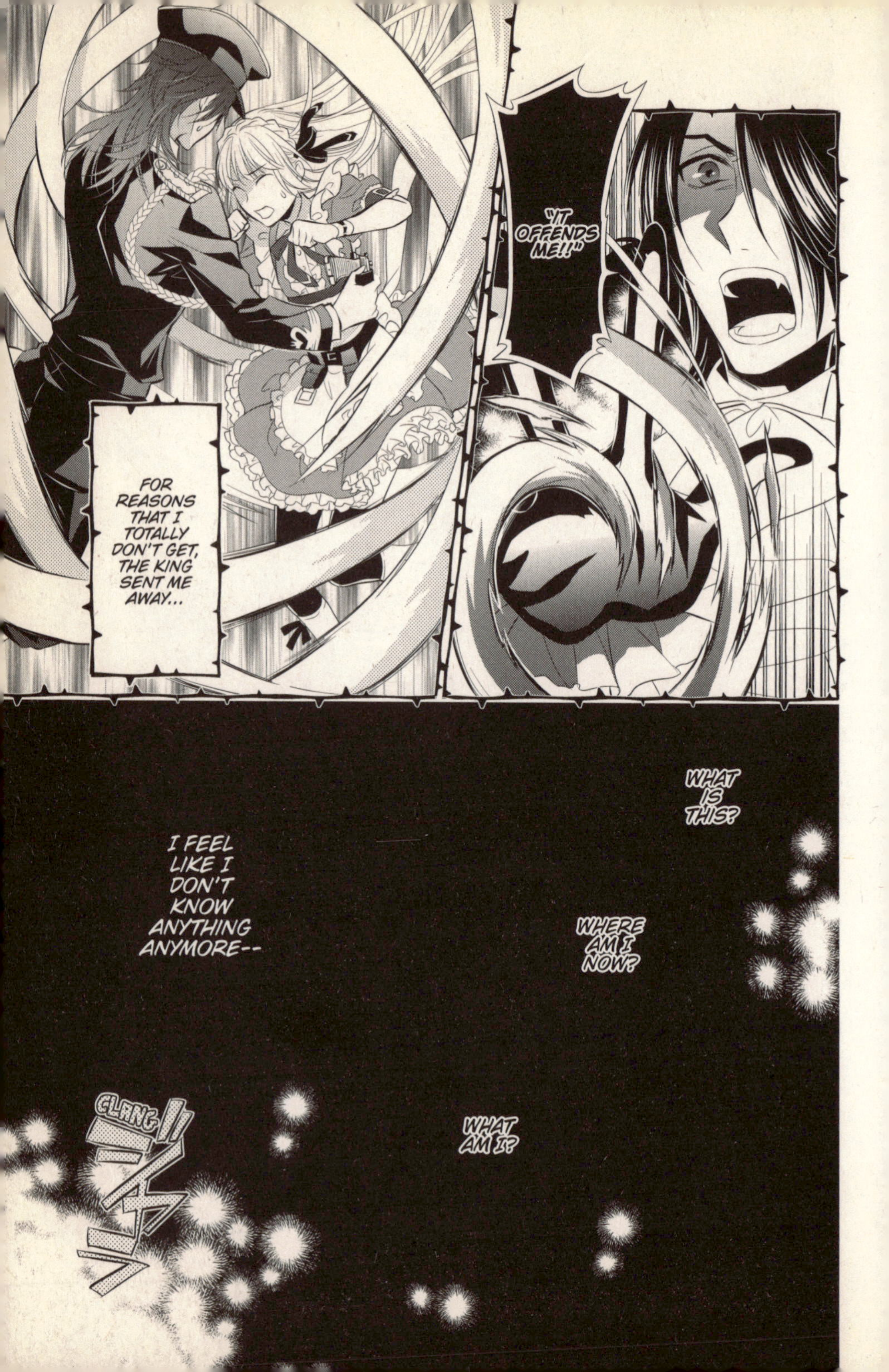
"IT OFFENDS ME!!"
FOR REASONS THAT I TOTALLY DON'T GET, THE KING SENT ME AWAY...
WHAT IS THIS?
WHERE AM I NOW?
I FEEL LIKE I DON'T KNOW ANYTHING ANYMORE--
WHAT AM I?
CLANG!!

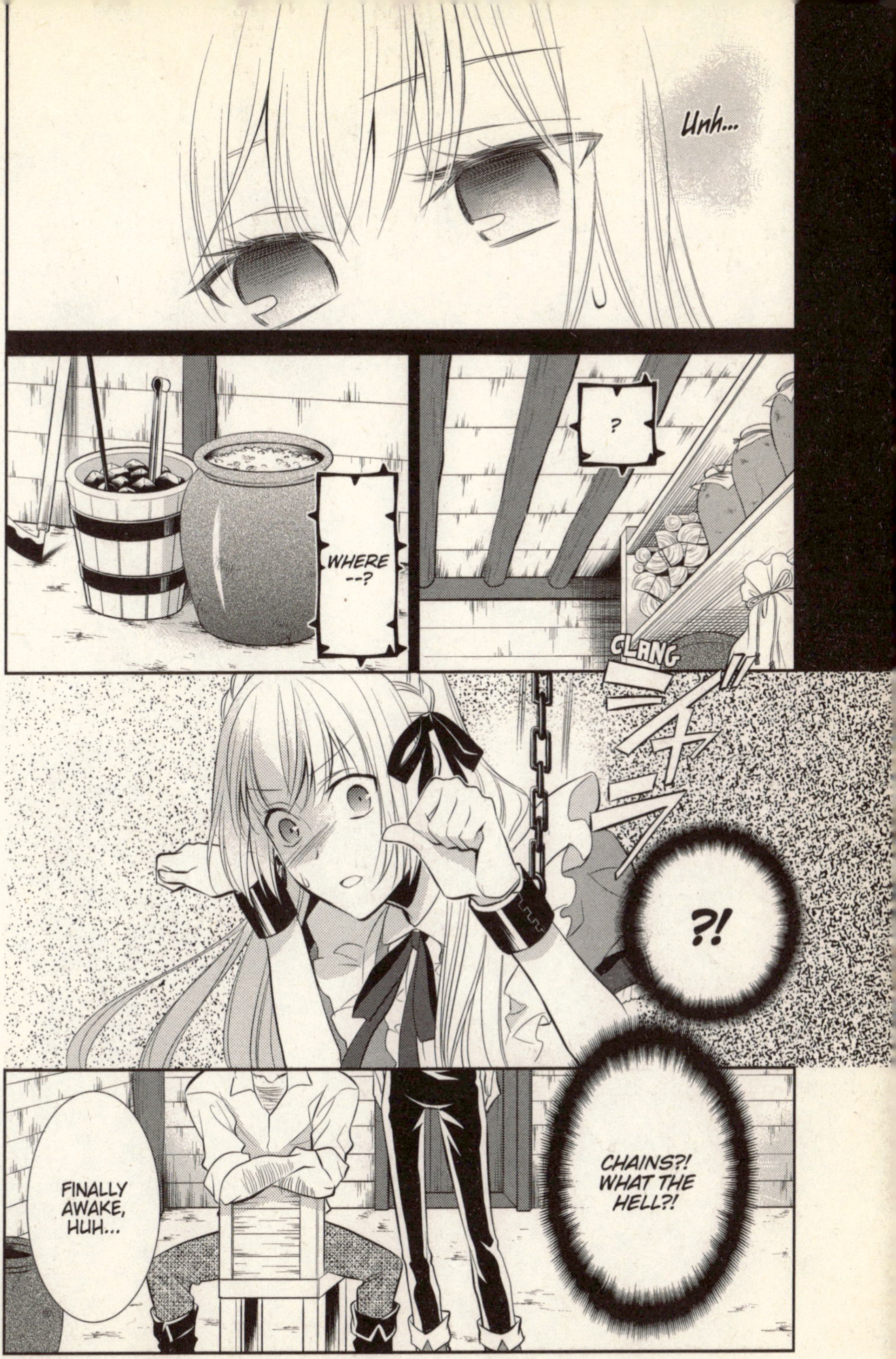
Unh...
?
WHERE --?
CLANG
?!
CHAINS?! WHAT THE HELL?!
FINALLY AWAKE, HUH...

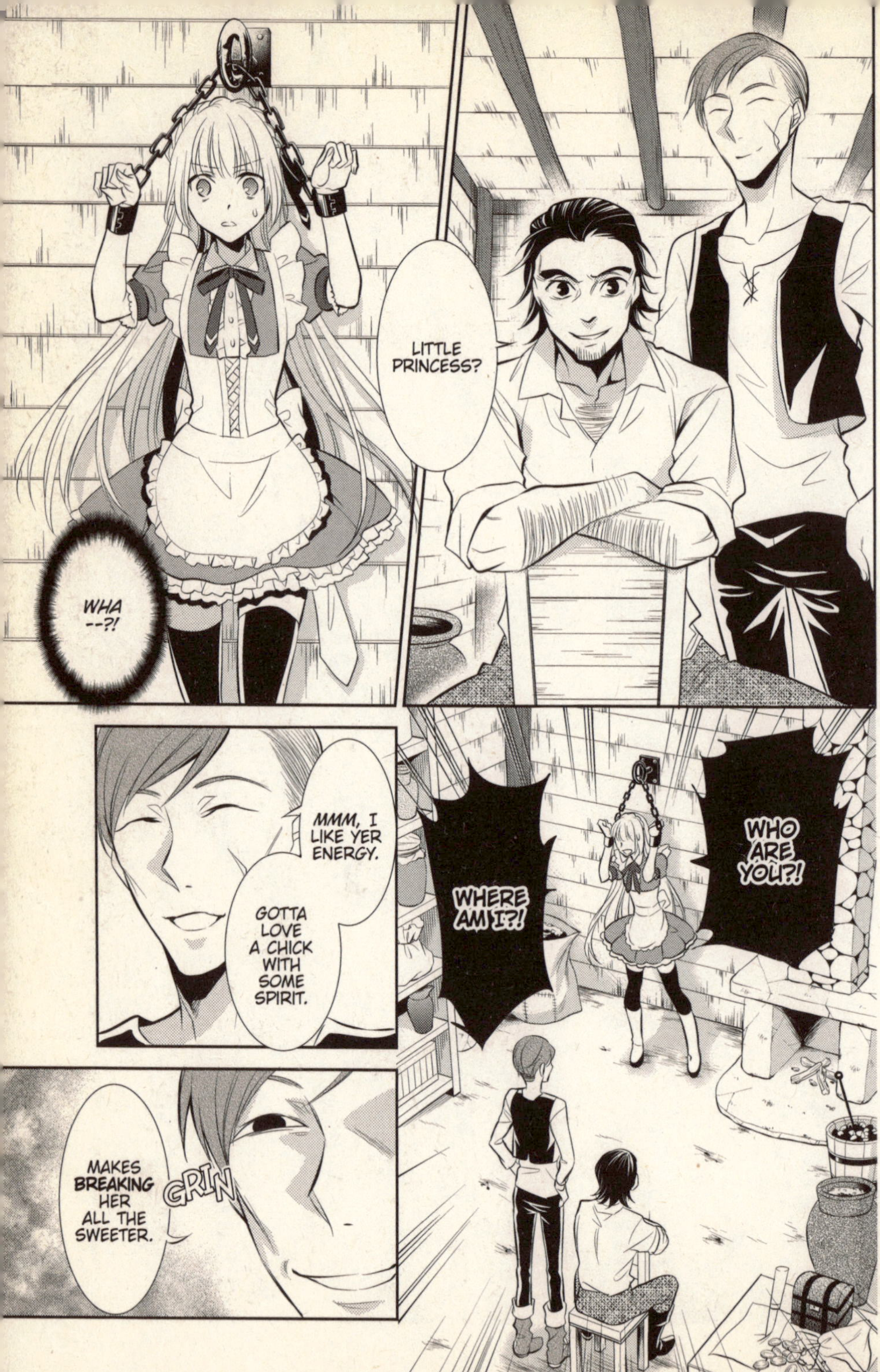
LITTLE PRINCESS?
WHA --?!
WHO ARE YOU?!
WHERE AM I?!
MMM, I LIKE YER ENERGY.
GOTTA LOVE A CHICK WITH SOME SPIRIT.
MAKES **BREAKING** HER ALL THE SWEETER.
GRIN

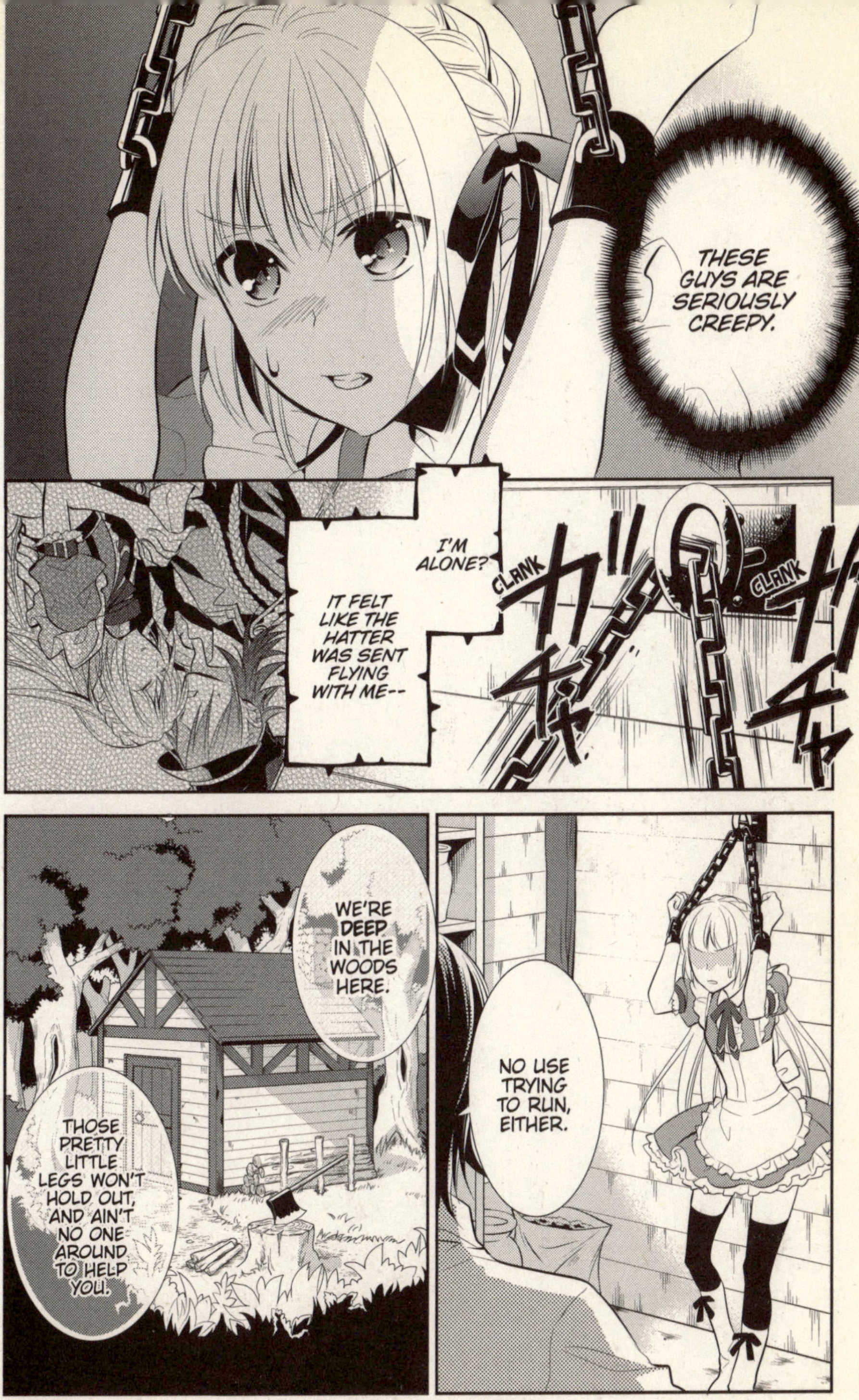
THESE GUYS ARE SERIOUSLY CREEPY.
ガチャ
CLANK
ガチャ
CLANK
I'M ALONE?
IT FELT LIKE THE HATTER WAS SENT FLYING WITH ME--
NO USE TRYING TO RUN, EITHER.
WE'RE DEEP IN THE WOODS HERE.
THOSE PRETTY LITTLE LEGS WON'T HOLD OUT, AND AIN'T NO ONE AROUND TO HELP YOU.

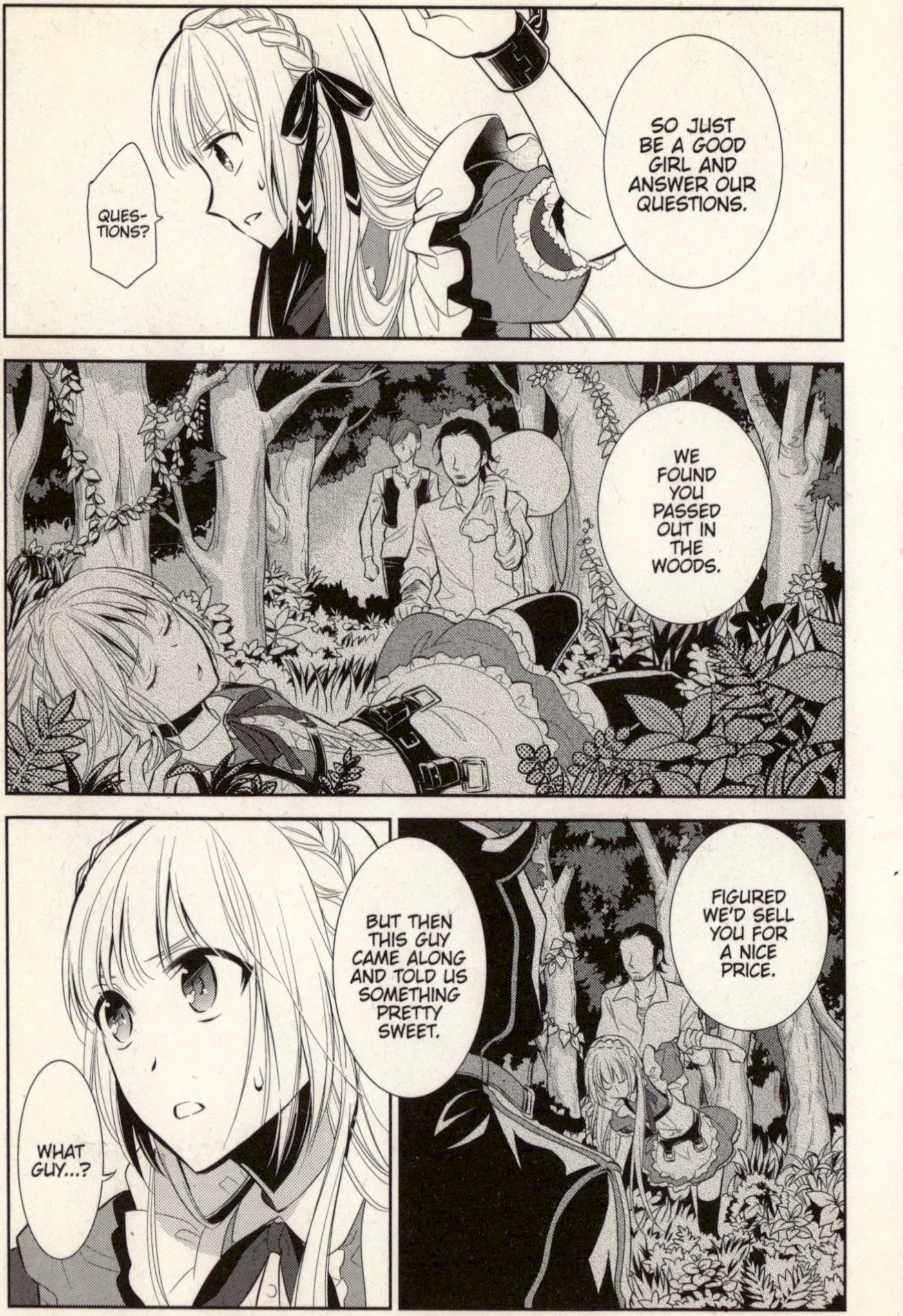
SO JUST BE A GOOD GIRL AND ANSWER OUR QUESTIONS.
QUES-TIONS?
WE FOUND YOU PASSED OUT IN THE WOODS.
FIGURED WE'D SELL YOU FOR A NICE PRICE.
BUT THEN THIS GUY CAME ALONG AND TOLD US SOMETHING PRETTY SWEET.
WHAT GUY...?

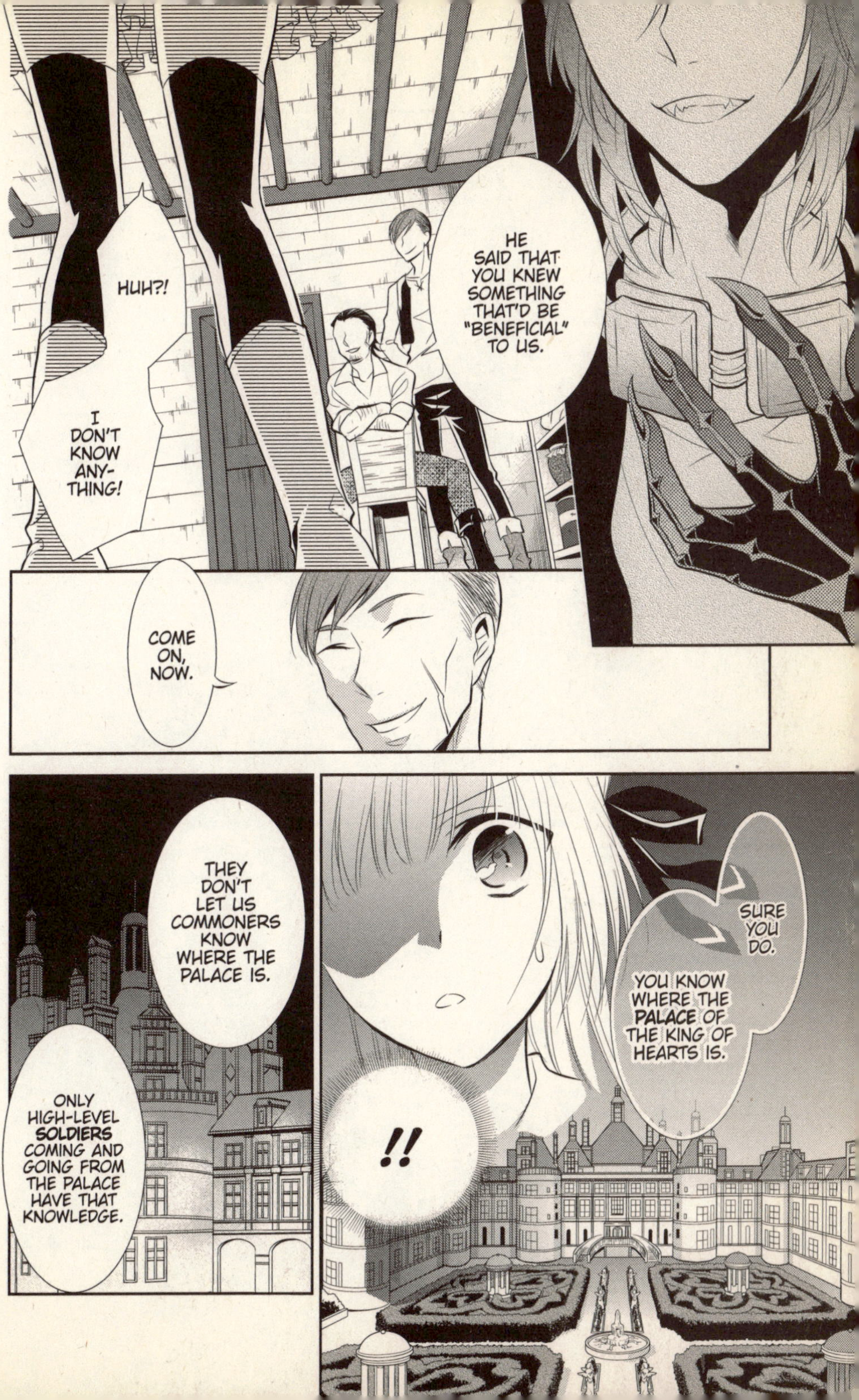
HE SAID THAT YOU KNEW SOMETHING THAT'D BE "BENEFICIAL" TO US.
HUH?!
I DON'T KNOW ANY-THING!
COME ON, NOW.
SURE YOU DO.
YOU KNOW WHERE THE **PALACE** OF THE KING OF HEARTS IS.
!!
THEY DON'T LET US COMMONERS KNOW WHERE THE PALACE IS.
ONLY HIGH-LEVEL **SOLDIERS** COMING AND GOING FROM THE PALACE HAVE THAT KNOWLEDGE.

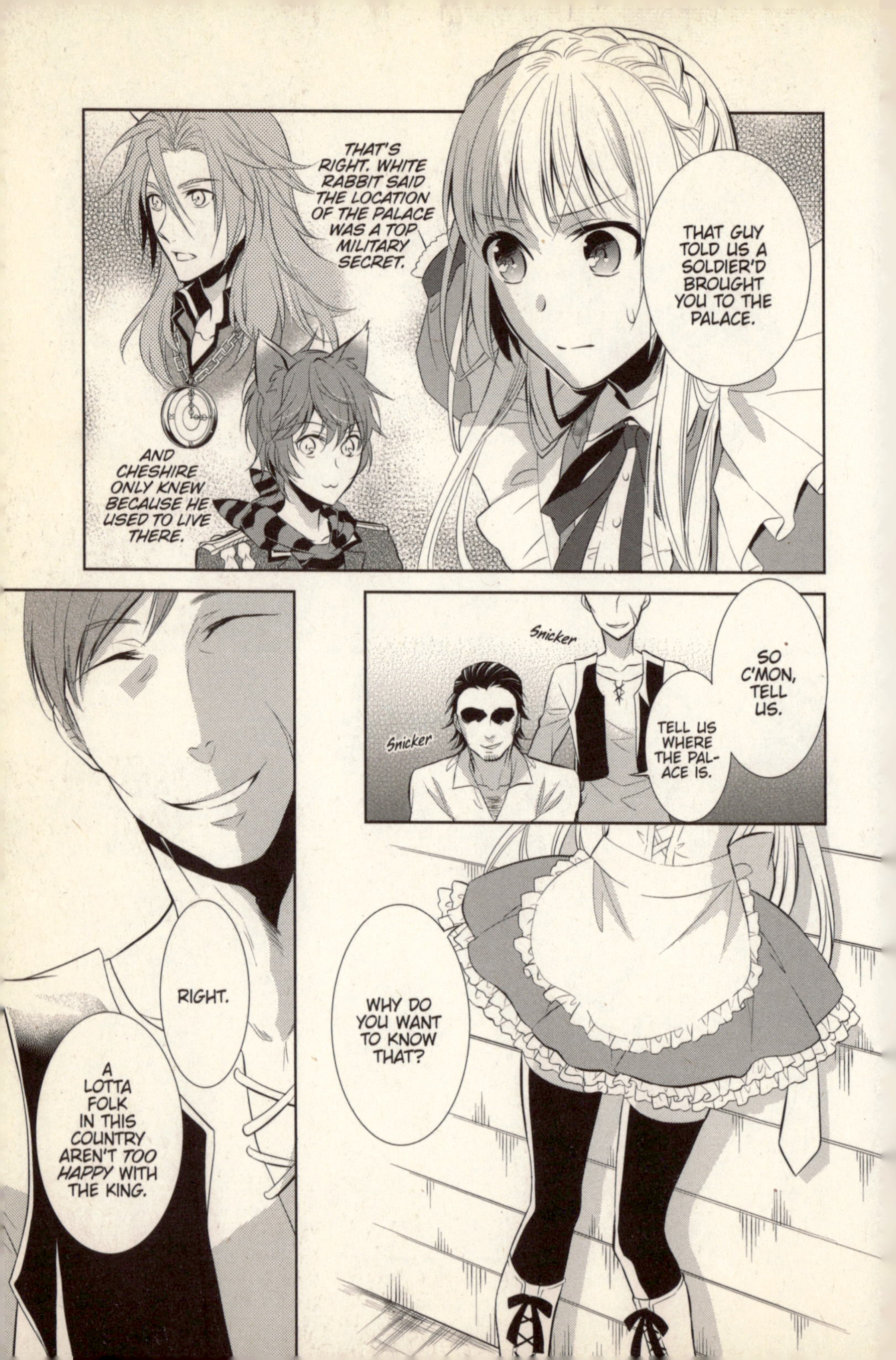
THAT GUY TOLD US A SOLDIER'D BROUGHT YOU TO THE PALACE.
THAT'S RIGHT. WHITE RABBIT SAID THE LOCATION OF THE PALACE WAS A TOP MILITARY SECRET.
AND CHESHIRE ONLY KNEW BECAUSE HE USED TO LIVE THERE.
Snicker
SO C'MON, TELL US.
TELL US WHERE THE PAL-ACE IS.
Snicker
WHY DO YOU WANT TO KNOW THAT?
RIGHT.
A LOTTA FOLK IN THIS COUNTRY AREN'T *TOO HAPPY* WITH THE KING.

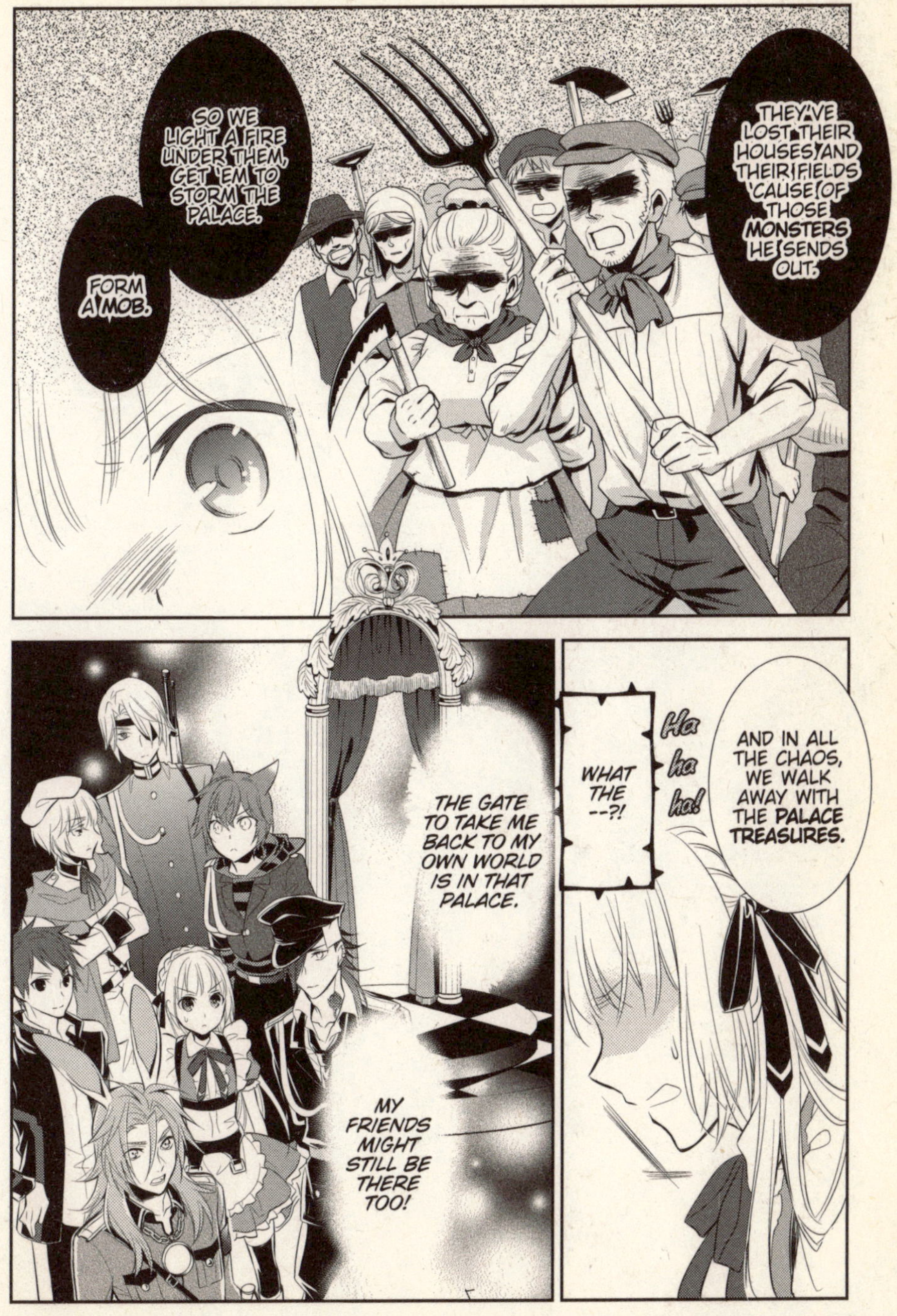
THEY'VE LOST THEIR HOUSES AND THEIR FIELDS 'CAUSE OF THOSE MONSTERS HE SENDS OUT.
SO WE LIGHT A FIRE UNDER THEM, GET 'EM TO STORM THE PALACE.
FORM A MOB.
AND IN ALL THE CHAOS, WE WALK AWAY WITH THE PALACE TREASURES.
Ha ha ha!
WHAT THE --?!
THE GATE TO TAKE ME BACK TO MY OWN WORLD IS IN THAT PALACE.
MY FRIENDS MIGHT STILL BE THERE TOO!

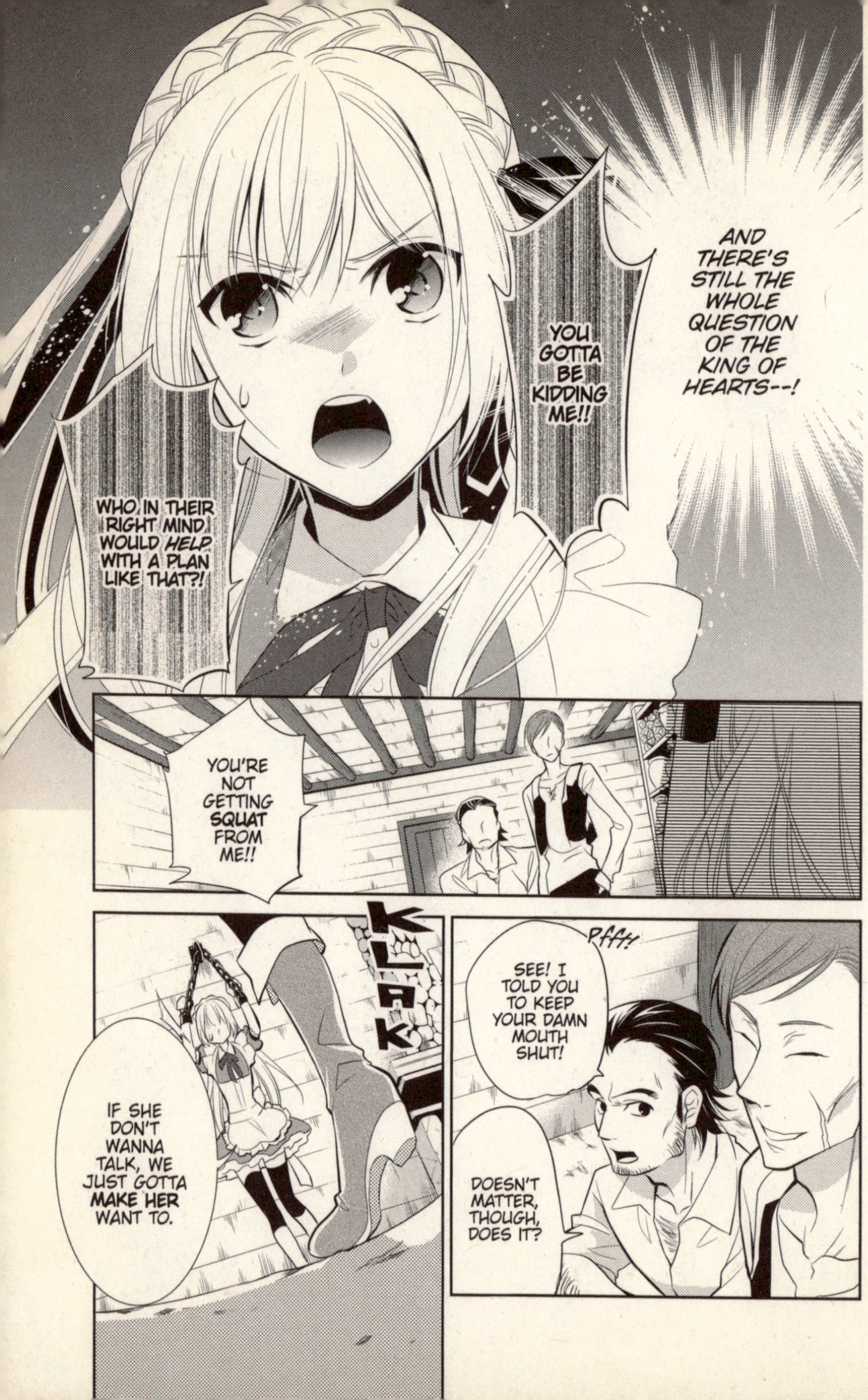
AND THERE'S STILL THE WHOLE QUESTION OF THE KING OF HEARTS--!
YOU GOTTA BE KIDDING ME!!
WHO IN THEIR RIGHT MIND WOULD *HELP* WITH A PLAN LIKE THAT?!
YOU'RE NOT GETTING **SQUAT** FROM ME!!
Pfft!
SEE! I TOLD YOU TO KEEP YOUR DAMN MOUTH SHUT!
DOESN'T MATTER, THOUGH, DOES IT?
KLAK
IF SHE DON'T WANNA TALK, WE JUST GOTTA **MAKE HER** WANT TO.

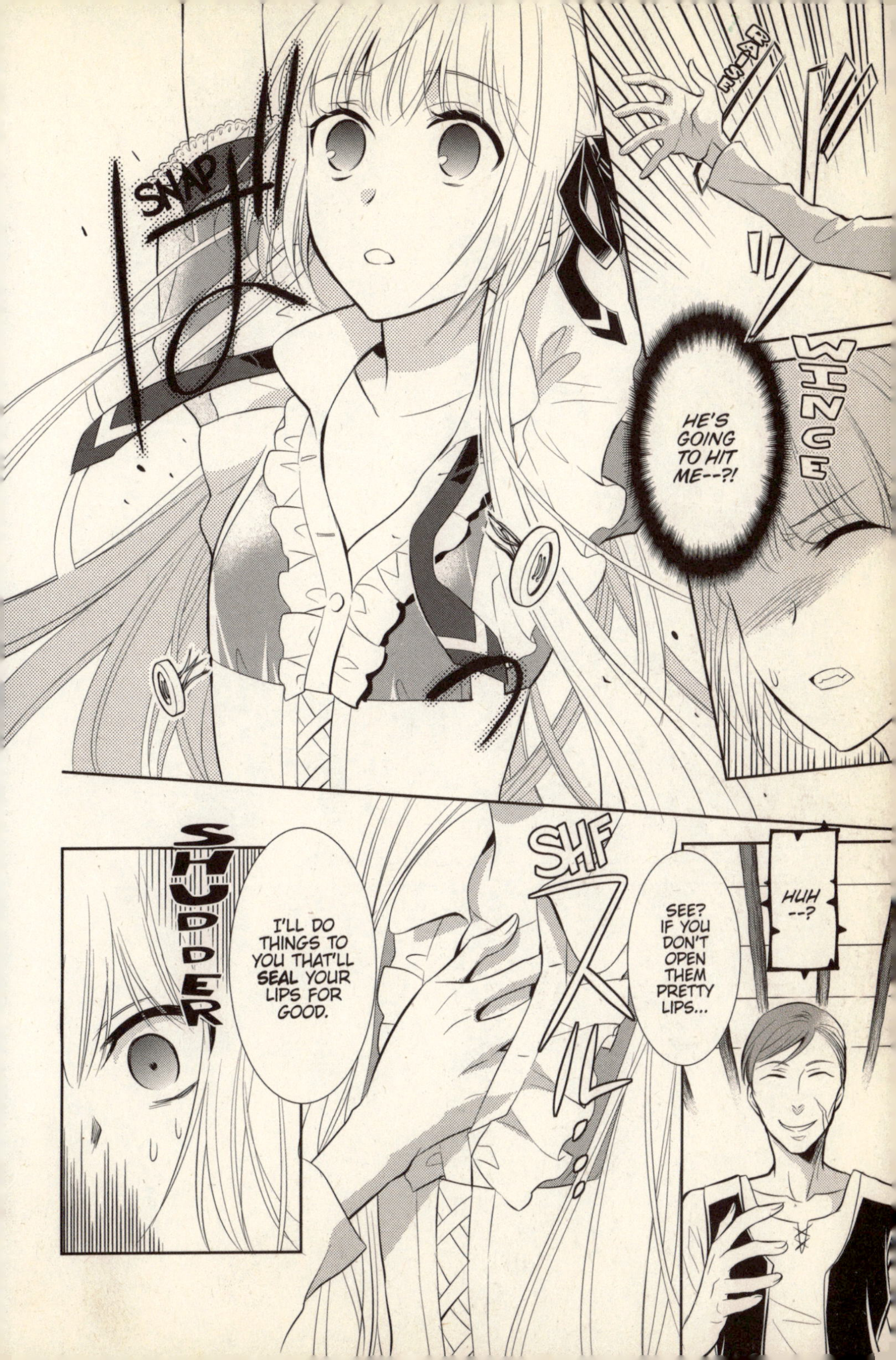
WINCE
HE'S GOING TO HIT ME--?!
SNAP
HUH --?
SEE? IF YOU DON'T OPEN THEM PRETTY LIPS...
SHF
I'LL DO THINGS TO YOU THAT'LL SEAL YOUR LIPS FOR GOOD.
SHUDDER

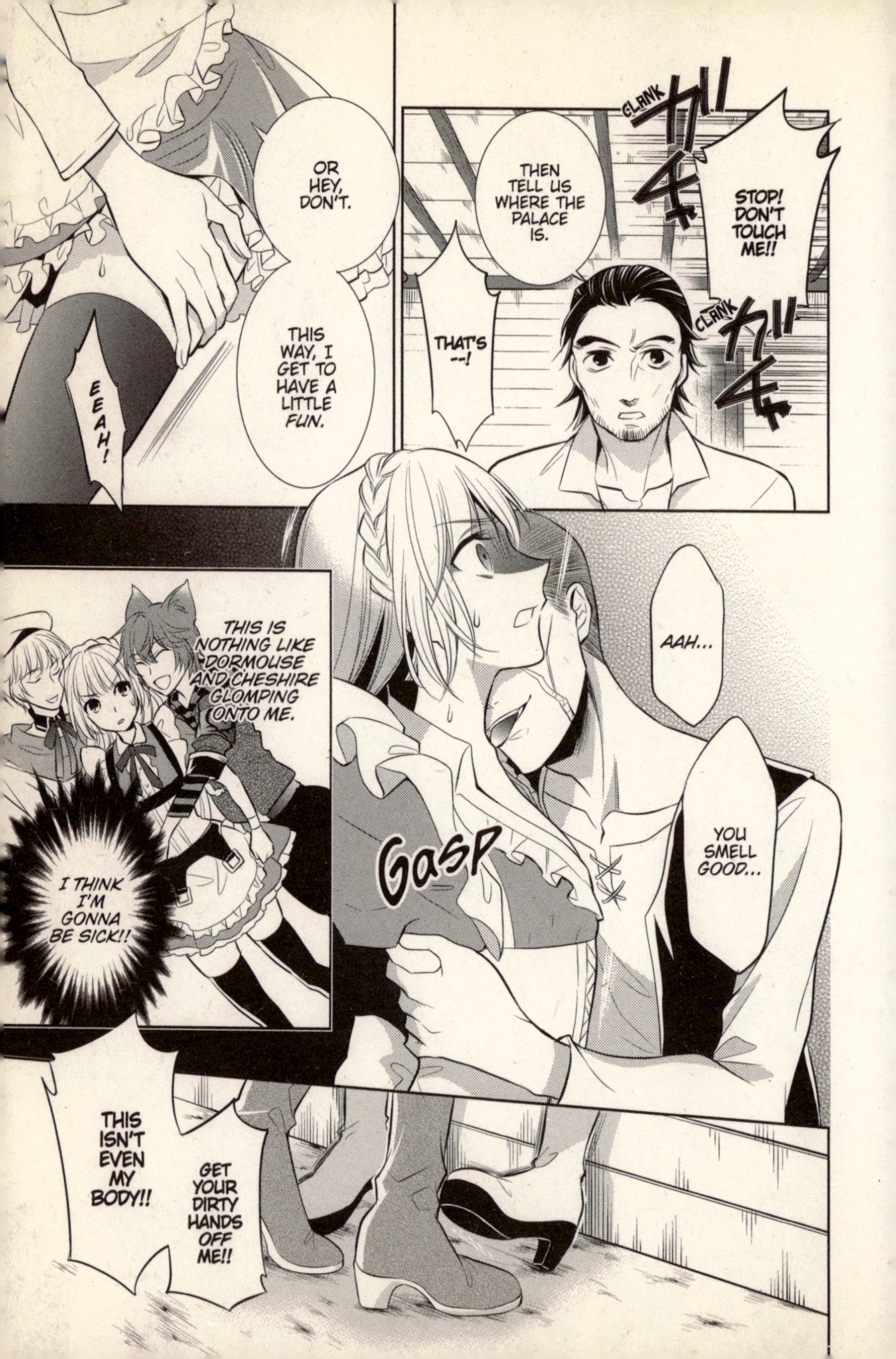
CLANK
STOP! DON'T TOUCH ME!!
THEN TELL US WHERE THE PALACE IS.
CLANK
THAT'S --!
OR HEY, DON'T.
THIS WAY, I GET TO HAVE A LITTLE FUN.
EEAH!
AAH...
YOU SMELL GOOD...
Gasp
THIS IS NOTHING LIKE DORMOUSE AND CHESHIRE GLOMPING ONTO ME.
I THINK I'M GONNA BE SICK!!
GET YOUR DIRTY HANDS OFF ME!!
THIS ISN'T EVEN MY BODY!!

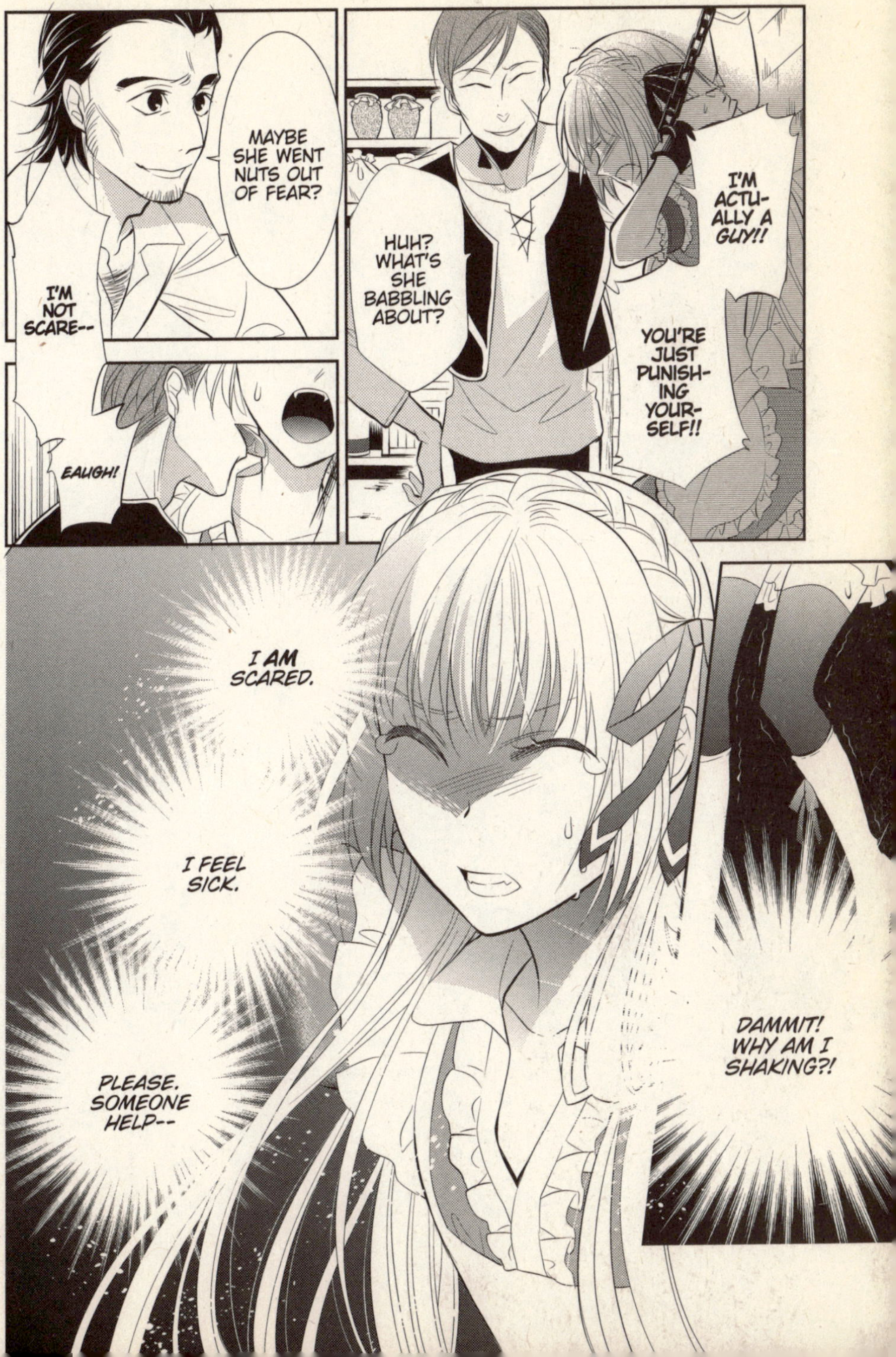
I'M ACTUALLY A GUY!!
YOU'RE JUST PUNISHING YOURSELF!!
HUH? WHAT'S SHE BABBLING ABOUT?
MAYBE SHE WENT NUTS OUT OF FEAR?
I'M NOT SCARE--
EAUGH!
DAMMIT! WHY AM I SHAKING?!
I AM SCARED.
I FEEL SICK.
PLEASE. SOMEONE HELP--

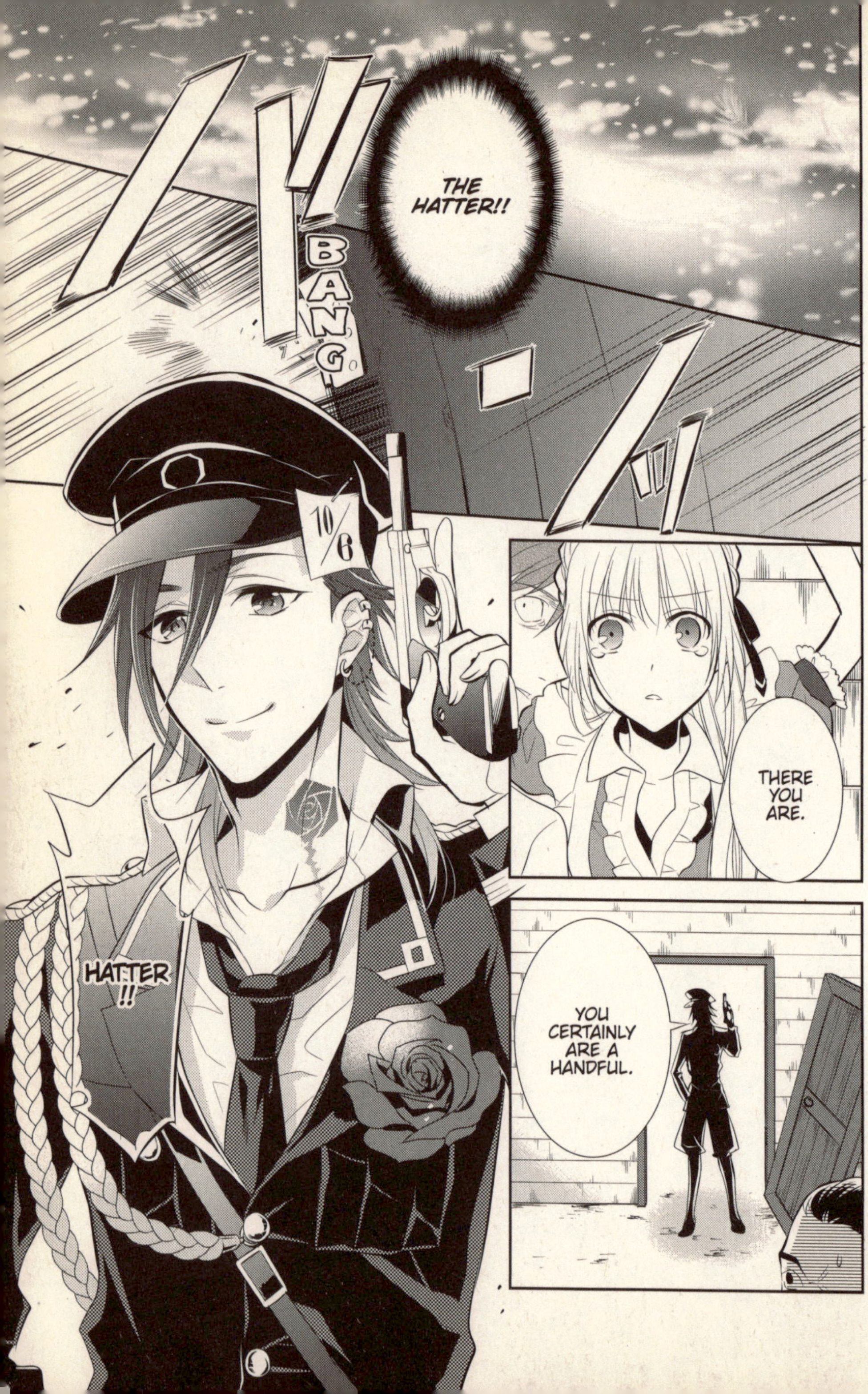
THE HATTER!!
BANG!
THERE YOU ARE.
YOU CERTAINLY ARE A HANDFUL.
HATTER!!

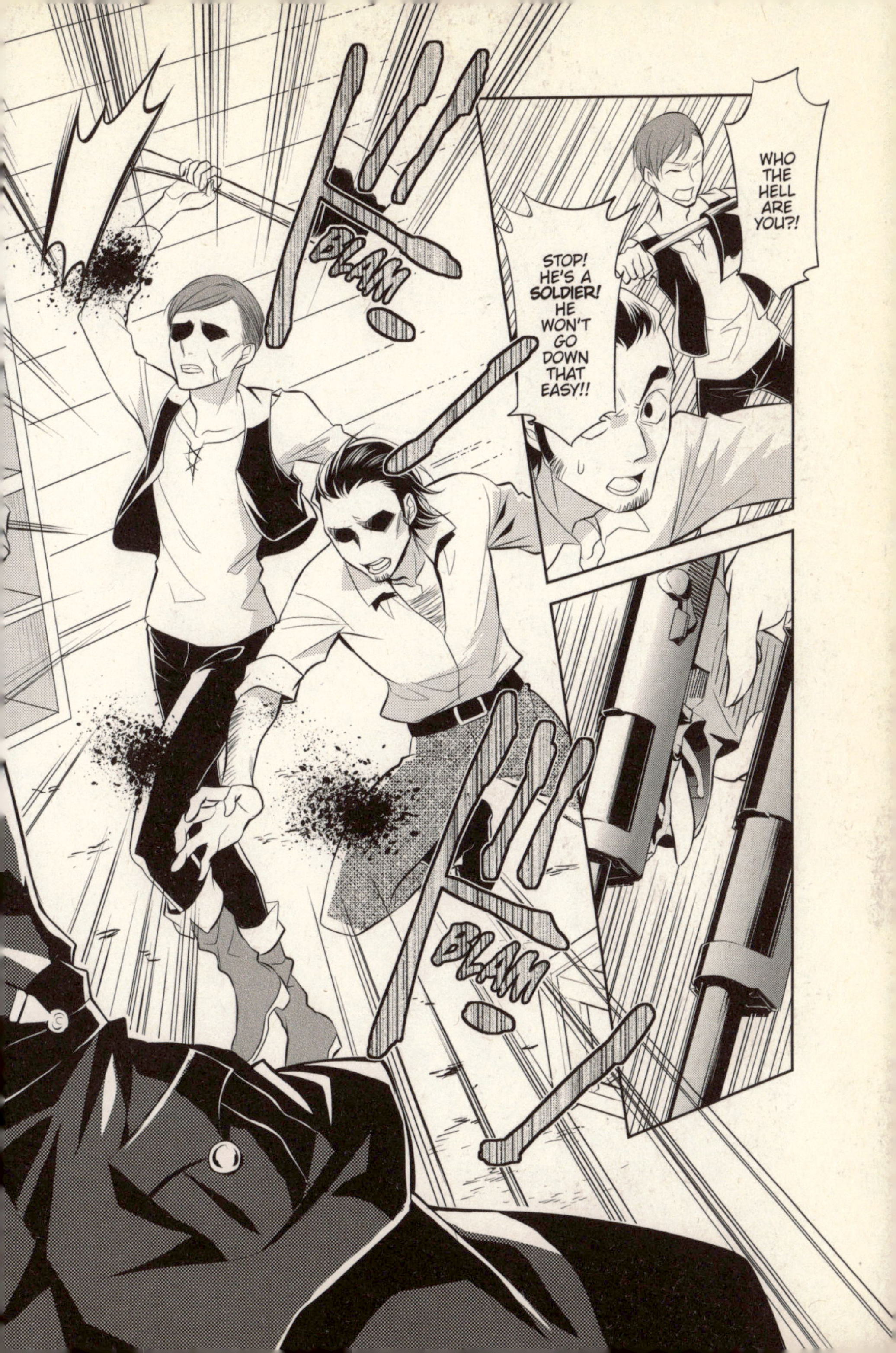
WHO THE HELL ARE YOU?!
STOP! HE'S A SOLDIER! HE WON'T GO DOWN THAT EASY!!
BLAM
BLAM

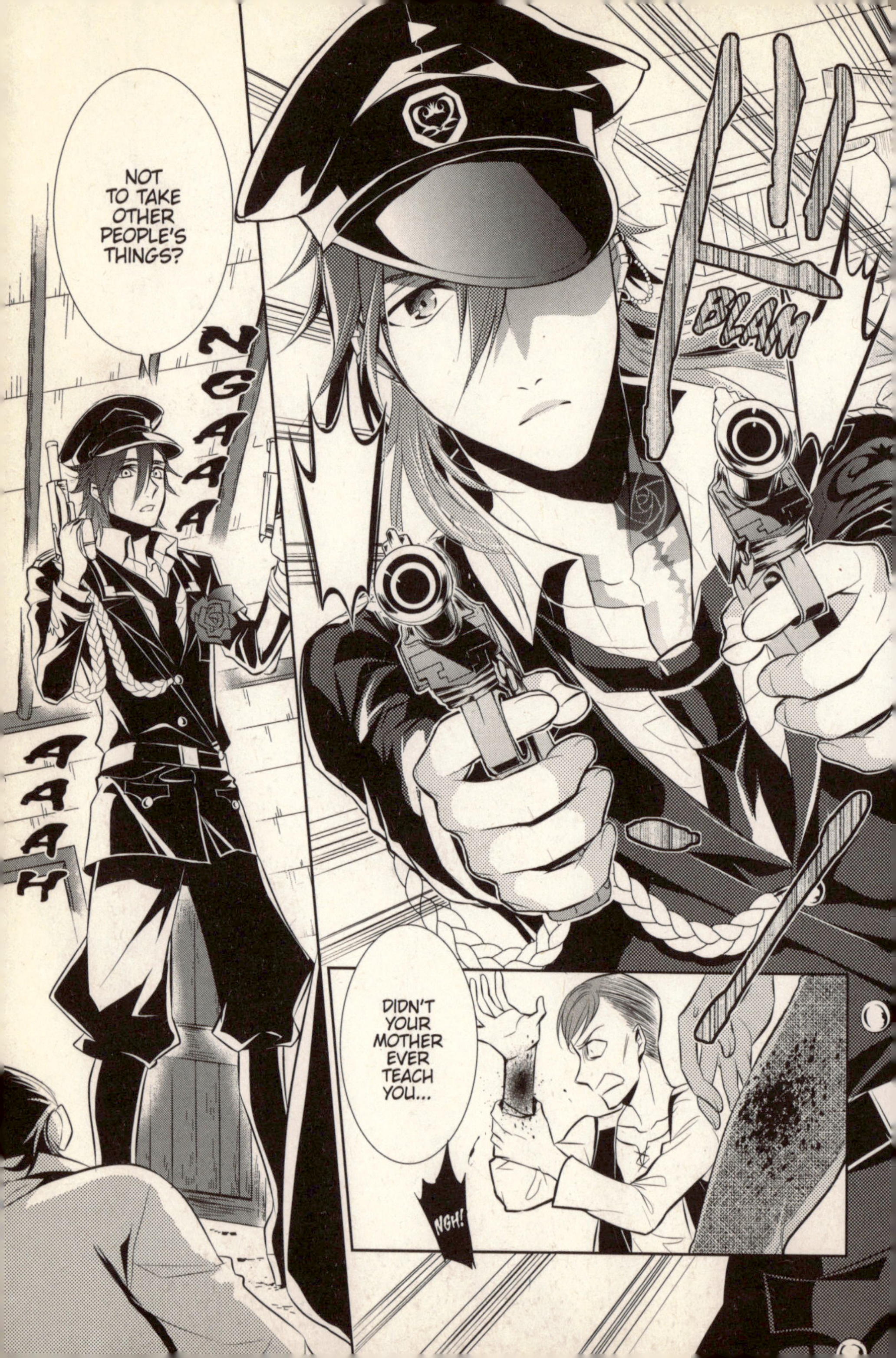
BLAM
DIDN'T YOUR MOTHER EVER TEACH YOU...
NGH!
NOT TO TAKE OTHER PEOPLE'S THINGS?
NGAAAA
AAAAH

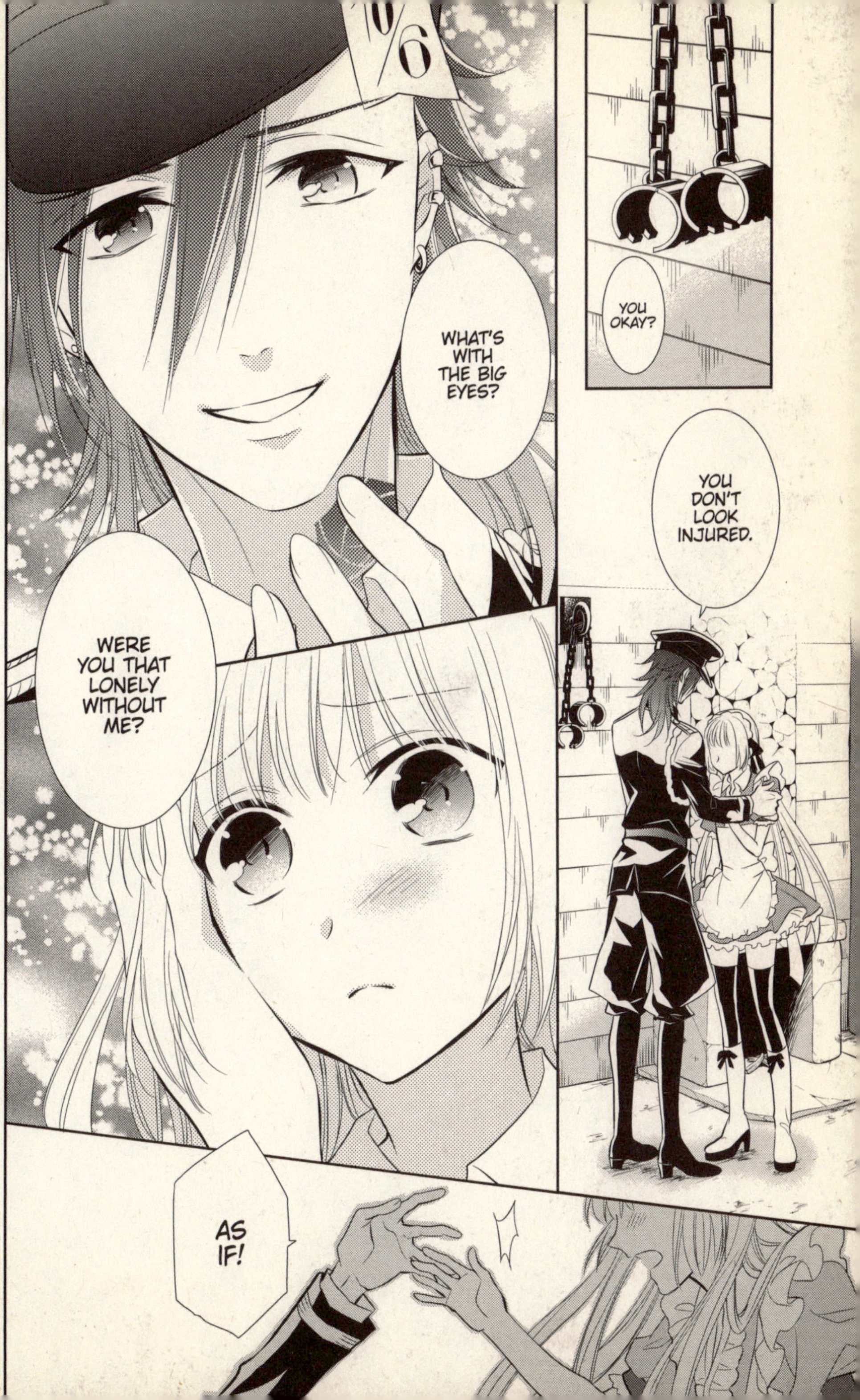
YOU OKAY?
YOU DON'T LOOK INJURED.
WHAT'S WITH THE BIG EYES?
WERE YOU THAT LONELY WITHOUT ME?
AS IF!

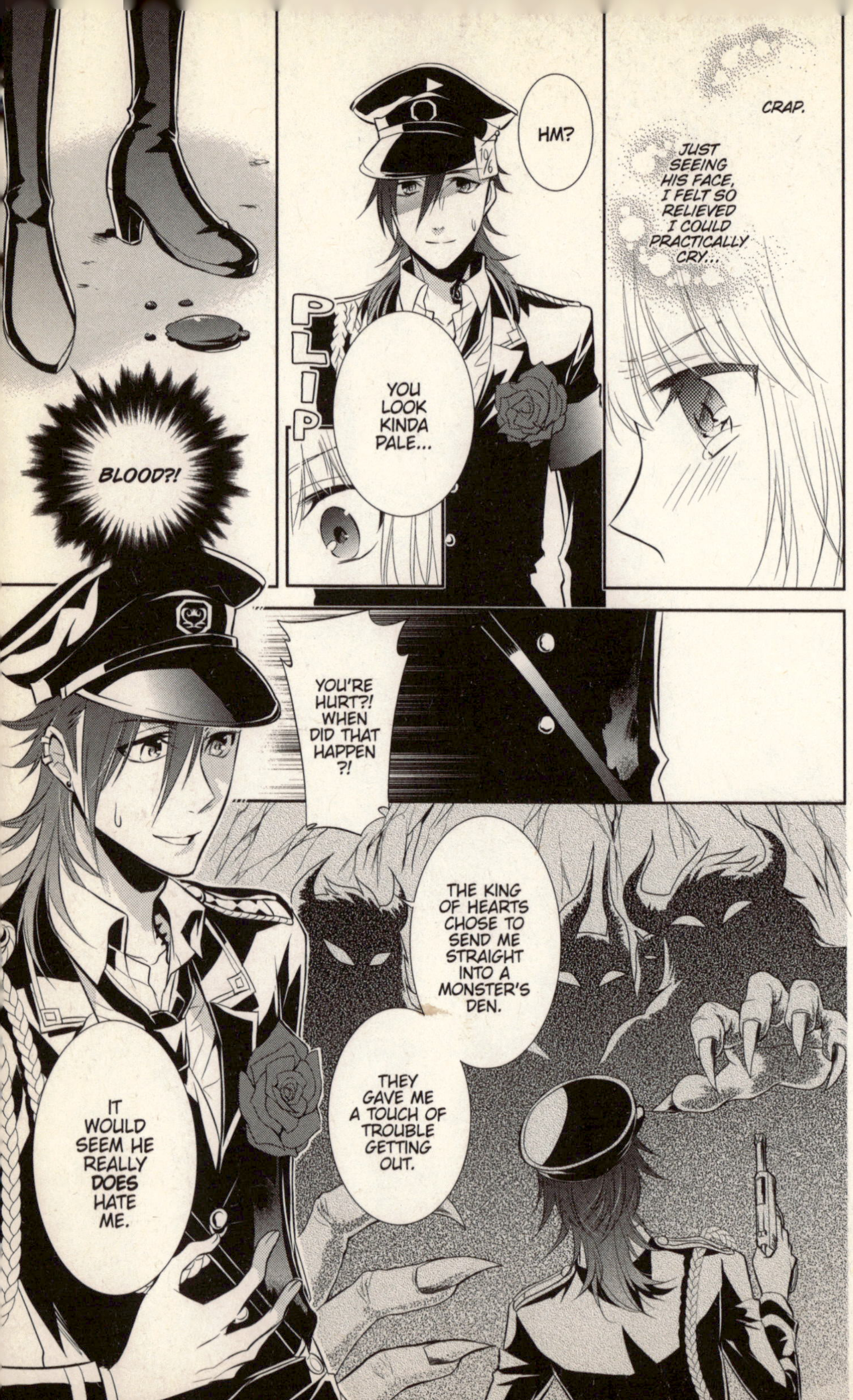
CRAP.
JUST SEEING HIS FACE, I FELT SO RELIEVED I COULD PRACTICALLY CRY...
HM?
PLIP
YOU LOOK KINDA PALE...
BLOOD?!
YOU'RE HURT?! WHEN DID THAT HAPPEN?!
THE KING OF HEARTS CHOSE TO SEND ME STRAIGHT INTO A MONSTER'S DEN.
THEY GAVE ME A TOUCH OF TROUBLE GETTING OUT.
IT WOULD SEEM HE REALLY DOES HATE ME.

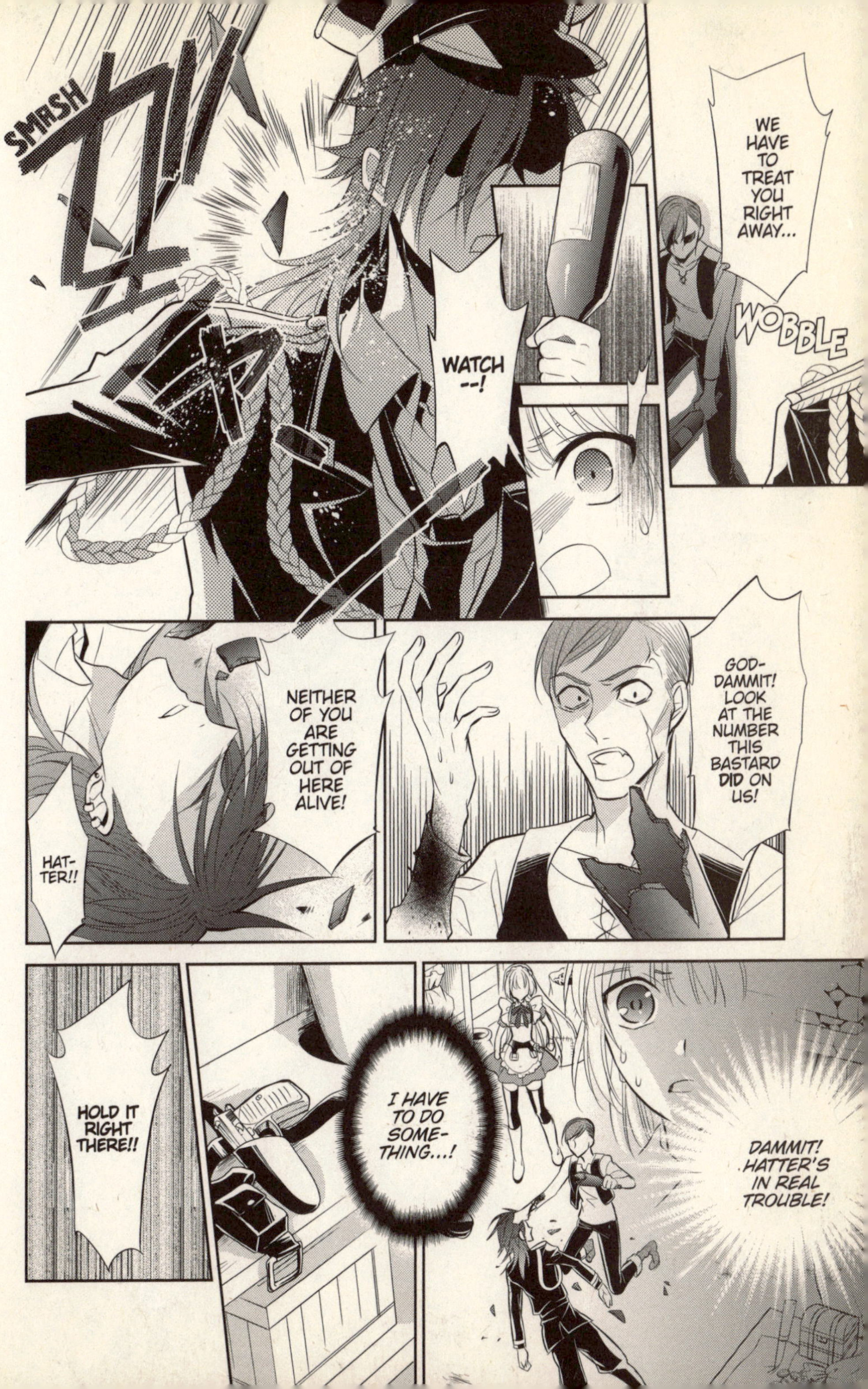
WE HAVE TO TREAT YOU RIGHT AWAY...
WOBBLE
WATCH --!
SMASH
GOD-DAMMIT! LOOK AT THE NUMBER THIS BASTARD DID ON US!
NEITHER OF YOU ARE GETTING OUT OF HERE ALIVE!
HAT-TER!!
DAMMIT! HATTER'S IN REAL TROUBLE!
I HAVE TO DO SOME-THING...!
HOLD IT RIGHT THERE!!

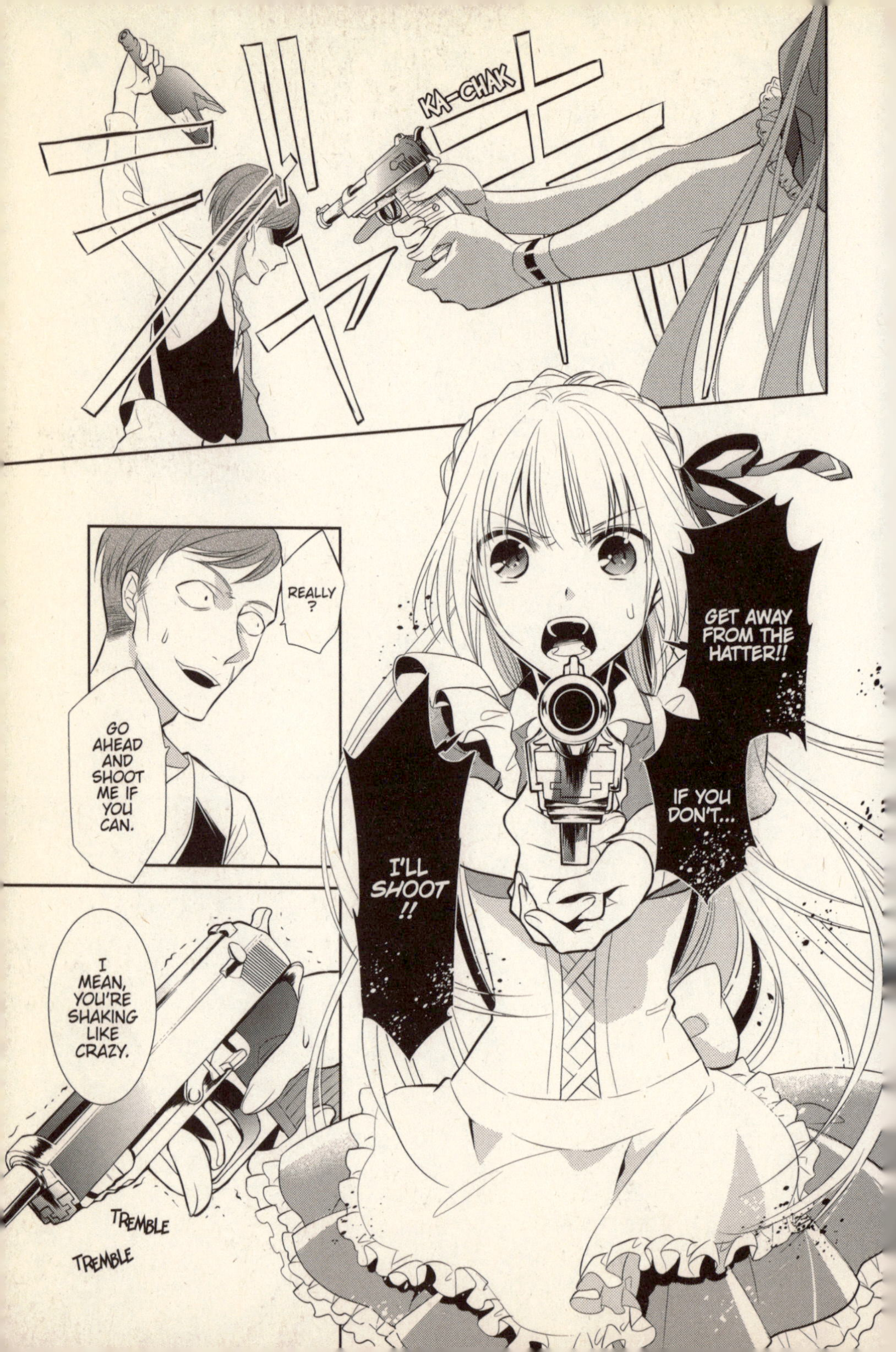
KA-CHAK
GET AWAY FROM THE HATTER!!
IF YOU DON'T...
I'LL SHOOT!!
REALLY?
GO AHEAD AND SHOOT ME IF YOU CAN.
I MEAN, YOU'RE SHAKING LIKE CRAZY.
TREMBLE
TREMBLE

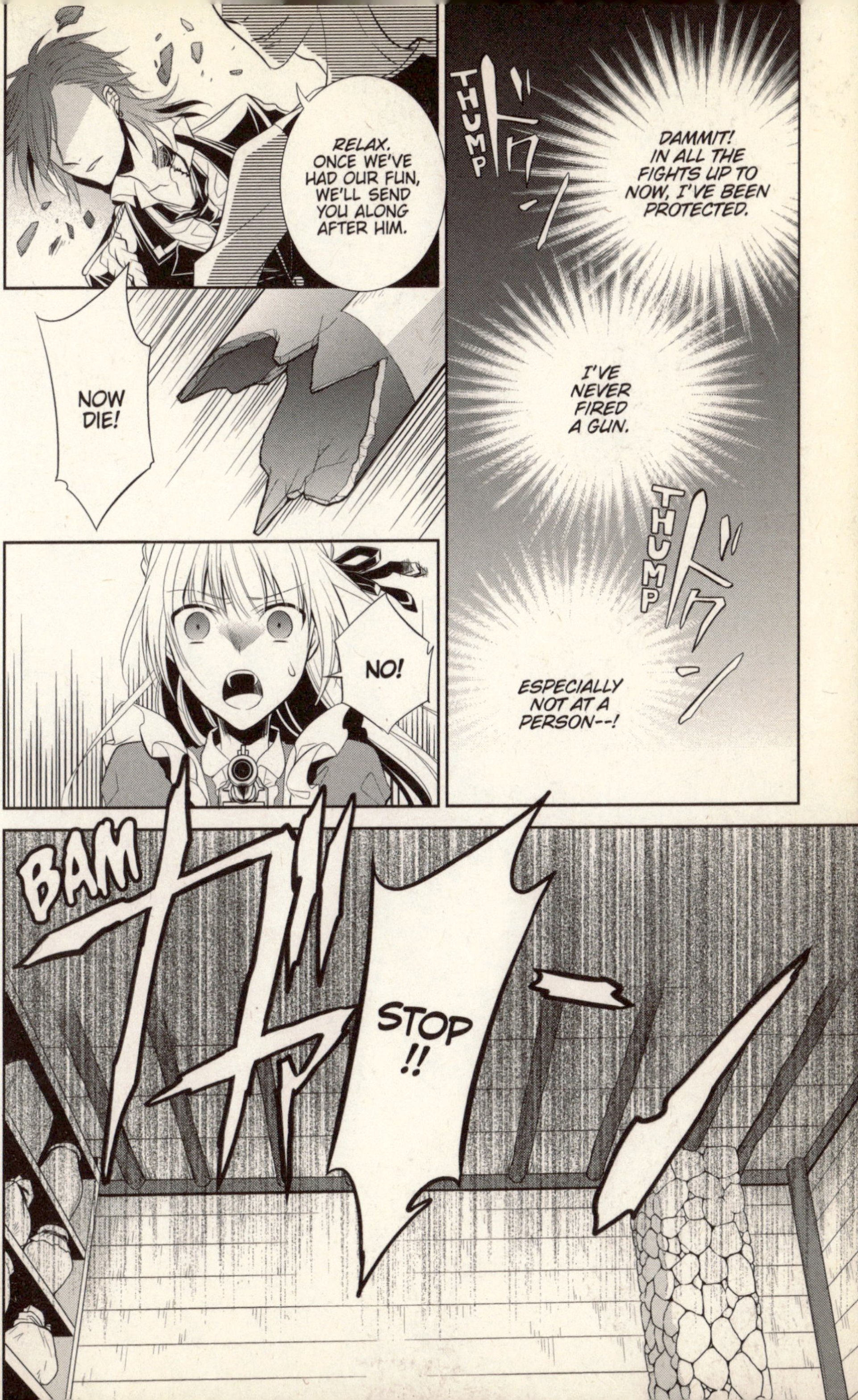
THUMP
DAMMIT! IN ALL THE FIGHTS UP TO NOW, I'VE BEEN PROTECTED.
I'VE NEVER FIRED A GUN.
THUMP
ESPECIALLY NOT AT A PERSON--!
RELAX. ONCE WE'VE HAD OUR FUN, WE'LL SEND YOU ALONG AFTER HIM.
NOW DIE!
NO!
BAM
STOP !!

KOFF

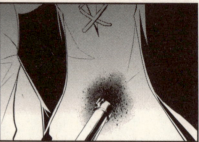

YOU SHOULDN'T HAVE WASTED YOUR CHANCE.

KLAK

NEXT TIME, DON'T CHIT-CHAT SO MUCH.

SLUMP

THUD

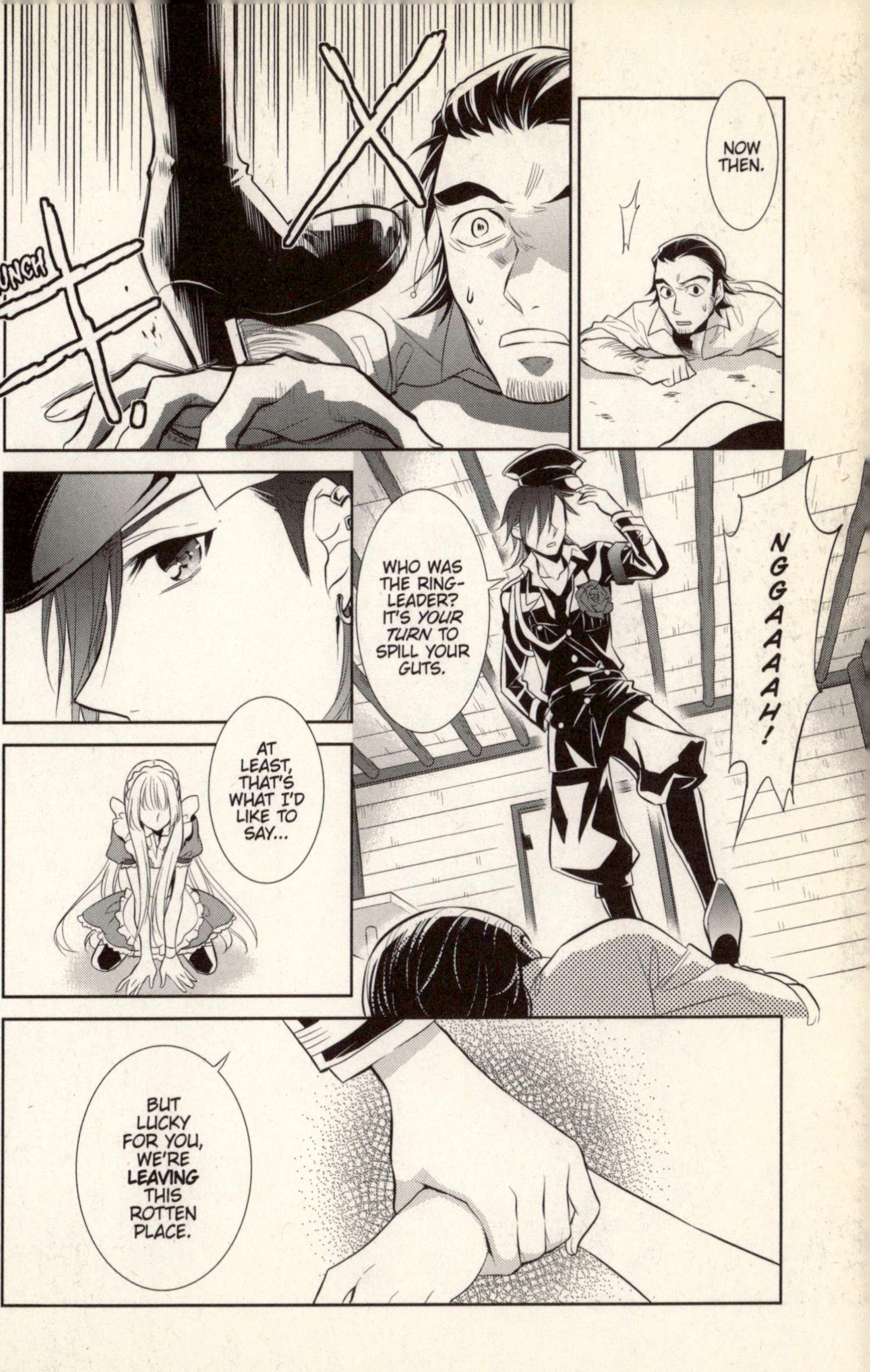
NOW THEN.
CRUNCH
NGGAAAAAH!
WHO WAS THE RING-LEADER? IT'S *YOUR TURN* TO SPILL YOUR GUTS.
AT LEAST, THAT'S WHAT I'D LIKE TO SAY...
BUT LUCKY FOR YOU, WE'RE **LEAVING** THIS ROTTEN PLACE.

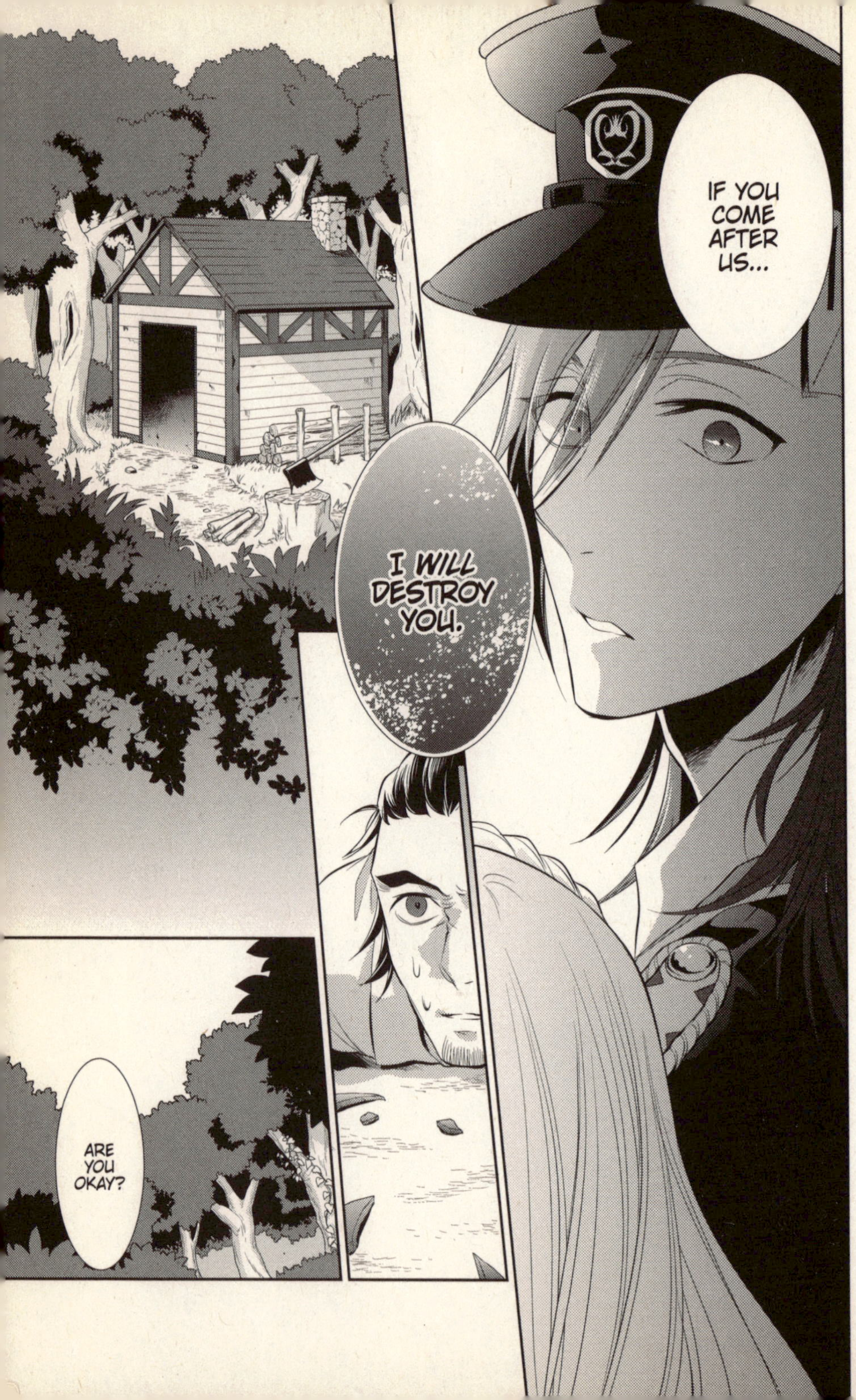
IF YOU COME AFTER US...
I WILL DESTROY YOU.
ARE YOU OKAY?

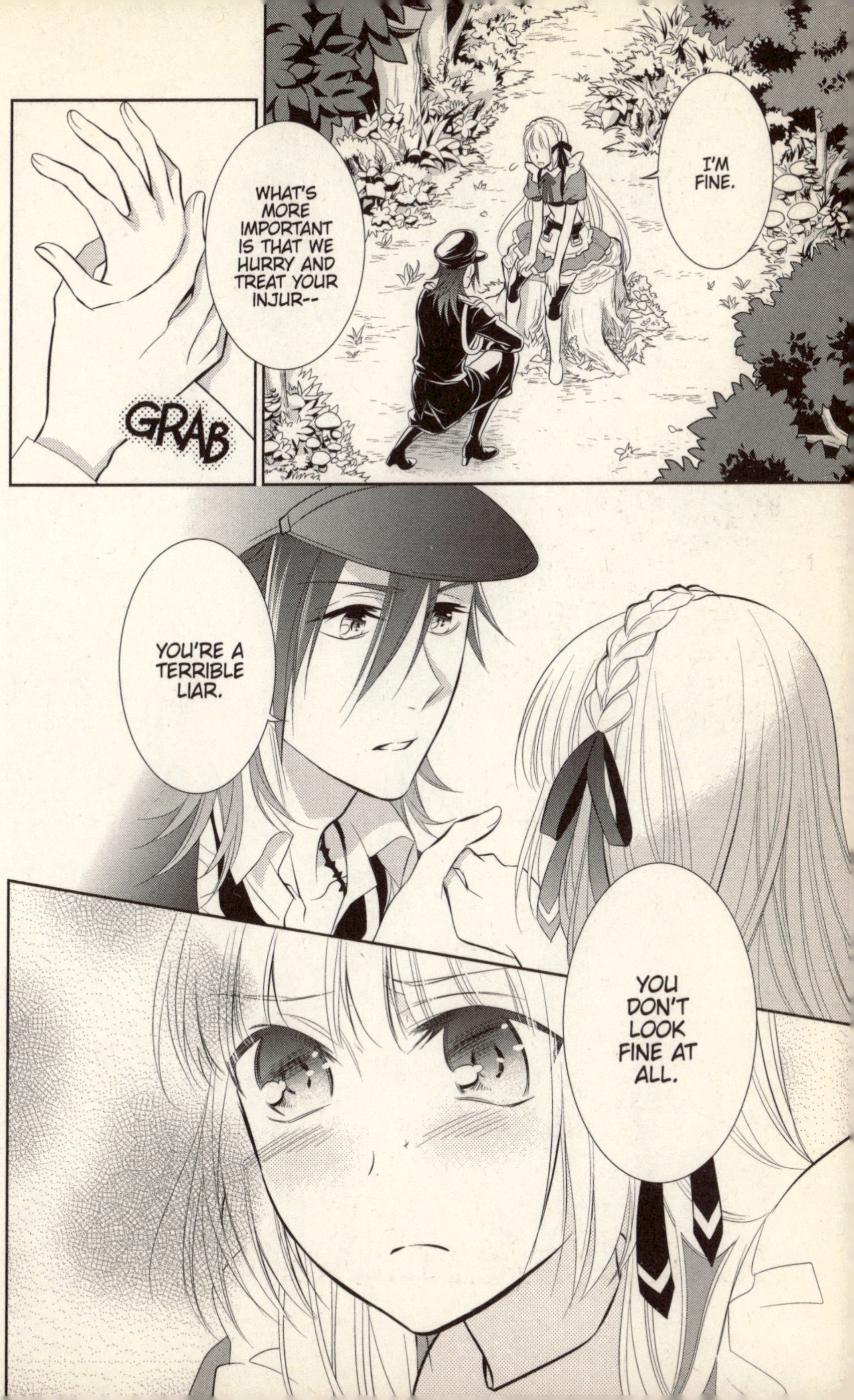
I'M FINE.
WHAT'S MORE IMPORTANT IS THAT WE HURRY AND TREAT YOUR INJUR--
GRAB
YOU'RE A TERRIBLE LIAR.
YOU DON'T LOOK FINE AT ALL.

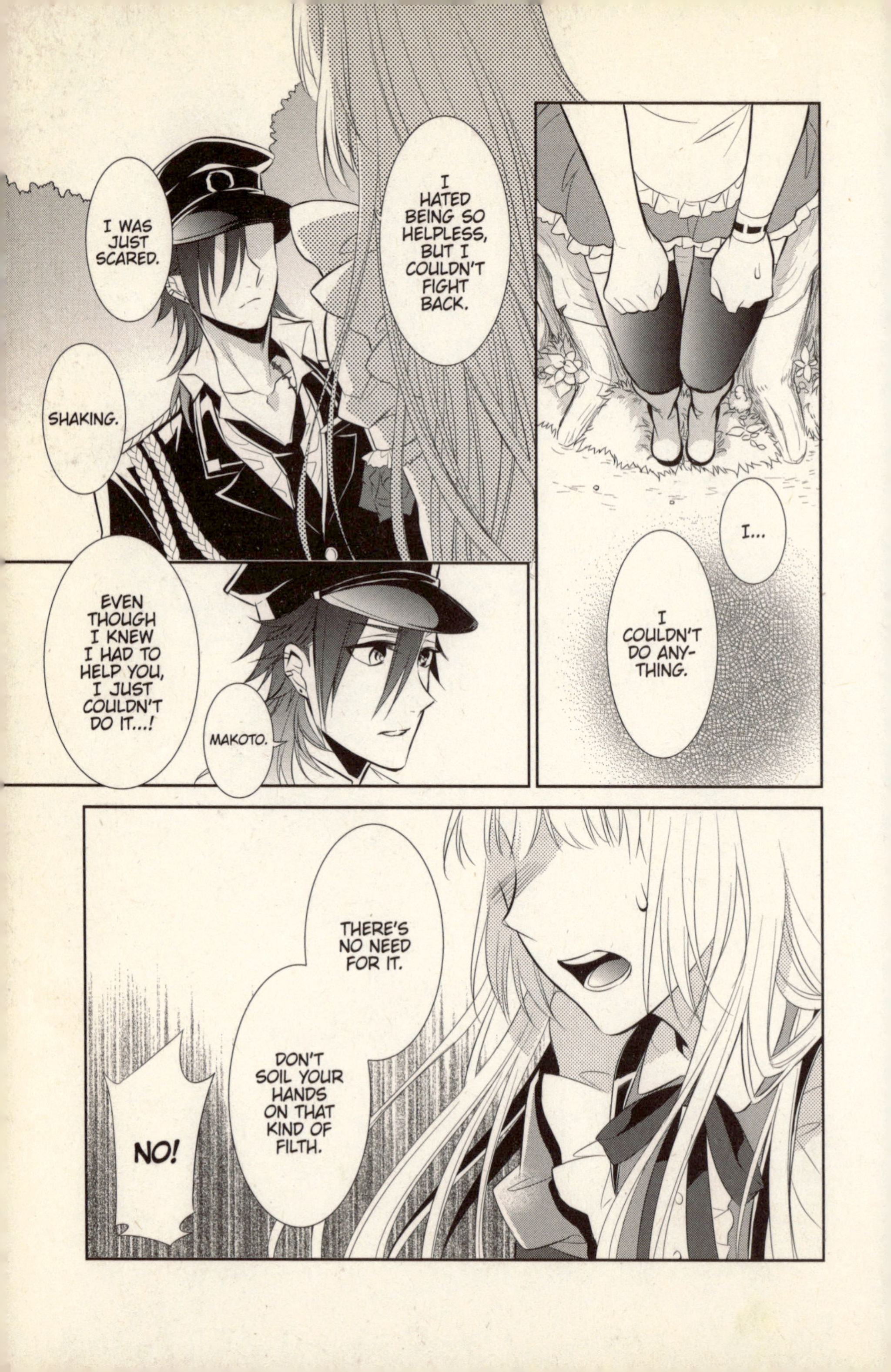
I...
I COULDN'T DO ANY-THING.
I HATED BEING SO HELPLESS, BUT I COULDN'T FIGHT BACK.
I WAS JUST SCARED.
SHAKING.
EVEN THOUGH I KNEW I HAD TO HELP YOU, I JUST COULDN'T DO IT...!
MAKOTO.
THERE'S NO NEED FOR IT.
DON'T SOIL YOUR HANDS ON THAT KIND OF FILTH.
NO!

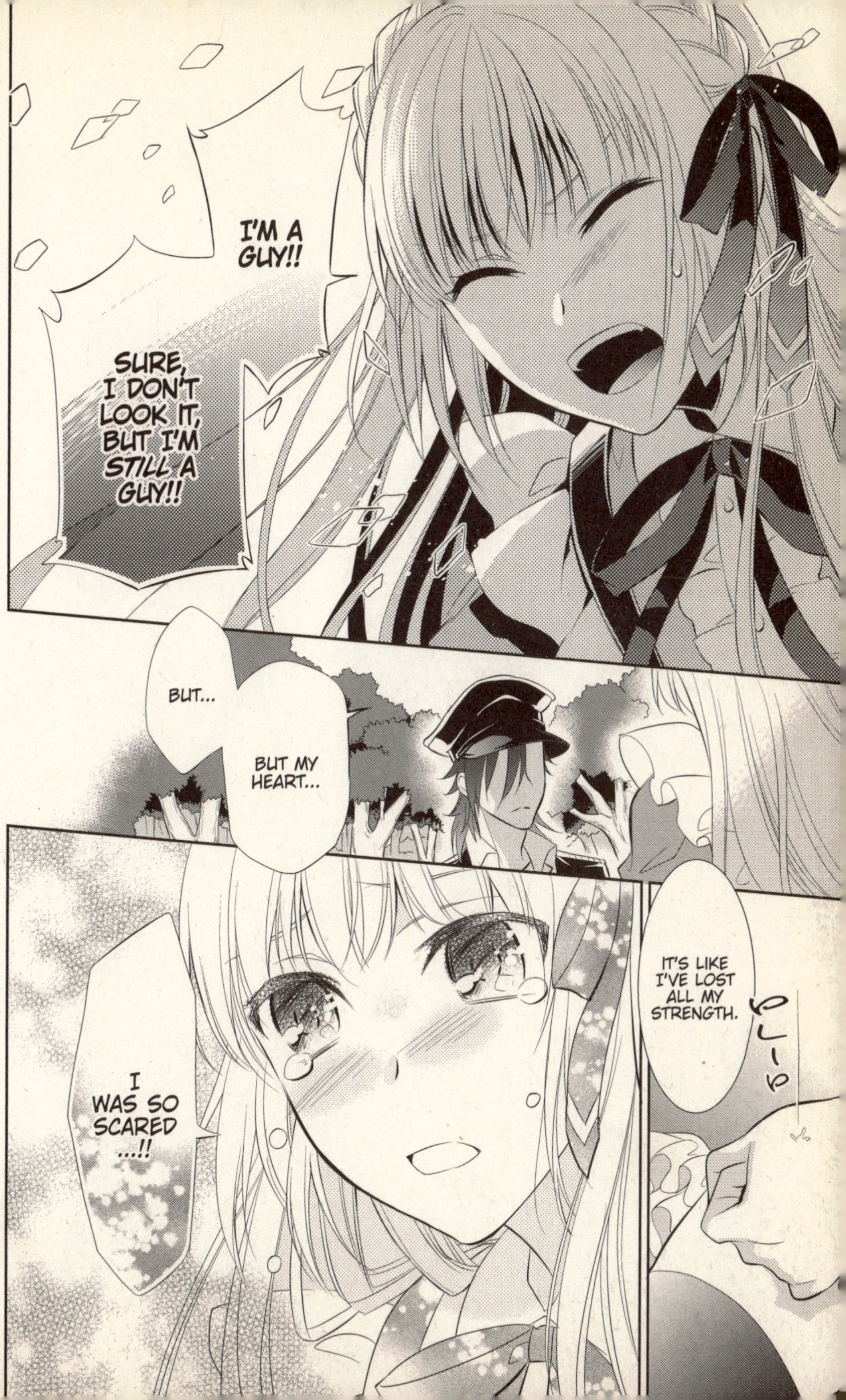
I'M A GUY!!
SURE, I DON'T LOOK IT, BUT I'M STILL A GUY!!
BUT...
BUT MY HEART...
IT'S LIKE I'VE LOST ALL MY STRENGTH.
I WAS SO SCARED ...!!

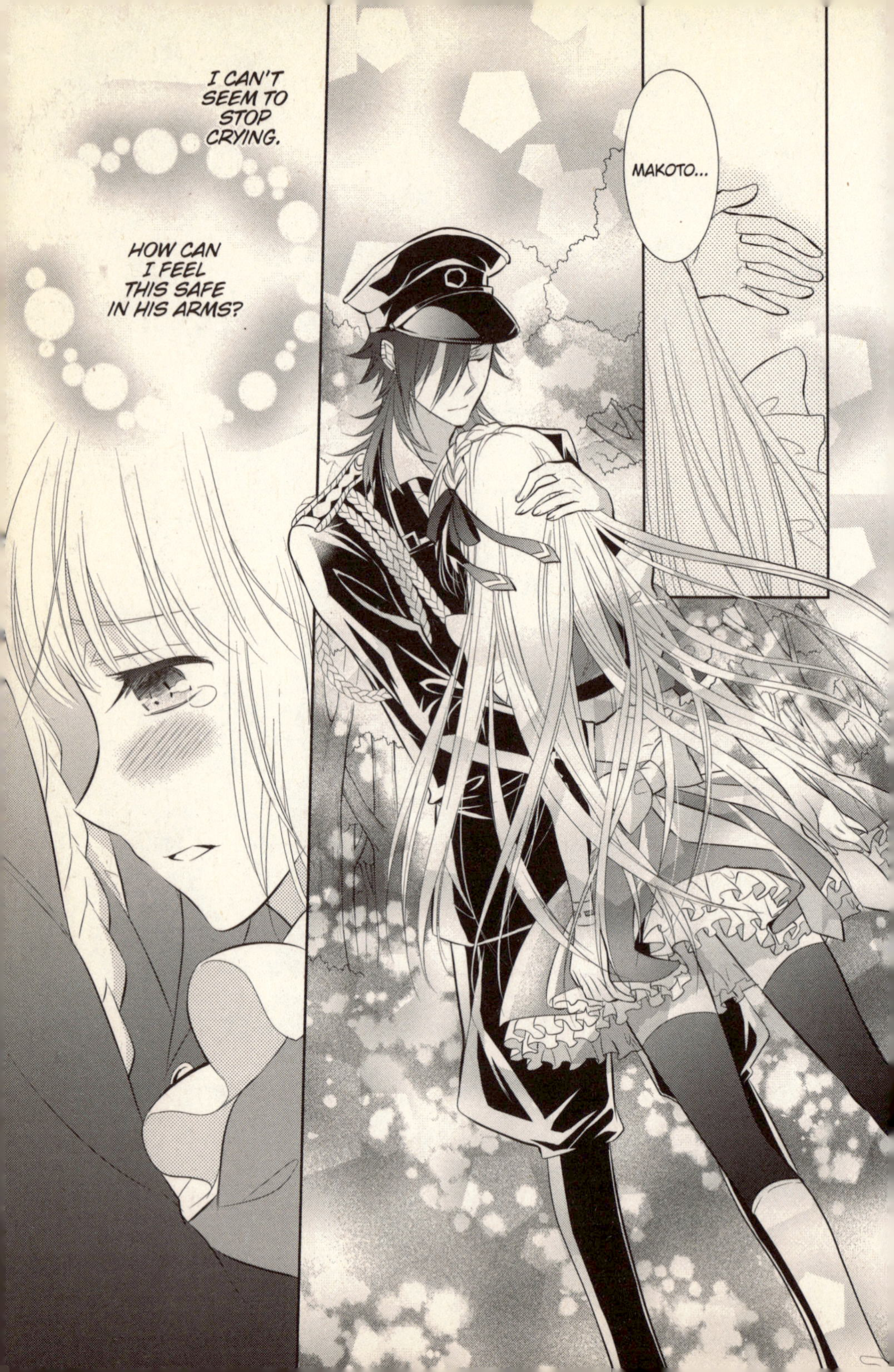
MAKOTO...
I CAN'T SEEM TO STOP CRYING.
HOW CAN I FEEL THIS SAFE IN HIS ARMS?

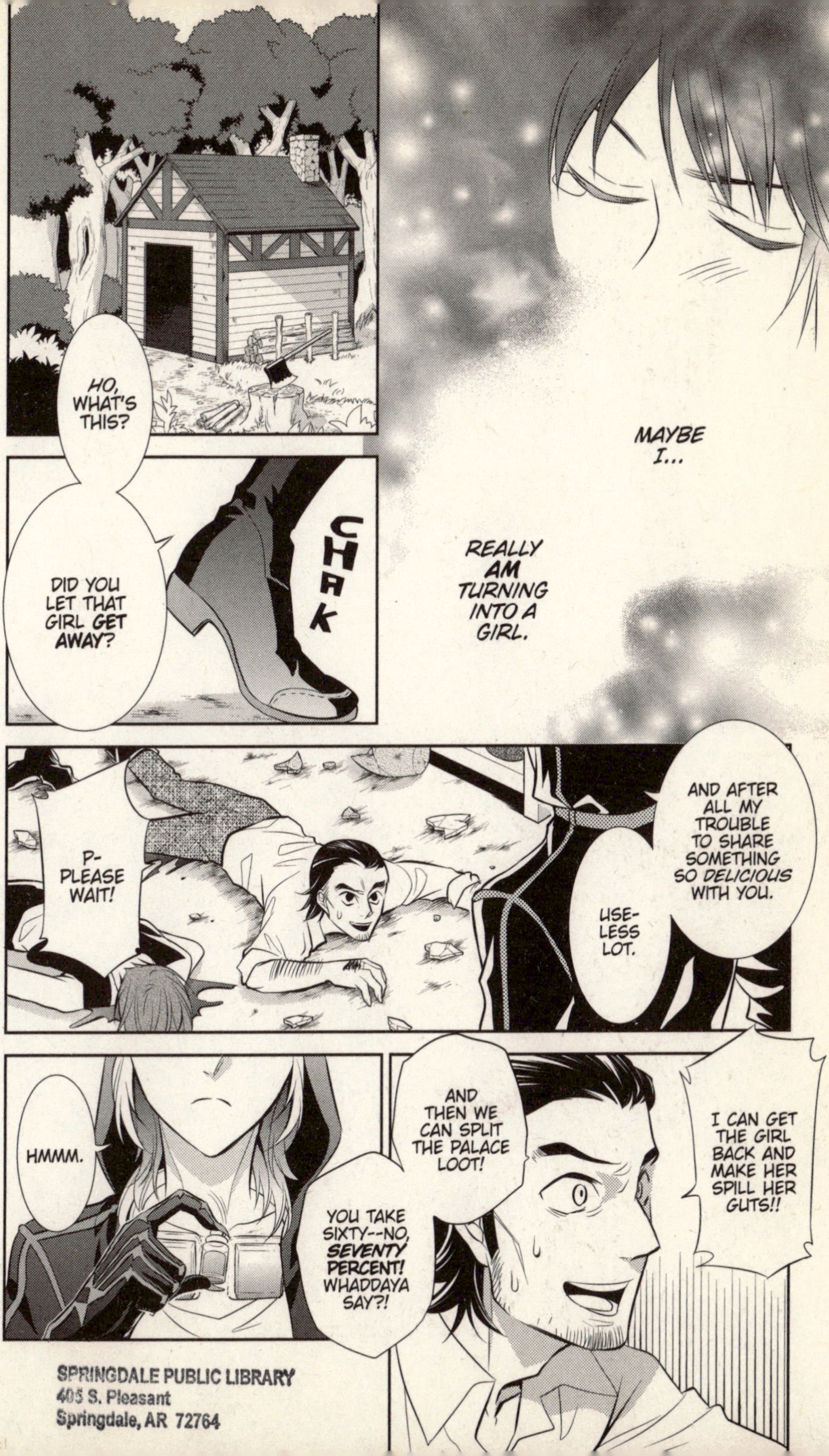
MAYBE I...
REALLY AM TURNING INTO A GIRL.
HO, WHAT'S THIS?
DID YOU LET THAT GIRL GET AWAY?
CHAK
AND AFTER ALL MY TROUBLE TO SHARE SOMETHING SO DELICIOUS WITH YOU.
USE-LESS LOT.
P-PLEASE WAIT!
I CAN GET THE GIRL BACK AND MAKE HER SPILL HER GUTS!!
AND THEN WE CAN SPLIT THE PALACE LOOT!
YOU TAKE SIXTY--NO, SEVENTY PERCENT! WHADDAYA SAY?!
HMMM.

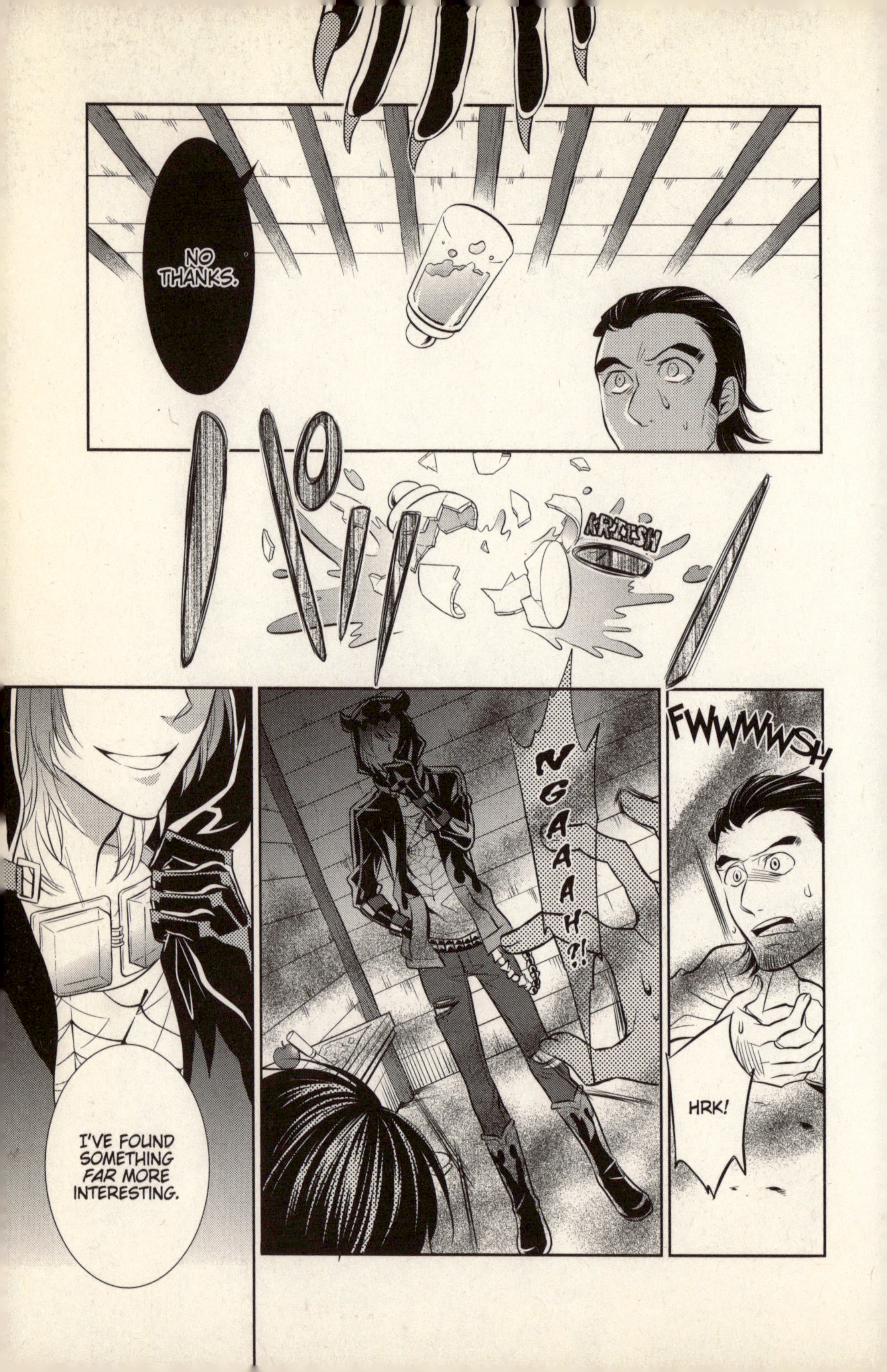
NO THANKS.
KRIISH
FWWWWSH
HRK!
NGAAAAH?!
I'VE FOUND SOMETHING *FAR* MORE INTERESTING.

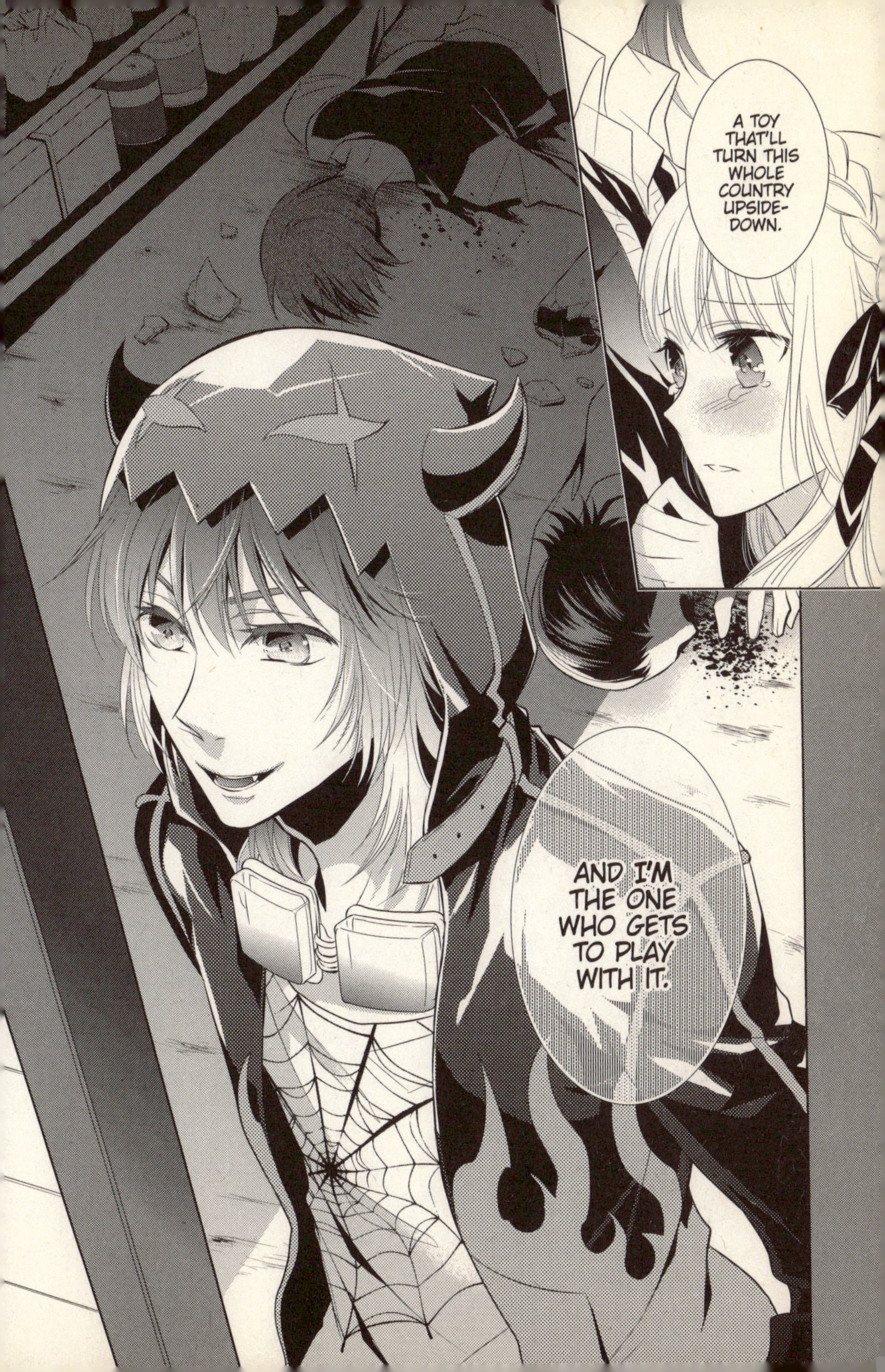
A TOY THAT'LL TURN THIS WHOLE COUNTRY UPSIDE-DOWN.
AND I'M THE ONE WHO GETS TO PLAY WITH IT.

I AM ALICE

I AM ALICE

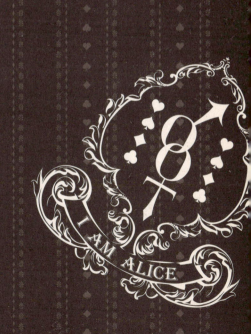

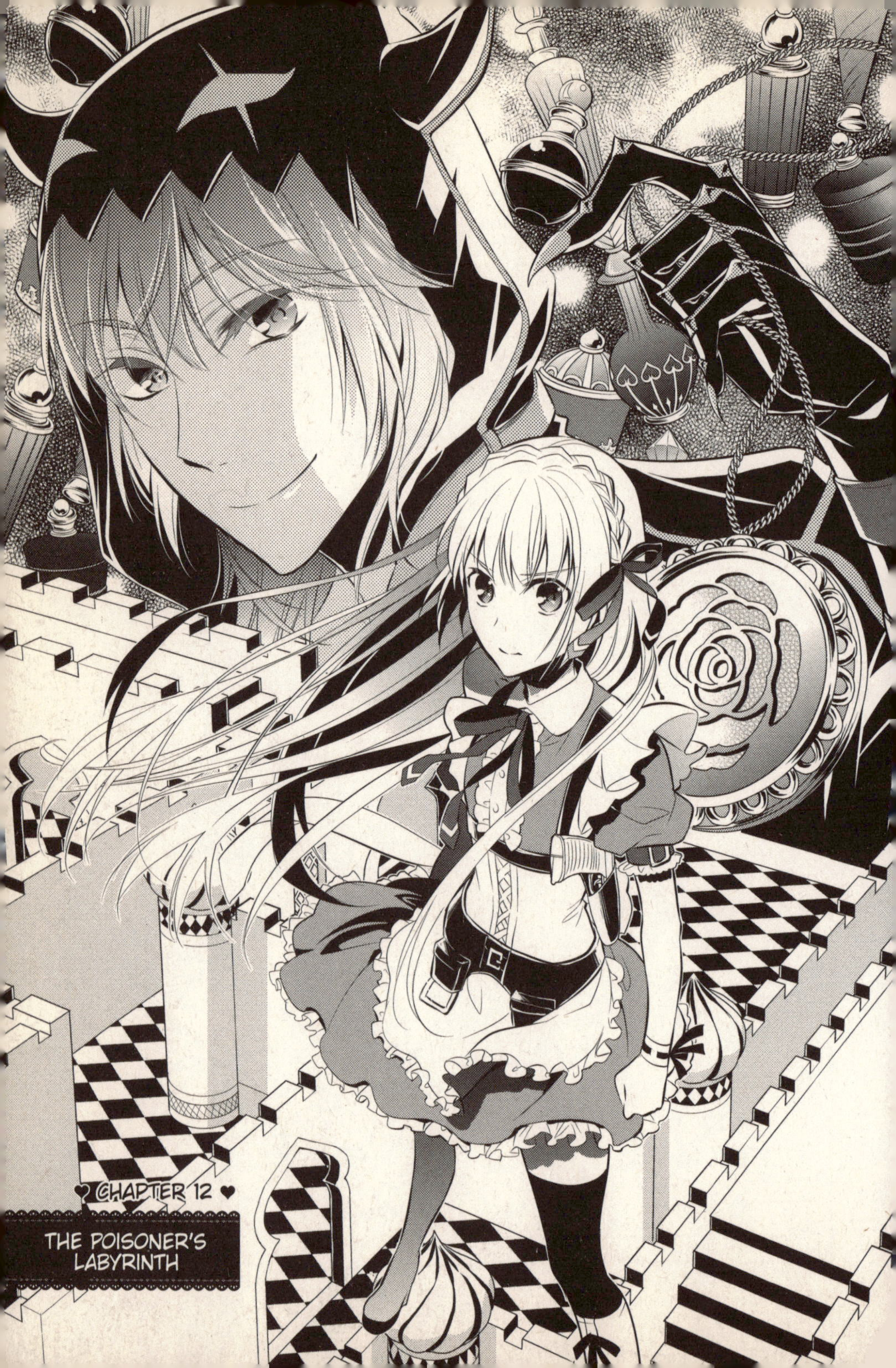
CHAPTER 12
THE POISONER'S LABYRINTH

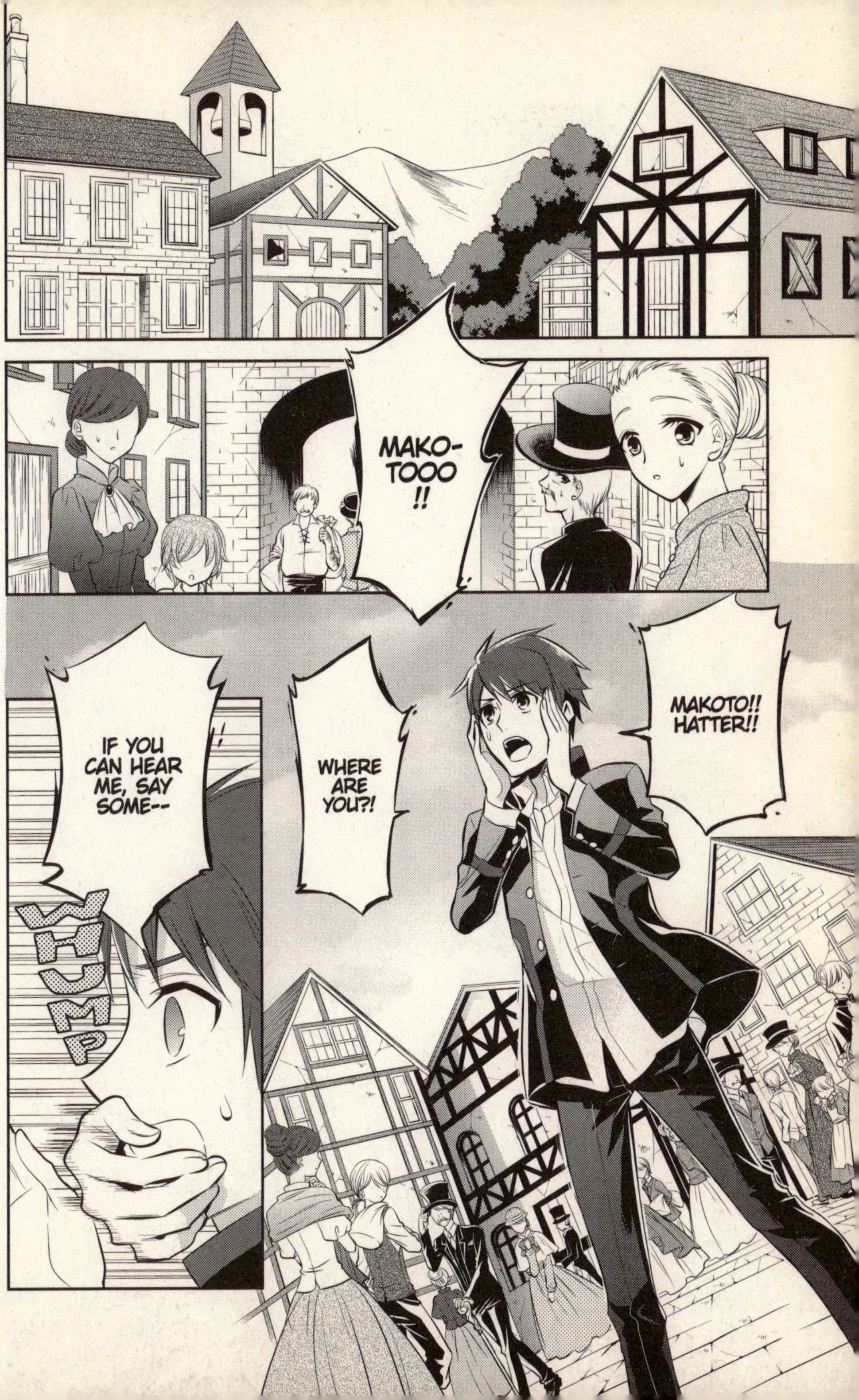
MAKO-TOOO!!
MAKOTO!! HATTER!!
WHERE ARE YOU?!
IF YOU CAN HEAR ME, SAY SOME--
WHUMP

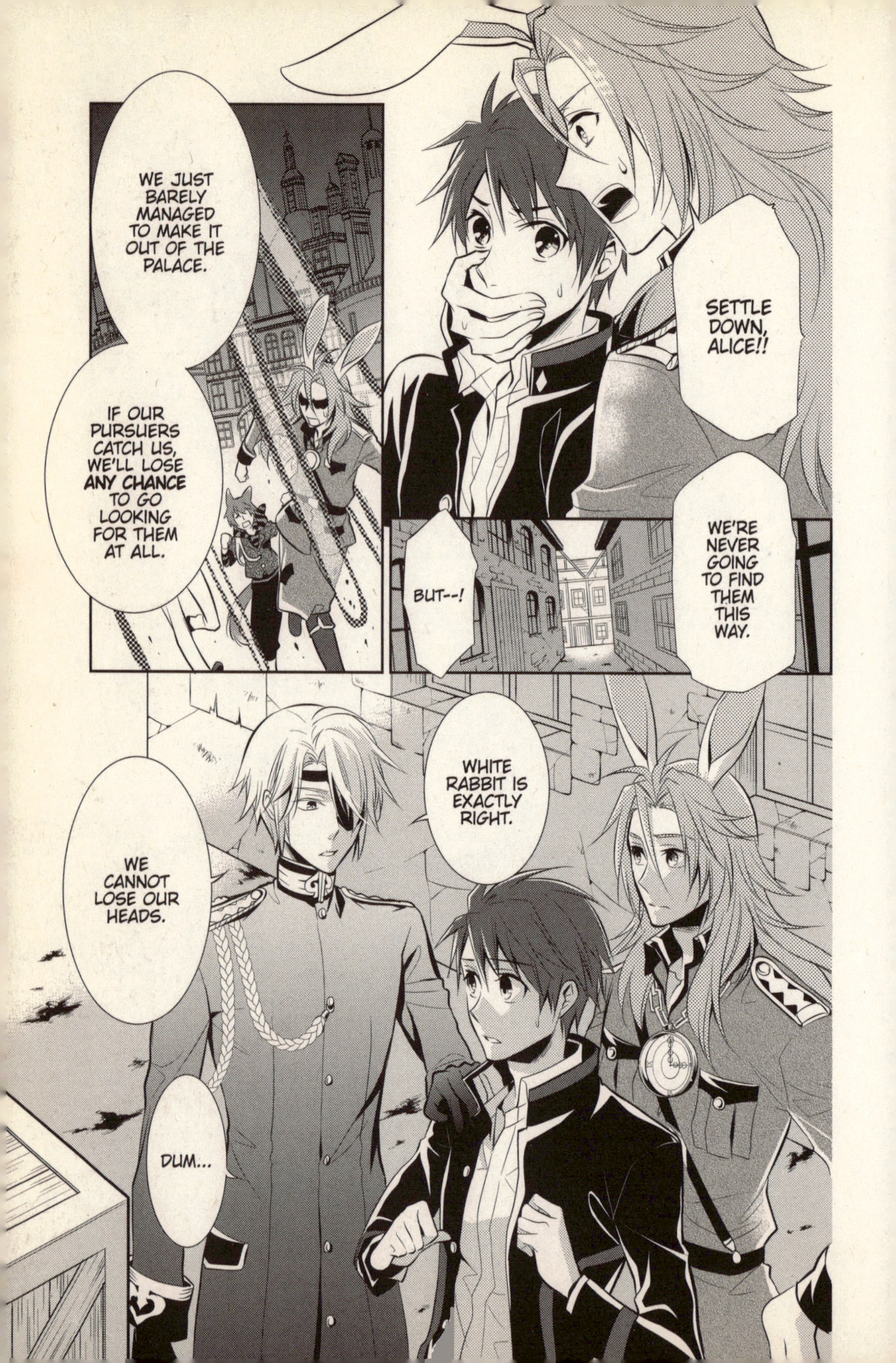
SETTLE DOWN, ALICE!!
WE'RE NEVER GOING TO FIND THEM THIS WAY.
BUT--!
WE JUST BARELY MANAGED TO MAKE IT OUT OF THE PALACE.
IF OUR PURSUERS CATCH US, WE'LL LOSE **ANY CHANCE** TO GO LOOKING FOR THEM AT ALL.
WHITE RABBIT IS EXACTLY RIGHT.
WE CANNOT LOSE OUR HEADS.
DUM...

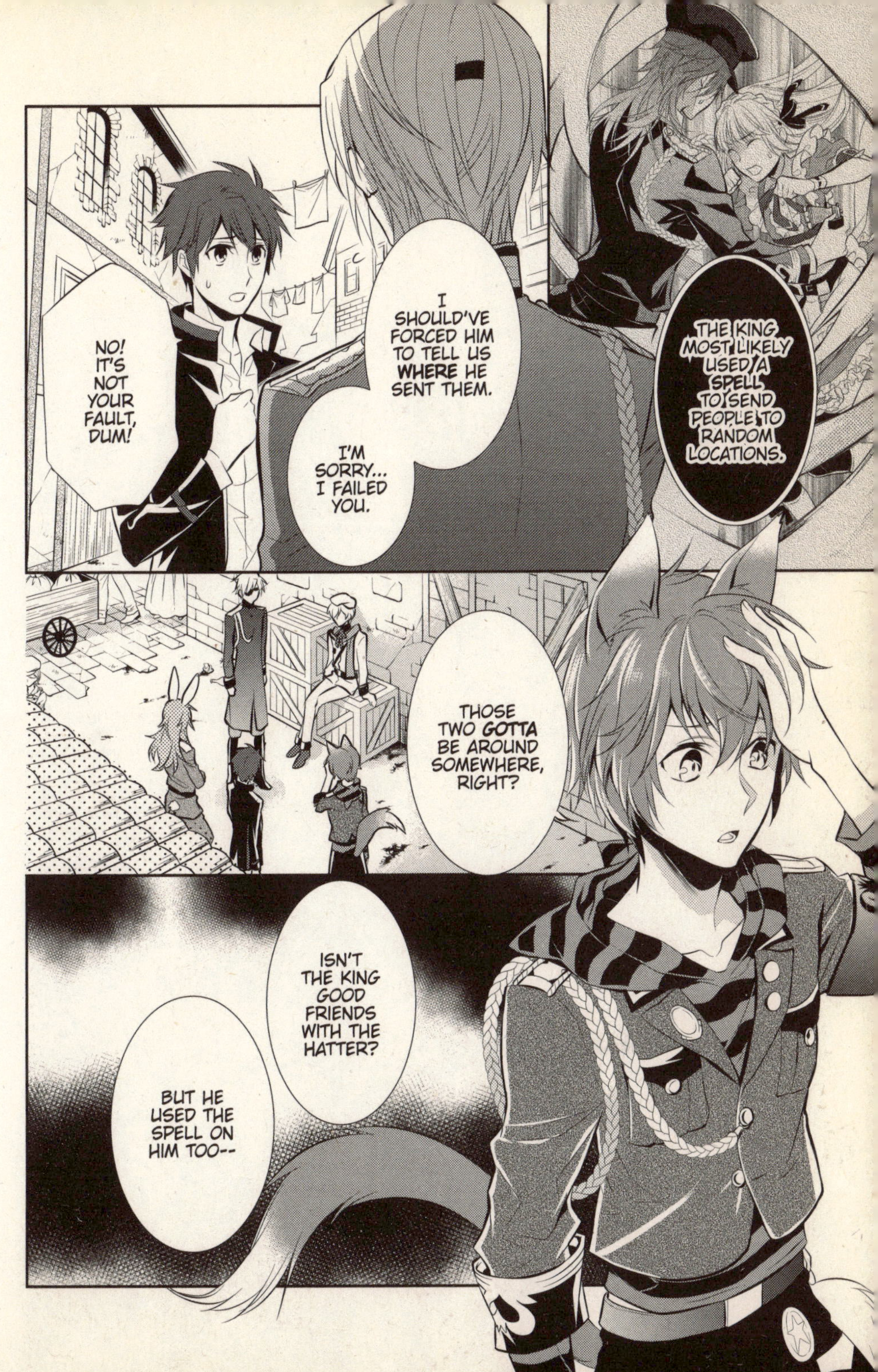
THE KING MOST LIKELY USED A SPELL TO SEND PEOPLE TO RANDOM LOCATIONS.
I SHOULD'VE FORCED HIM TO TELL US **WHERE** HE SENT THEM.
I'M SORRY... I FAILED YOU.
NO! IT'S NOT YOUR FAULT, DUM!
THOSE TWO **GOTTA** BE AROUND SOMEWHERE, RIGHT?
ISN'T THE KING GOOD FRIENDS WITH THE HATTER?
BUT HE USED THE SPELL ON HIM TOO--

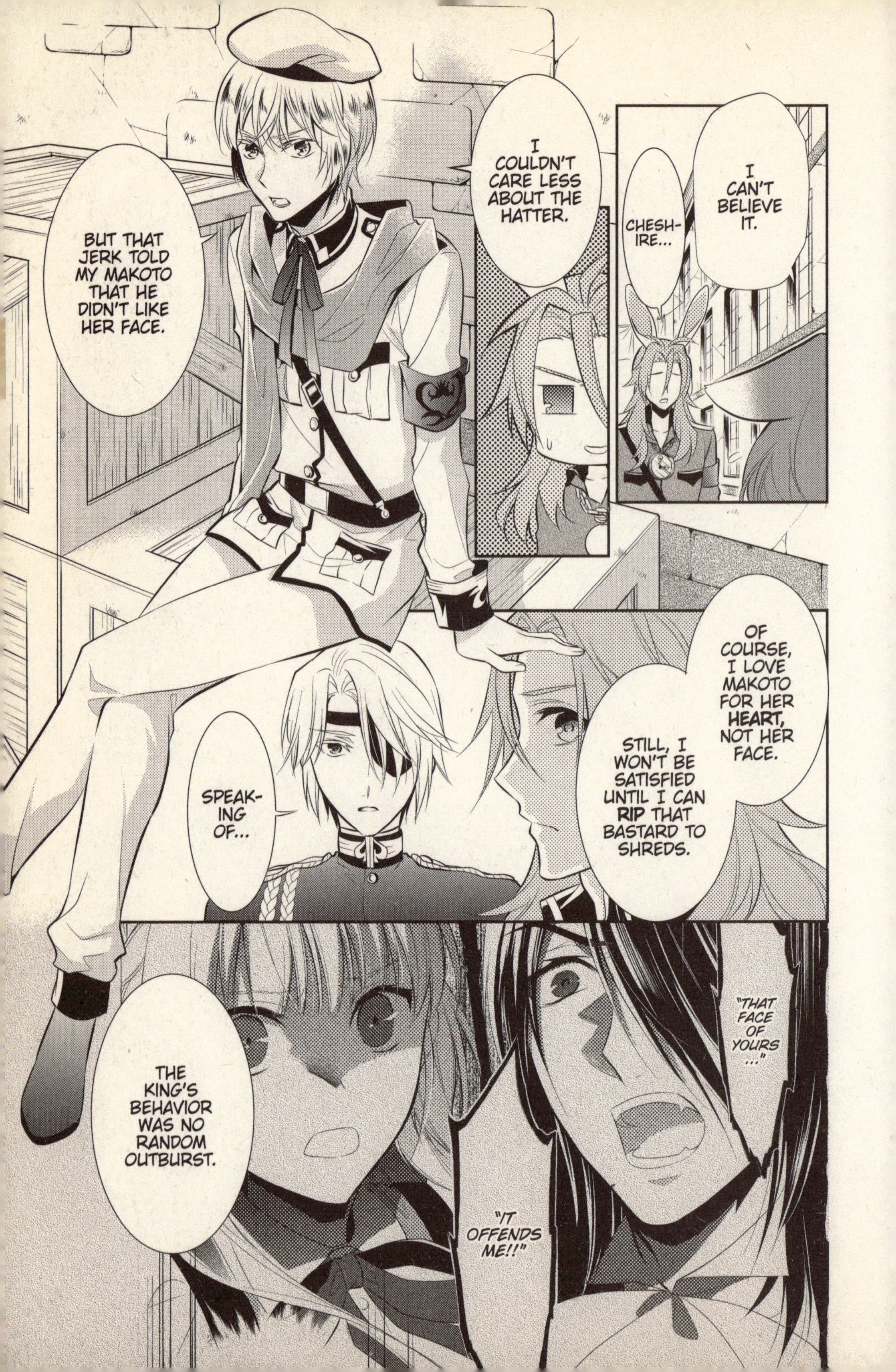
I CAN'T BELIEVE IT.
CHESHIRE...
I COULDN'T CARE LESS ABOUT THE HATTER.
BUT THAT JERK TOLD MY MAKOTO THAT HE DIDN'T LIKE HER FACE.
OF COURSE, I LOVE MAKOTO FOR HER HEART, NOT HER FACE.
STILL, I WON'T BE SATISFIED UNTIL I CAN RIP THAT BASTARD TO SHREDS.
SPEAK-ING OF...
"THAT FACE OF YOURS..."
"IT OFFENDS ME!!"
THE KING'S BEHAVIOR WAS NO RANDOM OUTBURST.

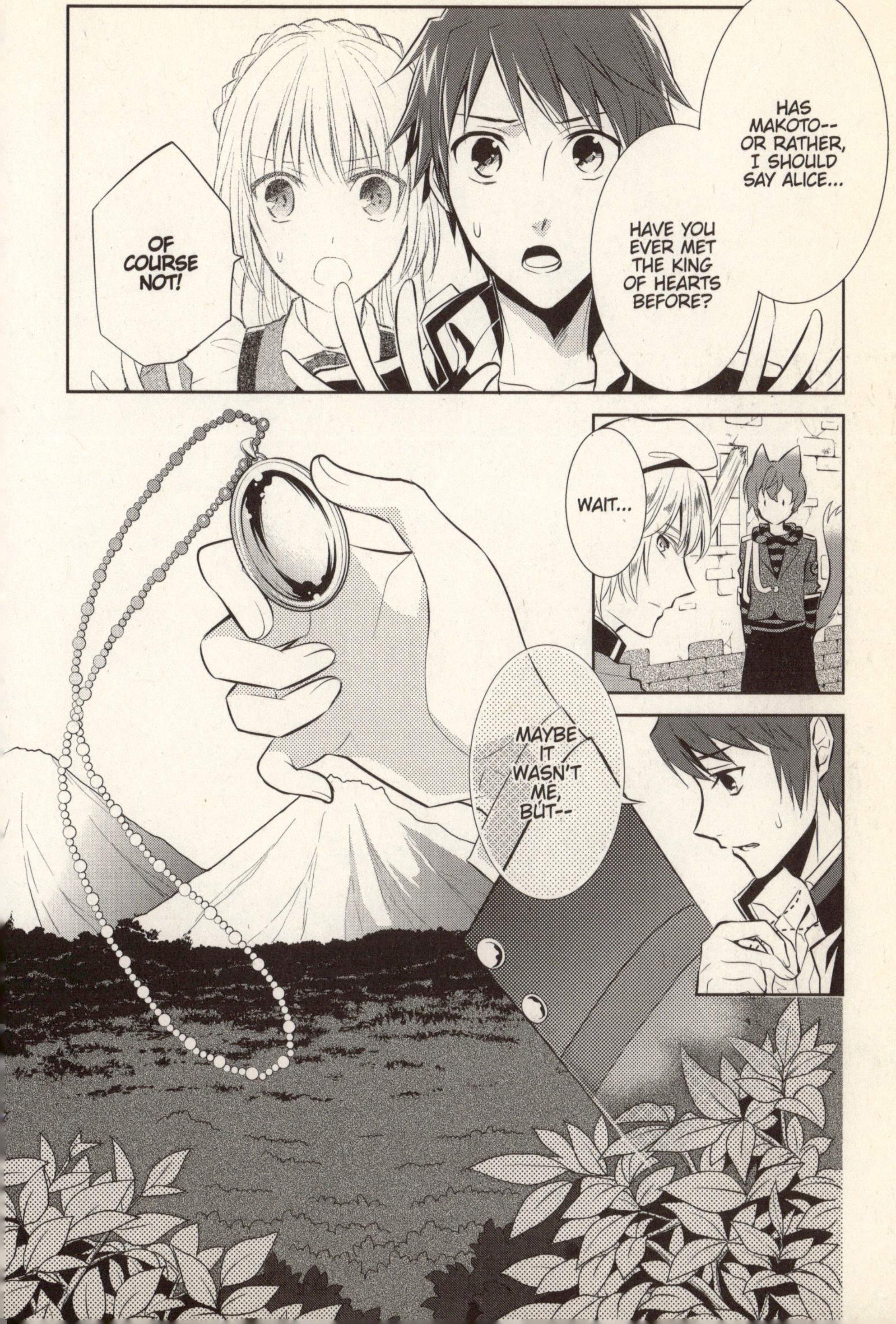
HAS MAKOTO-- OR RATHER, I SHOULD SAY ALICE...
HAVE YOU EVER MET THE KING OF HEARTS BEFORE?
OF COURSE NOT!
WAIT...
MAYBE IT WASN'T ME, BUT--

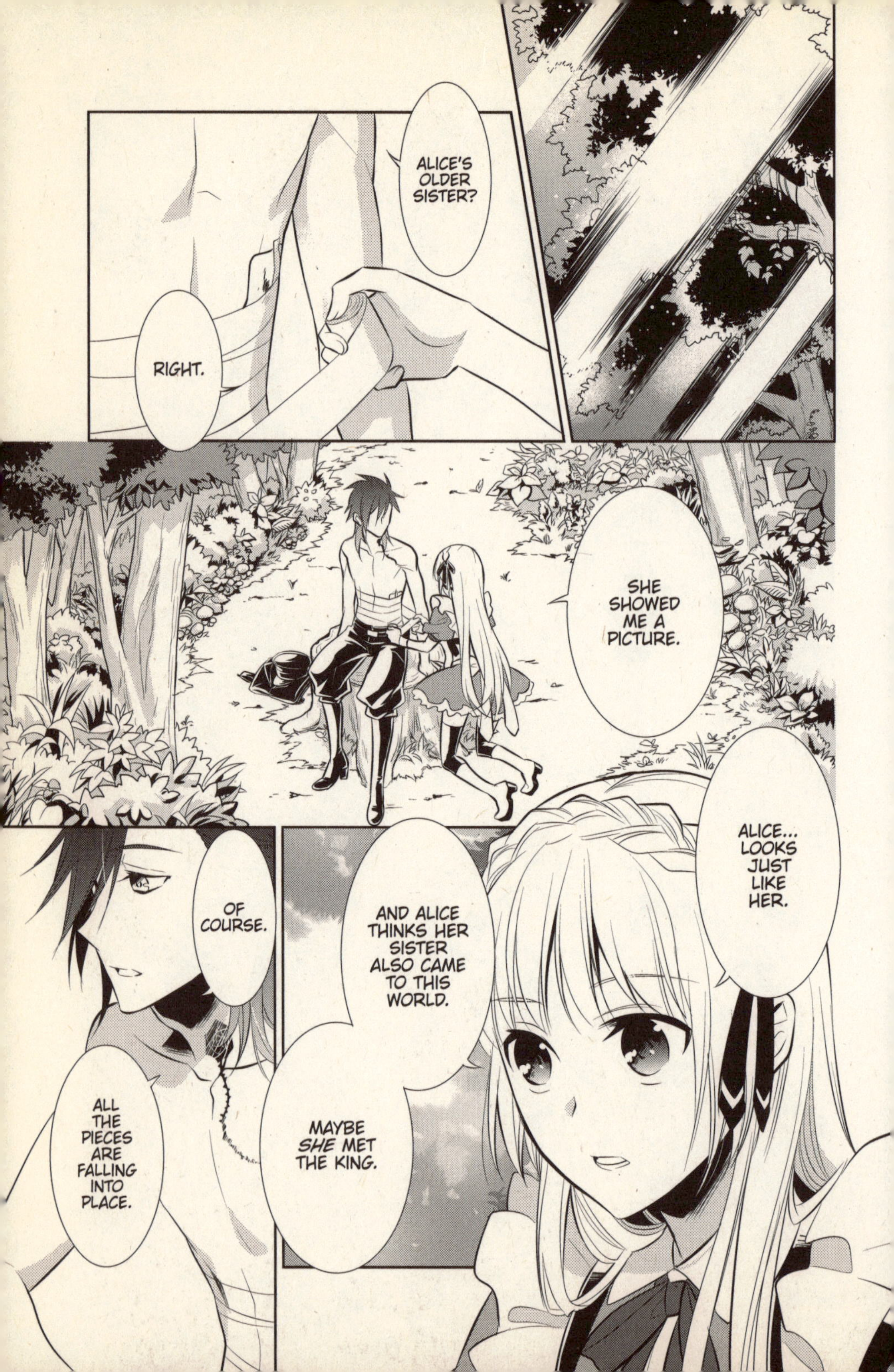
ALICE'S OLDER SISTER?
RIGHT.
SHE SHOWED ME A PICTURE.
ALICE... LOOKS JUST LIKE HER.
AND ALICE THINKS HER SISTER ALSO CAME TO THIS WORLD.
MAYBE *SHE* MET THE KING.
OF COURSE.
ALL THE PIECES ARE FALLING INTO PLACE.

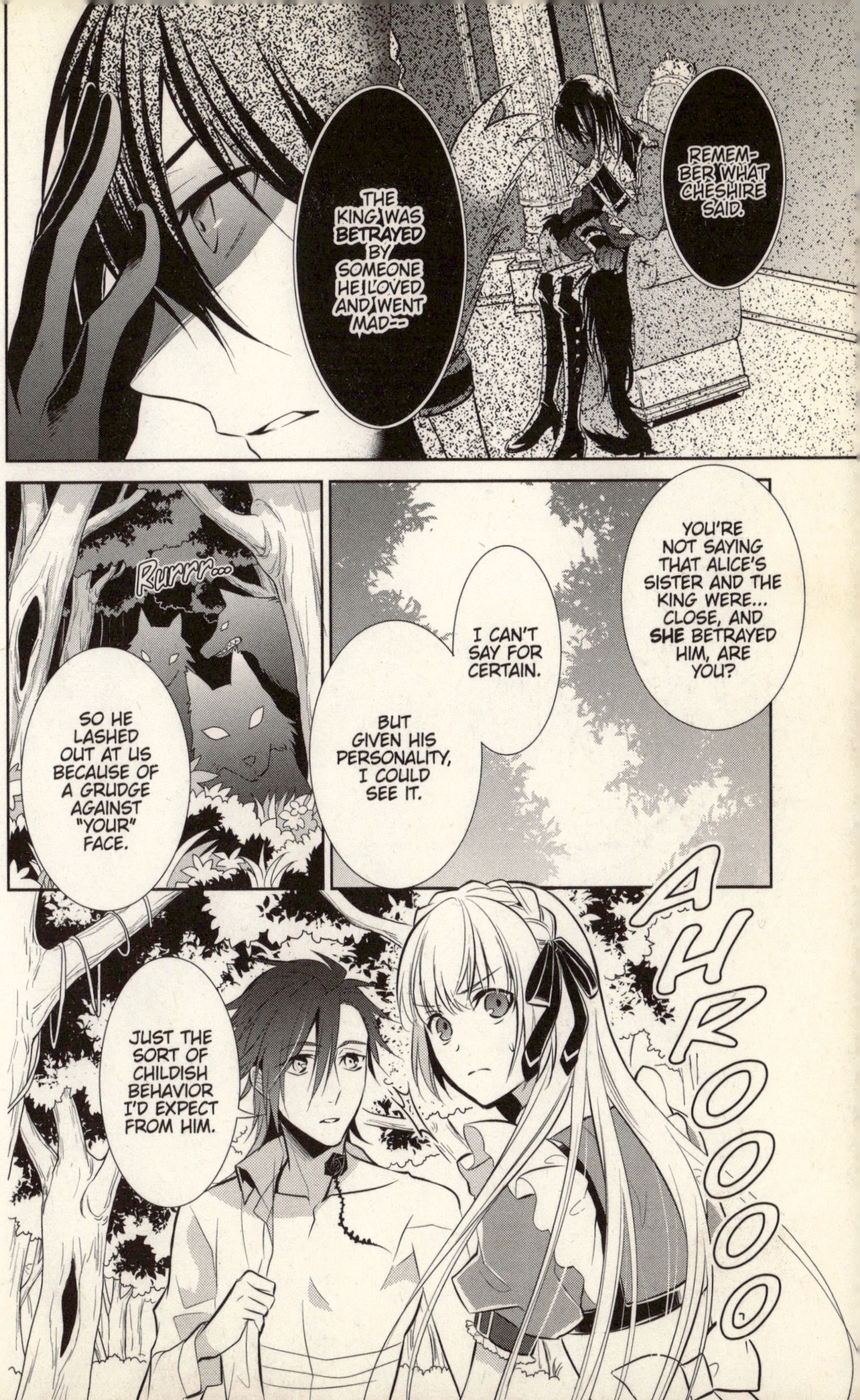
REMEMBER WHAT CHESHIRE SAID.
THE KING WAS BETRAYED BY SOMEONE HE LOVED AND WENT MAD--
YOU'RE NOT SAYING THAT ALICE'S SISTER AND THE KING WERE... CLOSE, AND SHE BETRAYED HIM, ARE YOU?
I CAN'T SAY FOR CERTAIN.
BUT GIVEN HIS PERSONALITY, I COULD SEE IT.
Rurrr...
SO HE LASHED OUT AT US BECAUSE OF A GRUDGE AGAINST "YOUR" FACE.
AHROOOOO
JUST THE SORT OF CHILDISH BEHAVIOR I'D EXPECT FROM HIM.

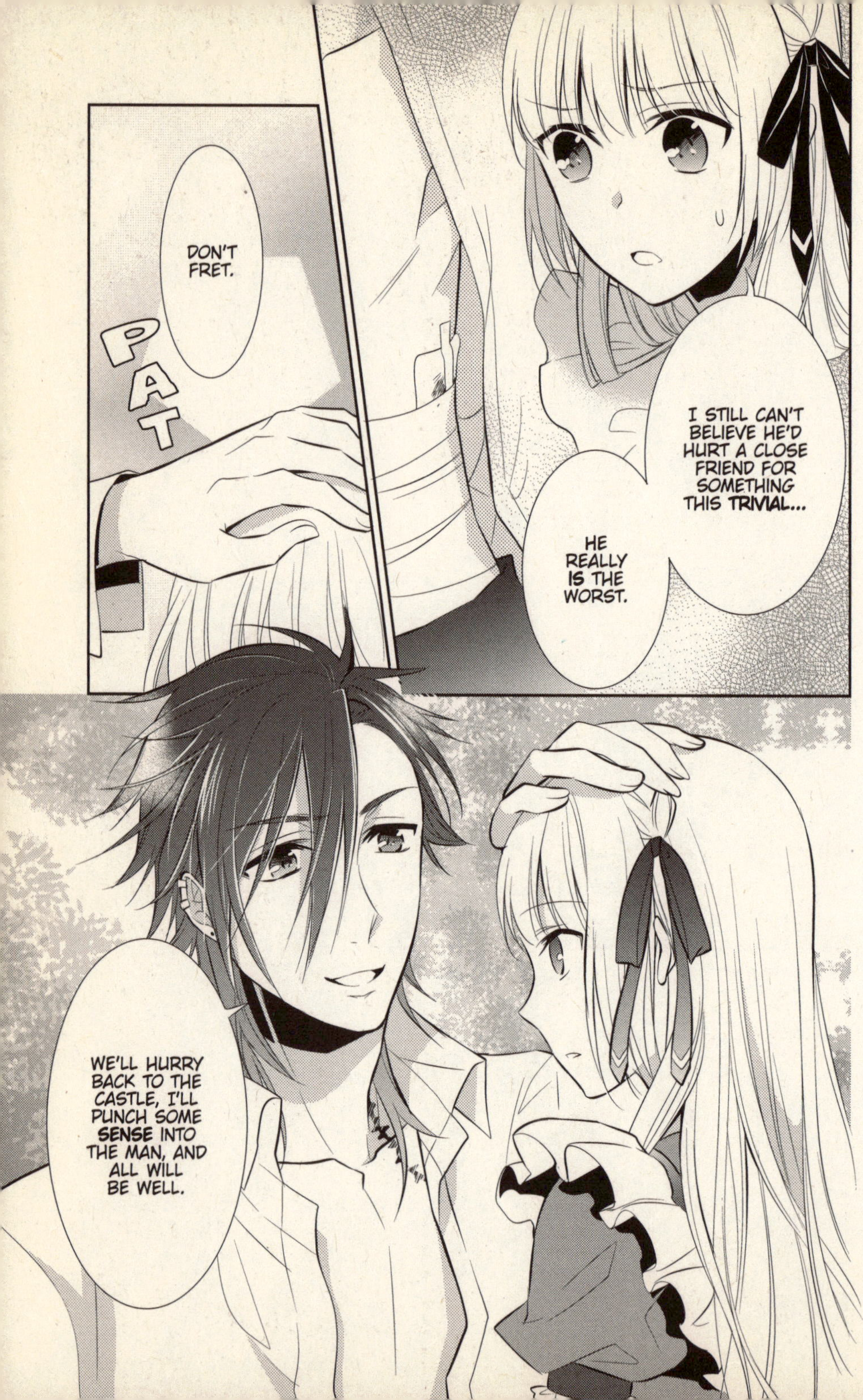
I STILL CAN'T BELIEVE HE'D HURT A CLOSE FRIEND FOR SOMETHING THIS **TRIVIAL...**
HE REALLY **IS** THE WORST.
DON'T FRET.
PAT
WE'LL HURRY BACK TO THE CASTLE, I'LL PUNCH SOME **SENSE** INTO THE MAN, AND ALL WILL BE WELL.

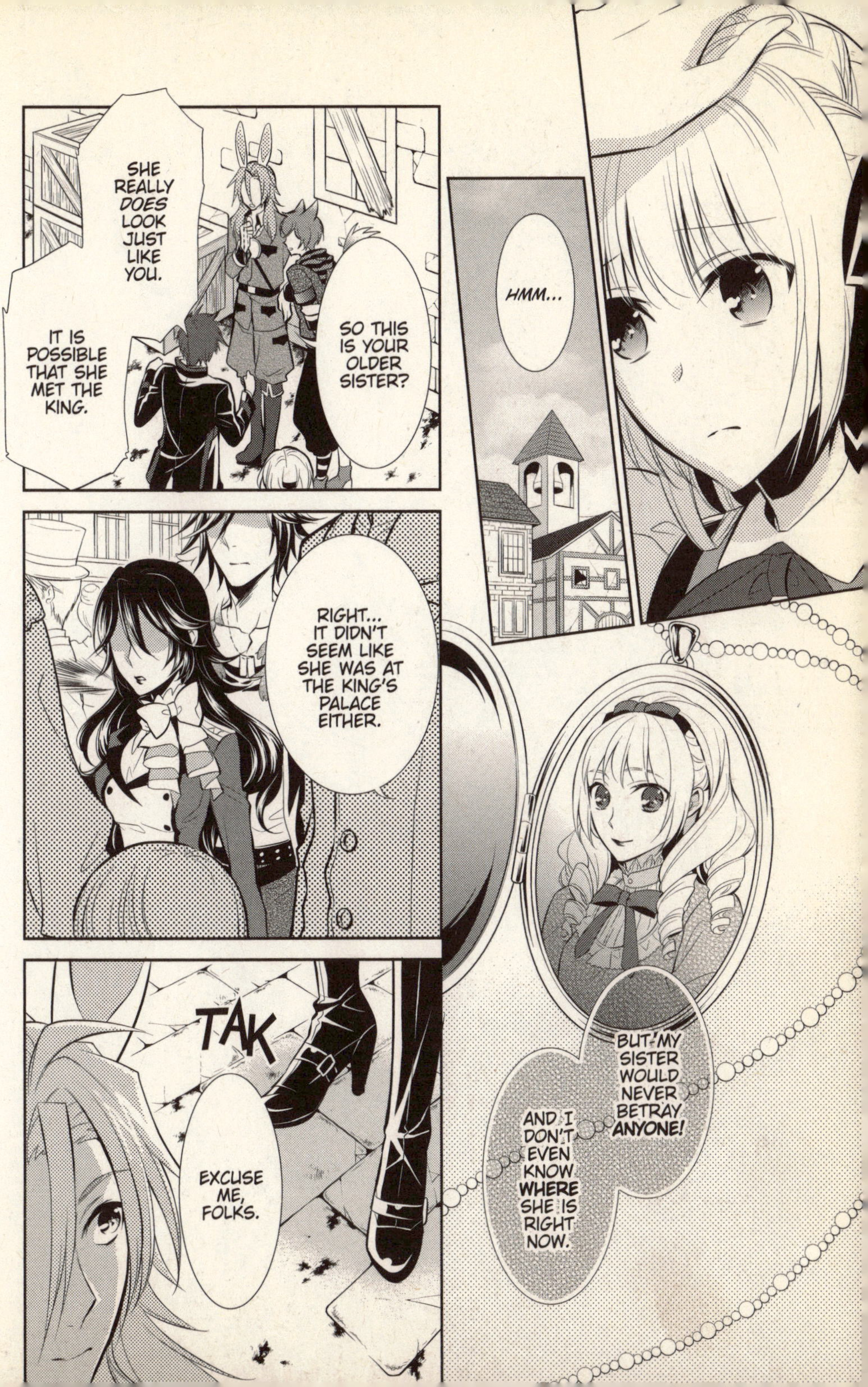
HMM...
BUT MY SISTER WOULD NEVER BETRAY ANYONE!
AND I DON'T EVEN KNOW WHERE SHE IS RIGHT NOW.
SO THIS IS YOUR OLDER SISTER?
SHE REALLY DOES LOOK JUST LIKE YOU.
IT IS POSSIBLE THAT SHE MET THE KING.
RIGHT... IT DIDN'T SEEM LIKE SHE WAS AT THE KING'S PALACE EITHER.
TAK
EXCUSE ME, FOLKS.

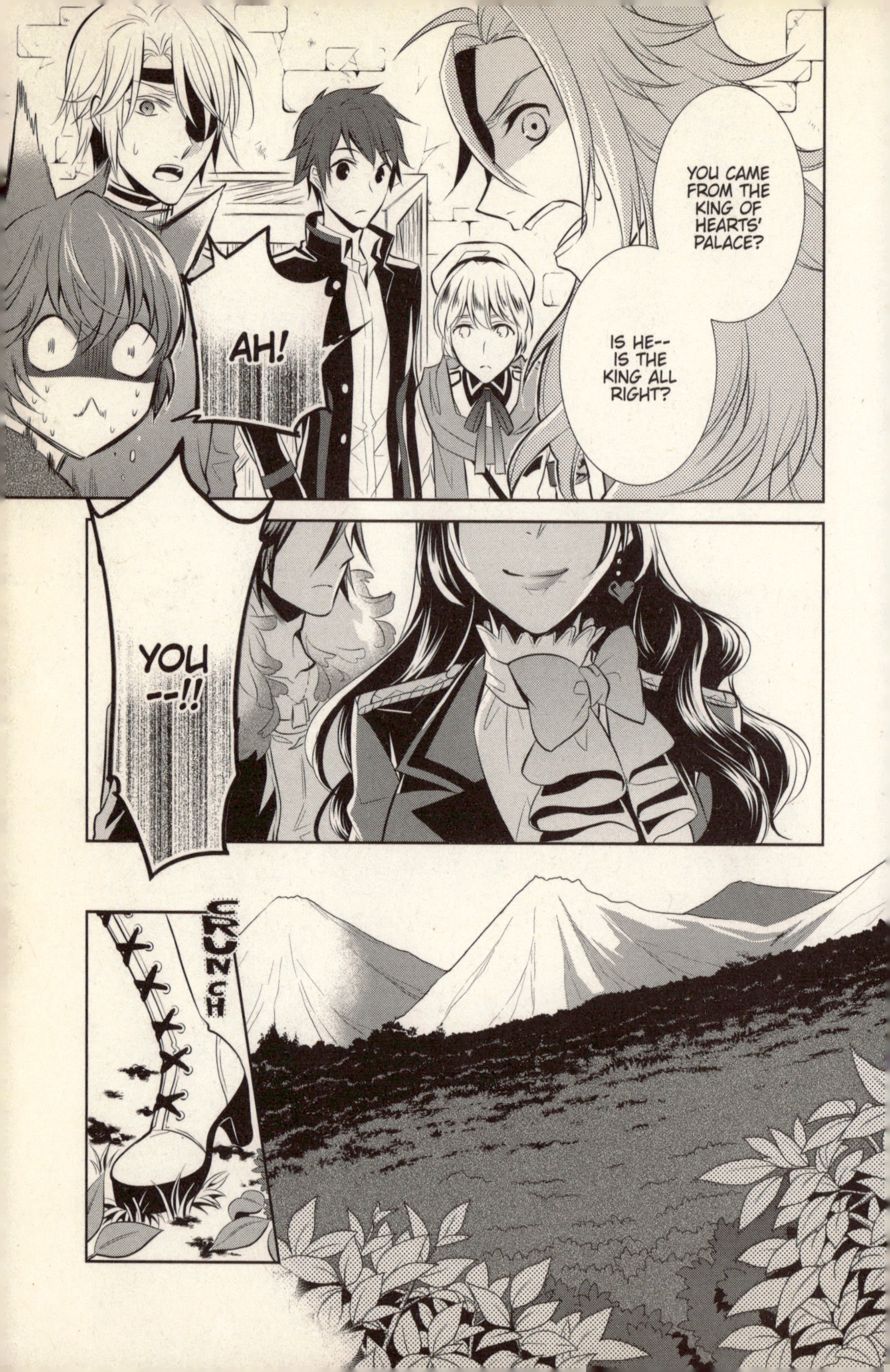
YOU CAME FROM THE KING OF HEARTS' PALACE?
IS HE-- IS THE KING ALL RIGHT?
AH!
YOU --!!
CRUNCH

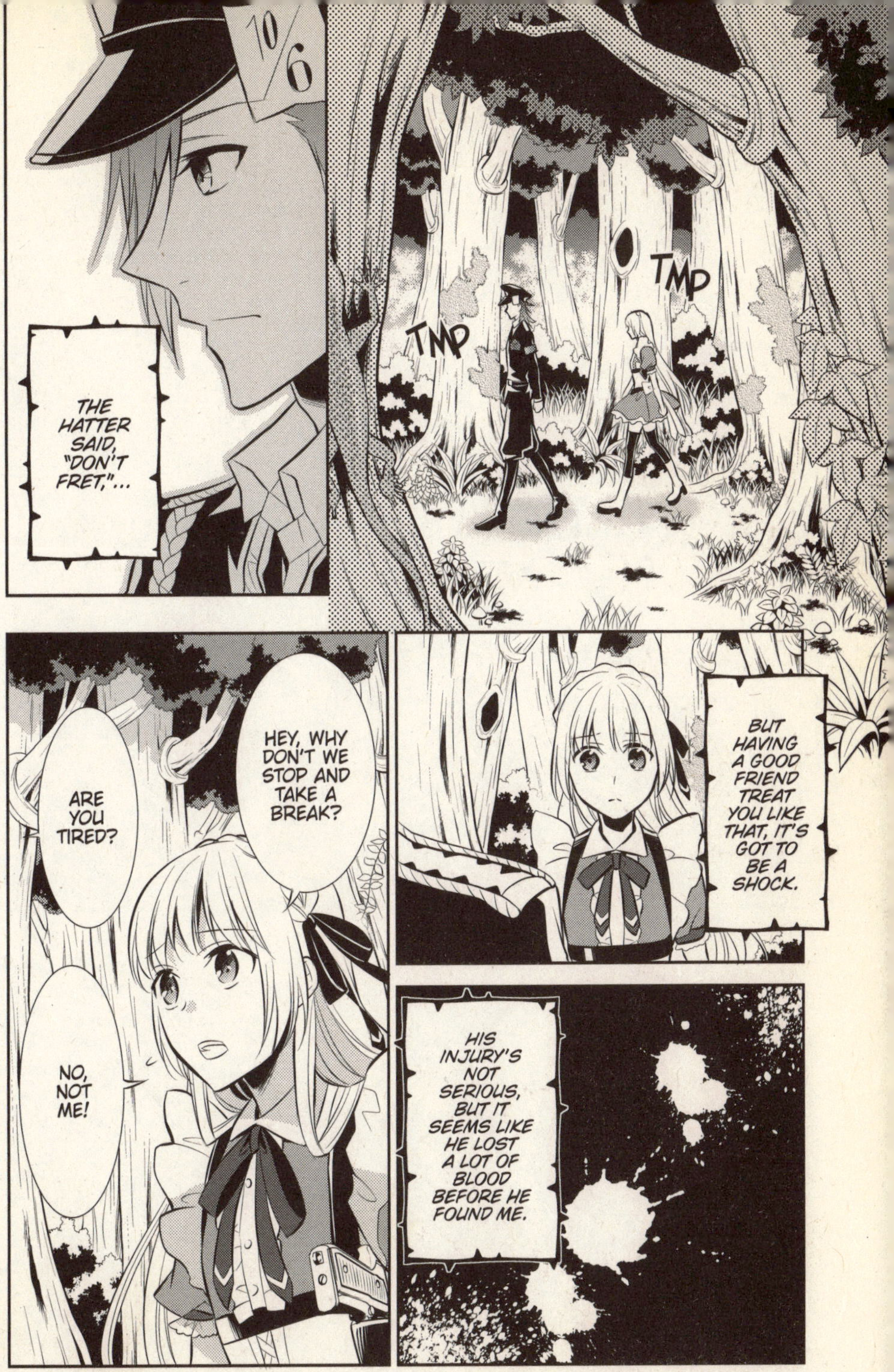
TMP
TMP
THE HATTER SAID, "DON'T FRET,"...
BUT HAVING A GOOD FRIEND TREAT YOU LIKE THAT, IT'S GOT TO BE A SHOCK.
HIS INJURY'S NOT SERIOUS, BUT IT SEEMS LIKE HE LOST A LOT OF BLOOD BEFORE HE FOUND ME.
HEY, WHY DON'T WE STOP AND TAKE A BREAK?
ARE YOU TIRED?
NO, NOT ME!

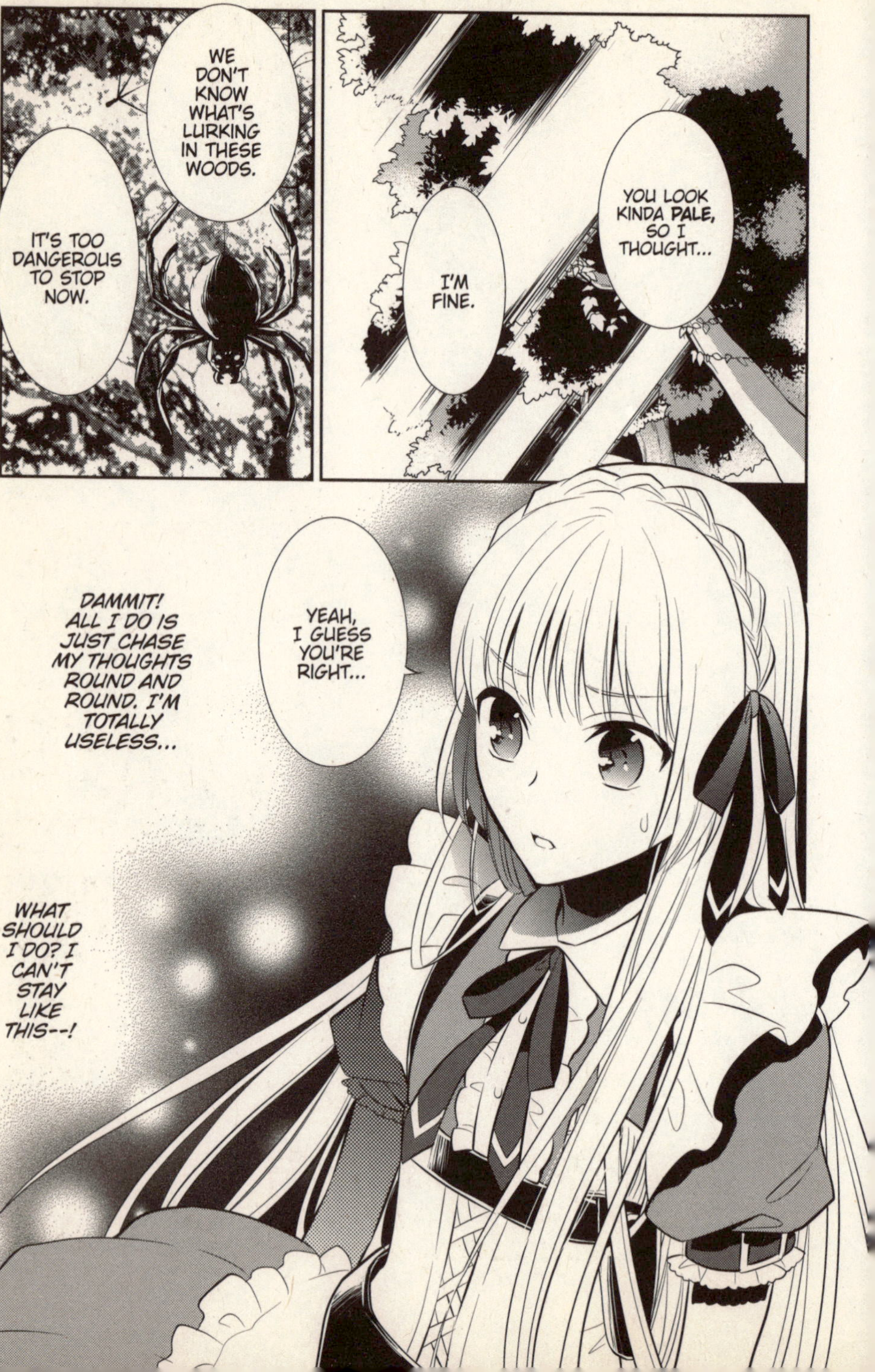
YOU LOOK KINDA PALE, SO I THOUGHT...
I'M FINE.
WE DON'T KNOW WHAT'S LURKING IN THESE WOODS.
IT'S TOO DANGEROUS TO STOP NOW.
YEAH, I GUESS YOU'RE RIGHT...
DAMMIT! ALL I DO IS JUST CHASE MY THOUGHTS ROUND AND ROUND. I'M TOTALLY USELESS...
WHAT SHOULD I DO? I CAN'T STAY LIKE THIS--!

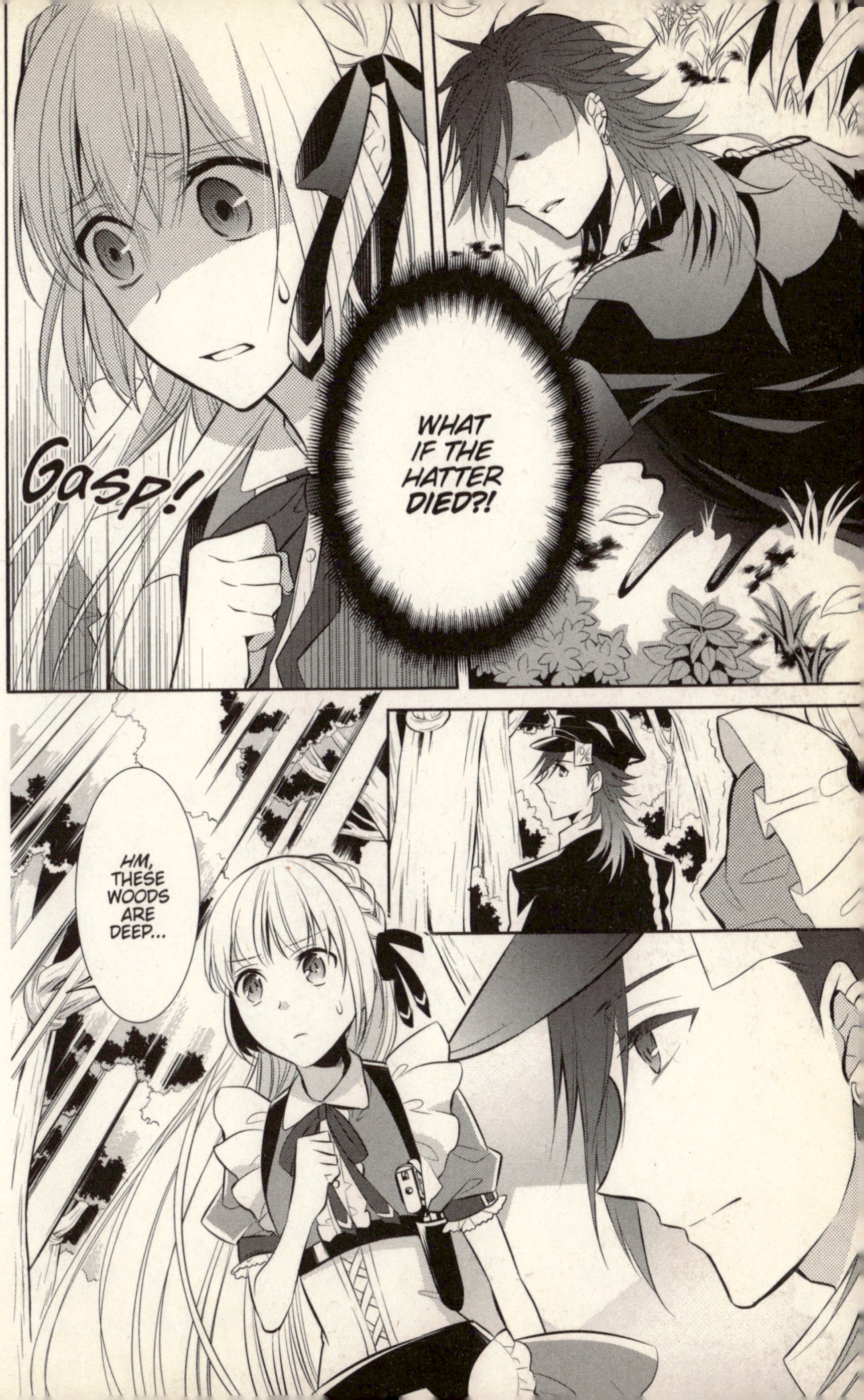
WHAT IF THE HATTER DIED?!
Gasp!
HM, THESE WOODS ARE DEEP...

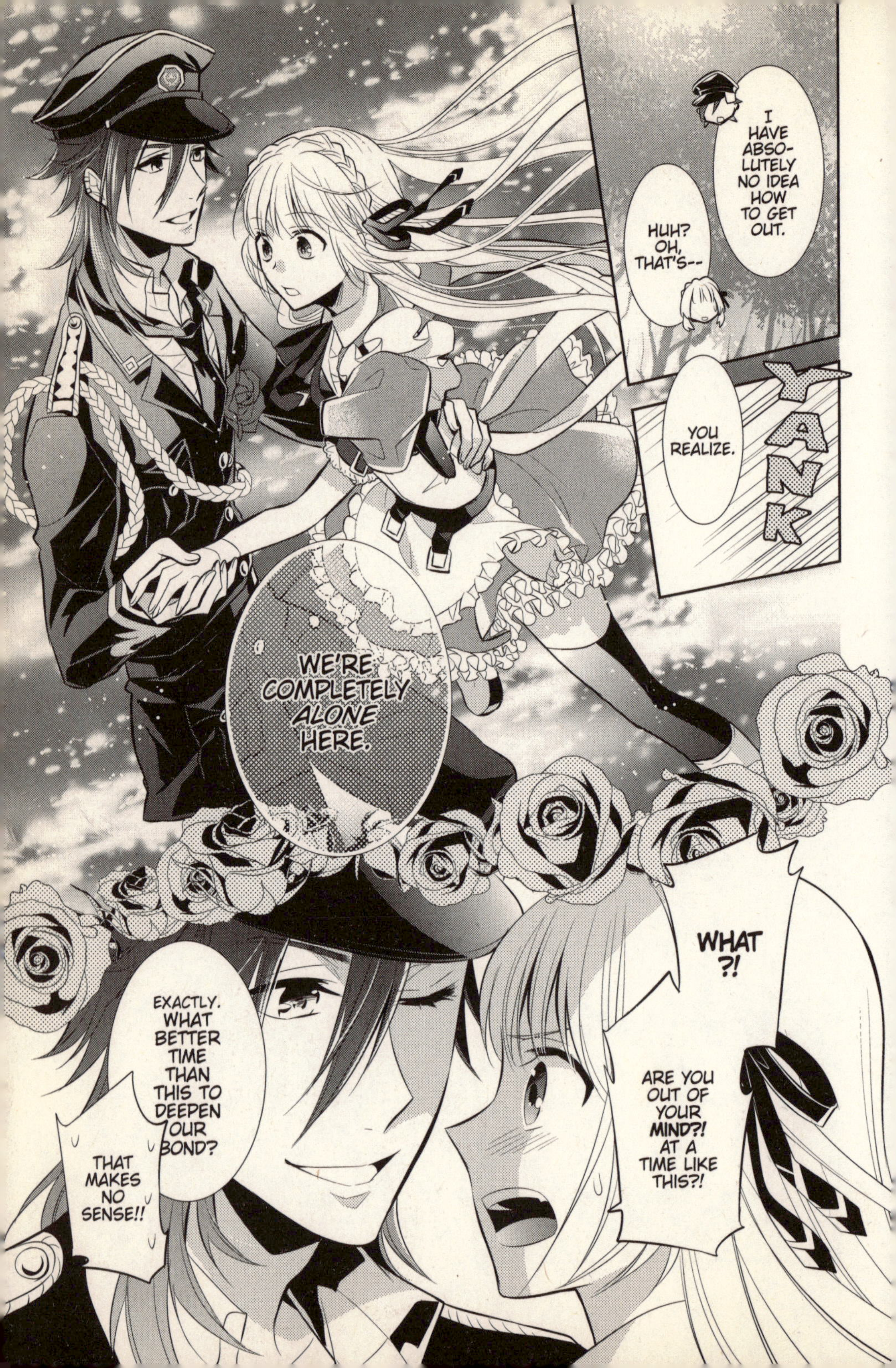
I HAVE ABSOLUTELY NO IDEA HOW TO GET OUT.
HUH? OH, THAT'S--
YANK
YOU REALIZE.
WE'RE COMPLETELY ALONE HERE.
WHAT?!
EXACTLY. WHAT BETTER TIME THAN THIS TO DEEPEN OUR BOND?
ARE YOU OUT OF YOUR MIND?! AT A TIME LIKE THIS?!
THAT MAKES NO SENSE!!

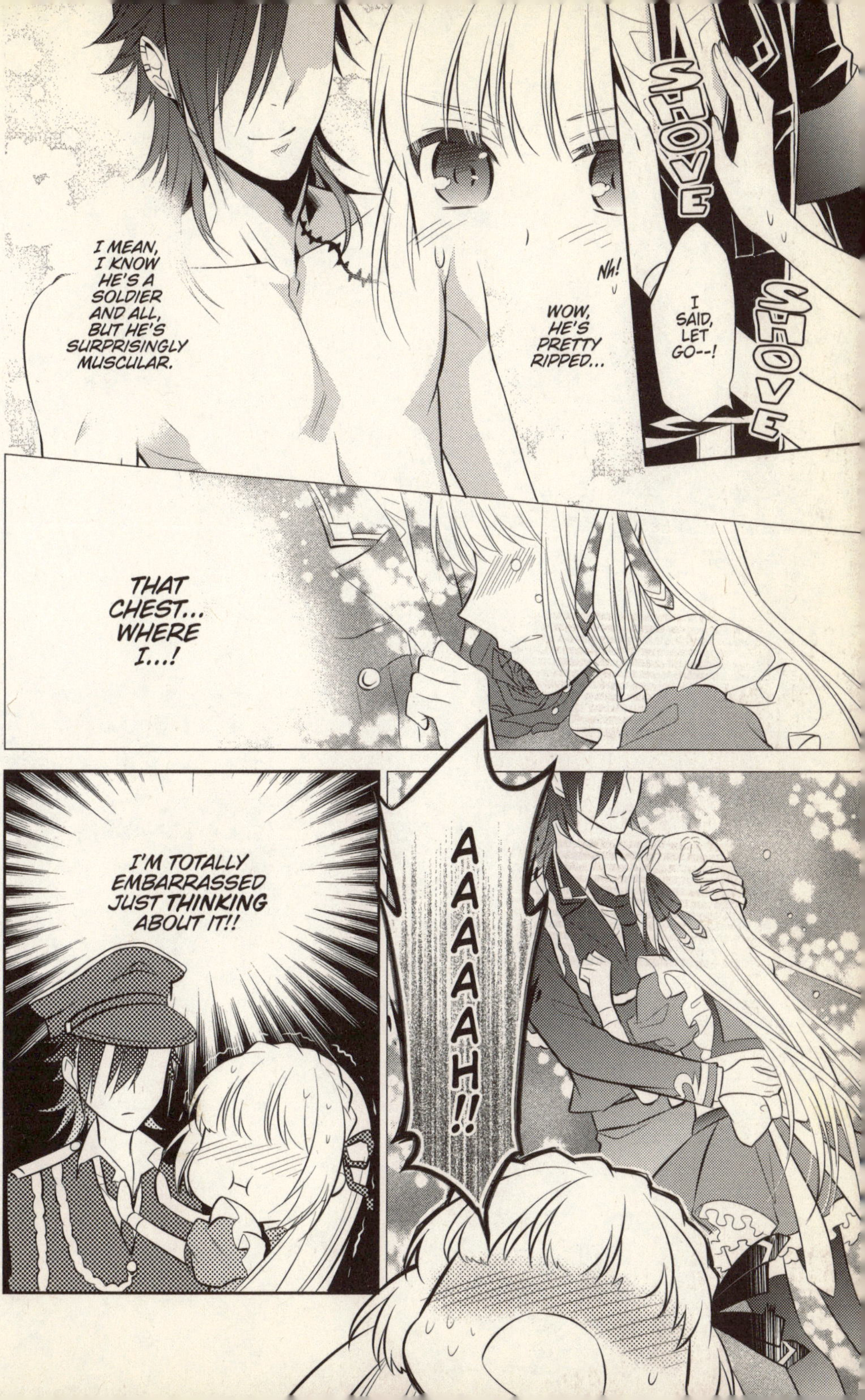
SHOVE
SHOVE
SHOVE
I SAID, LET GO--!
Nh!
WOW, HE'S PRETTY RIPPED...
I MEAN, I KNOW HE'S A SOLDIER AND ALL, BUT HE'S SURPRISINGLY MUSCULAR.
THAT CHEST... WHERE I...!
AAAAAAH!!
I'M TOTALLY EMBARRASSED JUST THINKING ABOUT IT!!

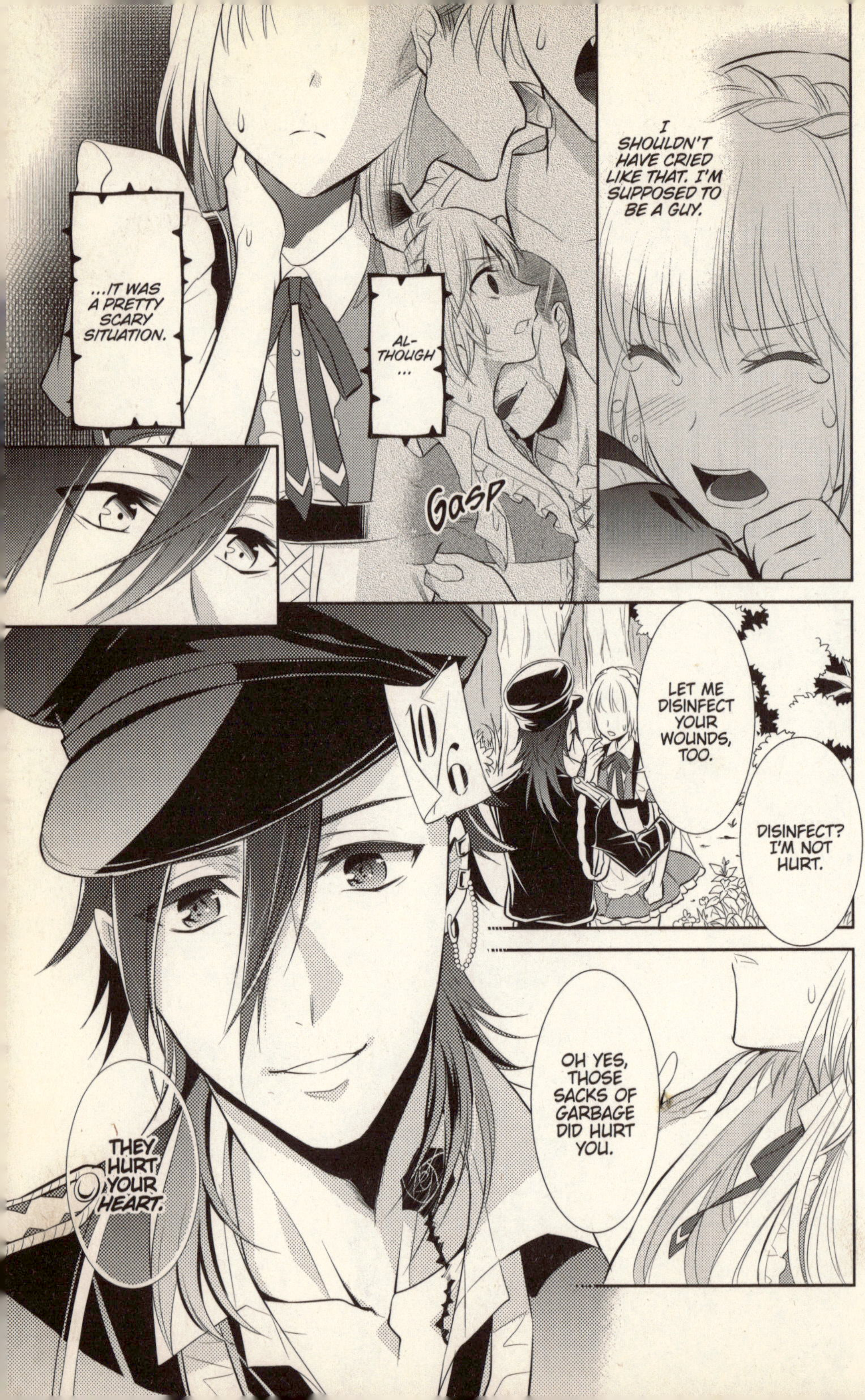
I SHOULDN'T HAVE CRIED LIKE THAT. I'M SUPPOSED TO BE A GUY.
ALTHOUGH...
...IT WAS A PRETTY SCARY SITUATION.
GASP
LET ME DISINFECT YOUR WOUNDS, TOO.
DISINFECT? I'M NOT HURT.
OH YES, THOSE SACKS OF GARBAGE DID HURT YOU.
10/6
THEY HURT YOUR HEART.

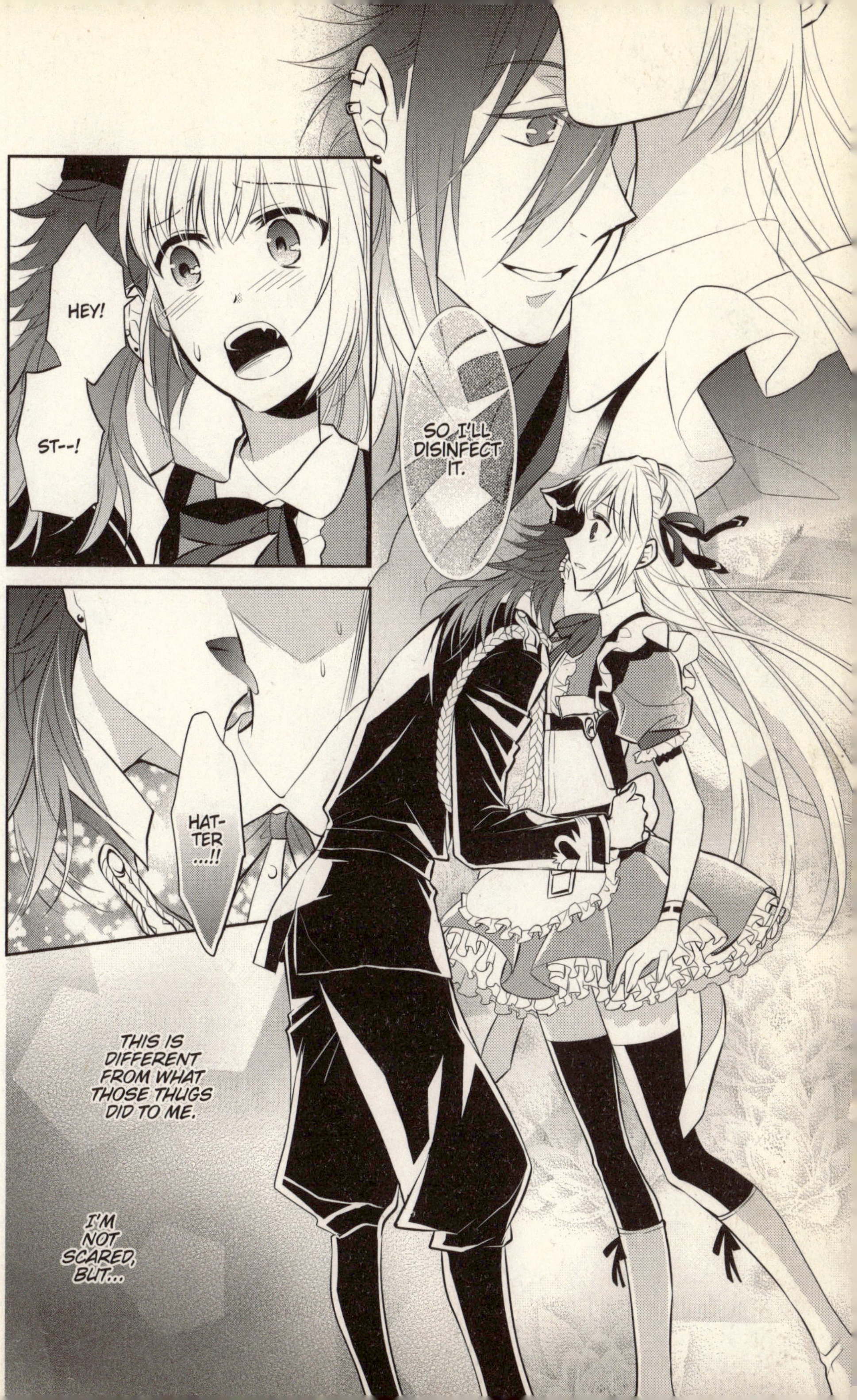
SO I'LL DISINFECT IT.
HEY!
ST--!
HAT-TER ...!!
THIS IS DIFFERENT FROM WHAT THOSE THUGS DID TO ME.
I'M NOT SCARED, BUT...

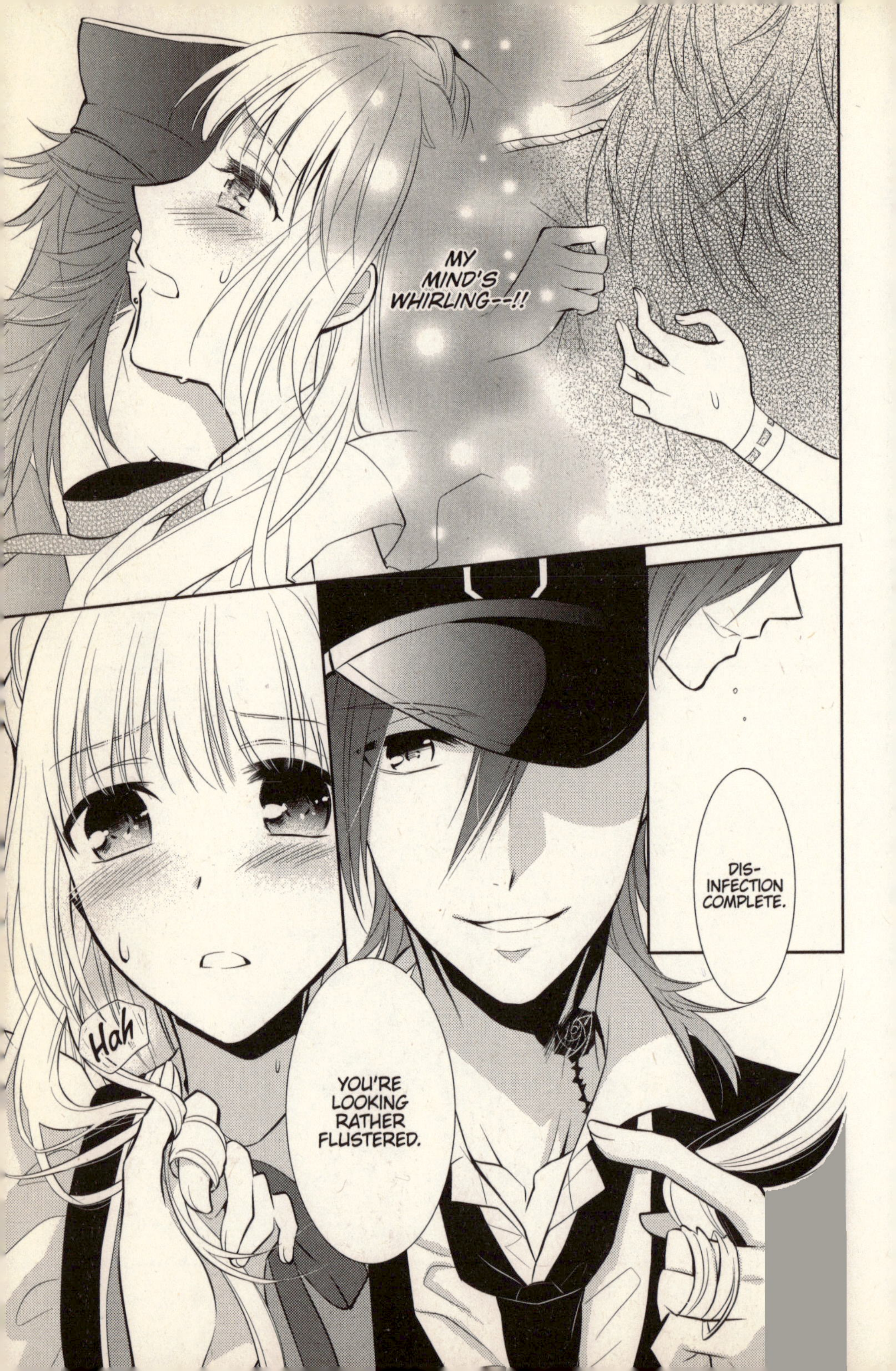
MY MIND'S WHIRLING--!!
DIS-INFECTION COMPLETE.
YOU'RE LOOKING RATHER FLUSTERED.
Hah

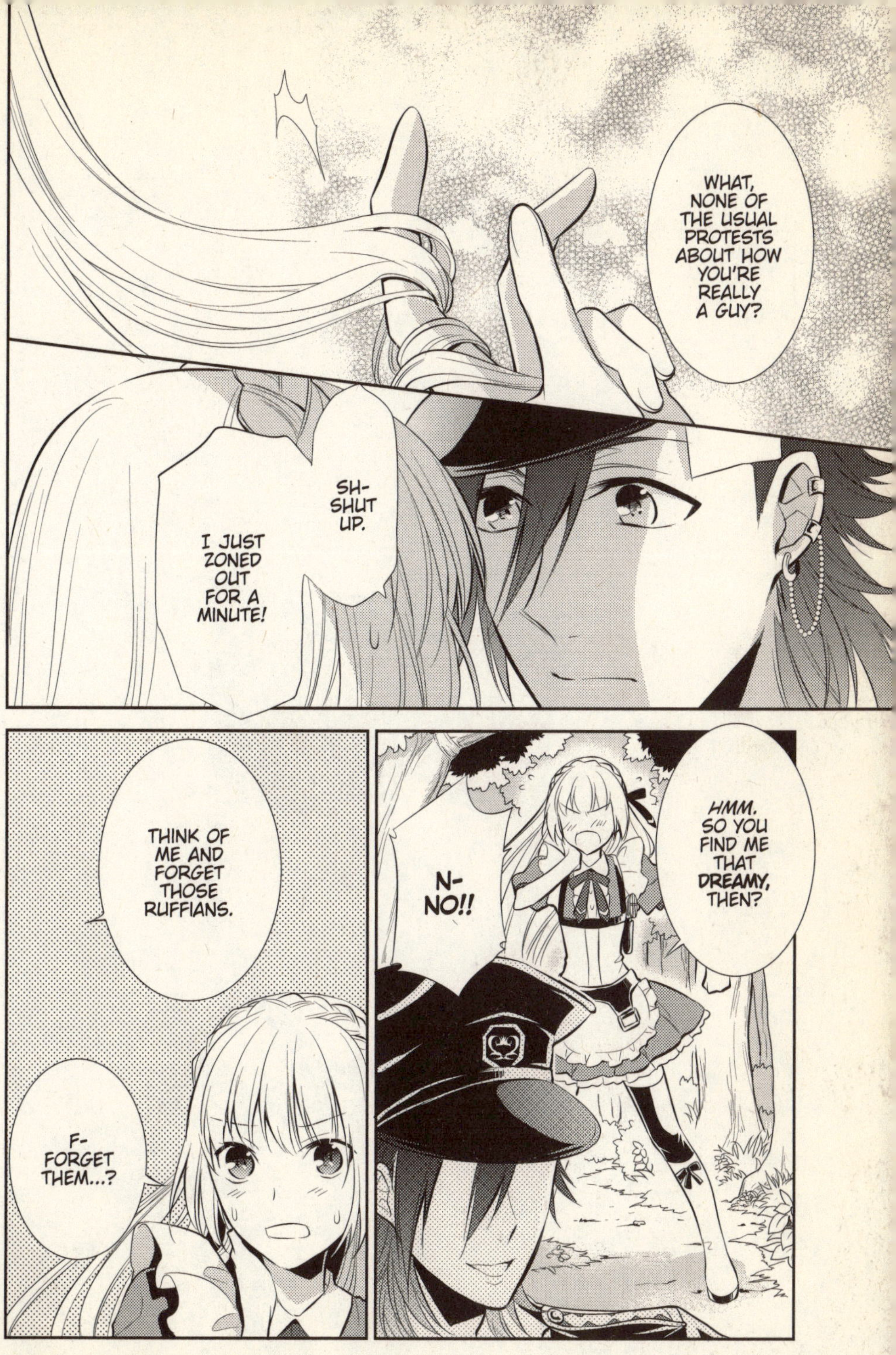
WHAT, NONE OF THE USUAL PROTESTS ABOUT HOW YOU'RE REALLY A GUY?
SH-SHUT UP.
I JUST ZONED OUT FOR A MINUTE!
HMM. SO YOU FIND ME THAT **DREAMY,** THEN?
N-NO!!
THINK OF ME AND FORGET THOSE RUFFIANS.
F-FORGET THEM...?

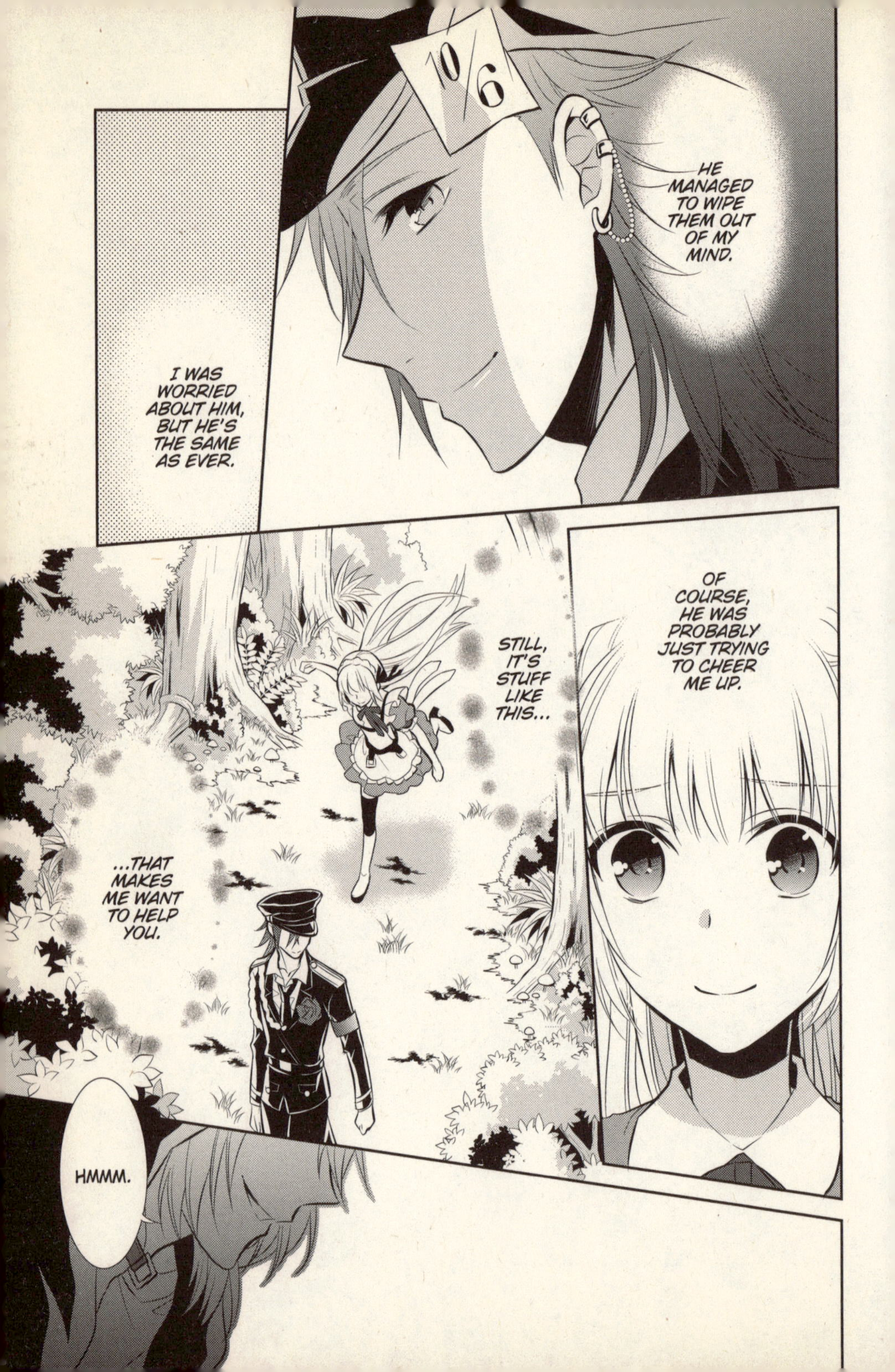
HE MANAGED TO WIPE THEM OUT OF MY MIND.
I WAS WORRIED ABOUT HIM, BUT HE'S THE SAME AS EVER.
OF COURSE, HE WAS PROBABLY JUST TRYING TO CHEER ME UP.
STILL, IT'S STUFF LIKE THIS...
...THAT MAKES ME WANT TO HELP YOU.
HMMM.

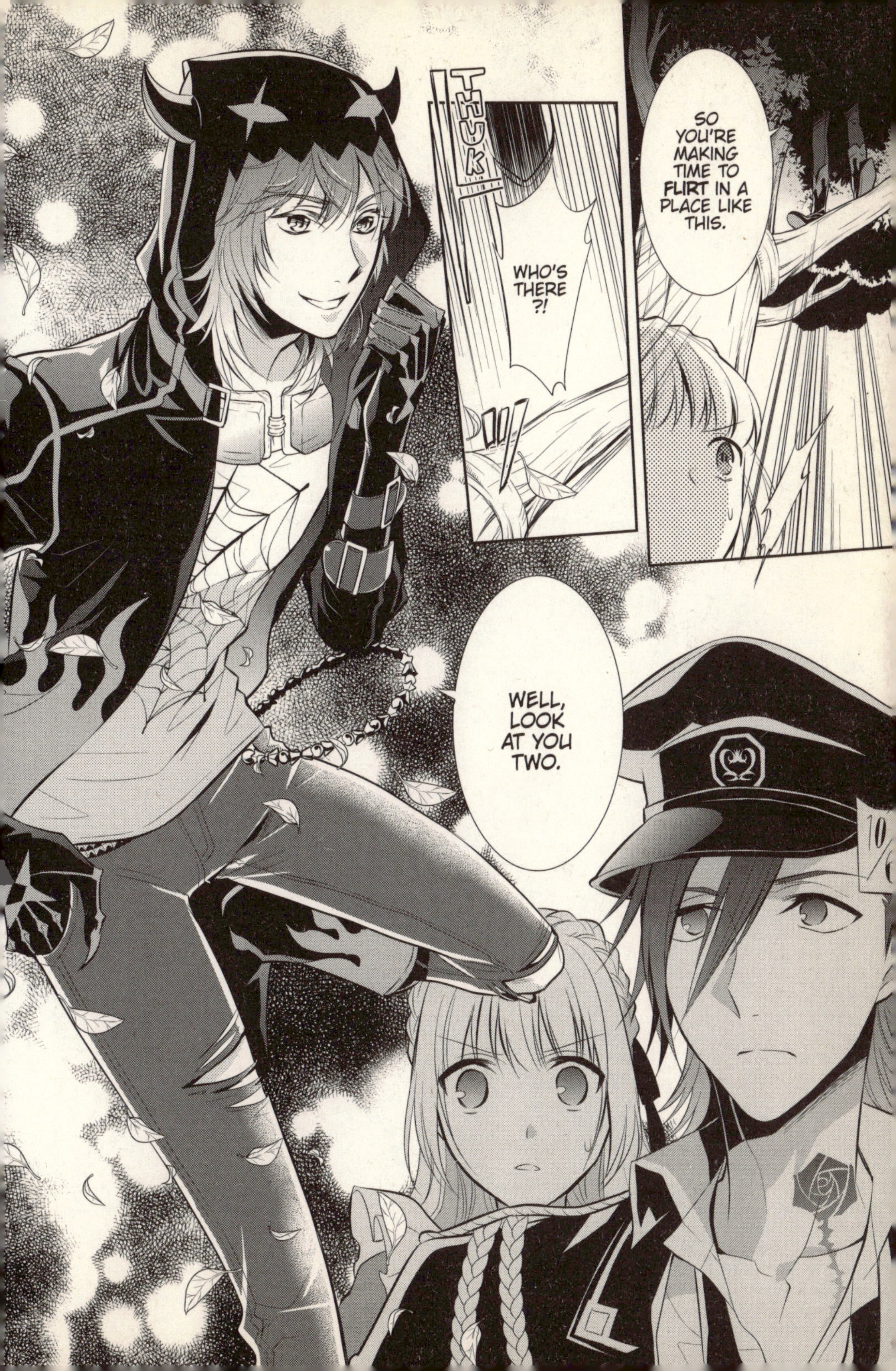
SO YOU'RE MAKING TIME TO FLIRT IN A PLACE LIKE THIS.
THUK
WHO'S THERE?!
WELL, LOOK AT YOU TWO.

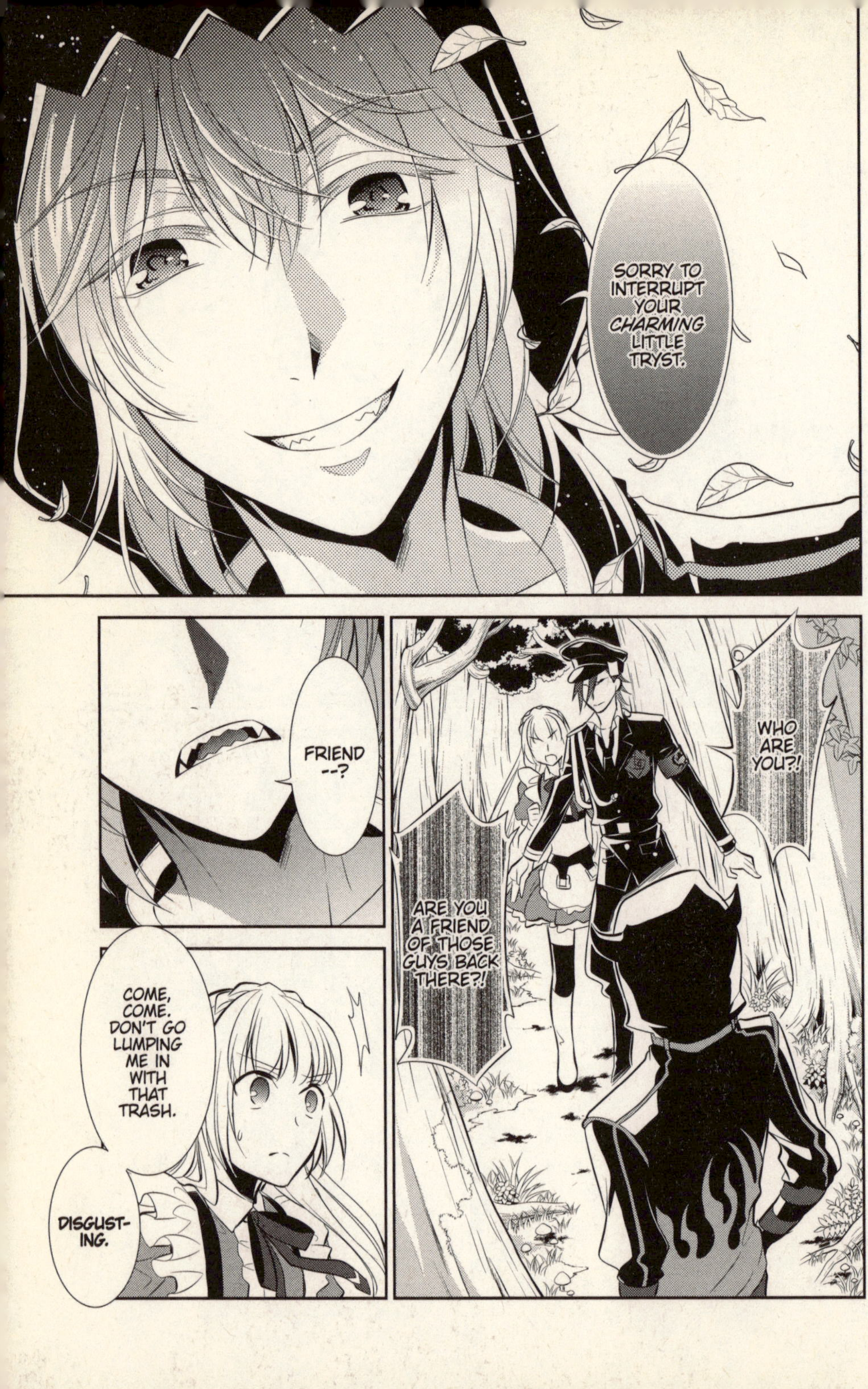
SORRY TO INTERRUPT YOUR CHARMING LITTLE TRYST.
WHO ARE YOU?!
ARE YOU A FRIEND OF THOSE GUYS BACK THERE?!
FRIEND --?
COME, COME. DON'T GO LUMPING ME IN WITH THAT TRASH.
DISGUSTING.

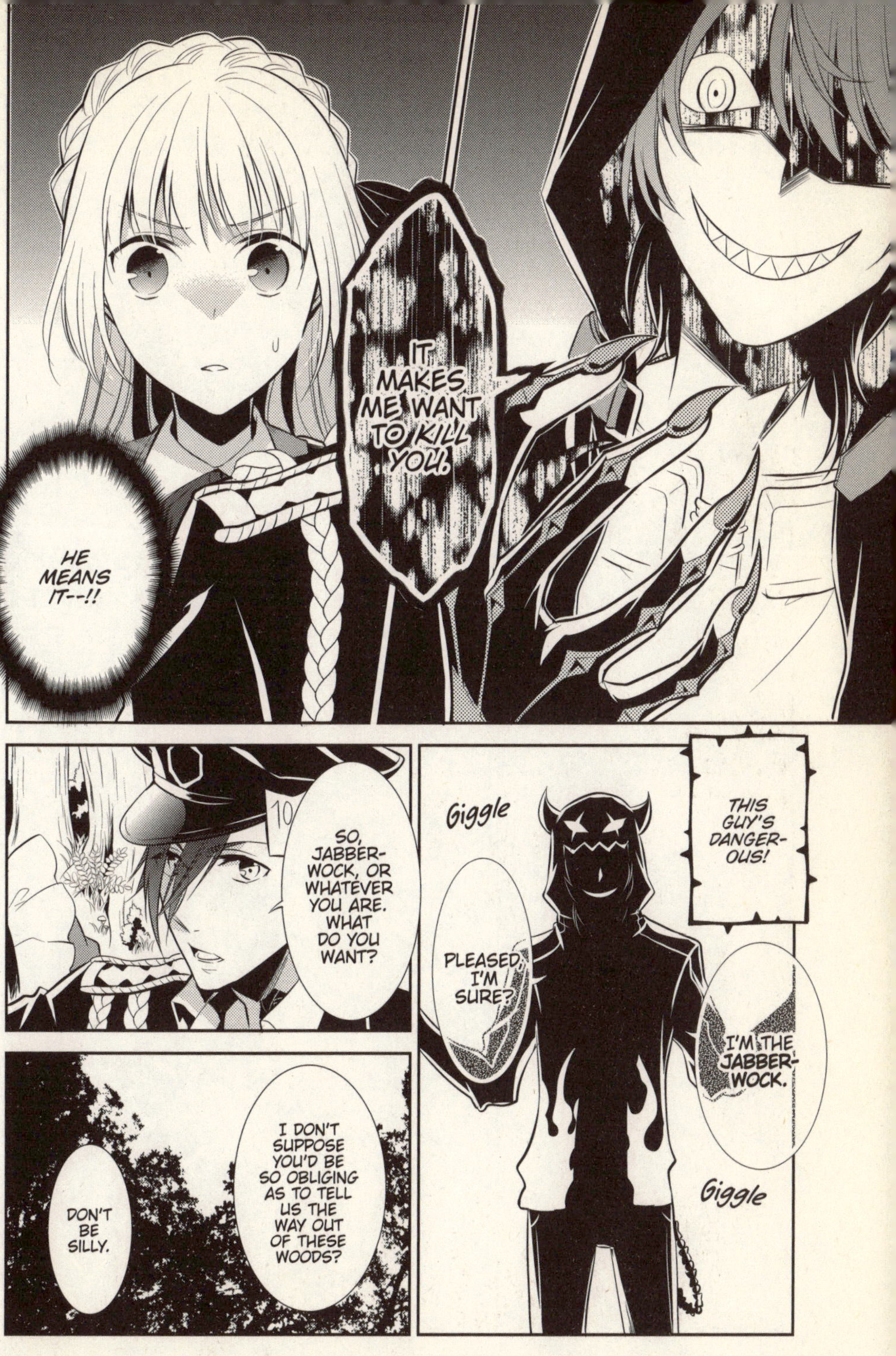
IT MAKES ME WANT TO KILL YOU.
HE MEANS IT--!!
THIS GUY'S DANGER-OUS!
Giggle
I'M THE JABBER-WOCK.
PLEASED, I'M SURE?
Giggle
SO, JABBER-WOCK, OR WHATEVER YOU ARE. WHAT DO YOU WANT?
I DON'T SUPPOSE YOU'D BE SO OBLIGING AS TO TELL US THE WAY OUT OF THESE WOODS?
DON'T BE SILLY.

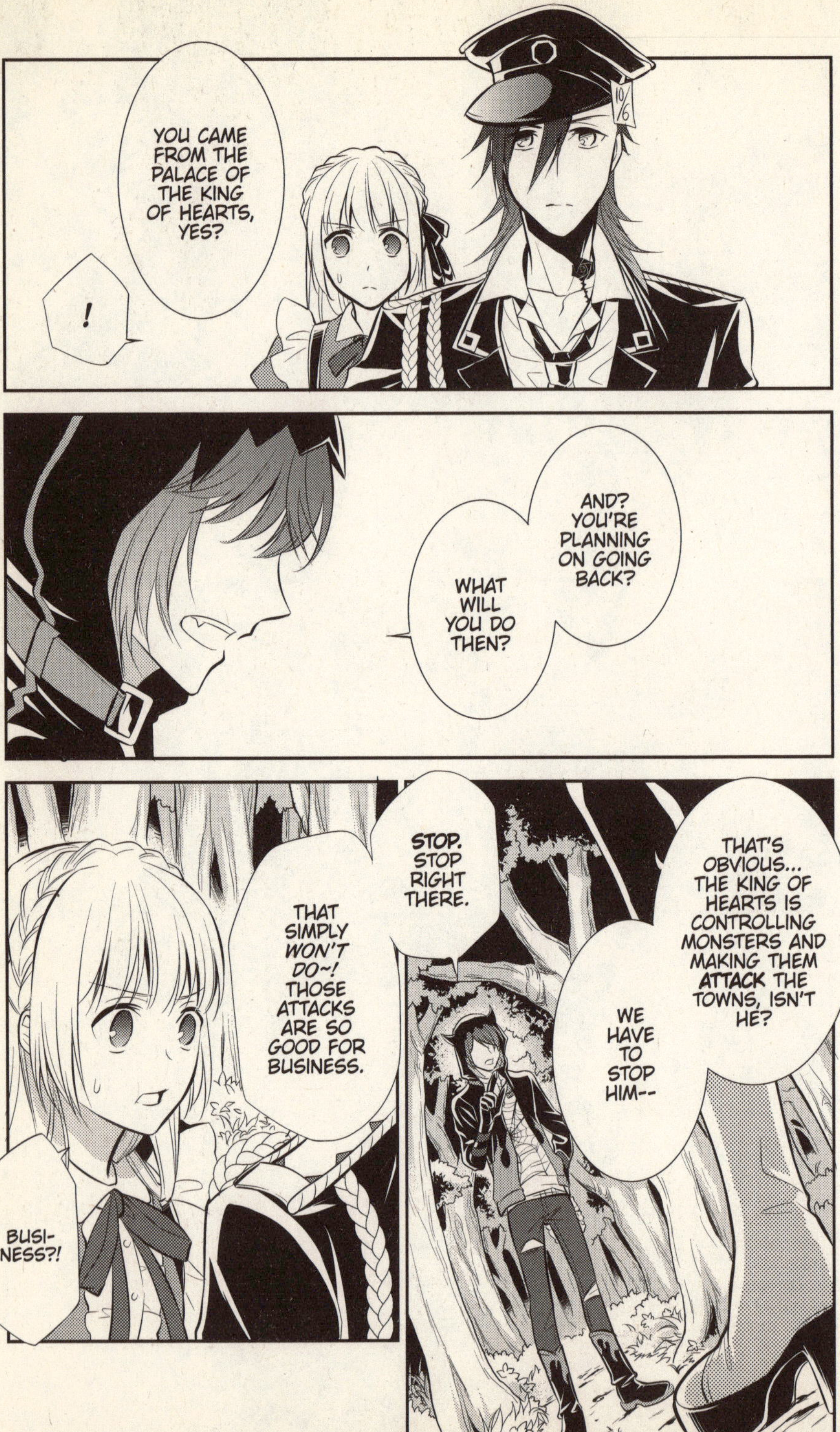
YOU CAME FROM THE PALACE OF THE KING OF HEARTS, YES?
!
AND? YOU'RE PLANNING ON GOING BACK?
WHAT WILL YOU DO THEN?
THAT'S OBVIOUS... THE KING OF HEARTS IS CONTROLLING MONSTERS AND MAKING THEM ATTACK THE TOWNS, ISN'T HE?
WE HAVE TO STOP HIM--
STOP. STOP RIGHT THERE.
THAT SIMPLY WON'T DO~! THOSE ATTACKS ARE SO GOOD FOR BUSINESS.
BUSI-NESS?!

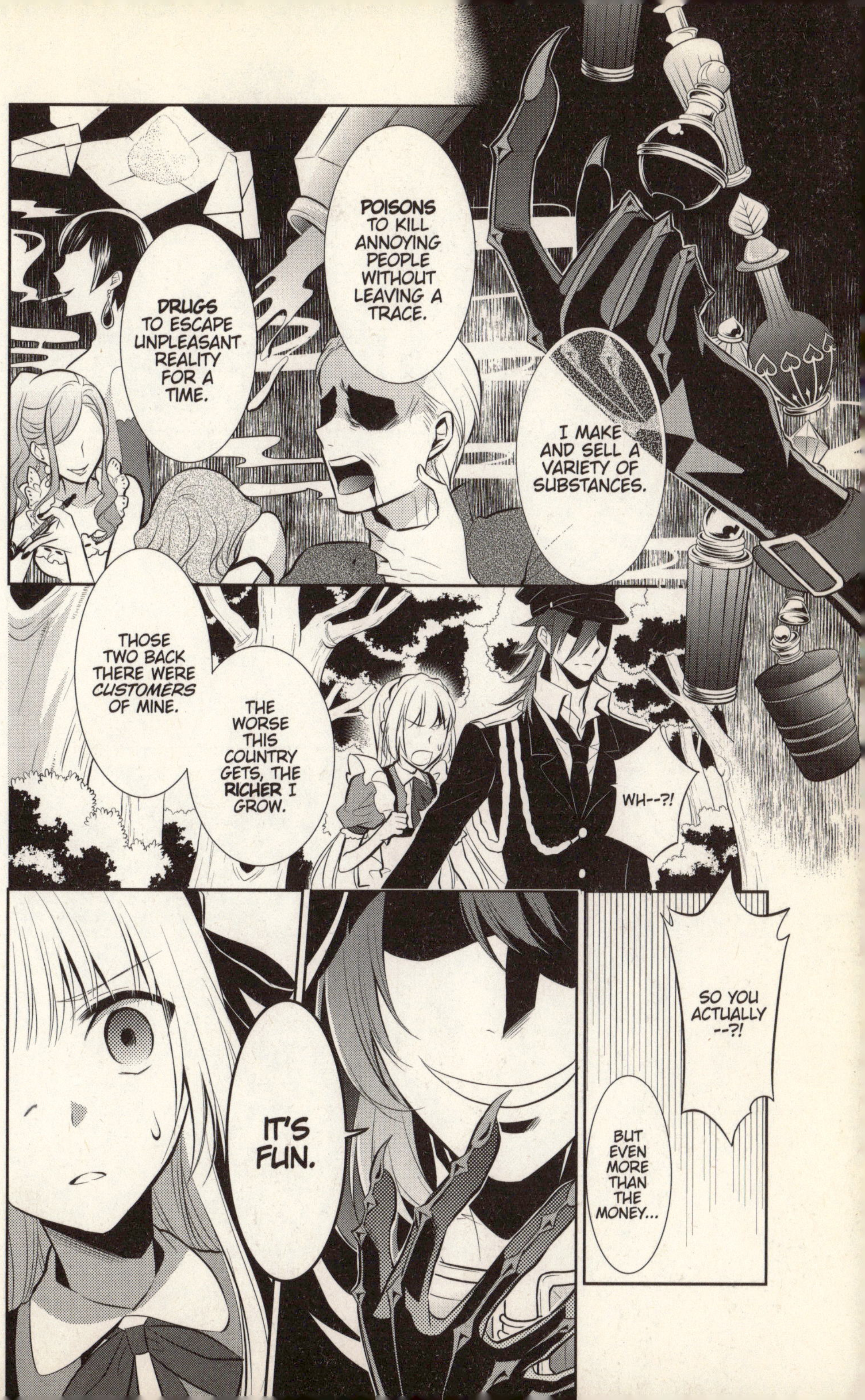
I MAKE AND SELL A VARIETY OF SUBSTANCES.
POISONS TO KILL ANNOYING PEOPLE WITHOUT LEAVING A TRACE.
DRUGS TO ESCAPE UNPLEASANT REALITY FOR A TIME.
THOSE TWO BACK THERE WERE CUSTOMERS OF MINE.
THE WORSE THIS COUNTRY GETS, THE RICHER I GROW.
WH--?!
SO YOU ACTUALLY --?!
BUT EVEN MORE THAN THE MONEY...
IT'S FUN.

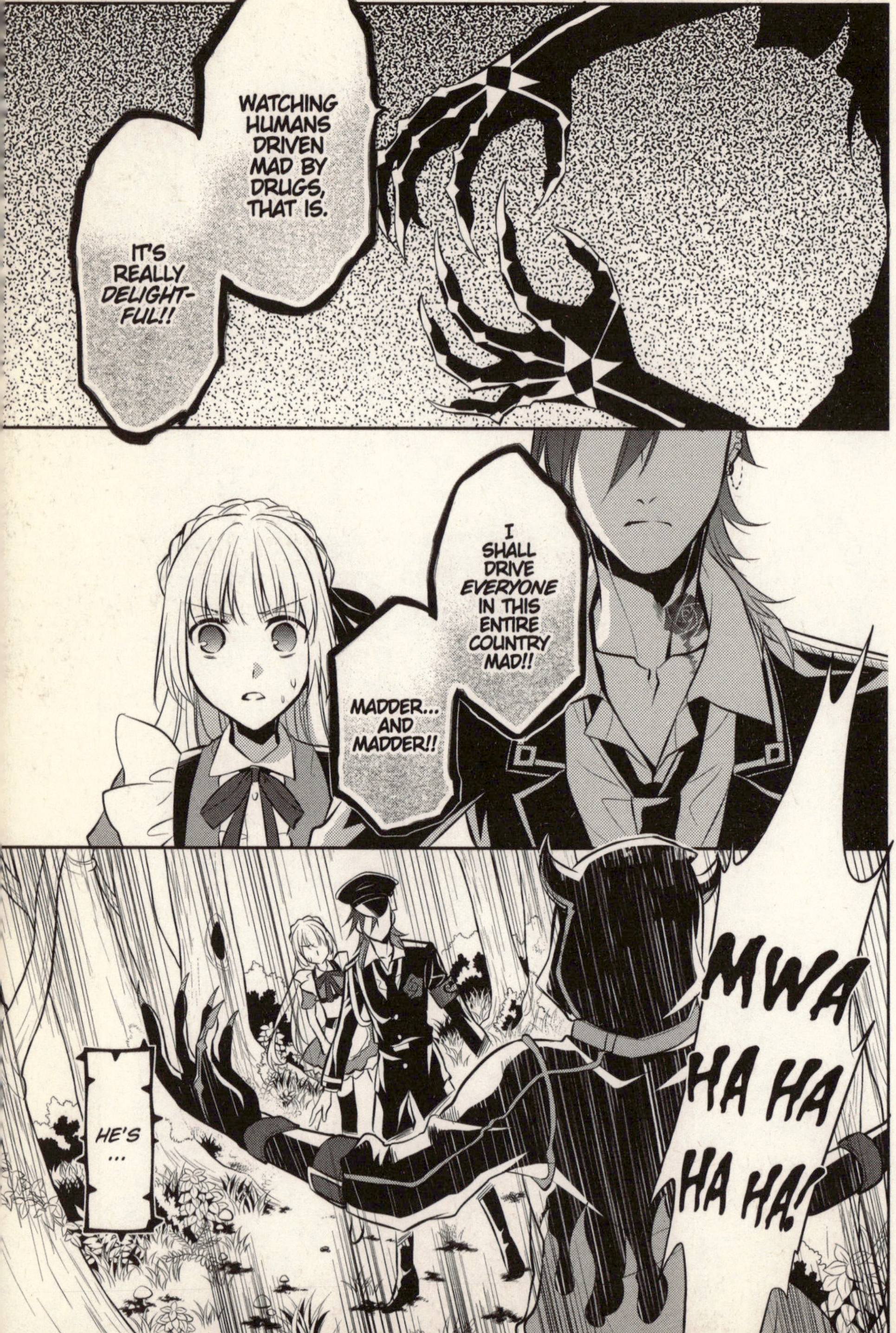
WATCHING HUMANS DRIVEN MAD BY DRUGS, THAT IS.
IT'S REALLY DELIGHT-FUL!!
I SHALL DRIVE EVERYONE IN THIS ENTIRE COUNTRY MAD!!
MADDER... AND MADDER!!
MWA HA HA HA HA!
HE'S ...

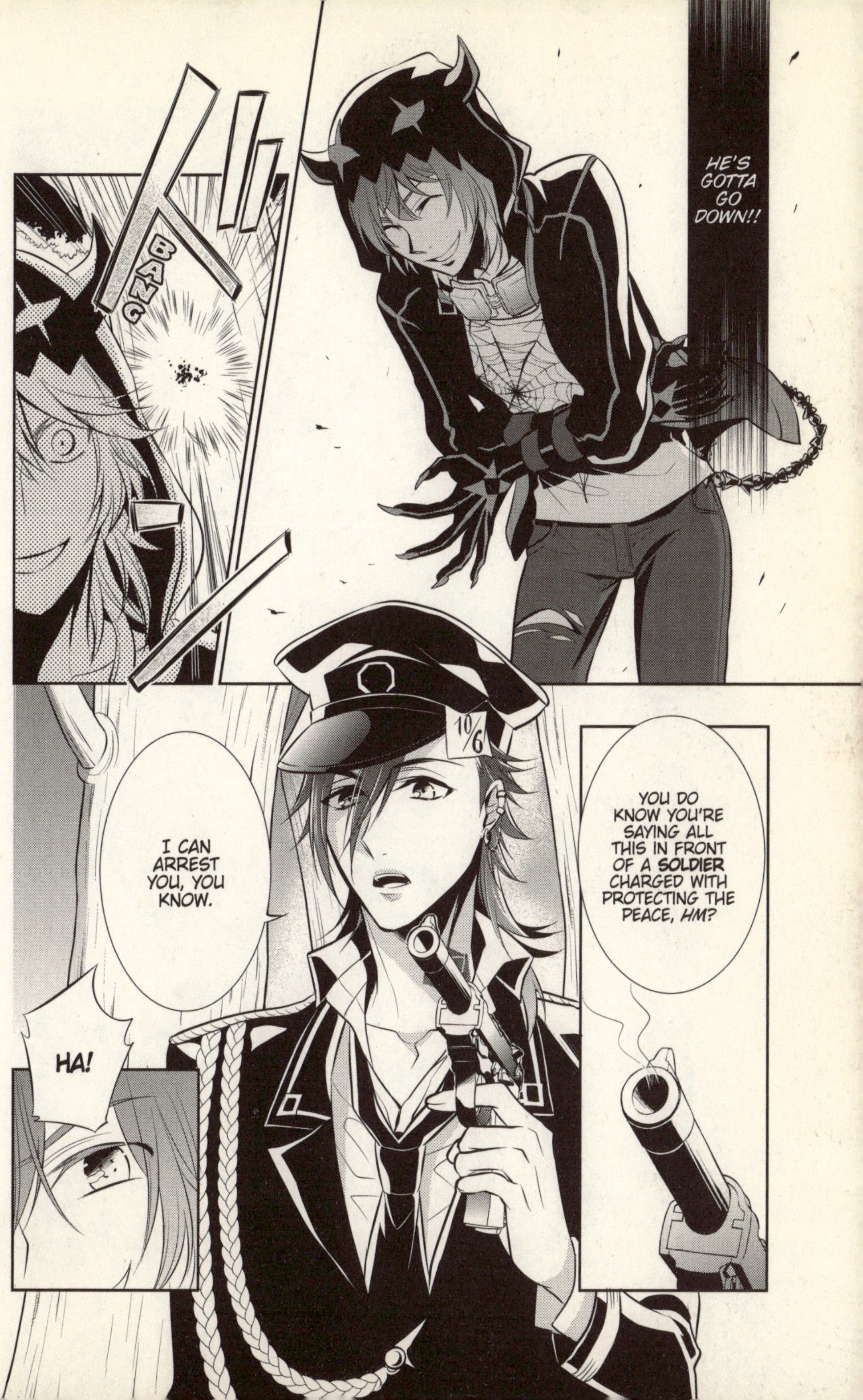
HE'S GOTTA GO DOWN!!
BANG
YOU DO KNOW YOU'RE SAYING ALL THIS IN FRONT OF A **SOLDIER** CHARGED WITH PROTECTING THE PEACE, *HM?*
I CAN ARREST YOU, YOU KNOW.
HA!

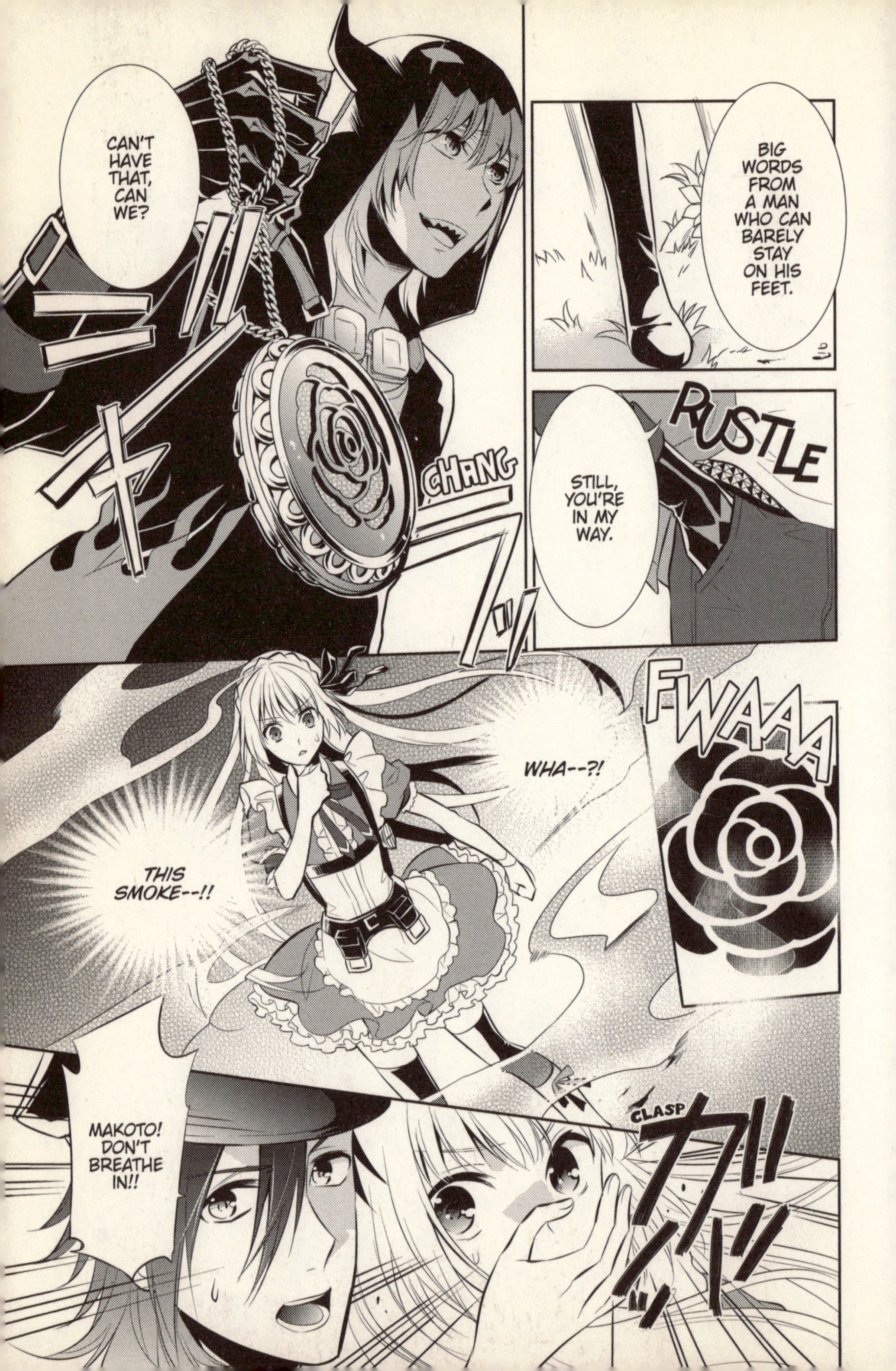
BIG WORDS FROM A MAN WHO CAN BARELY STAY ON HIS FEET.
RUSTLE
STILL, YOU'RE IN MY WAY.
CAN'T HAVE THAT, CAN WE?
CHANG
FWAAA
WHA--?!
THIS SMOKE--!!
CLASP
MAKOTO! DON'T BREATHE IN!!

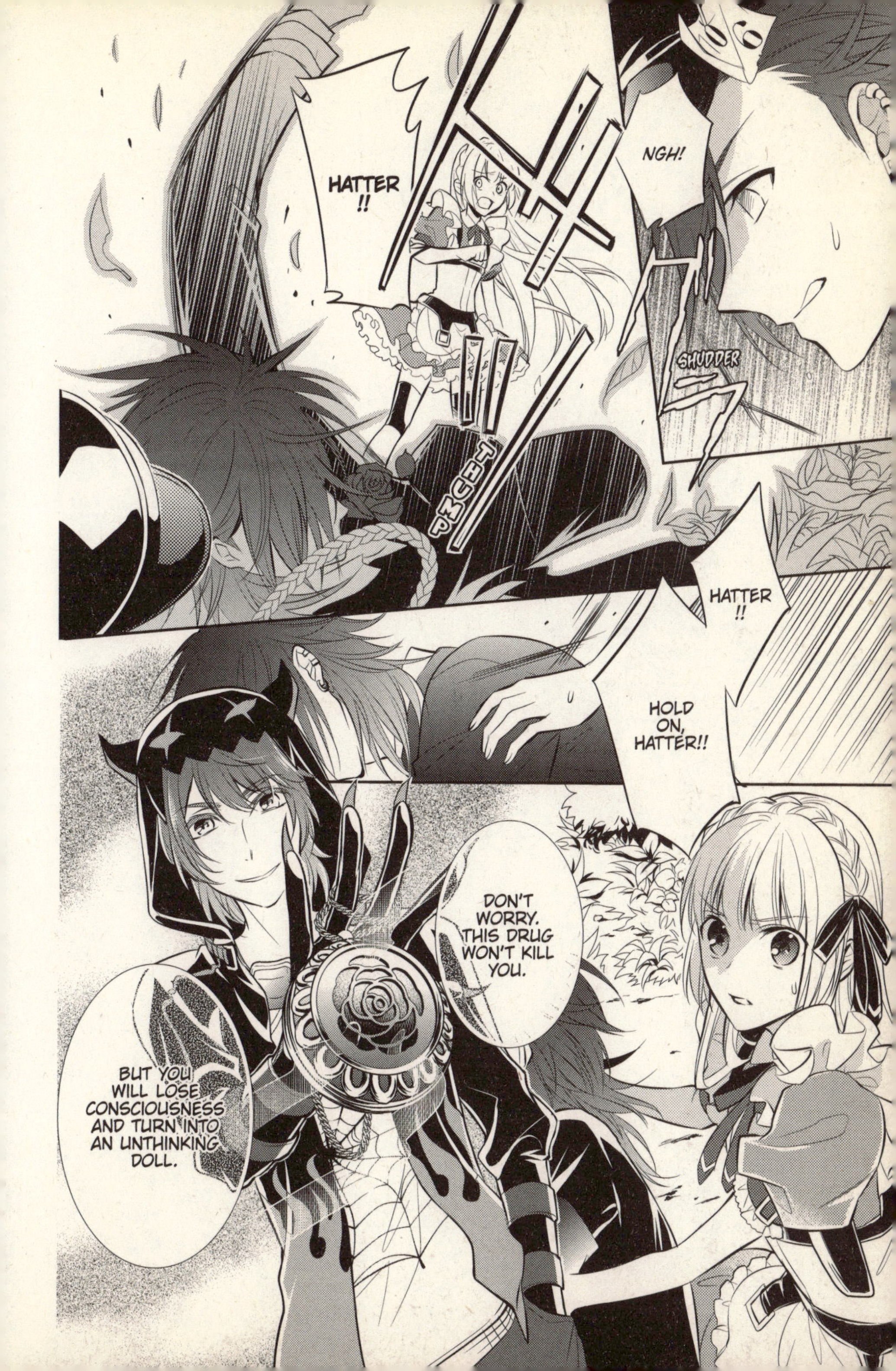
NGH!
SHUDDER
HATTER!!
THUMP
HATTER!!
HOLD ON, HATTER!!
DON'T WORRY. THIS DRUG WON'T KILL YOU.
BUT YOU WILL LOSE CONSCIOUSNESS AND TURN INTO AN UNTHINKING DOLL.

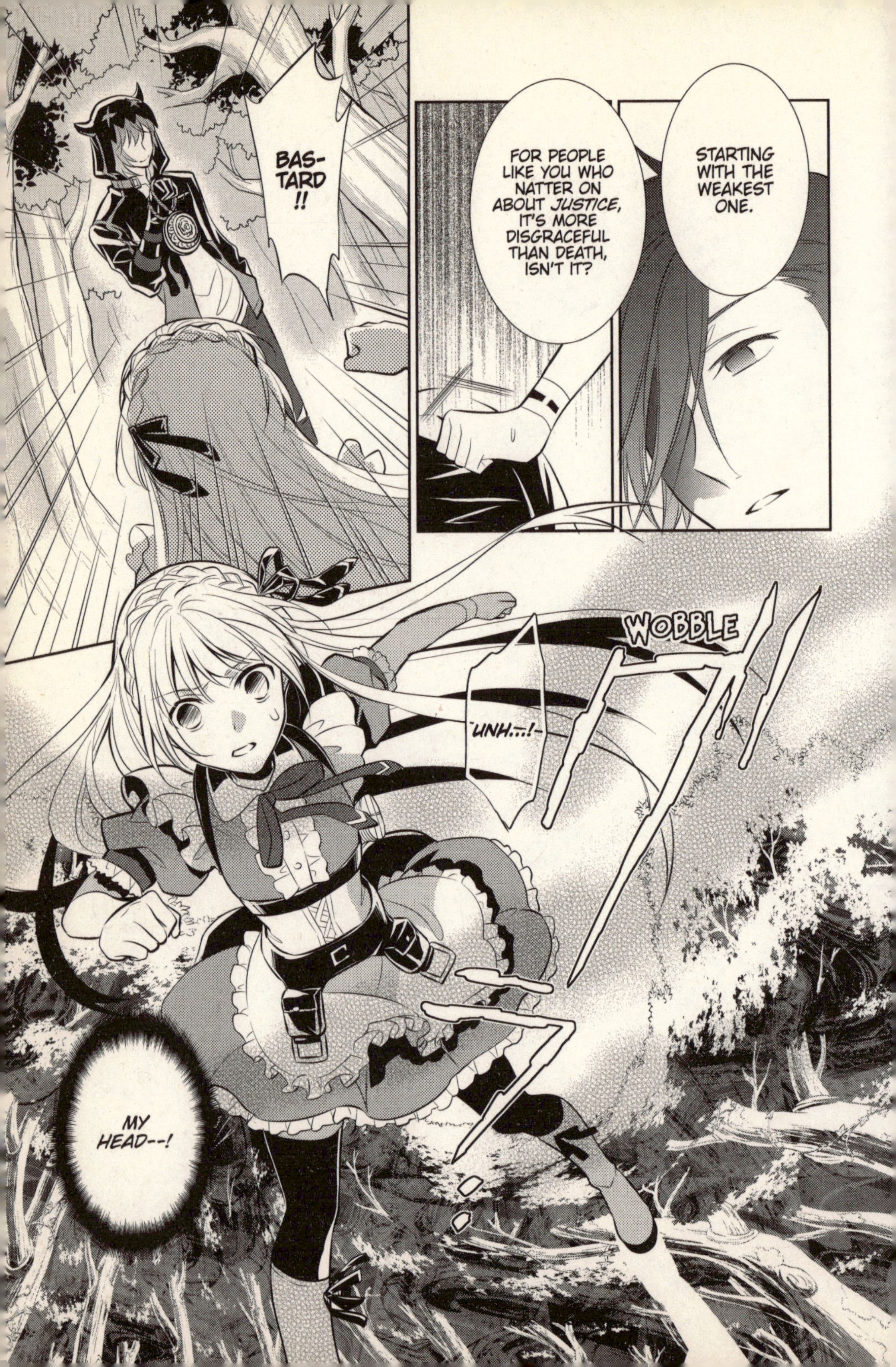
STARTING WITH THE WEAKEST ONE.
FOR PEOPLE LIKE YOU WHO NATTER ON ABOUT JUSTICE, IT'S MORE DISGRACEFUL THAN DEATH, ISN'T IT?
BAS-TARD!!
WOBBLE
UNH...!
MY HEAD--!

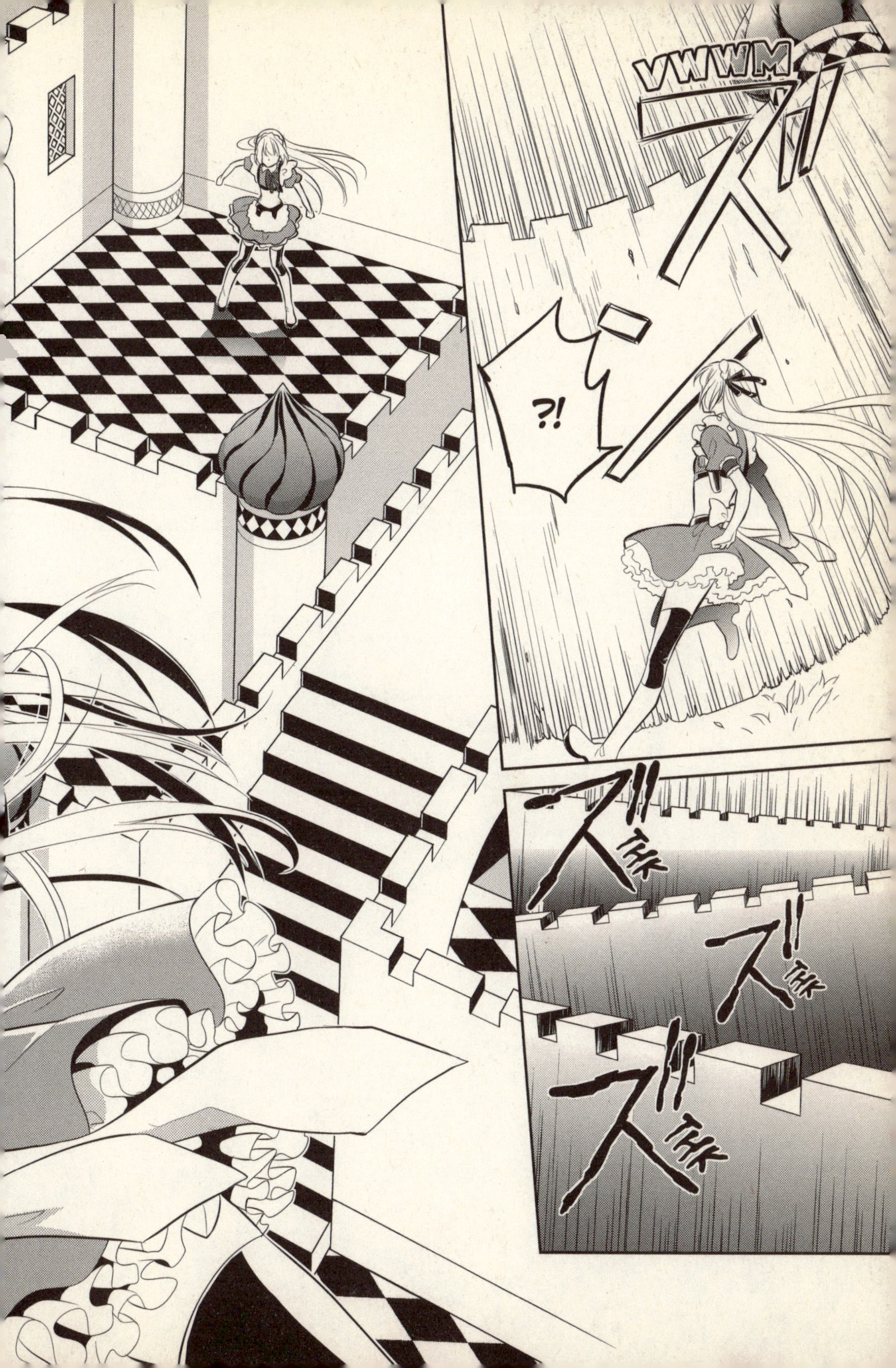
VWWM
?!
THK
THK
THK

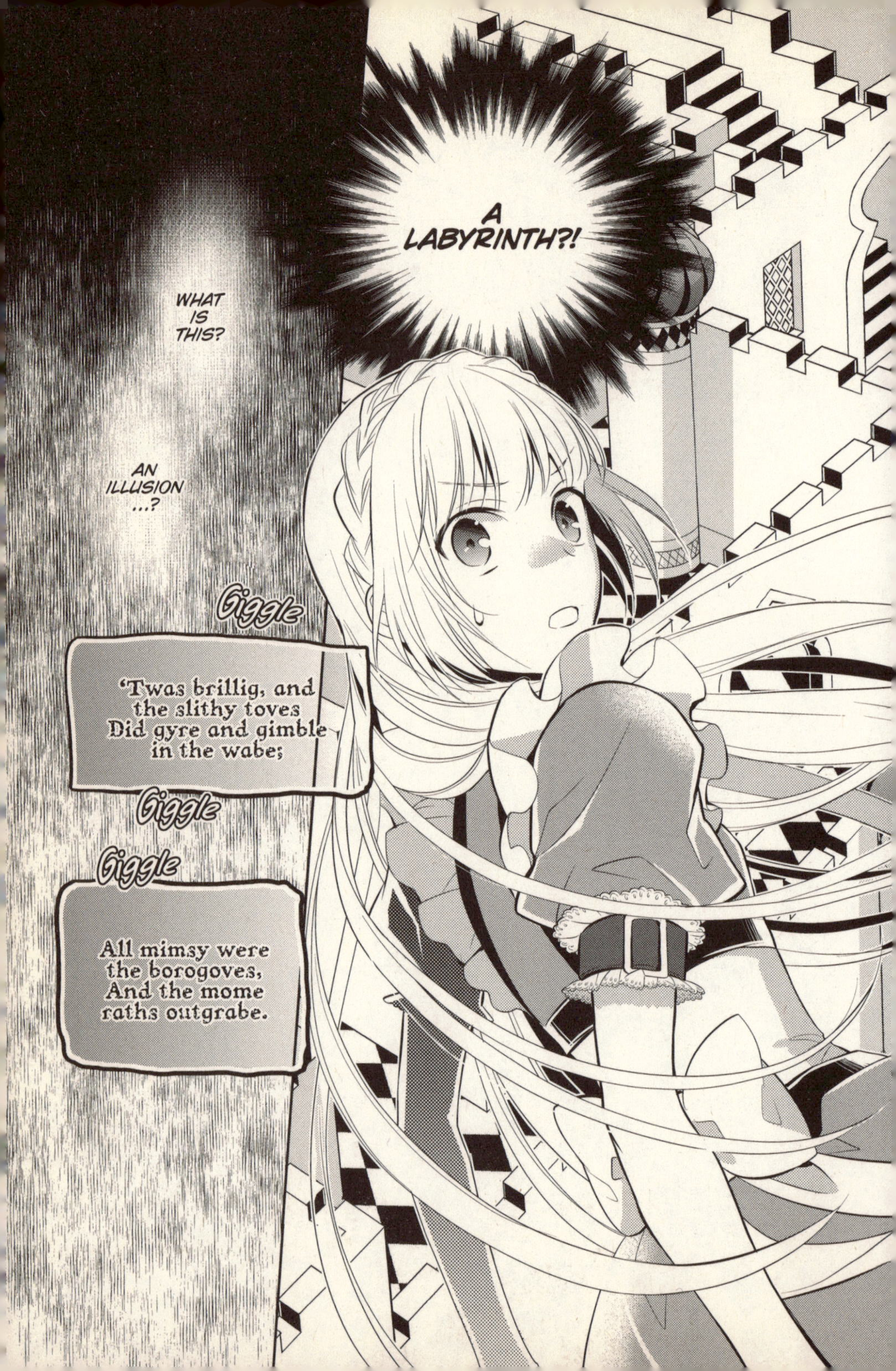
A LABYRINTH?!
WHAT IS THIS?
AN ILLUSION ...?
Giggle
'Twas brillig, and the slithy toves Did gyre and gimble in the wabe;
Giggle
Giggle
All mimsy were the borogoves, And the mome raths outgrabe.

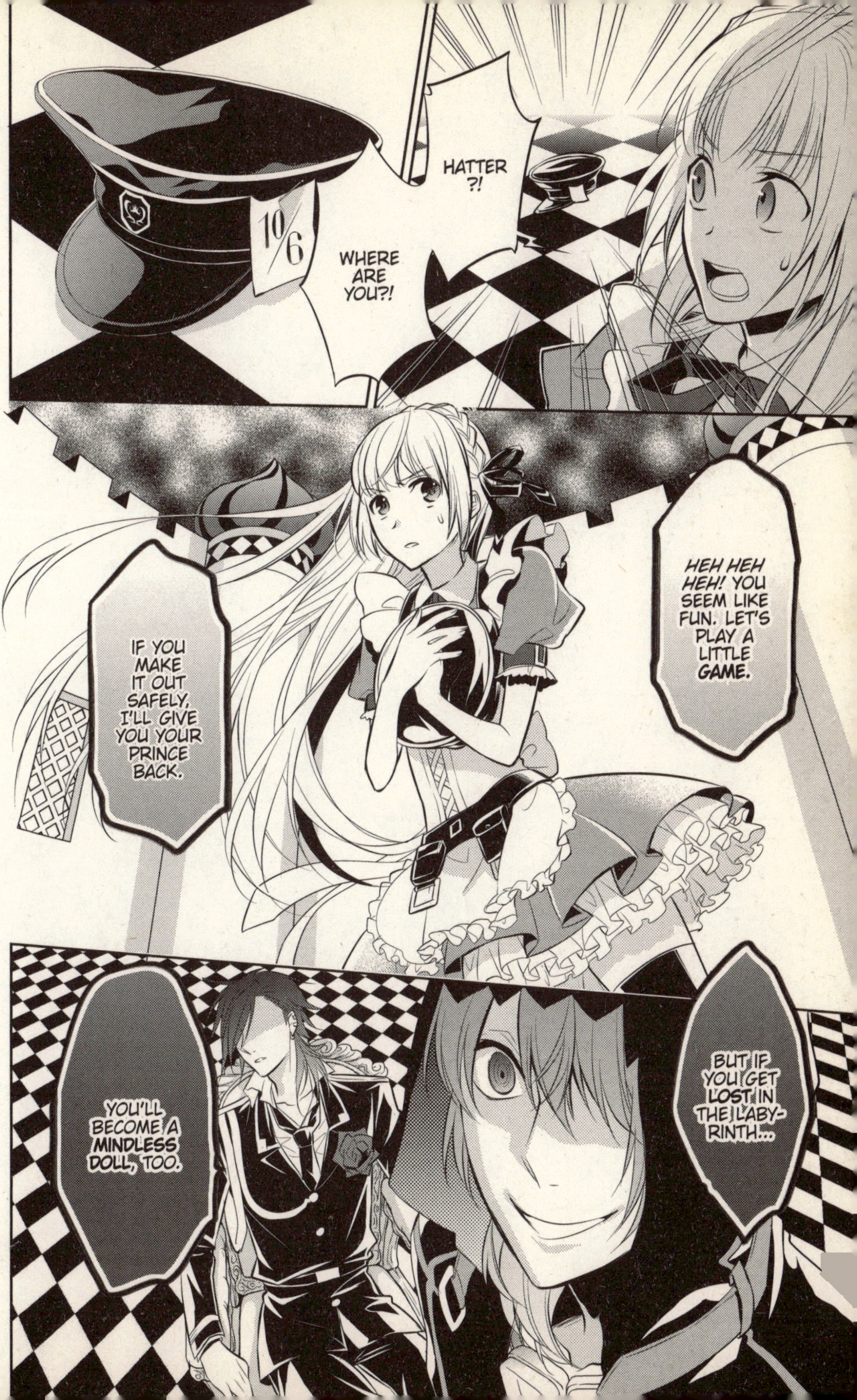
HATTER ?!
WHERE ARE YOU?!
10/6
HEH HEH HEH! YOU SEEM LIKE FUN. LET'S PLAY A LITTLE GAME.
IF YOU MAKE IT OUT SAFELY, I'LL GIVE YOU YOUR PRINCE BACK.
BUT IF YOU GET LOST IN THE LABYRINTH...
YOU'LL BECOME A MINDLESS DOLL, TOO.

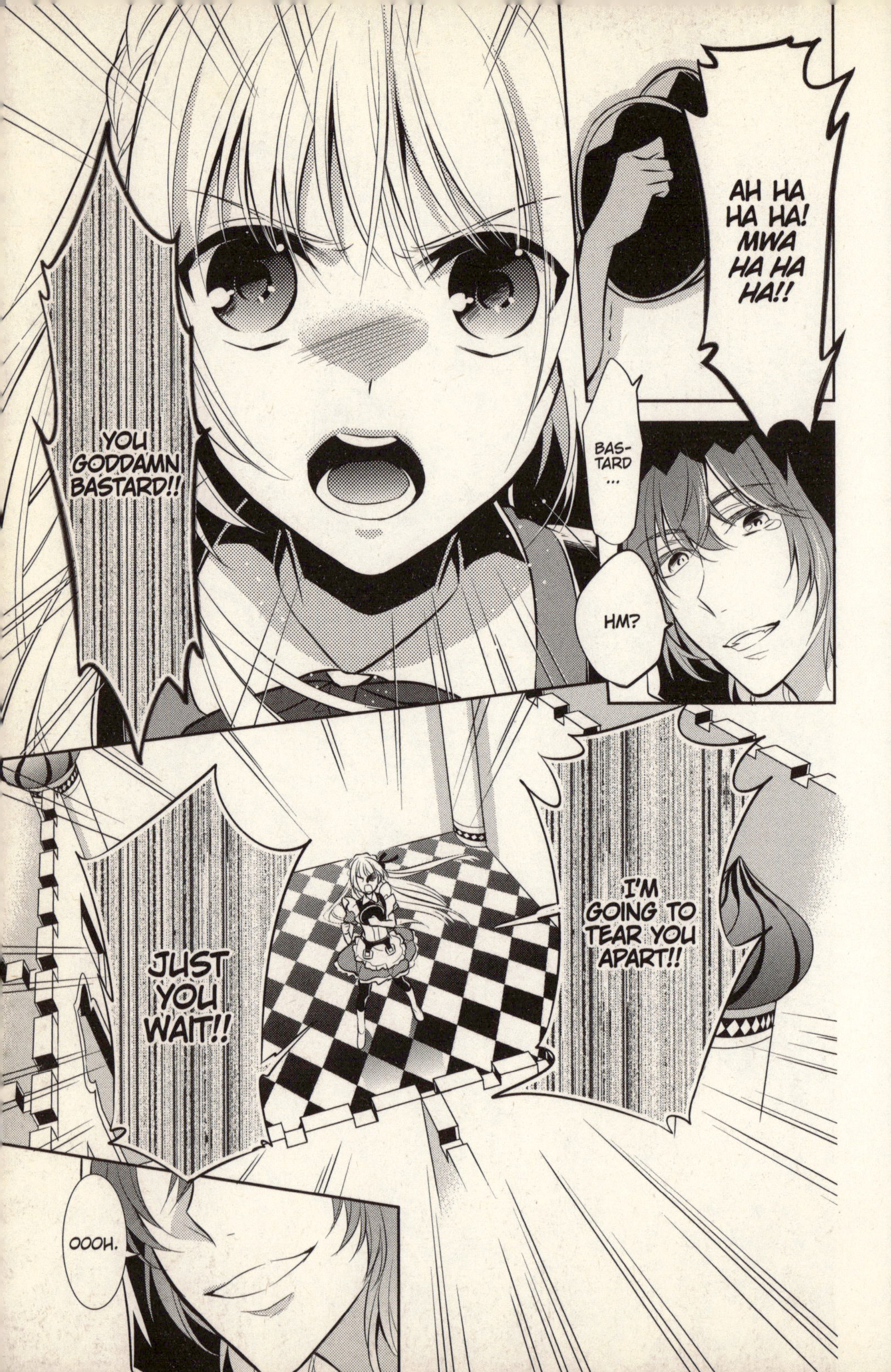
AH HA HA HA! MWA HA HA HA HA!!
BAS-TARD ...
HM?
YOU GODDAMN BASTARD!!
I'M GOING TO TEAR YOU APART!!
JUST YOU WAIT!!
OOOH.

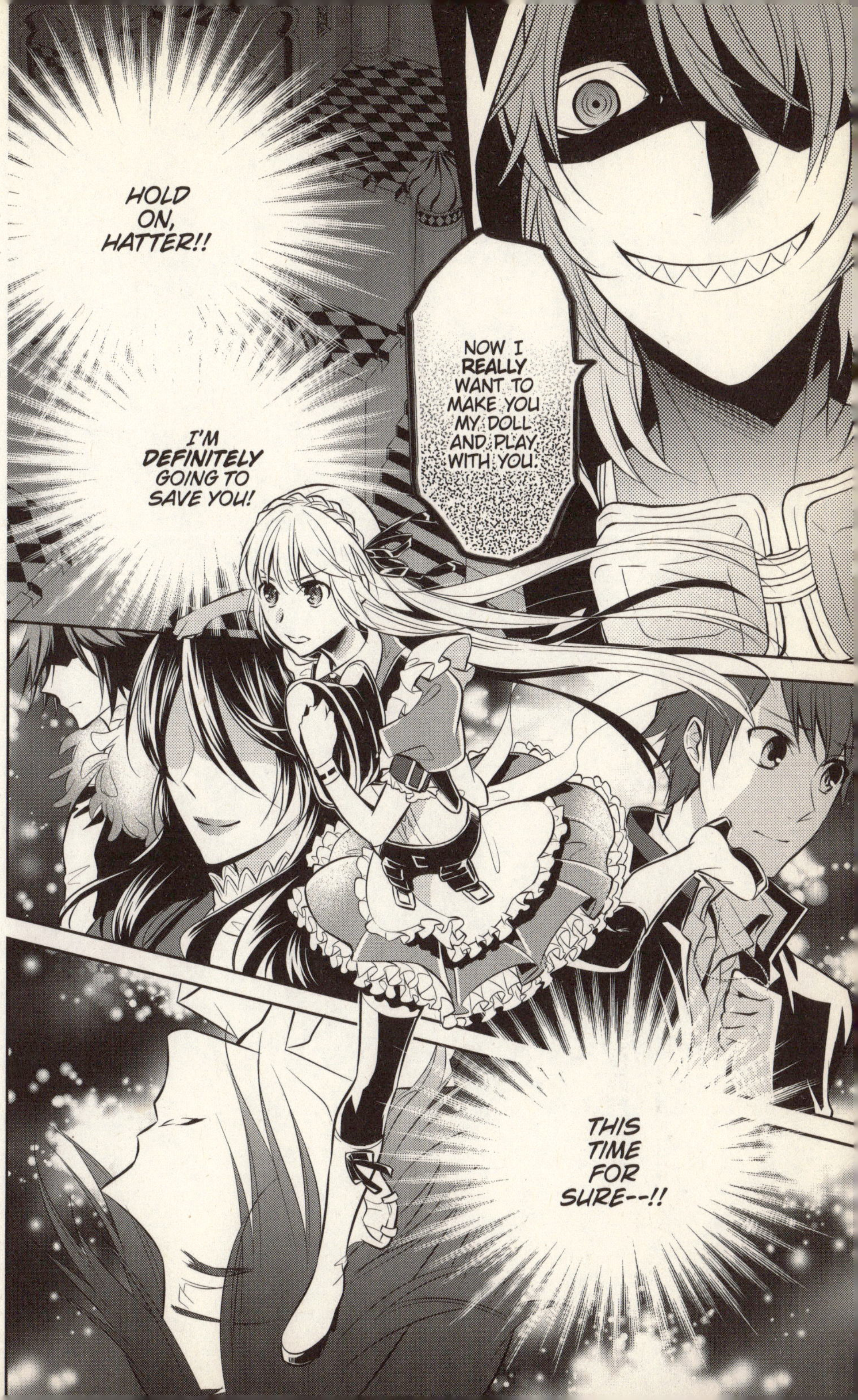
NOW I REALLY WANT TO MAKE YOU MY DOLL AND PLAY WITH YOU.
HOLD ON, HATTER!!
I'M DEFINITELY GOING TO SAVE YOU!
THIS TIME FOR SURE--!!

I AM ALICE

I AM ALICE

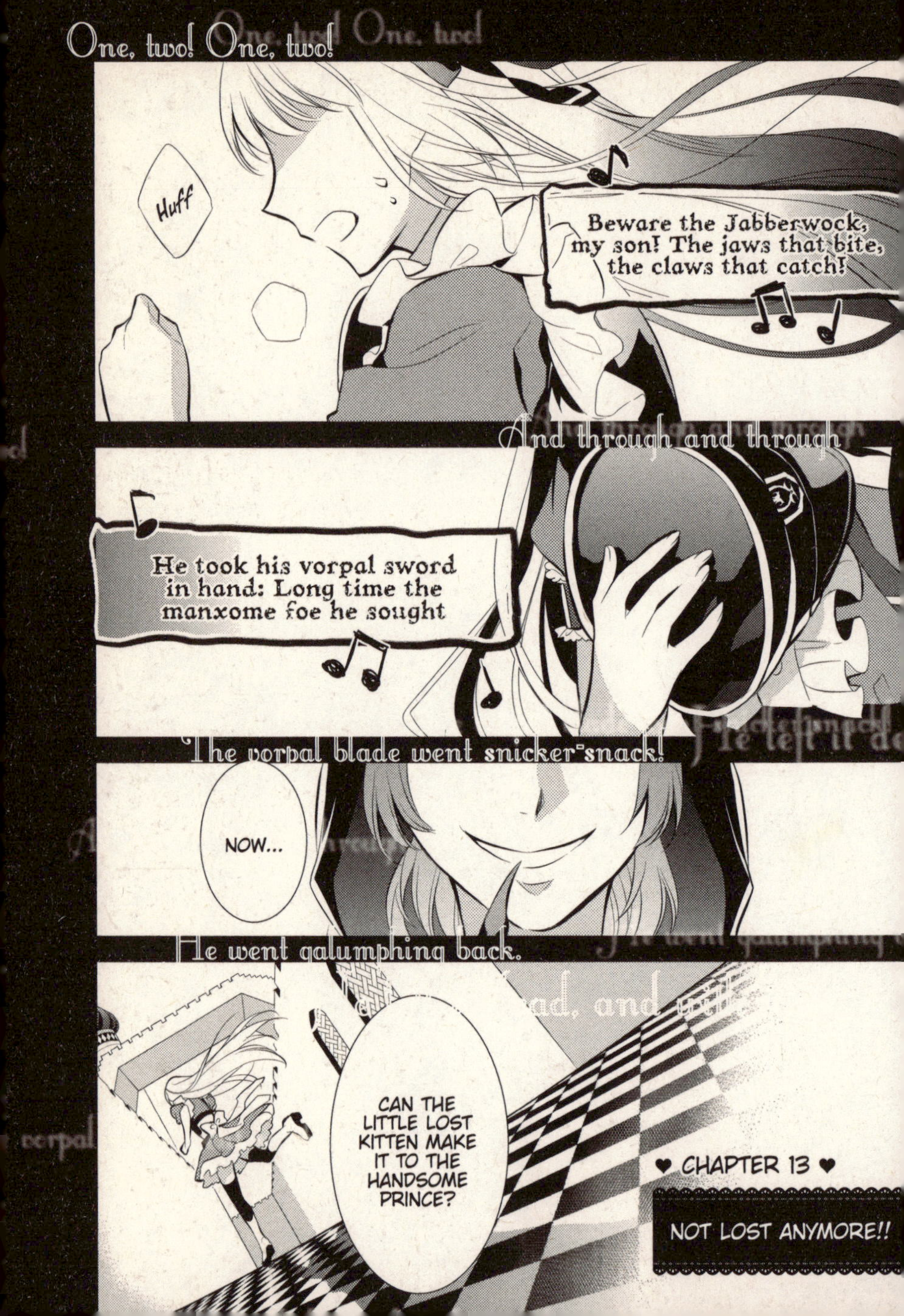

One, two! One, two!
Beware the Jabberwock, my son! The jaws that bite, the claws that catch!
Huff
And through and through
He took his vorpal sword in hand: Long time the manxome foe he sought
The vorpal blade went snicker-snack!
NOW...
He went galumphing back.
CAN THE LITTLE LOST KITTEN MAKE IT TO THE HANDSOME PRINCE?
♥ CHAPTER 13 ♥
NOT LOST ANYMORE!!

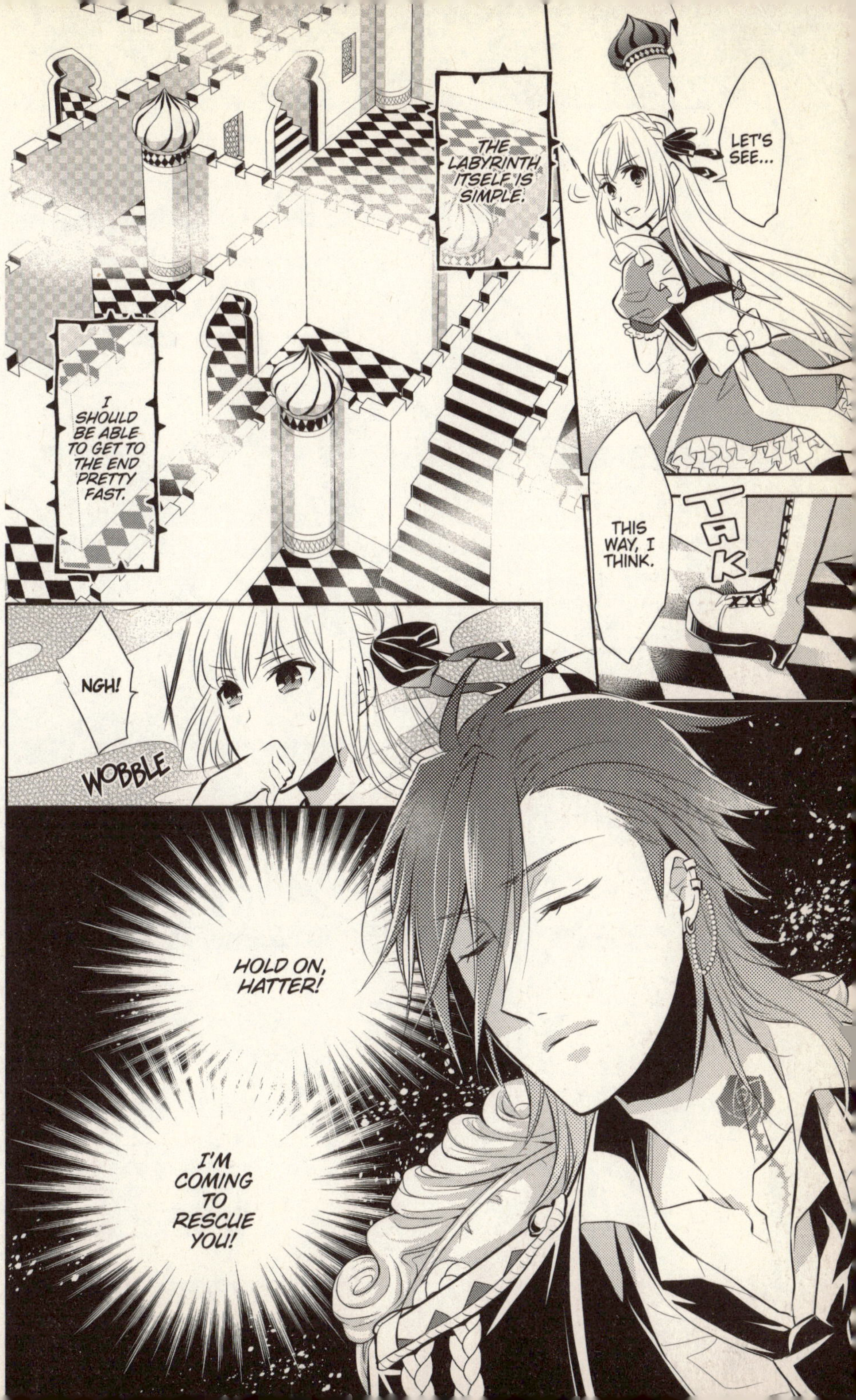
LET'S SEE...
THIS WAY, I THINK.
TAK
THE LABYRINTH ITSELF IS SIMPLE.
I SHOULD BE ABLE TO GET TO THE END PRETTY FAST.
NGH!
WOBBLE
HOLD ON, HATTER!
I'M COMING TO RESCUE YOU!

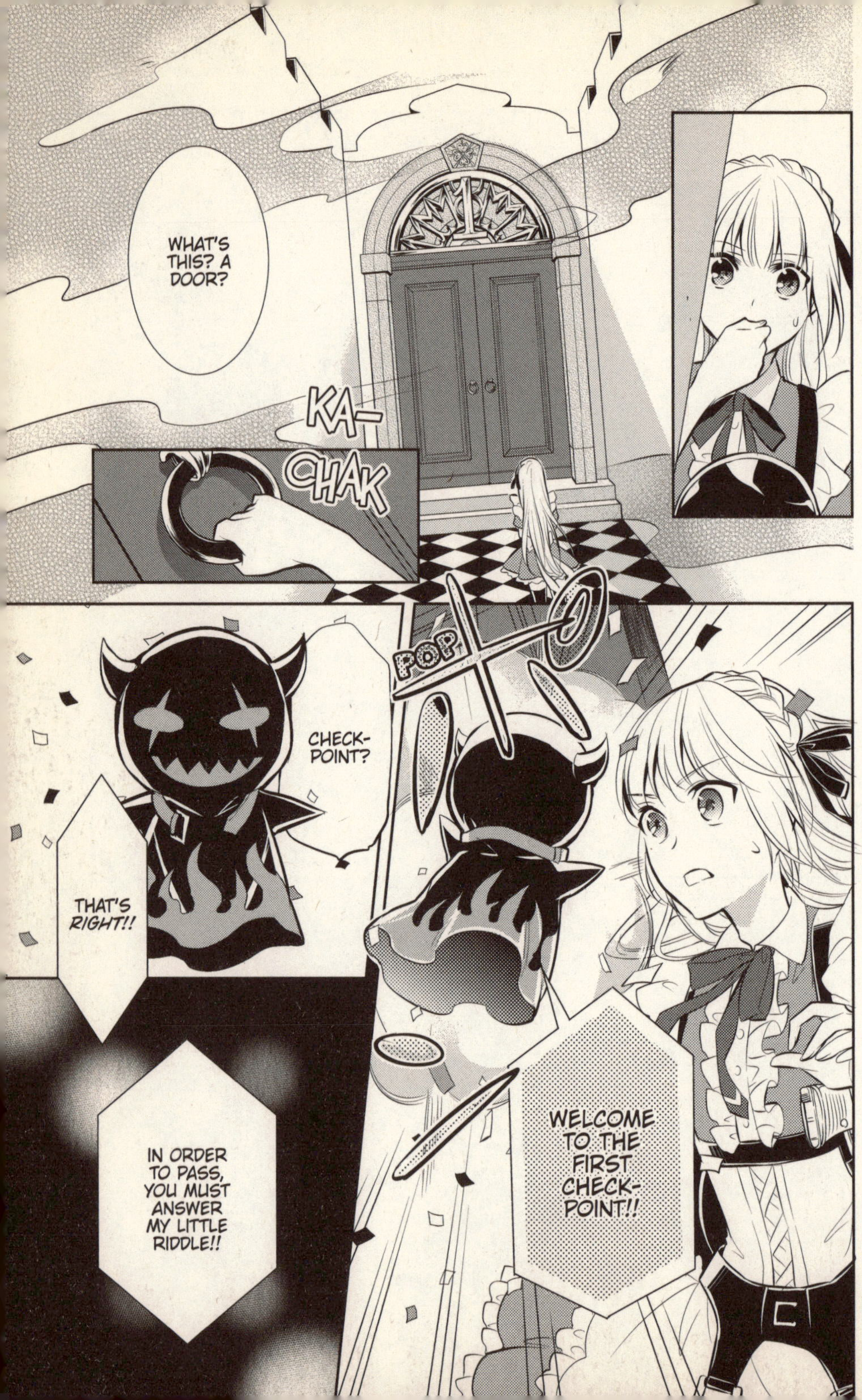
WHAT'S THIS? A DOOR?
KA-CHAK
POP
WELCOME TO THE FIRST CHECK-POINT!!
CHECK-POINT?
THAT'S RIGHT!!
IN ORDER TO PASS, YOU MUST ANSWER MY LITTLE RIDDLE!!

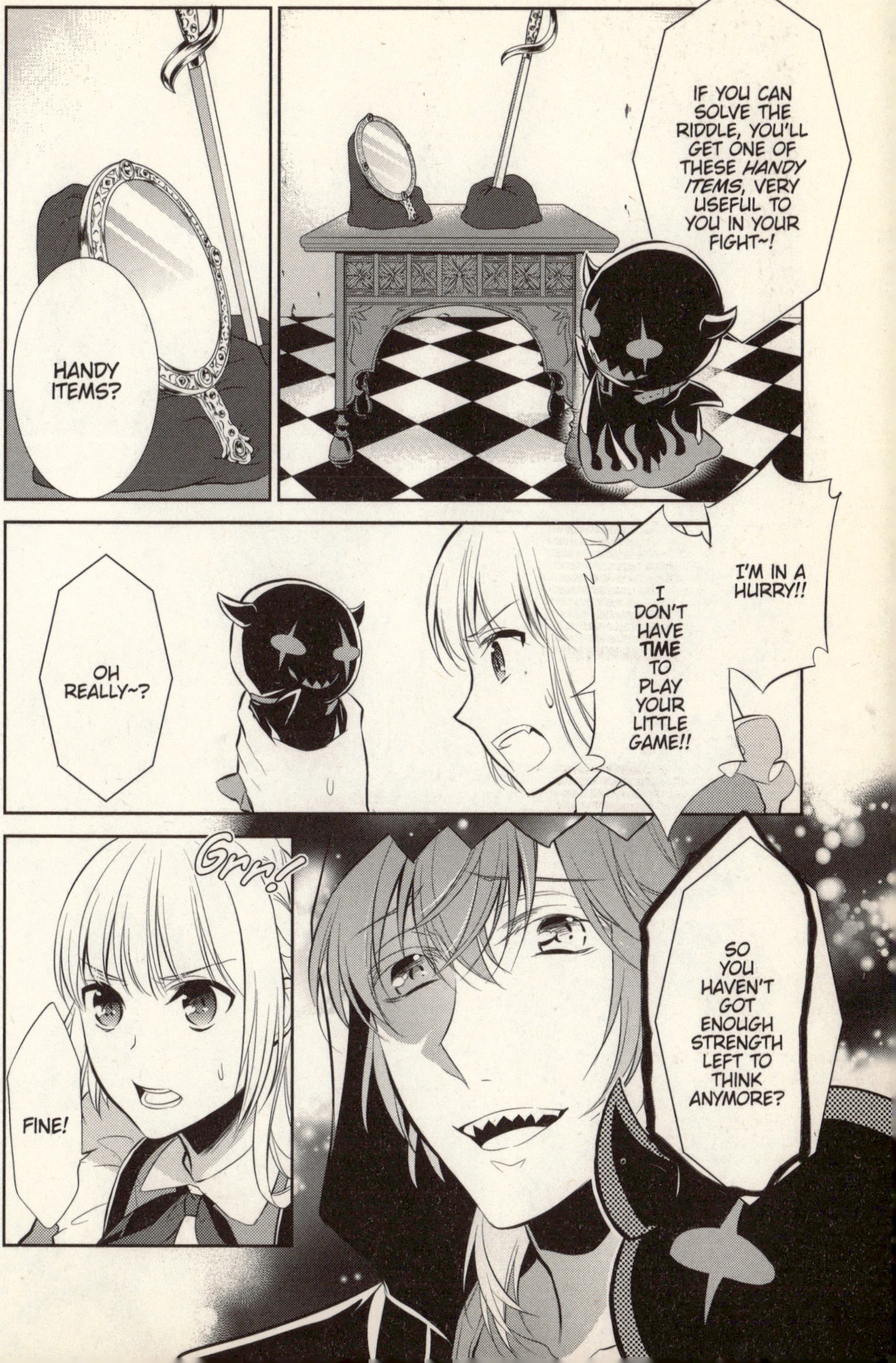
IF YOU CAN SOLVE THE RIDDLE, YOU'LL GET ONE OF THESE *HANDY ITEMS*, VERY USEFUL TO YOU IN YOUR FIGHT~!
HANDY ITEMS?
I'M IN A HURRY!!
I DON'T HAVE TIME TO PLAY YOUR LITTLE GAME!!
OH REALLY~?
SO YOU HAVEN'T GOT ENOUGH STRENGTH LEFT TO THINK ANYMORE?
Grrr!
FINE!

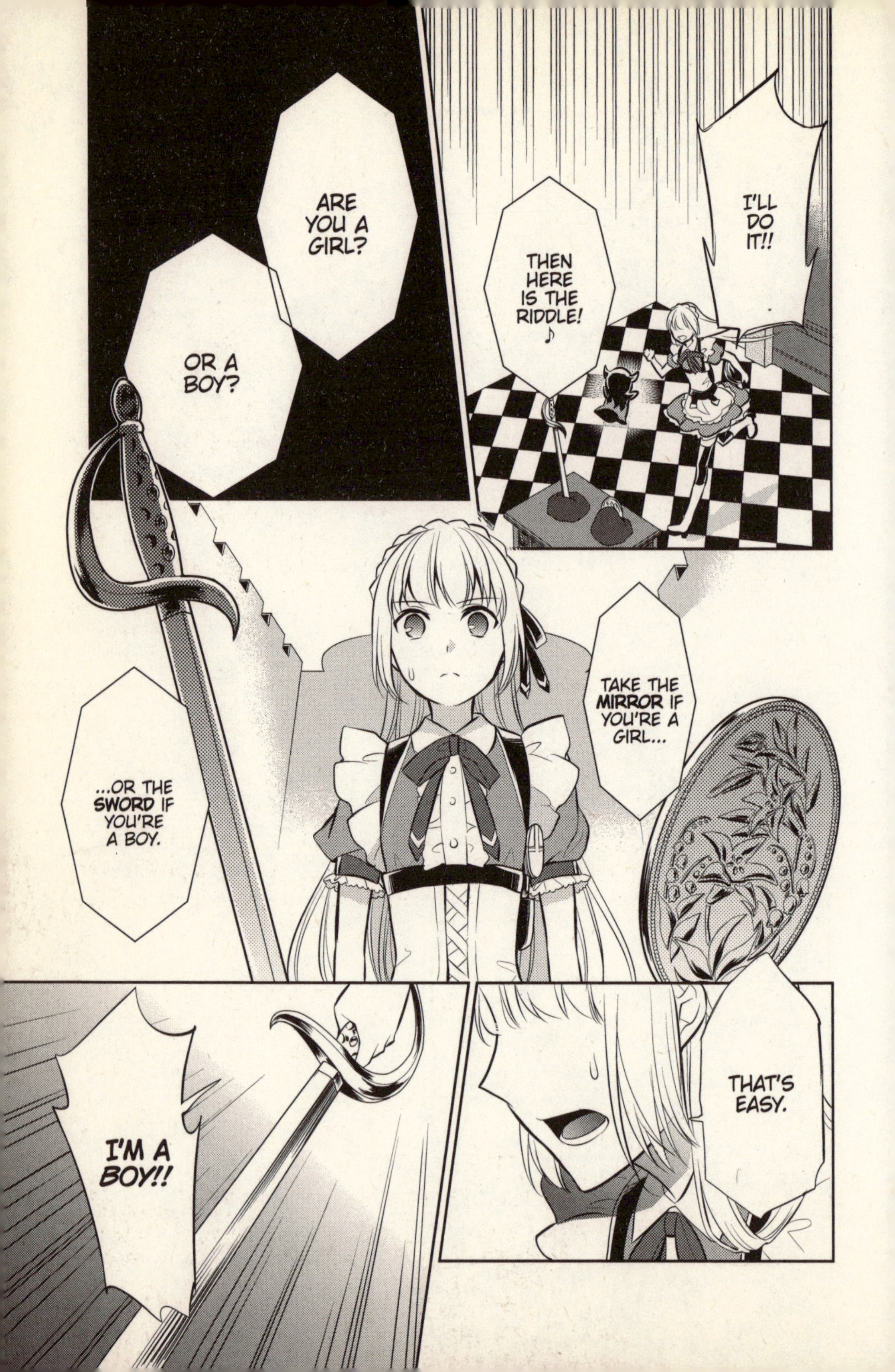
I'LL DO IT!!
THEN HERE IS THE RIDDLE! ♪
ARE YOU A GIRL?
OR A BOY?
TAKE THE MIRROR IF YOU'RE A GIRL...
...OR THE SWORD IF YOU'RE A BOY.
THAT'S EASY.
I'M A BOY!!

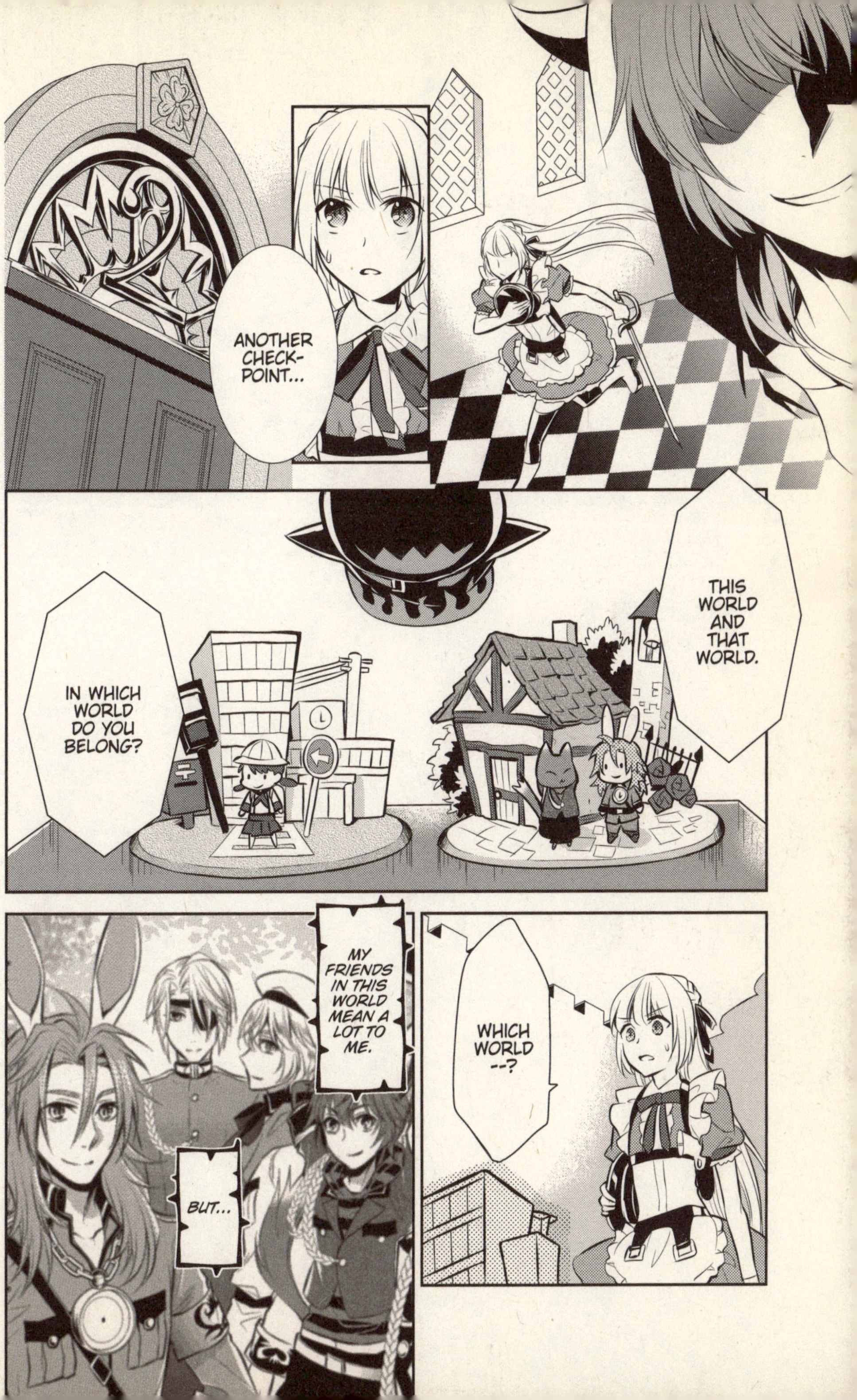
ANOTHER CHECK-POINT...
THIS WORLD AND THAT WORLD.
IN WHICH WORLD DO YOU BELONG?
WHICH WORLD --?
MY FRIENDS IN THIS WORLD MEAN A LOT TO ME.
BUT...

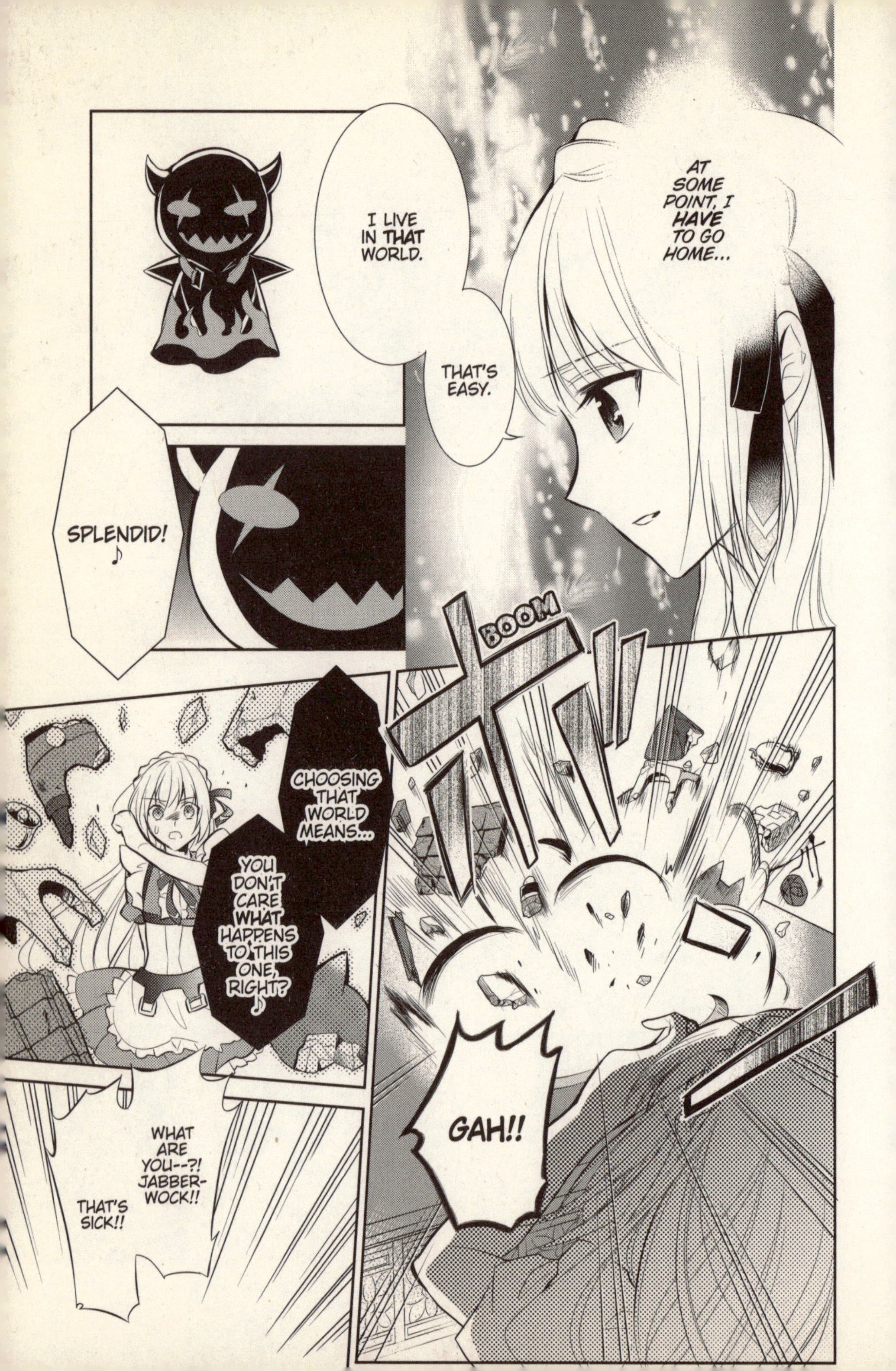
AT SOME POINT, I HAVE TO GO HOME...
I LIVE IN THAT WORLD.
THAT'S EASY.
SPLENDID! ♪
BOOM
GAH!!
CHOOSING THAT WORLD MEANS...
YOU DON'T CARE WHAT HAPPENS TO THIS ONE, RIGHT? ♪
WHAT ARE YOU--?! JABBERWOCK!!
THAT'S SICK!!

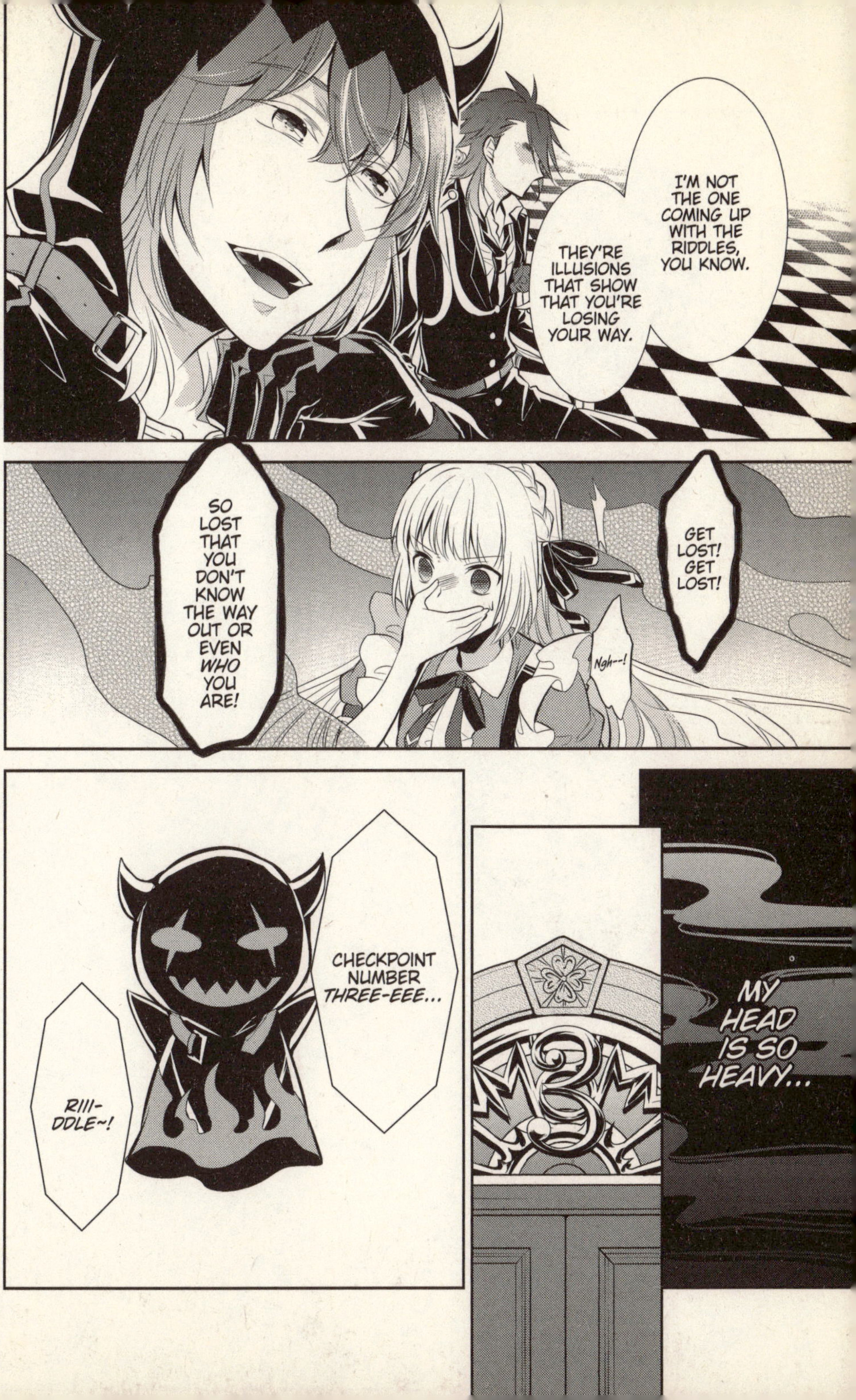
I'M NOT THE ONE COMING UP WITH THE RIDDLES, YOU KNOW.
THEY'RE ILLUSIONS THAT SHOW THAT YOU'RE LOSING YOUR WAY.
GET LOST! GET LOST!
Ngh--!
SO LOST THAT YOU DON'T KNOW THE WAY OUT OR EVEN *WHO* YOU ARE!
MY HEAD IS SO HEAVY...
CHECKPOINT NUMBER *THREE-EEE...*
RIII-DDLE~!

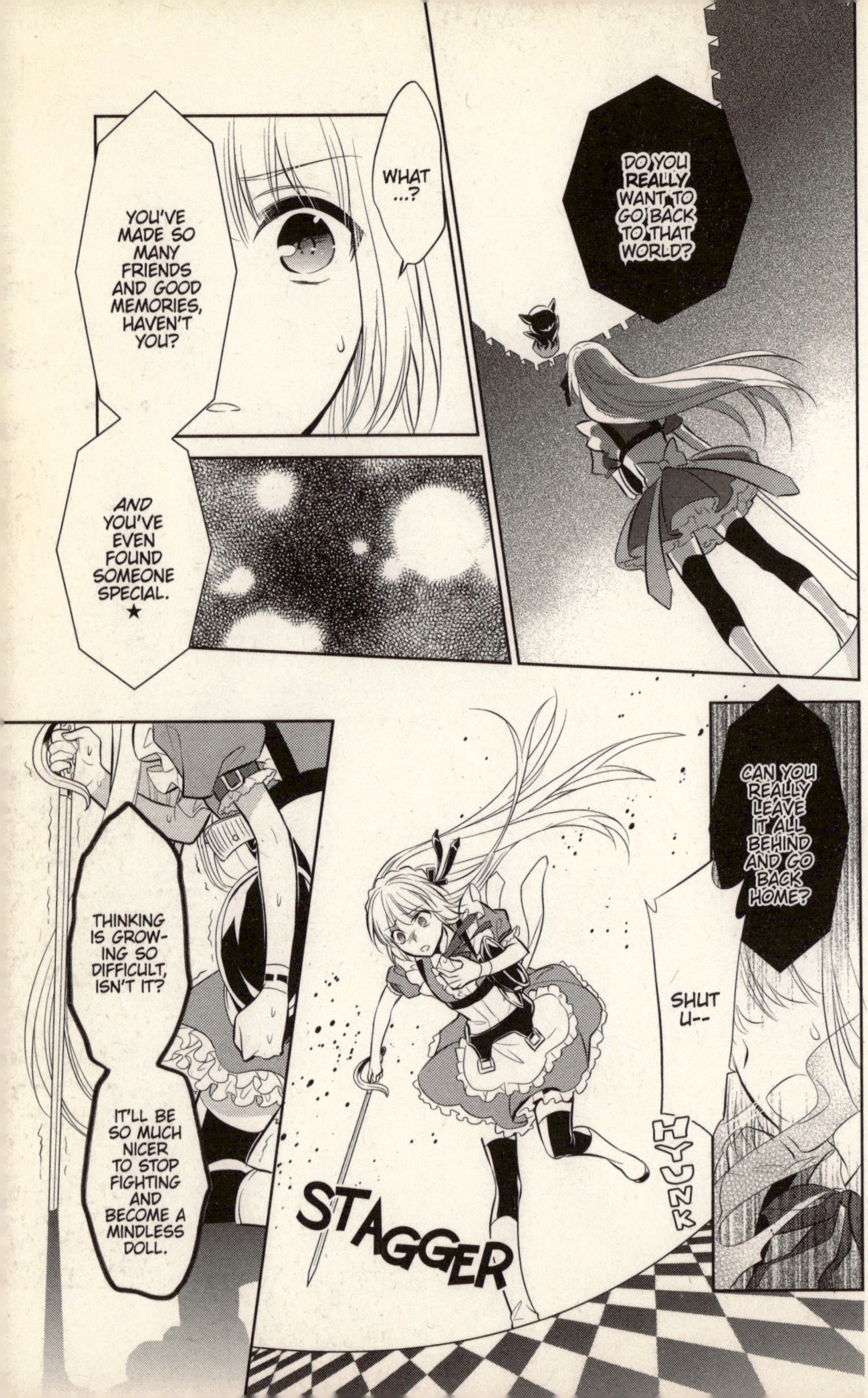
DO YOU REALLY WANT TO GO BACK TO THAT WORLD?
WHAT ...?
YOU'VE MADE SO MANY FRIENDS AND GOOD MEMORIES, HAVEN'T YOU?
AND YOU'VE EVEN FOUND SOMEONE SPECIAL. ★
CAN YOU REALLY LEAVE IT ALL BEHIND AND GO BACK HOME?
SHUT U--
HYUNK
STAGGER
THINKING IS GROW-ING SO DIFFICULT, ISN'T IT?
IT'LL BE SO MUCH NICER TO STOP FIGHTING AND BECOME A MINDLESS DOLL.

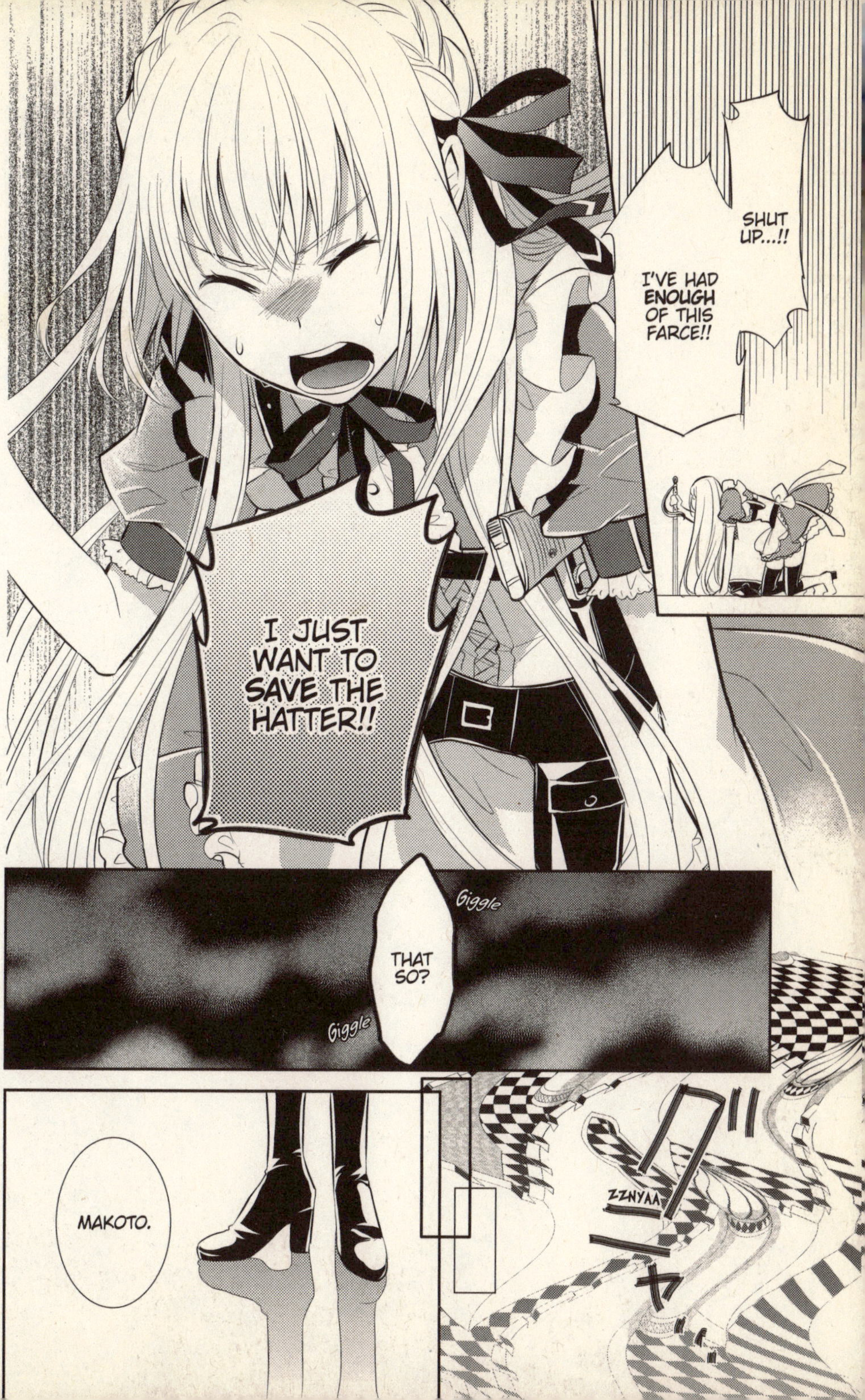
SHUT UP...!!
I'VE HAD ENOUGH OF THIS FARCE!!
I JUST WANT TO SAVE THE HATTER!!
Giggle
THAT SO?
Giggle
ZZNYAA
MAKOTO.

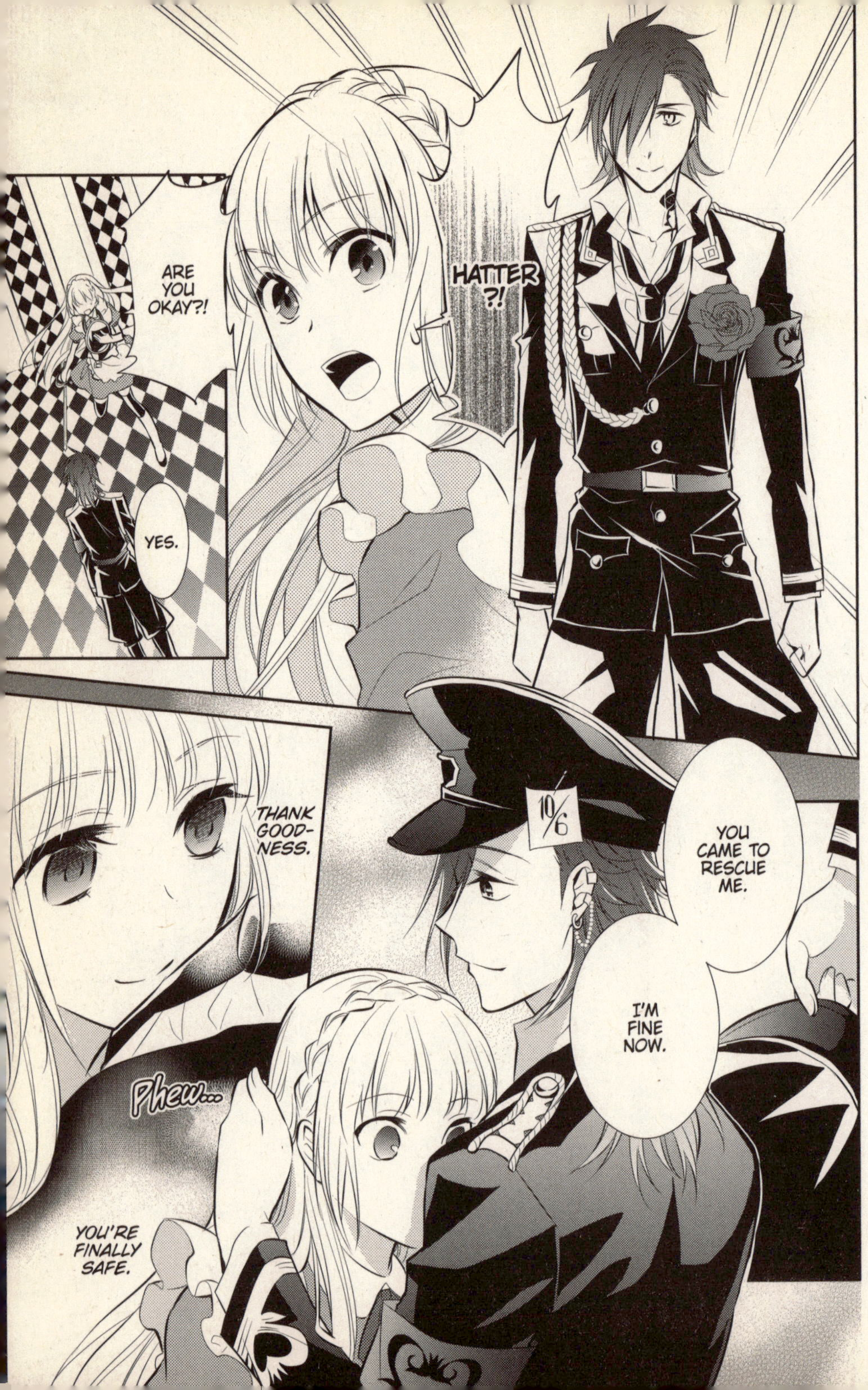
HATTER?!
ARE YOU OKAY?!
YES.
YOU CAME TO RESCUE ME.
I'M FINE NOW.
THANK GOODNESS.
Phew...
YOU'RE FINALLY SAFE.

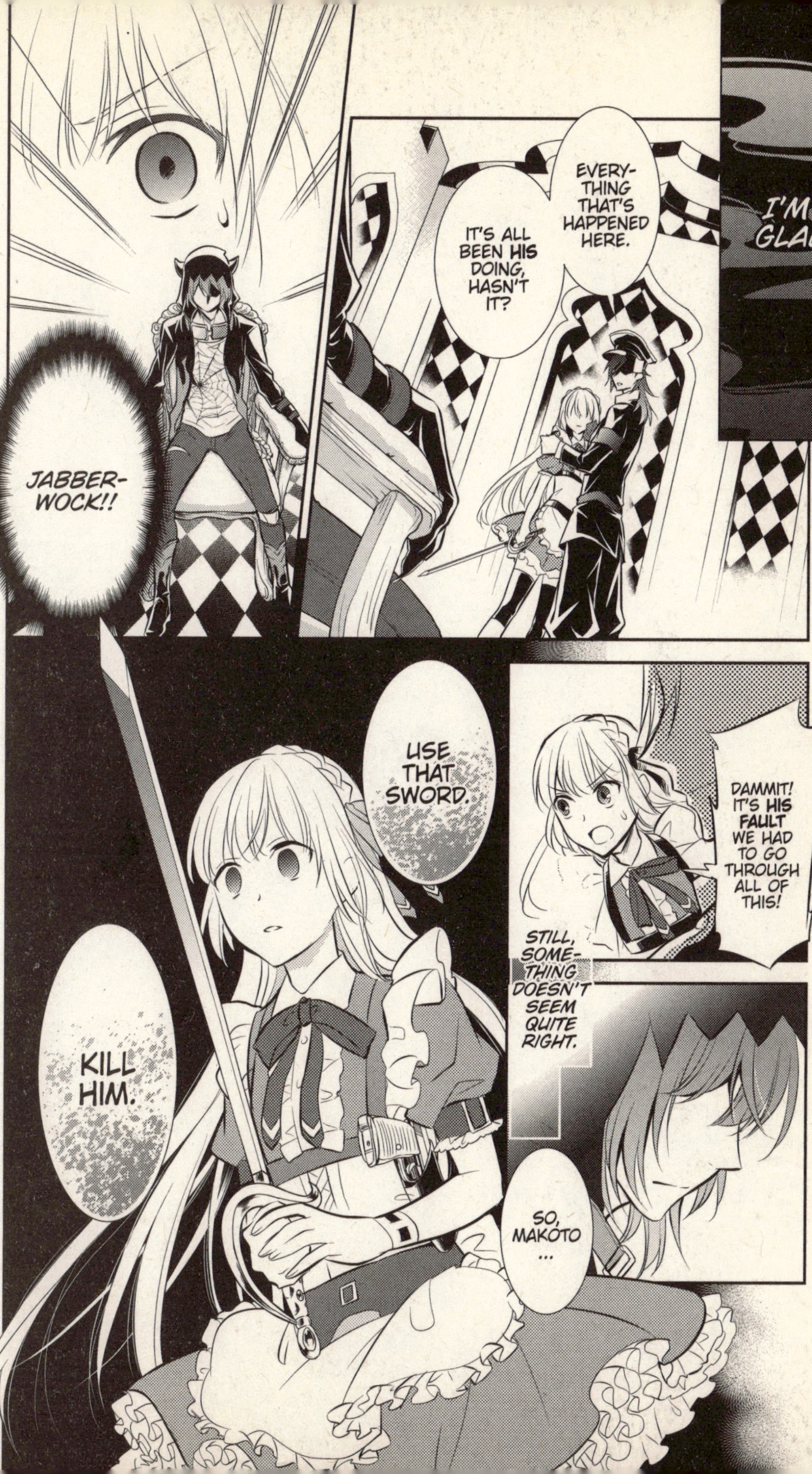

I'M SO GLAD...!
EVERY-THING THAT'S HAPPENED HERE.
IT'S ALL BEEN **HIS** DOING, HASN'T IT?
JABBER-WOCK!!
DAMMIT! IT'S **HIS FAULT** WE HAD TO GO THROUGH ALL OF THIS!
STILL, SOME-THING DOESN'T SEEM QUITE RIGHT.
SO, MAKOTO ...
USE THAT SWORD.
KILL HIM.

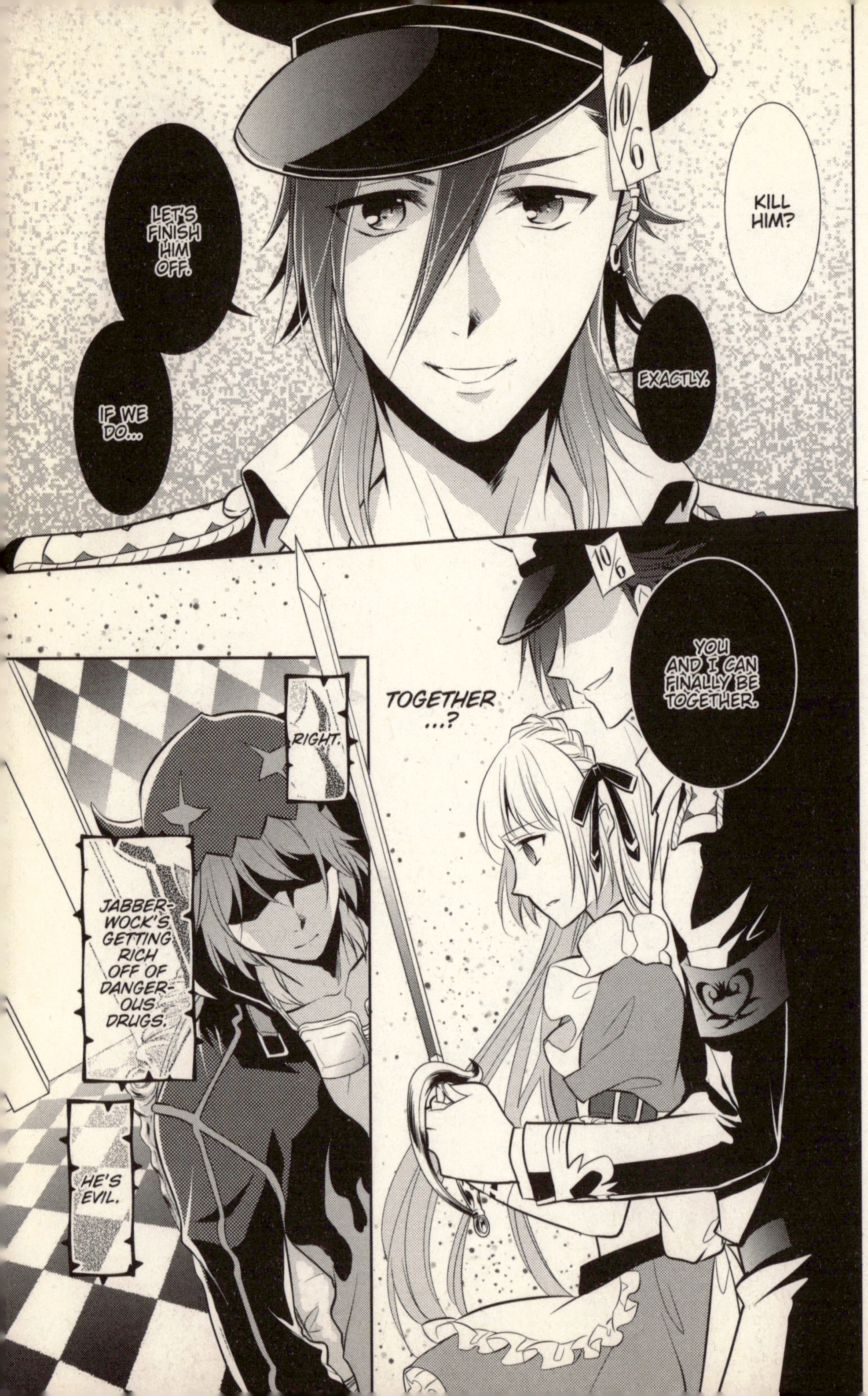
KILL HIM?
EXACTLY.
LET'S FINISH HIM OFF.
IF WE DO...
YOU AND I CAN FINALLY BE TOGETHER.
TOGETHER ...?
RIGHT.
JABBER-WOCK'S GETTING RICH OFF OF DANGER-OUS DRUGS.
HE'S EVIL.

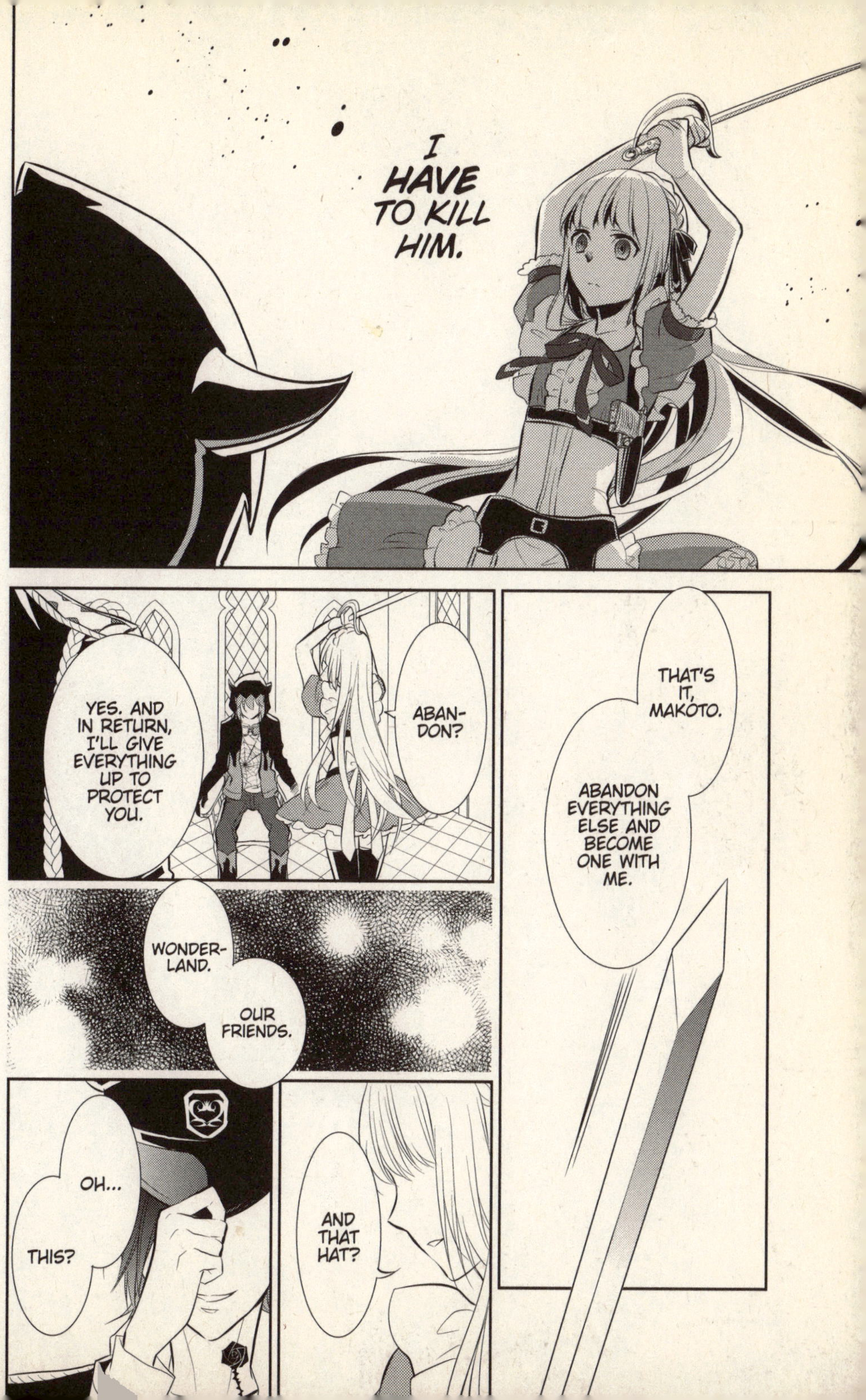
I HAVE TO KILL HIM.
THAT'S IT, MAKOTO.
ABANDON EVERYTHING ELSE AND BECOME ONE WITH ME.
ABAN-DON?
YES. AND IN RETURN, I'LL GIVE EVERYTHING UP TO PROTECT YOU.
WONDER-LAND.
OUR FRIENDS.
AND THAT HAT?
OH...
THIS?

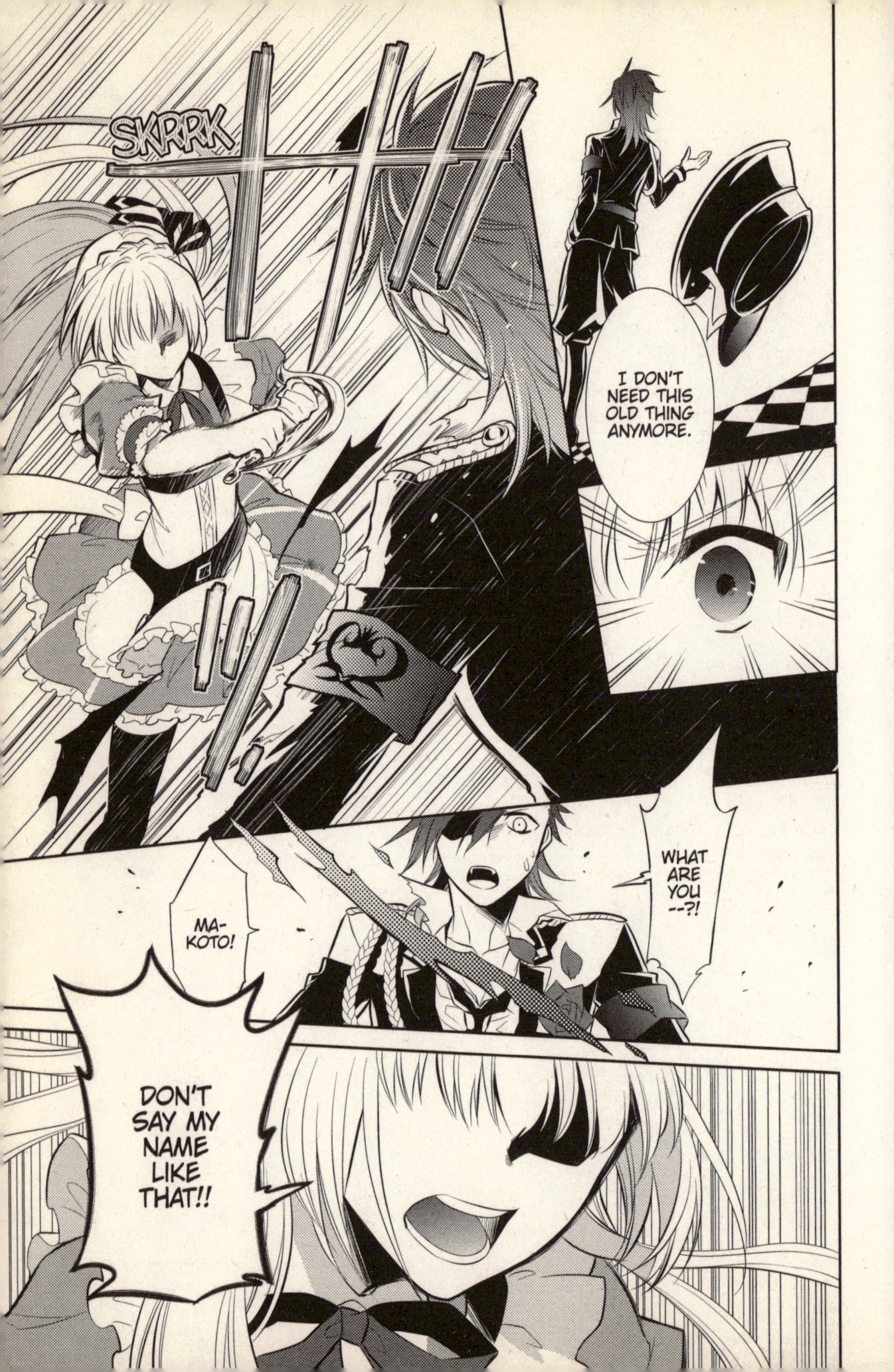
I DON'T NEED THIS OLD THING ANYMORE.
SKRRK
WHAT ARE YOU --?!
MA-KOTO!
DON'T SAY MY NAME LIKE THAT!!

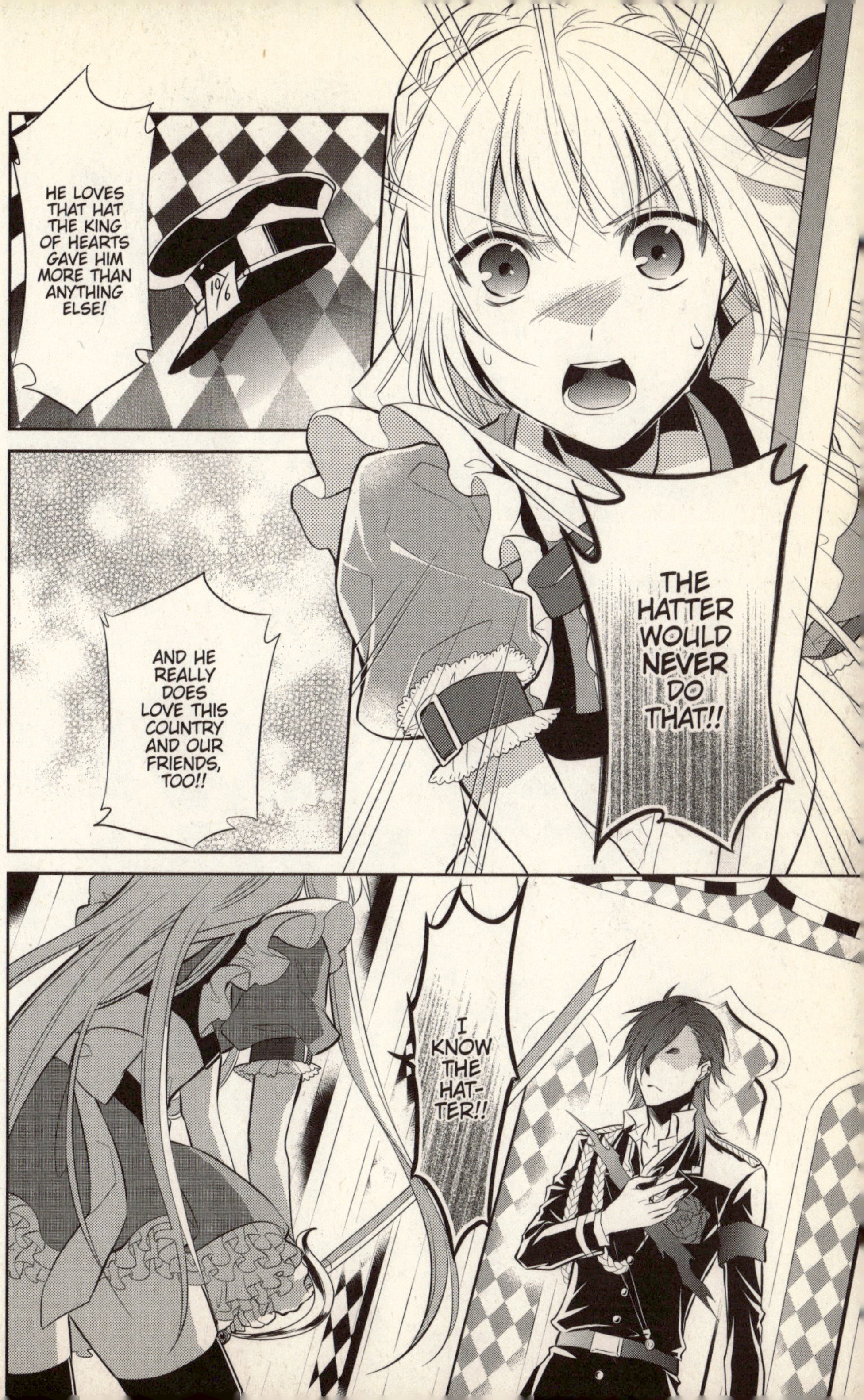
THE HATTER WOULD NEVER DO THAT!!
HE LOVES THAT HAT THE KING OF HEARTS GAVE HIM MORE THAN ANYTHING ELSE!
10/6
AND HE REALLY DOES LOVE THIS COUNTRY AND OUR FRIENDS, TOO!!
I KNOW THE HAT-TER!!

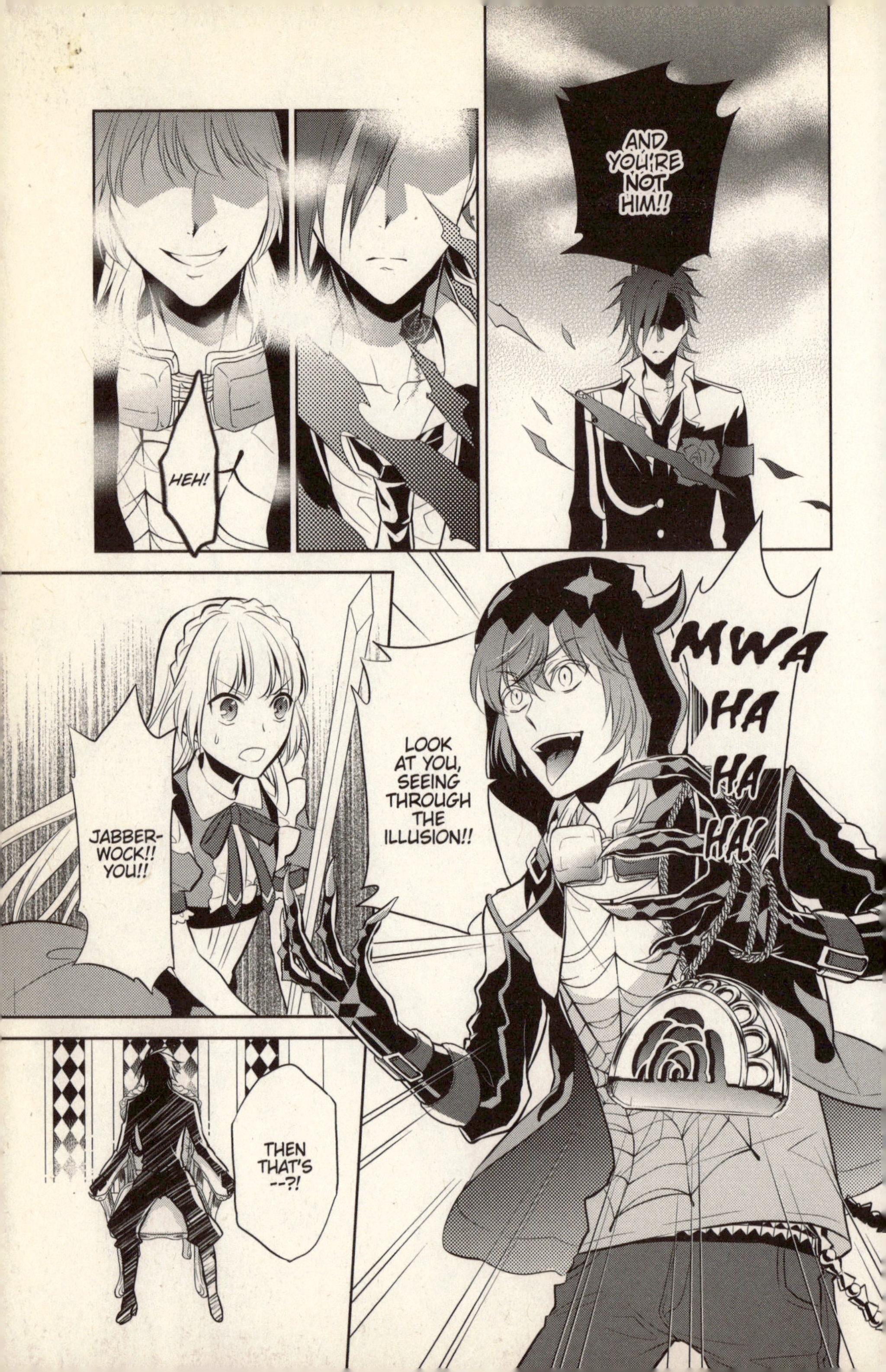
AND YOU'RE NOT HIM!!
HEH!
MWA HA HA HA HA!
LOOK AT YOU, SEEING THROUGH THE ILLUSION!!
JABBER-WOCK!! YOU!!
THEN THAT'S --?!

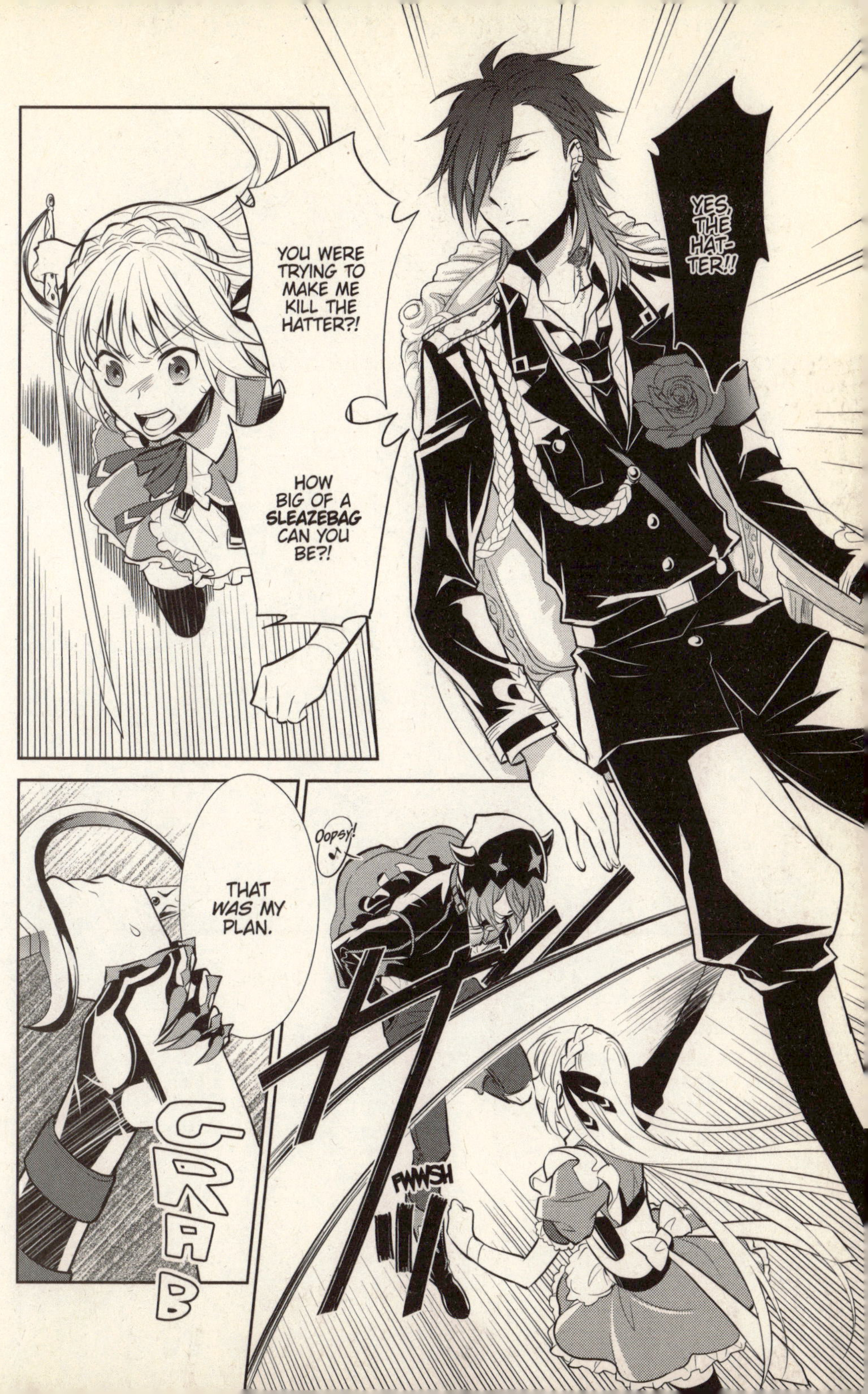
YES, THE HAT-TER!!
YOU WERE TRYING TO MAKE ME KILL THE HATTER?!
HOW BIG OF A SLEAZEBAG CAN YOU BE?!
Oopsy!
FWWSH
THAT WAS MY PLAN.
GRAB

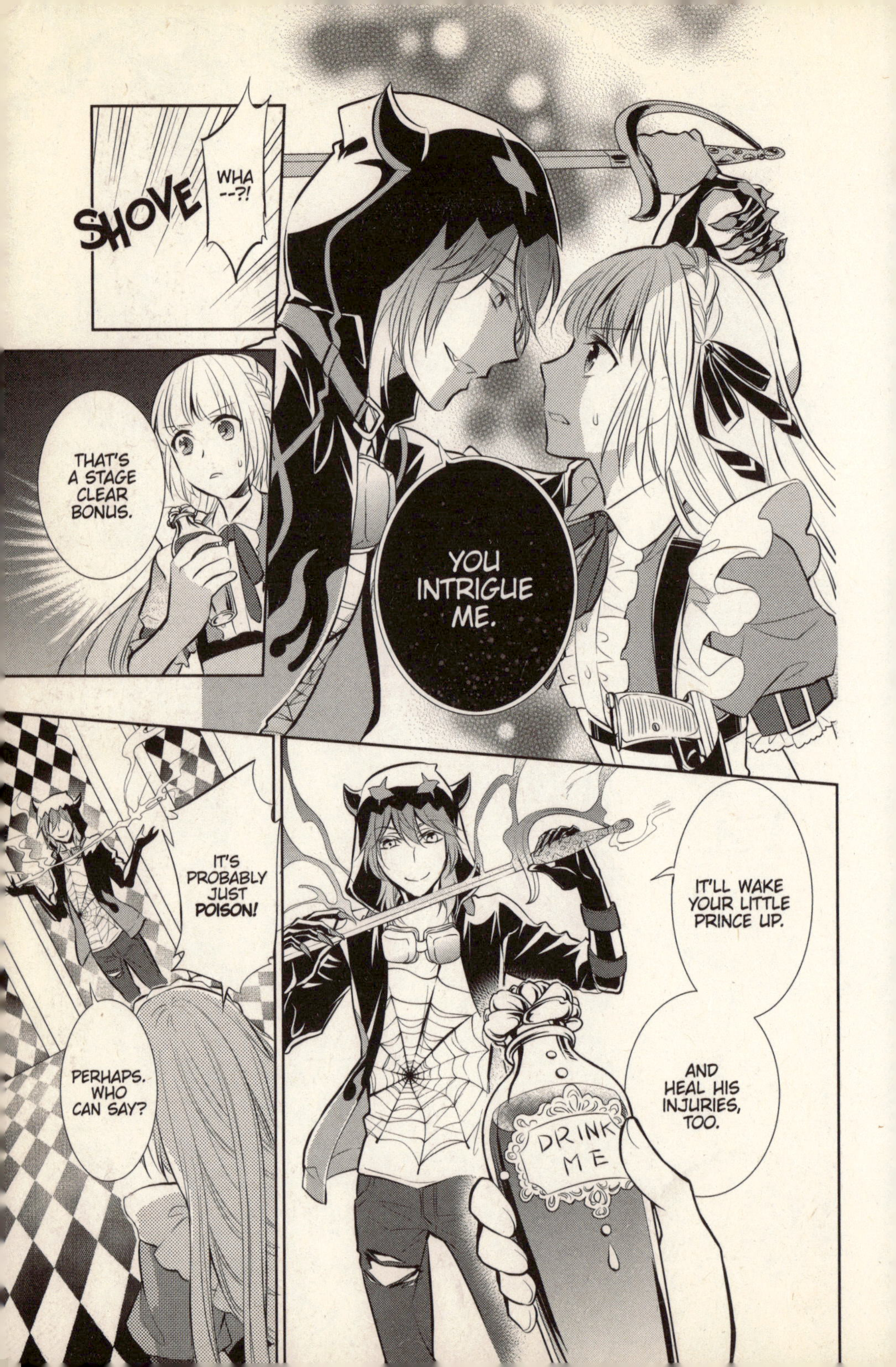
YOU INTRIGUE ME.
SHOVE
WHA--?!
THAT'S A STAGE CLEAR BONUS.
IT'LL WAKE YOUR LITTLE PRINCE UP.
AND HEAL HIS INJURIES, TOO.
DRINK ME
IT'S PROBABLY JUST POISON!
PERHAPS. WHO CAN SAY?

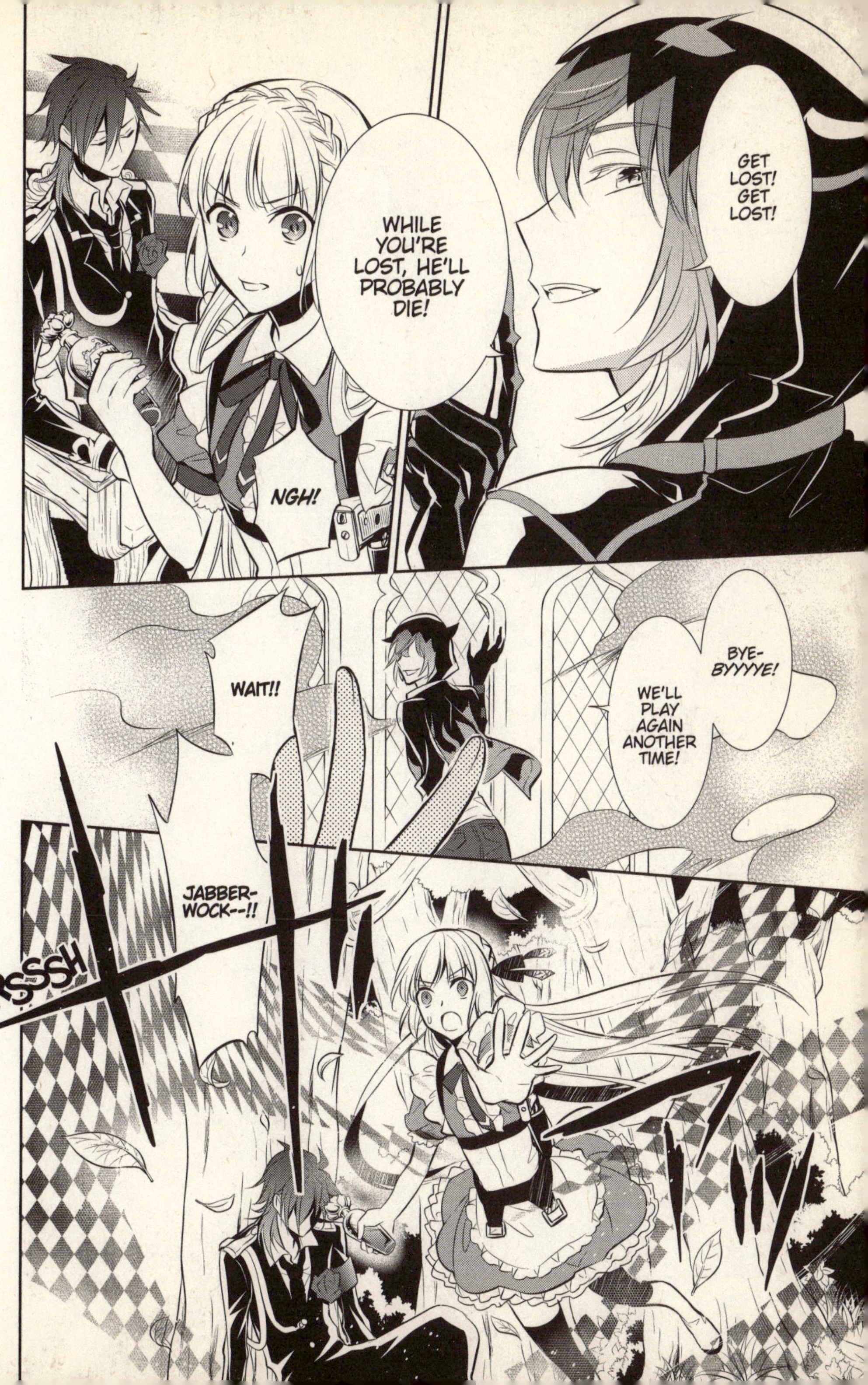
GET LOST! GET LOST!
WHILE YOU'RE LOST, HE'LL PROBABLY DIE!
NGH!
BYE-BYYYYE!
WE'LL PLAY AGAIN ANOTHER TIME!
WAIT!!
JABBER-WOCK--!!
KRSSSH

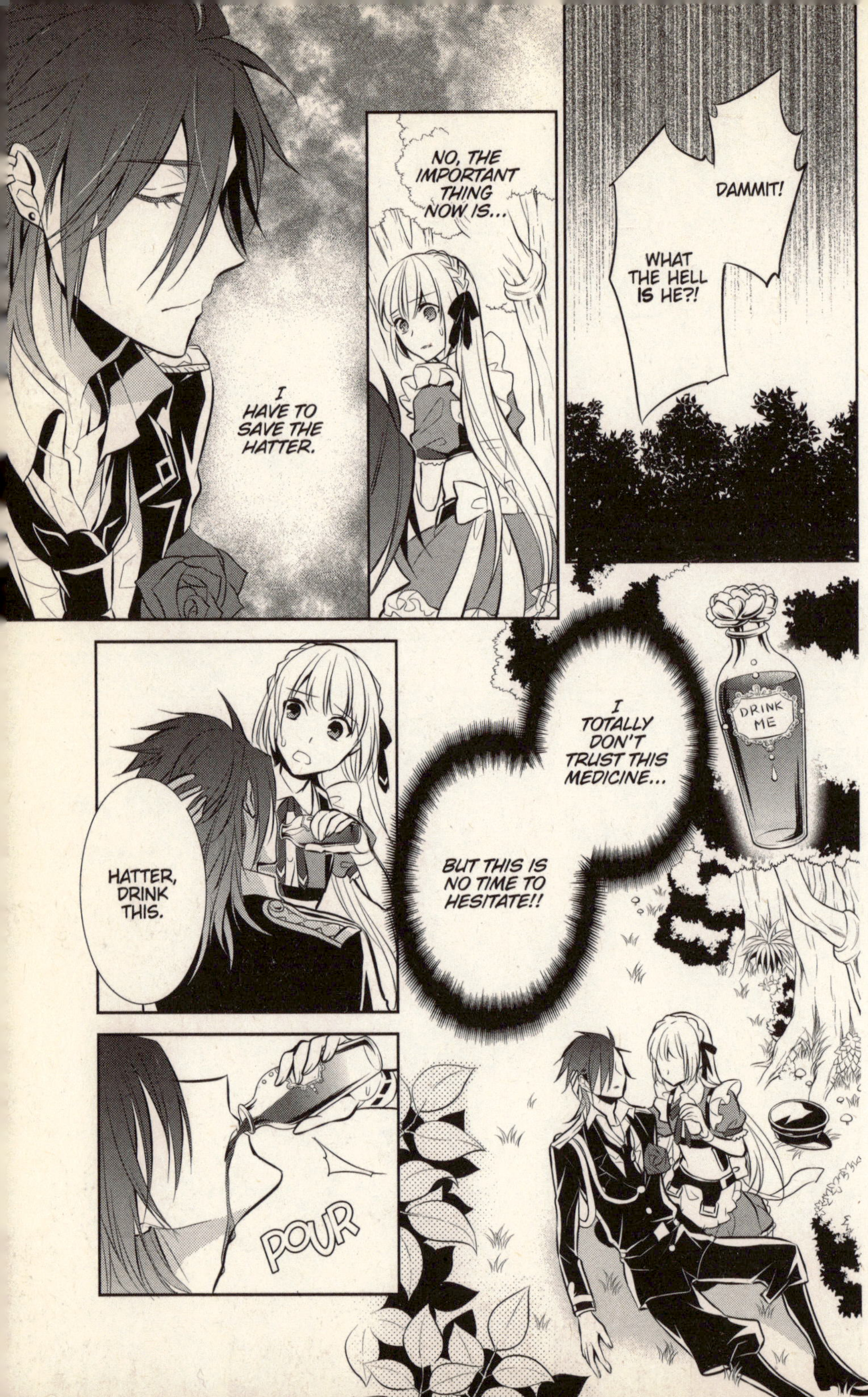
DAMMIT!
WHAT THE HELL IS HE?!
NO, THE IMPORTANT THING NOW IS...
I HAVE TO SAVE THE HATTER.
DRINK ME
I TOTALLY DON'T TRUST THIS MEDICINE...
BUT THIS IS NO TIME TO HESITATE!!
HATTER, DRINK THIS.
POUR

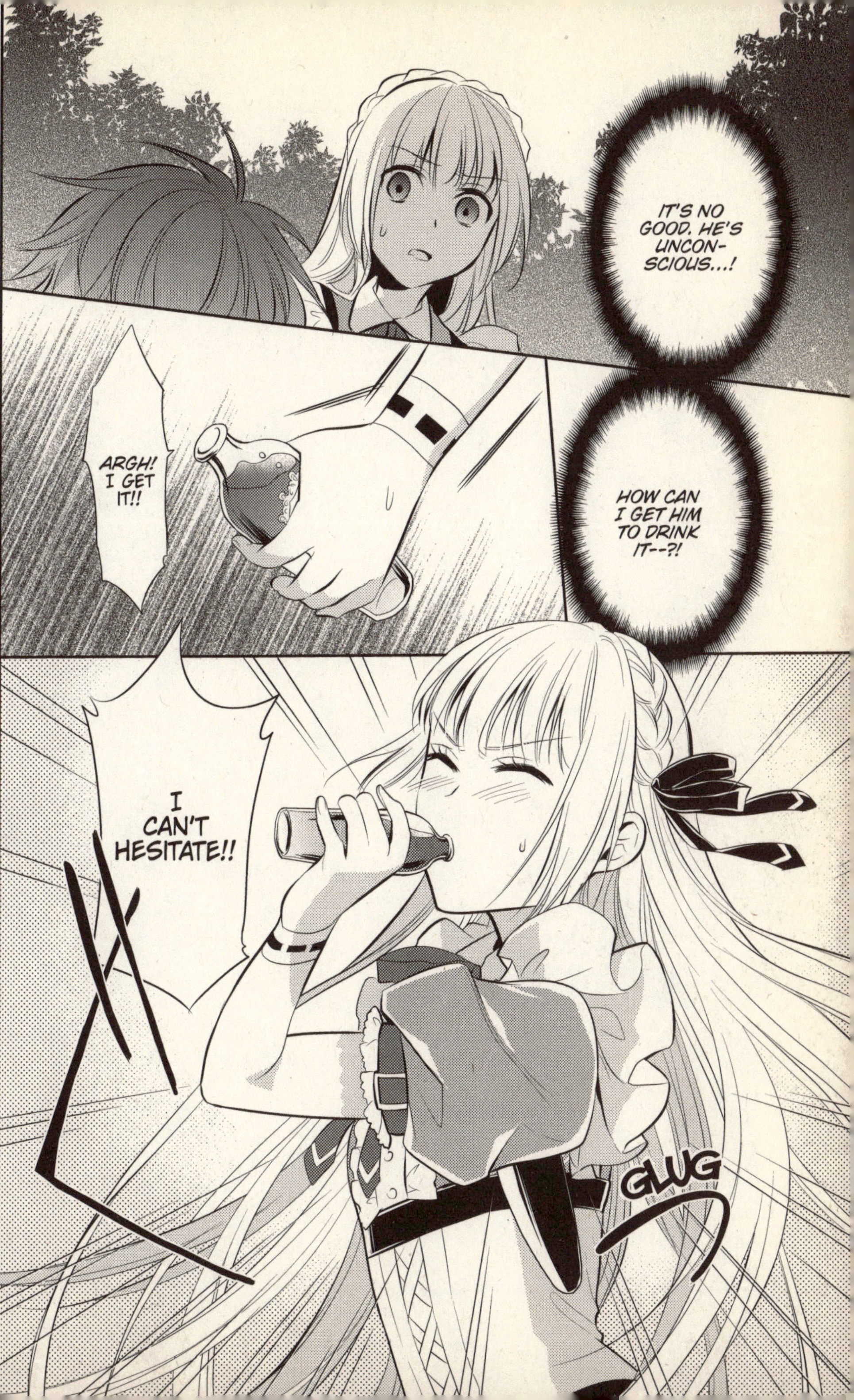
IT'S NO GOOD. HE'S UNCON-SCIOUS...!
HOW CAN I GET HIM TO DRINK IT--?!
ARGH! I GET IT!!
I CAN'T HESITATE!!
GLUG

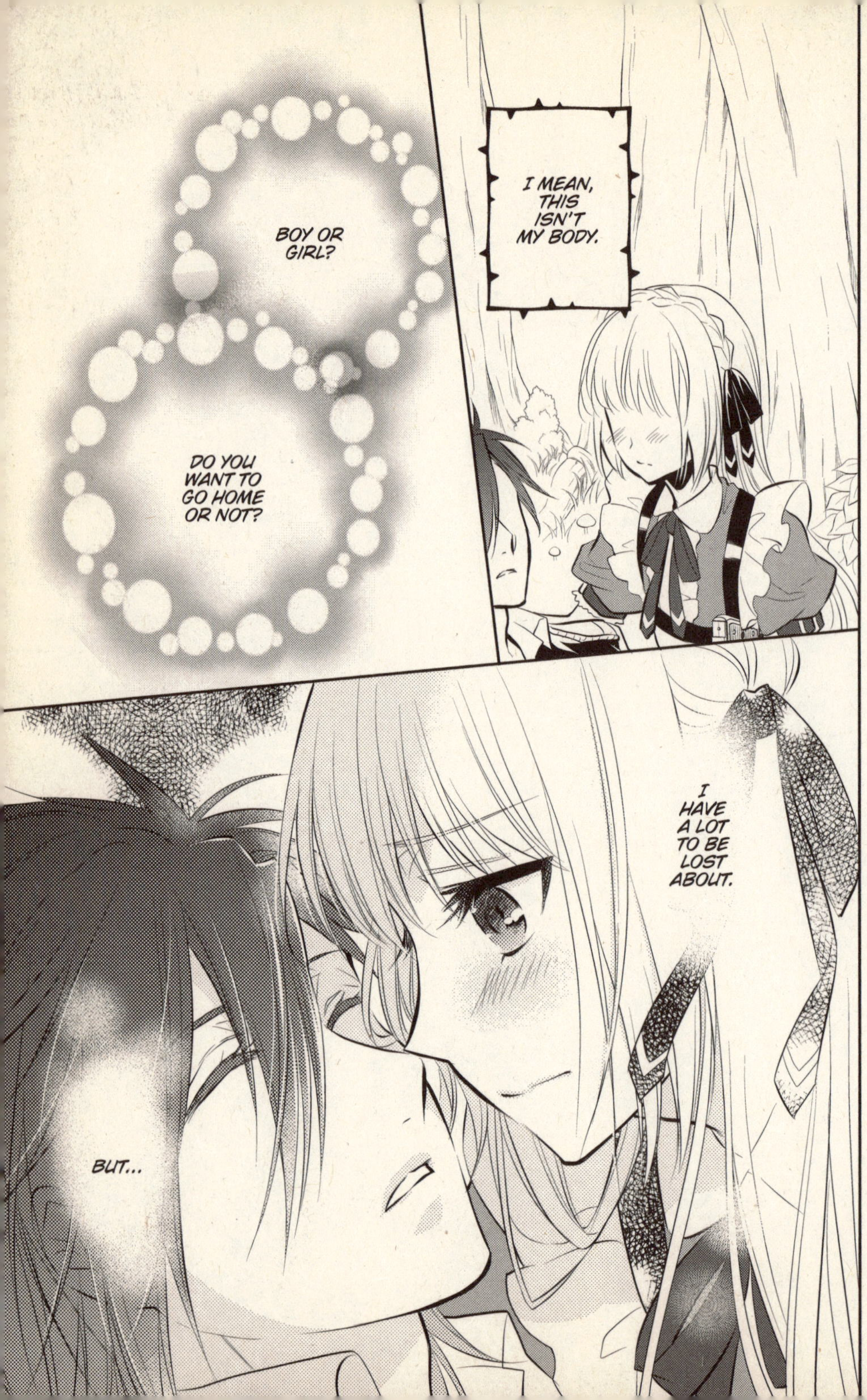
I MEAN, THIS ISN'T MY BODY.
BOY OR GIRL?
DO YOU WANT TO GO HOME OR NOT?
I HAVE A LOT TO BE LOST ABOUT.
BUT...

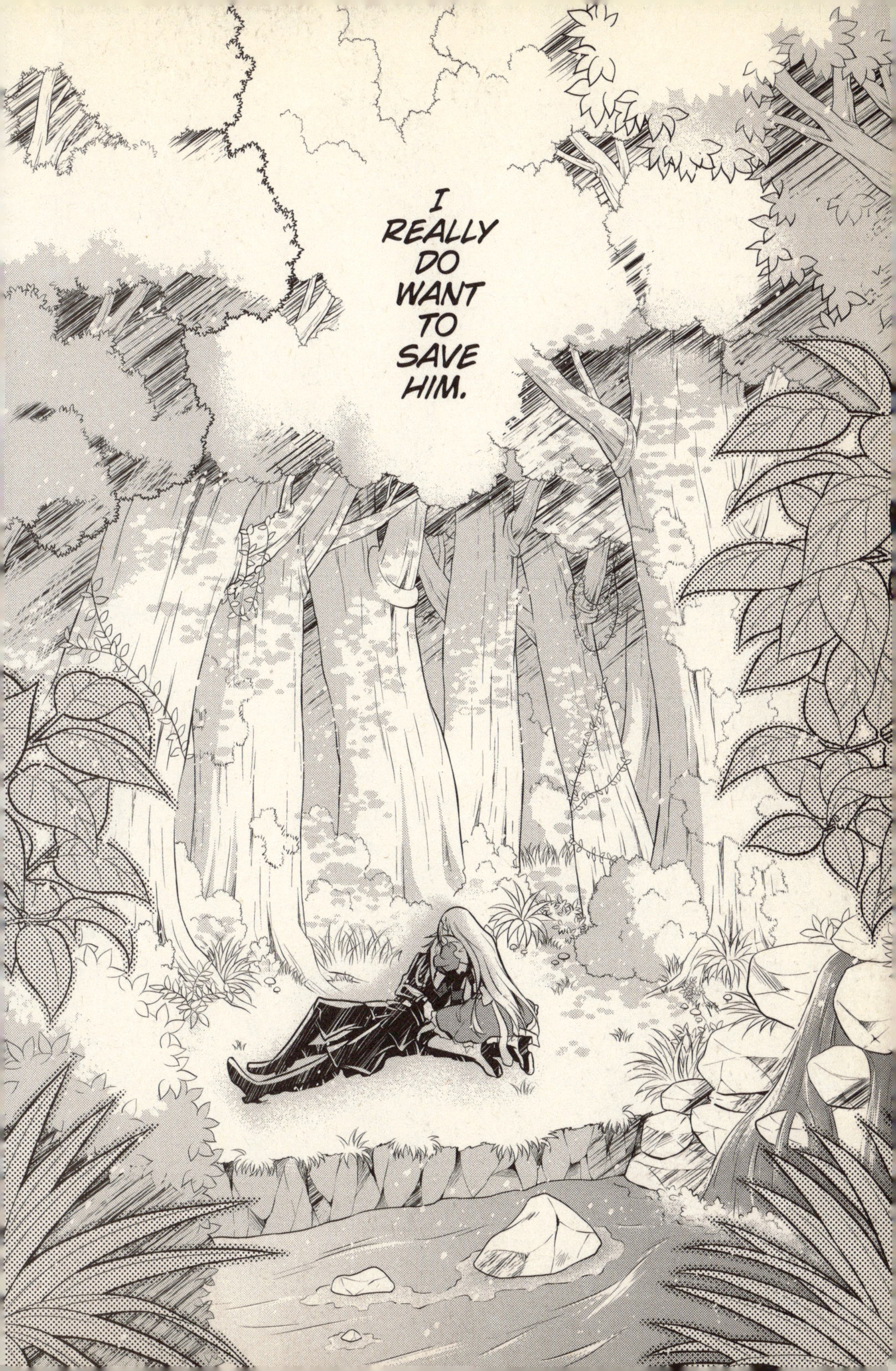
I REALLY DO WANT TO SAVE HIM.

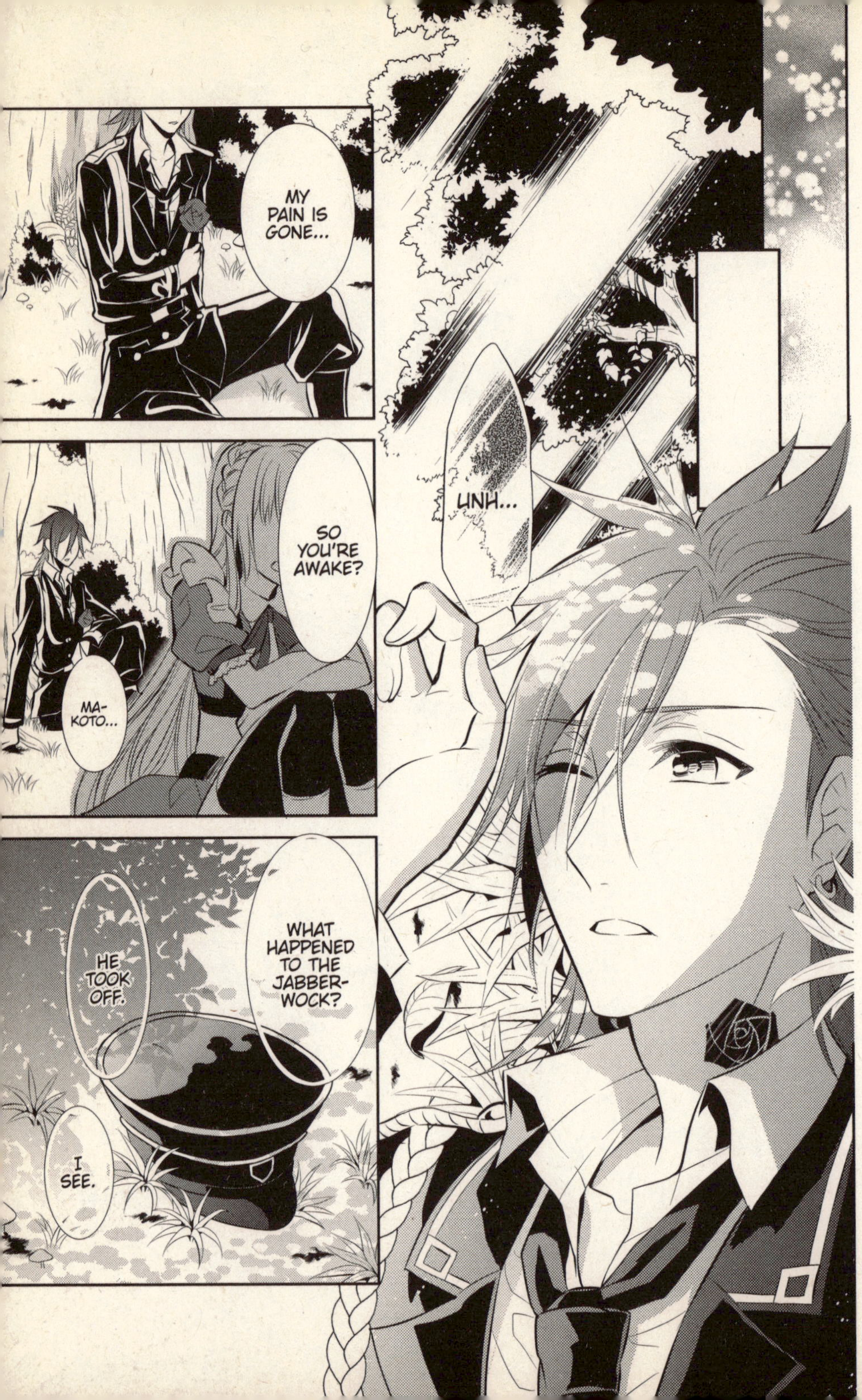
UNH...
MY PAIN IS GONE...
SO YOU'RE AWAKE?
MA-KOTO...
WHAT HAPPENED TO THE JABBER-WOCK?
HE TOOK OFF.
I SEE.

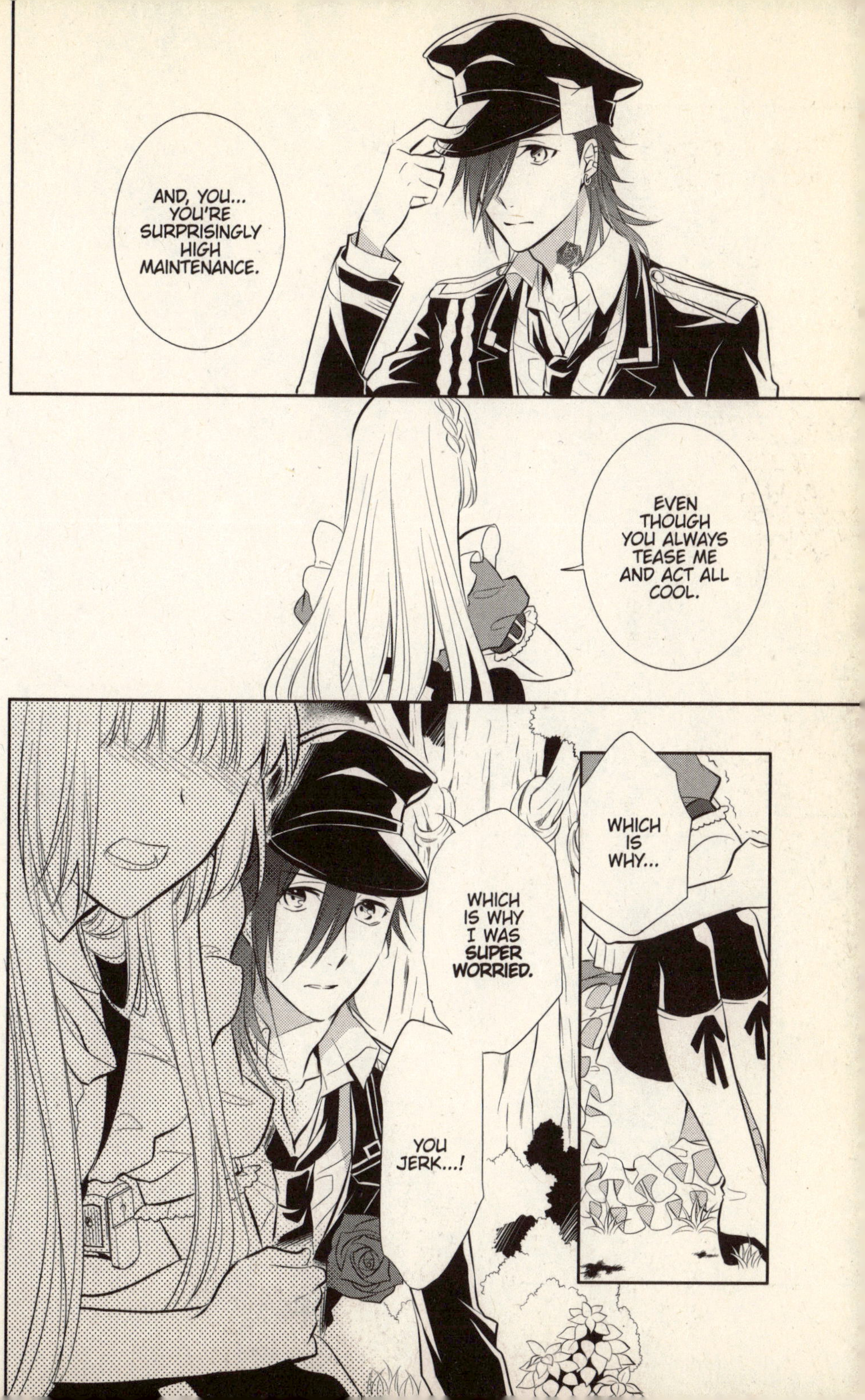
AND, YOU... YOU'RE SURPRISINGLY HIGH MAINTENANCE.
EVEN THOUGH YOU ALWAYS TEASE ME AND ACT ALL COOL.
WHICH IS WHY...
WHICH IS WHY I WAS **SUPER** WORRIED.
YOU JERK...!

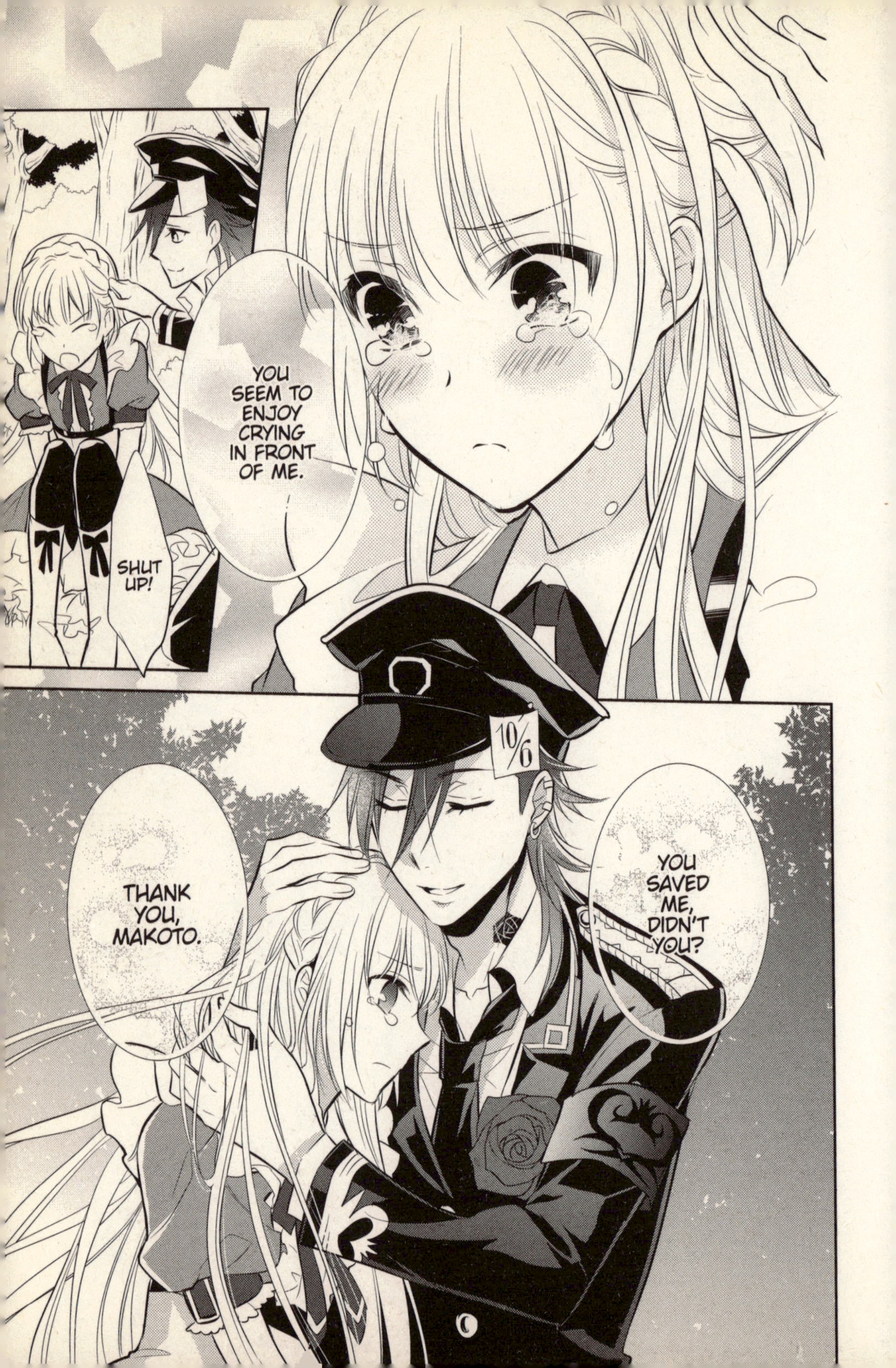
YOU SEEM TO ENJOY CRYING IN FRONT OF ME.
SHUT UP!
YOU SAVED ME, DIDN'T YOU?
THANK YOU, MAKOTO.

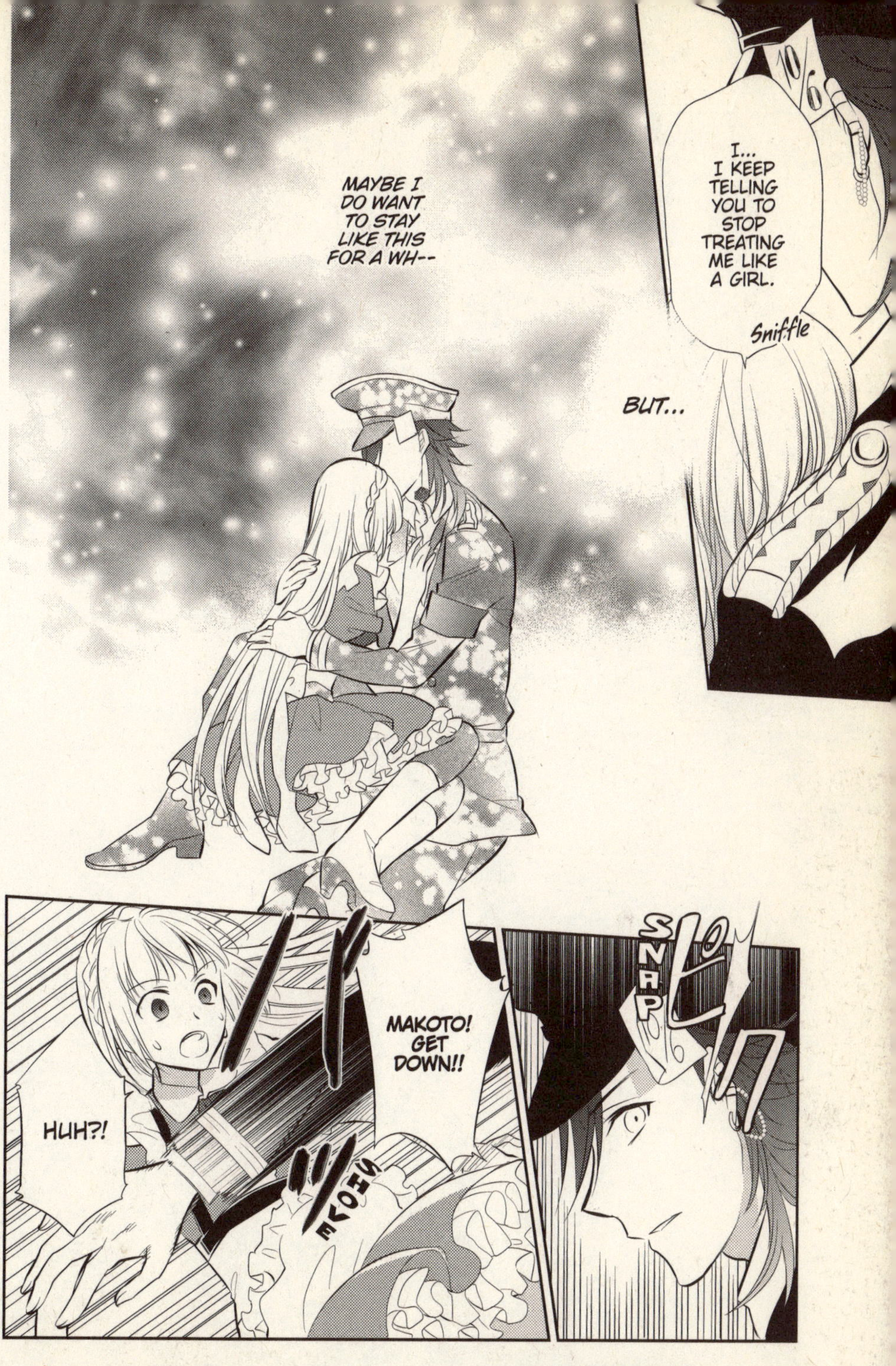
I... I KEEP TELLING YOU TO STOP TREATING ME LIKE A GIRL.
Sniffle
BUT...
MAYBE I DO WANT TO STAY LIKE THIS FOR A WH--
SNAP
MAKOTO! GET DOWN!!
HUH?!
SHOVE

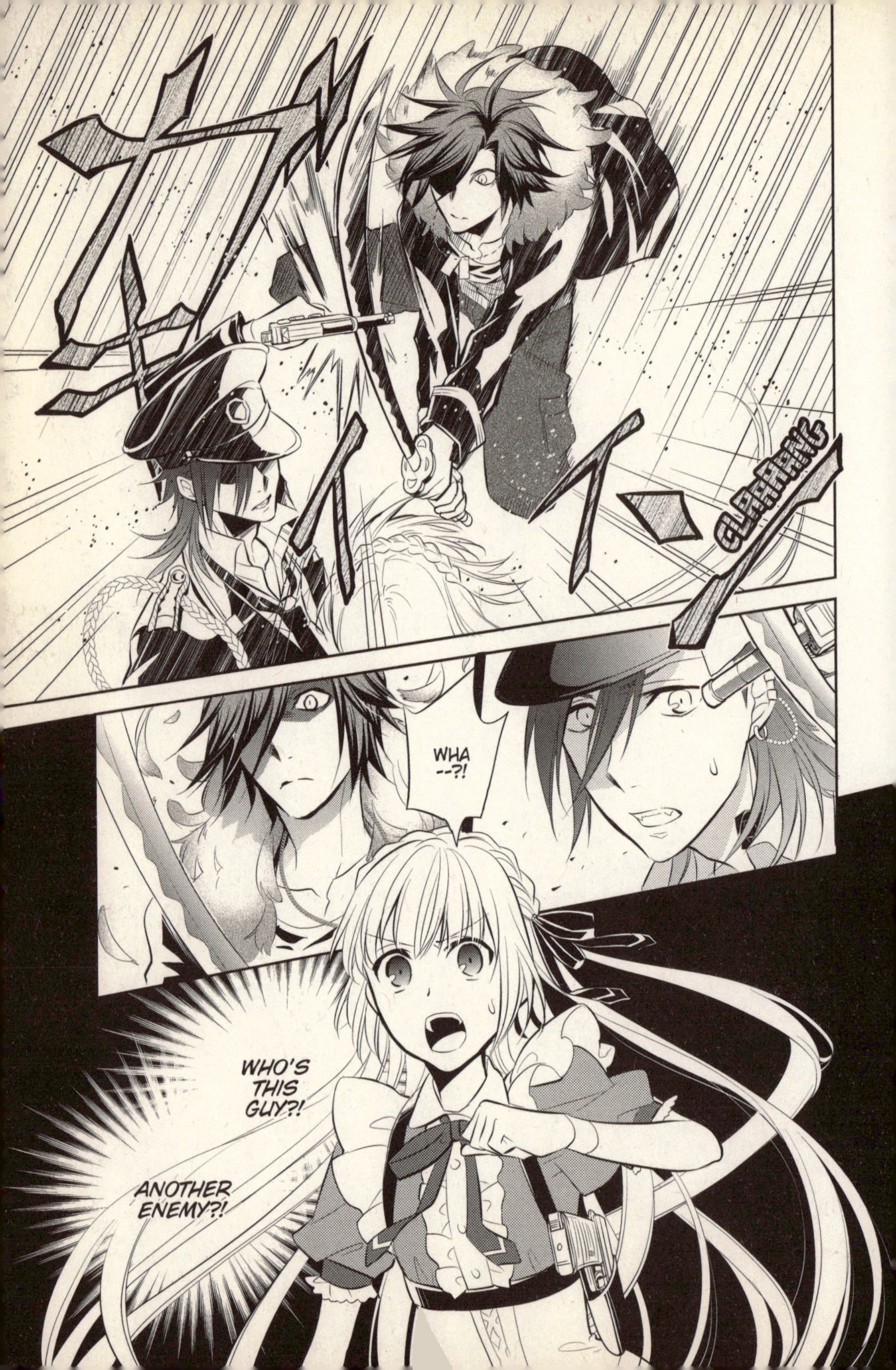
CLAAANG
WHA--?!
WHO'S THIS GUY?!
ANOTHER ENEMY?!

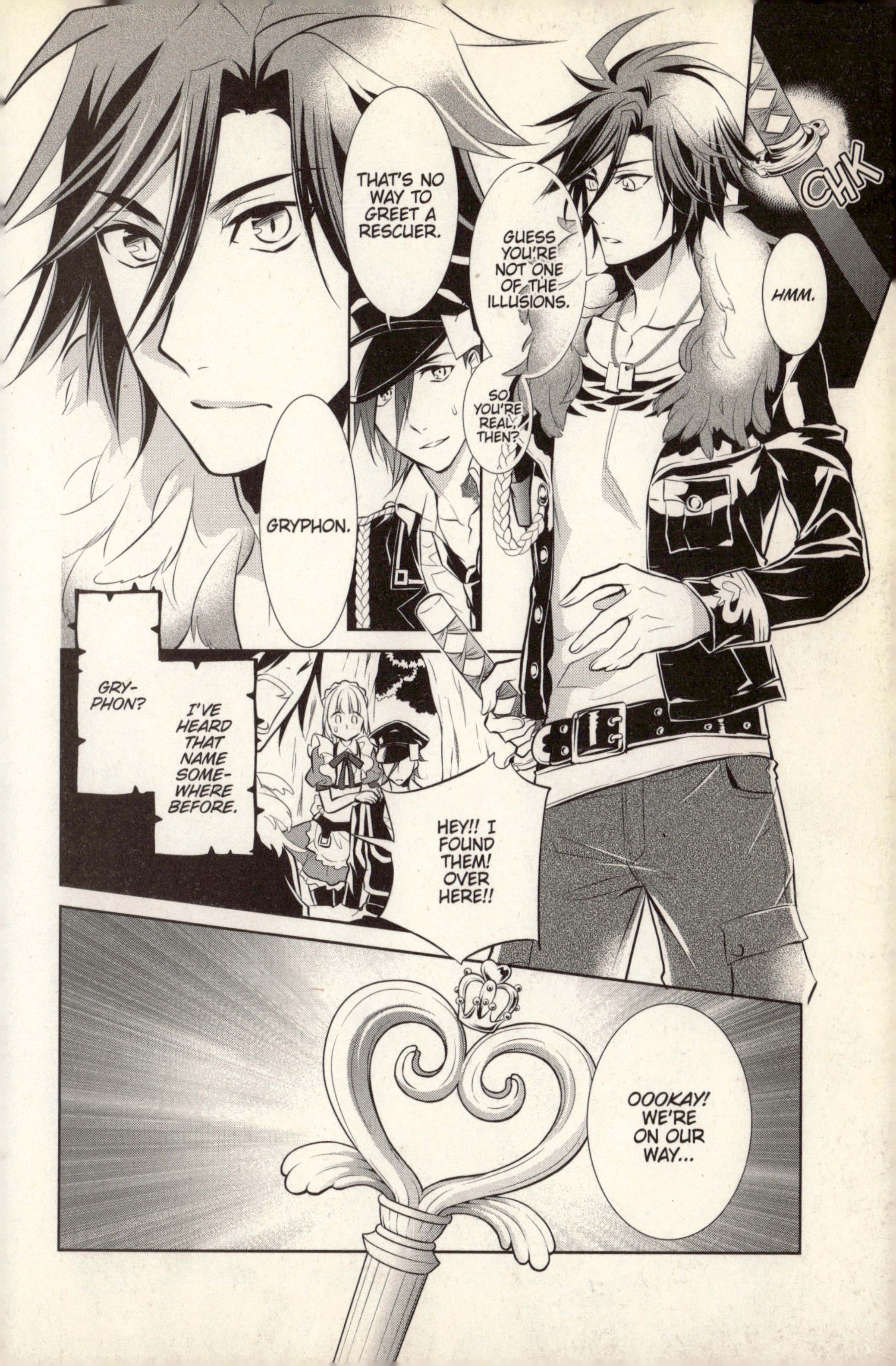
CHK
HMM.
GUESS YOU'RE NOT ONE OF THE ILLUSIONS.
SO YOU'RE REAL, THEN?
THAT'S NO WAY TO GREET A RESCUER.
GRYPHON.
GRY-PHON?
I'VE HEARD THAT NAME SOME-WHERE BEFORE.
HEY!! I FOUND THEM! OVER HERE!!
OOOKAY! WE'RE ON OUR WAY...

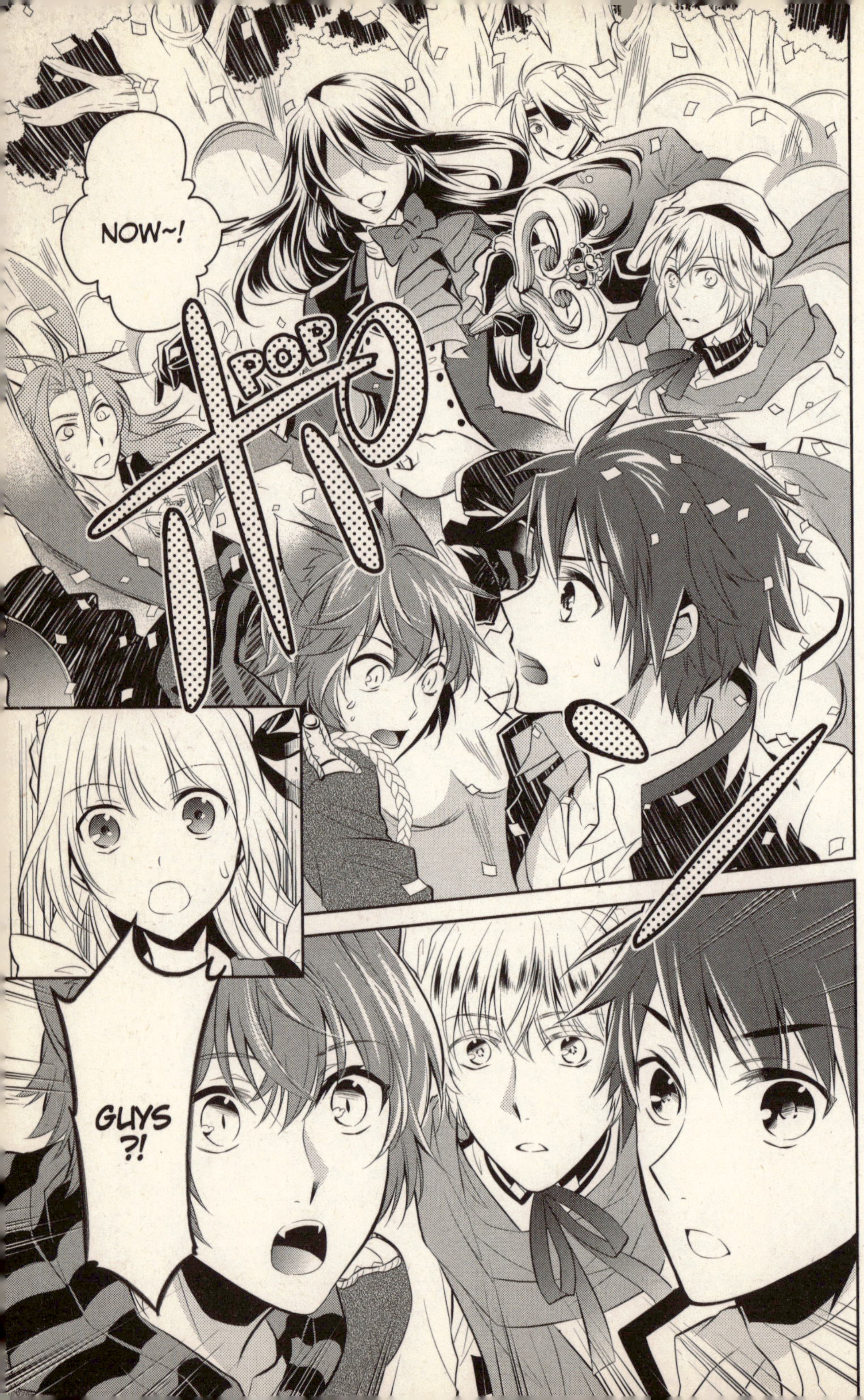
NOW~!
POP
GUYS ?!

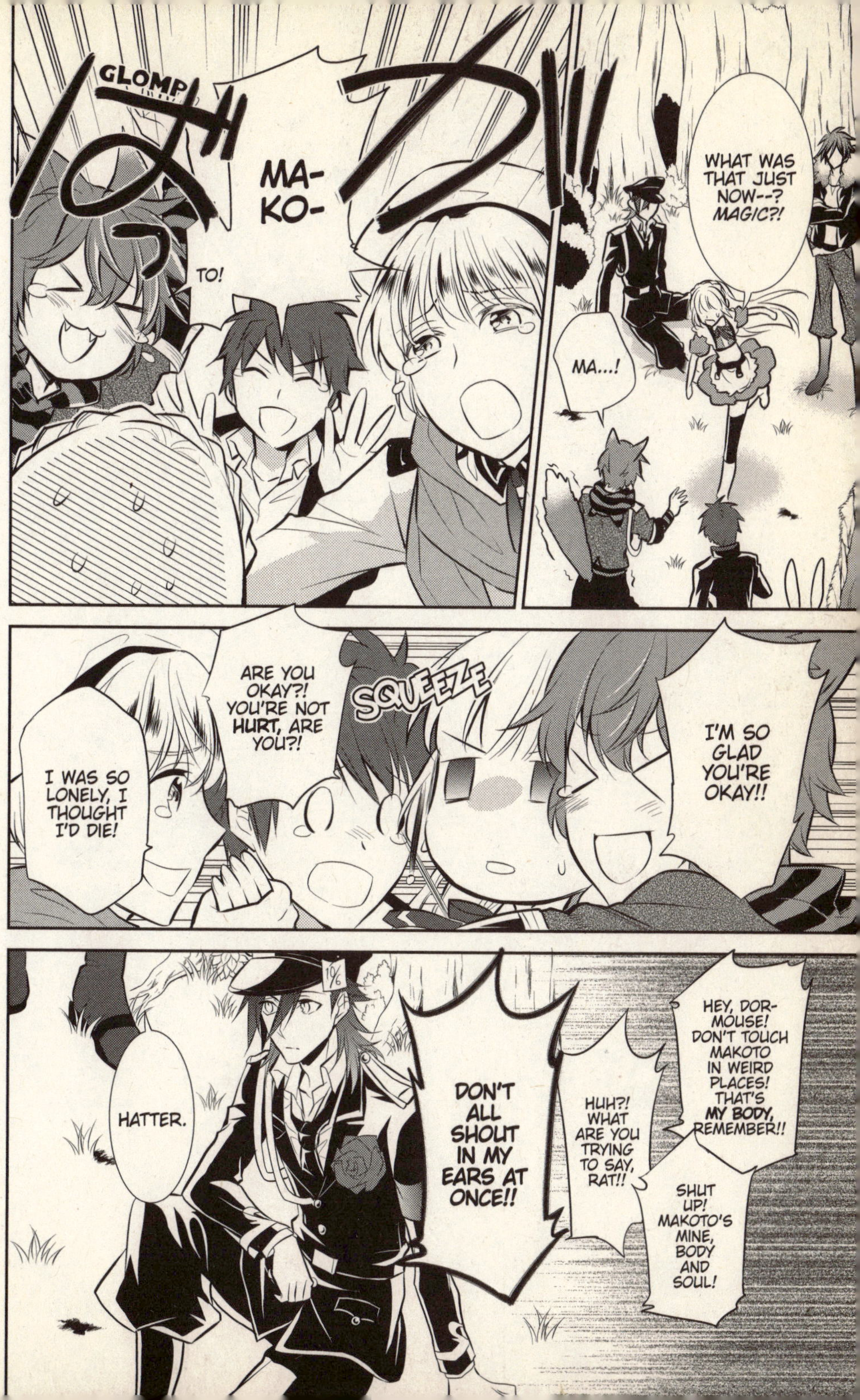
WHAT WAS THAT JUST NOW--? MAGIC?!
MA...!
GLOMP
MA-KO-
TO!
I'M SO GLAD YOU'RE OKAY!!
SQUEEZE
ARE YOU OKAY?! YOU'RE NOT HURT, ARE YOU?!
I WAS SO LONELY, I THOUGHT I'D DIE!
HEY, DOR-MOUSE! DON'T TOUCH MAKOTO IN WEIRD PLACES! THAT'S MY BODY, REMEMBER!!
HUH?! WHAT ARE YOU TRYING TO SAY, RAT!!
SHUT UP! MAKOTO'S MINE, BODY AND SOUL!
DON'T ALL SHOUT IN MY EARS AT ONCE!!
HATTER.

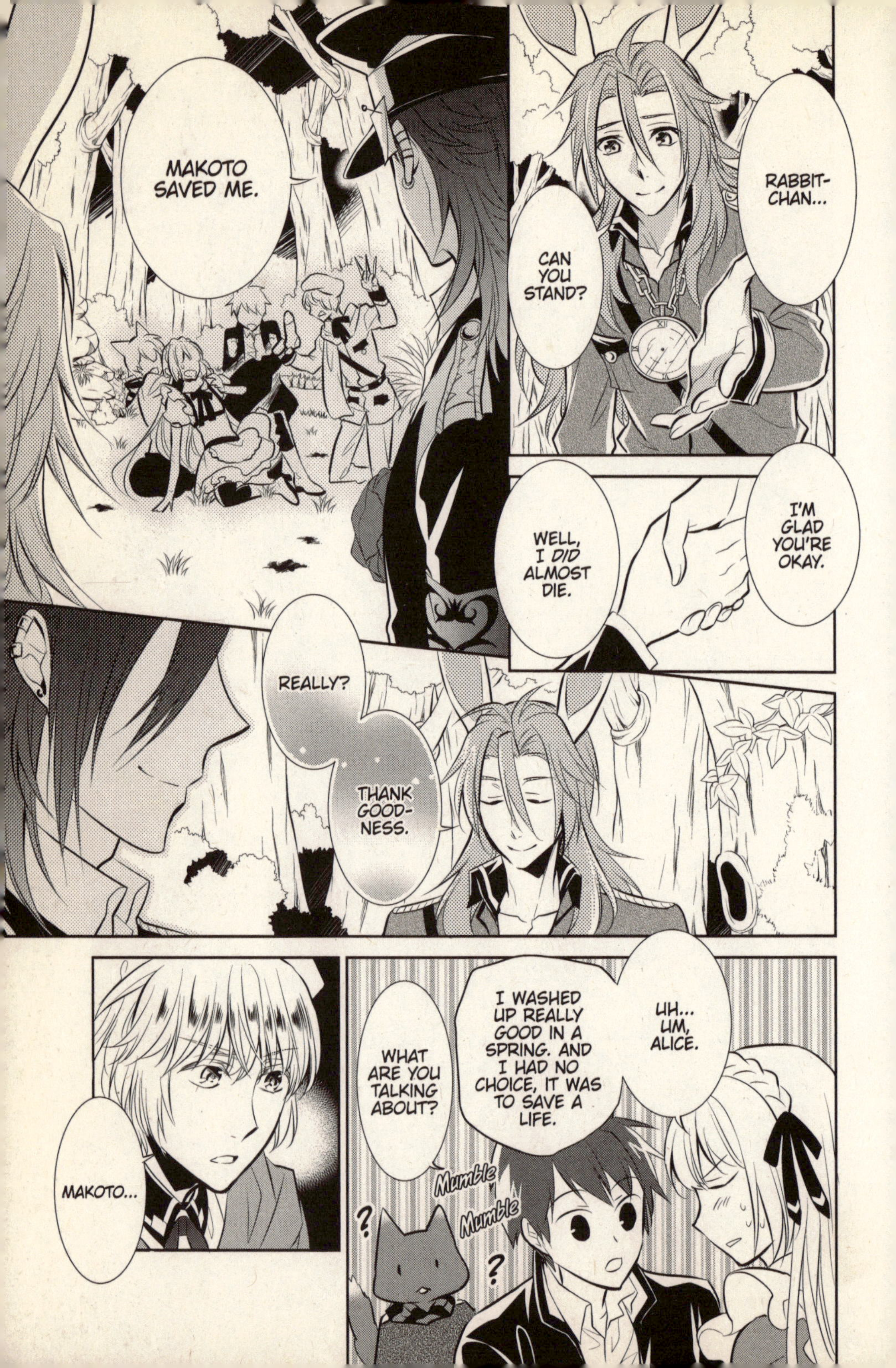
RABBIT-CHAN...
CAN YOU STAND?
I'M GLAD YOU'RE OKAY.
WELL, I *DID* ALMOST DIE.
MAKOTO SAVED ME.
REALLY?
THANK GOODNESS.
UH... UM, ALICE.
I WASHED UP REALLY GOOD IN A SPRING. AND I HAD NO CHOICE, IT WAS TO SAVE A LIFE.
WHAT ARE YOU TALKING ABOUT?
Mumble
Mumble
?
?
MAKOTO...

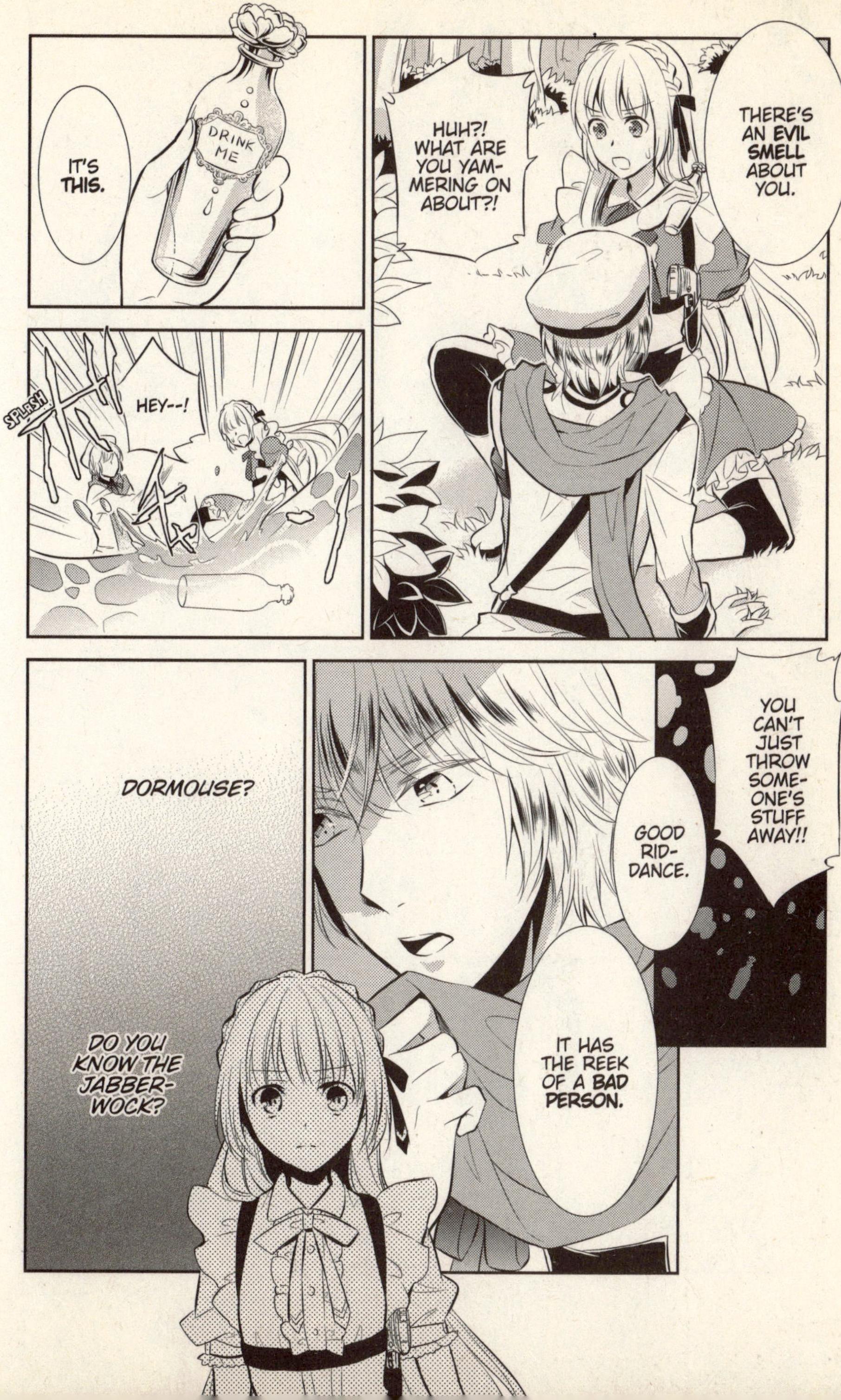
THERE'S AN EVIL SMELL ABOUT YOU.
HUH?! WHAT ARE YOU YAMMERING ON ABOUT?!
IT'S THIS.
DRINK ME
HEY--!
SPLASH
YOU CAN'T JUST THROW SOMEONE'S STUFF AWAY!!
GOOD RIDDANCE.
IT HAS THE REEK OF A BAD PERSON.
DORMOUSE?
DO YOU KNOW THE JABBERWOCK?

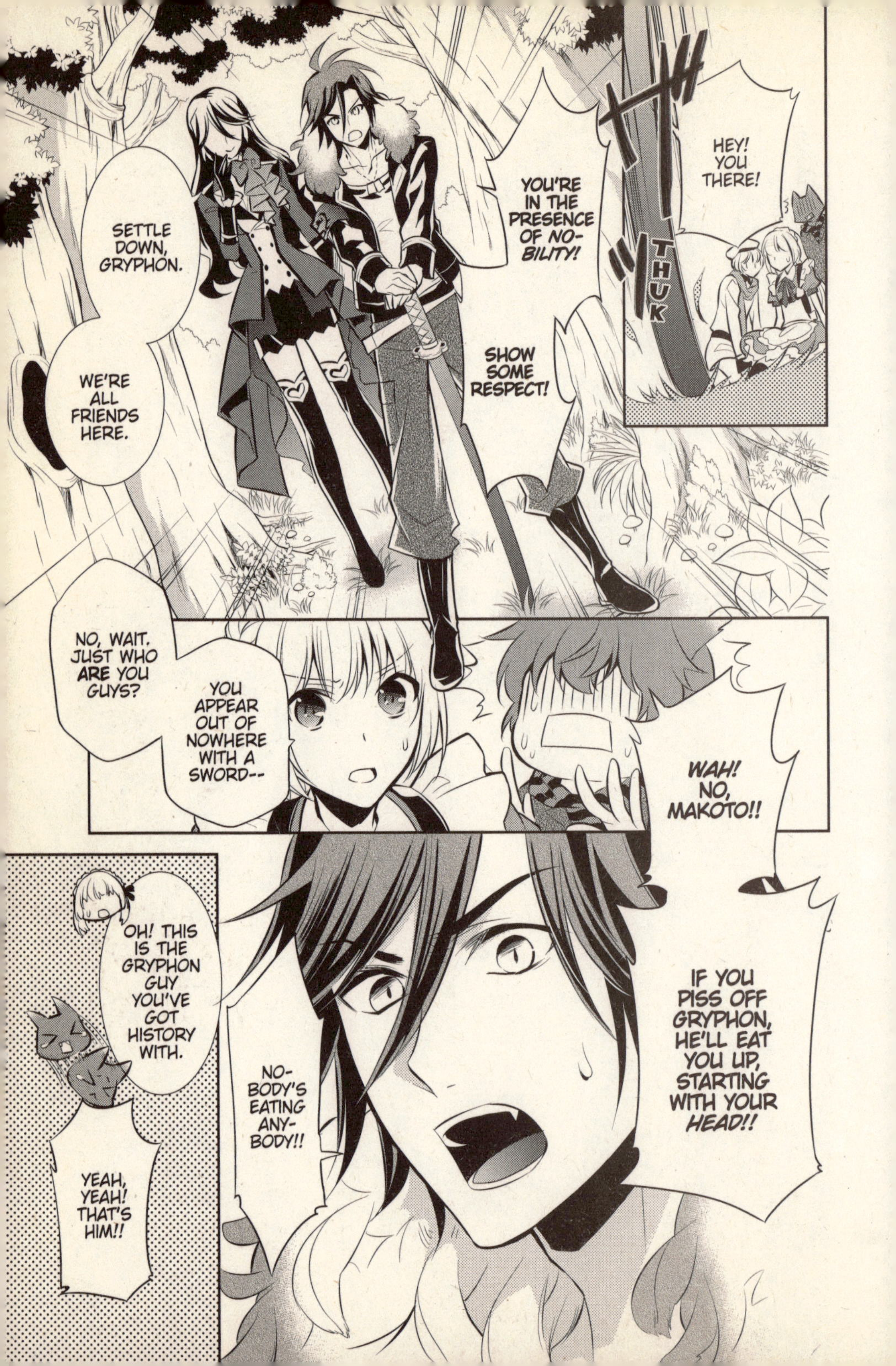
HEY! YOU THERE!
THUK
YOU'RE IN THE PRESENCE OF NO-BILITY!
SHOW SOME RESPECT!
SETTLE DOWN, GRYPHON.
WE'RE ALL FRIENDS HERE.
NO, WAIT. JUST WHO ARE YOU GUYS?
YOU APPEAR OUT OF NOWHERE WITH A SWORD--
WAH! NO, MAKOTO!!
IF YOU PISS OFF GRYPHON, HE'LL EAT YOU UP, STARTING WITH YOUR HEAD!!
NO-BODY'S EATING ANY-BODY!!
OH! THIS IS THE GRYPHON GUY YOU'VE GOT HISTORY WITH.
YEAH, YEAH! THAT'S HIM!!

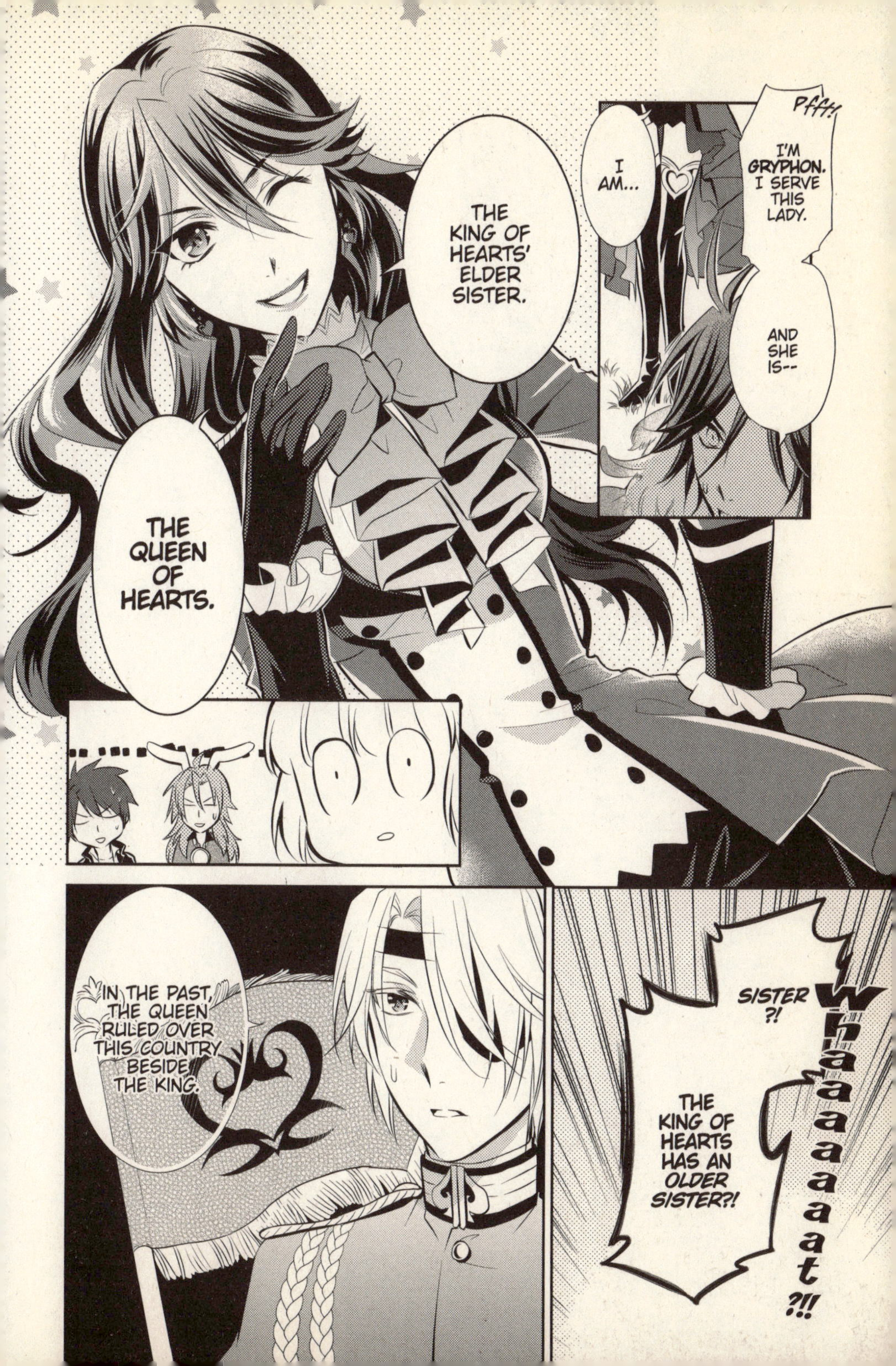
Pfff!
I'M GRYPHON. I SERVE THIS LADY.
AND SHE IS--
I AM...
THE KING OF HEARTS' ELDER SISTER.
THE QUEEN OF HEARTS.
Whaaaaaaat?!!
SISTER?!
THE KING OF HEARTS HAS AN OLDER SISTER?!
IN THE PAST, THE QUEEN RULED OVER THIS COUNTRY BESIDE THE KING.

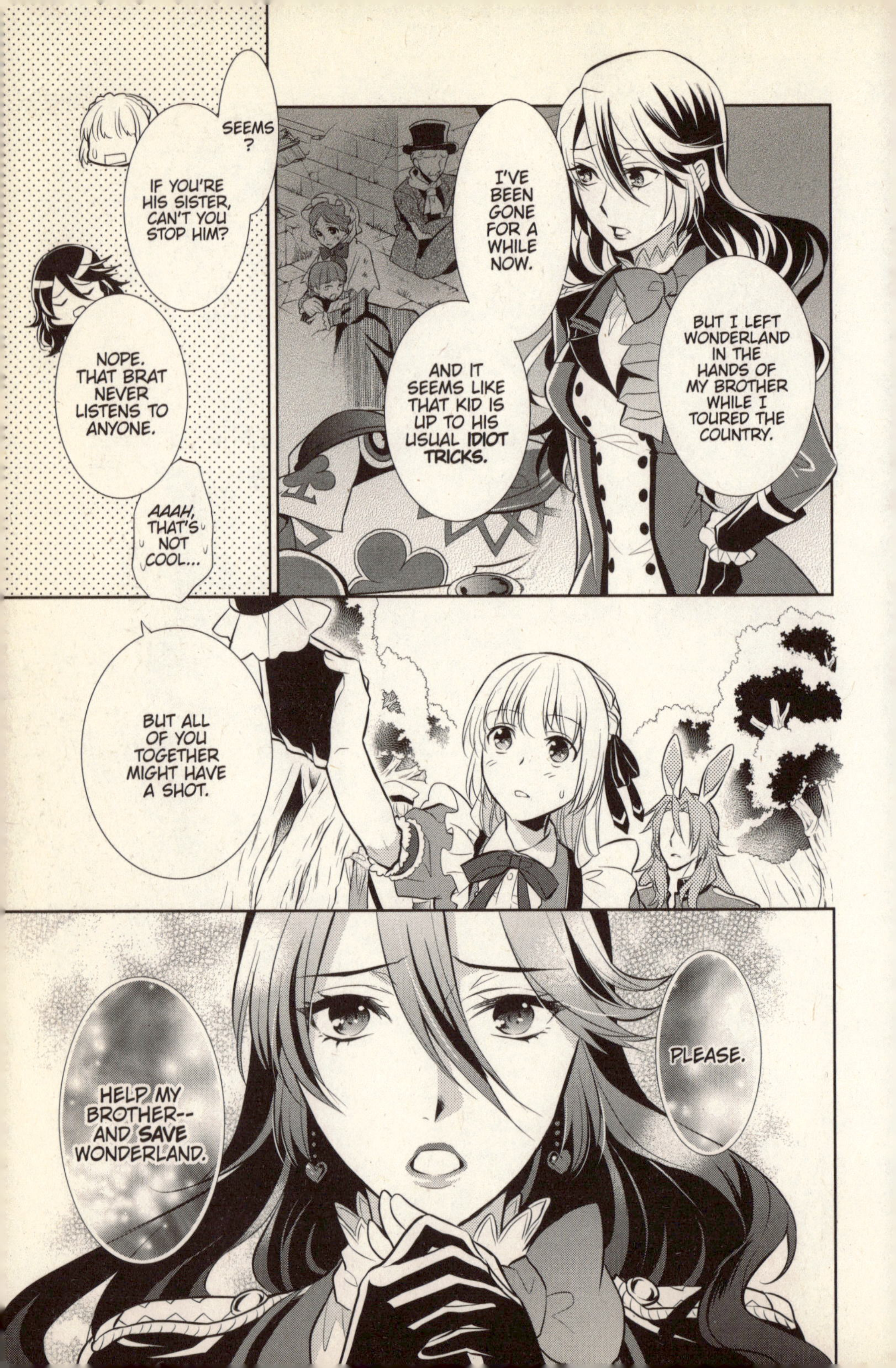

I'VE BEEN GONE FOR A WHILE NOW.
BUT I LEFT WONDERLAND IN THE HANDS OF MY BROTHER WHILE I TOURED THE COUNTRY.
AND IT SEEMS LIKE THAT KID IS UP TO HIS USUAL IDIOT TRICKS.
SEEMS?
IF YOU'RE HIS SISTER, CAN'T YOU STOP HIM?
NOPE. THAT BRAT NEVER LISTENS TO ANYONE.
AAAH, THAT'S NOT COOL...
BUT ALL OF YOU TOGETHER MIGHT HAVE A SHOT.
PLEASE.
HELP MY BROTHER-- AND SAVE WONDERLAND.

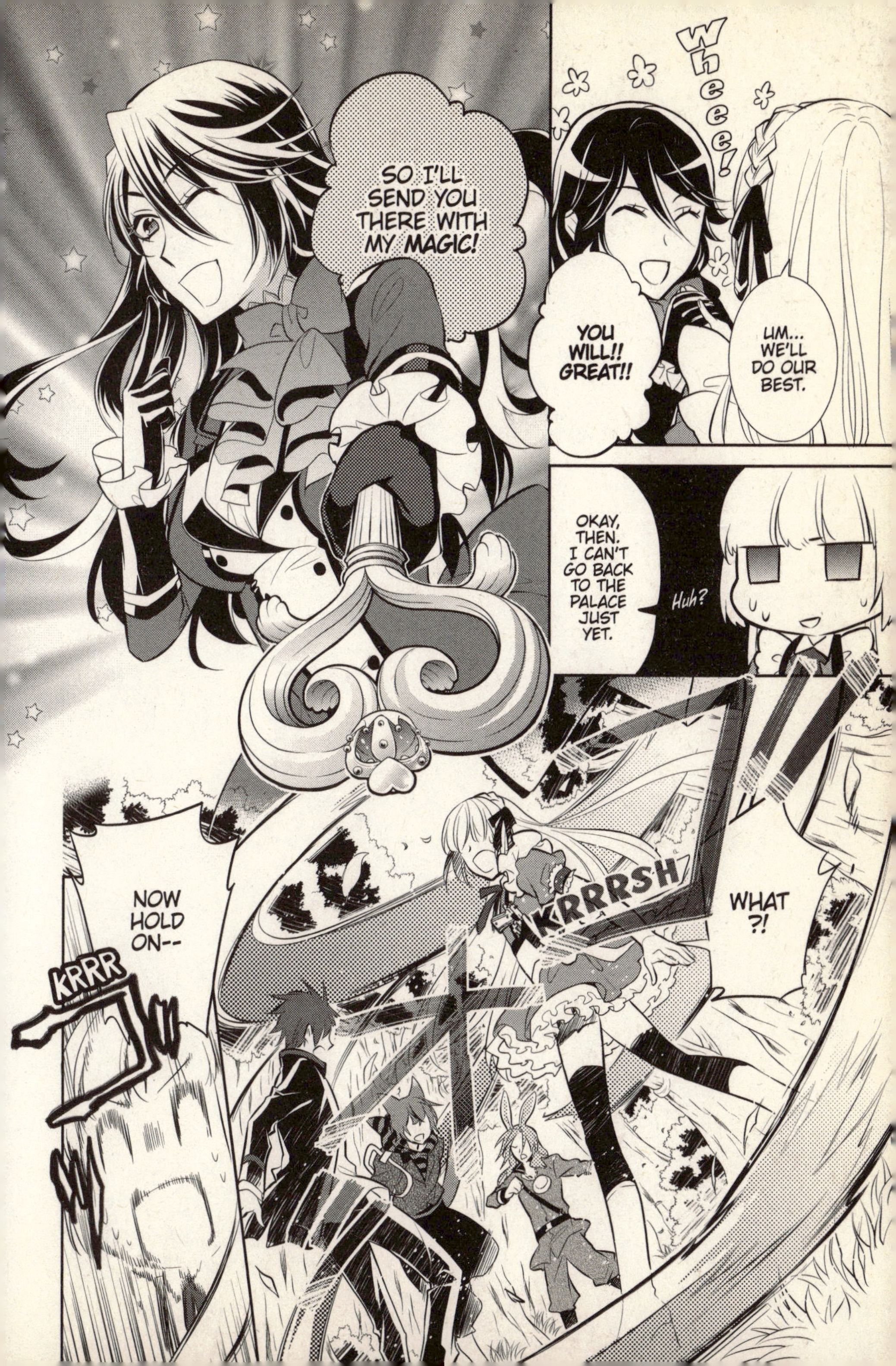
Wheee!
UM... WE'LL DO OUR BEST.
YOU WILL!! GREAT!!
OKAY, THEN. I CAN'T GO BACK TO THE PALACE JUST YET.
Huh?
SO I'LL SEND YOU THERE WITH MY MAGIC!
WHAT ?!
KRRRSH
NOW HOLD ON--
KRRR

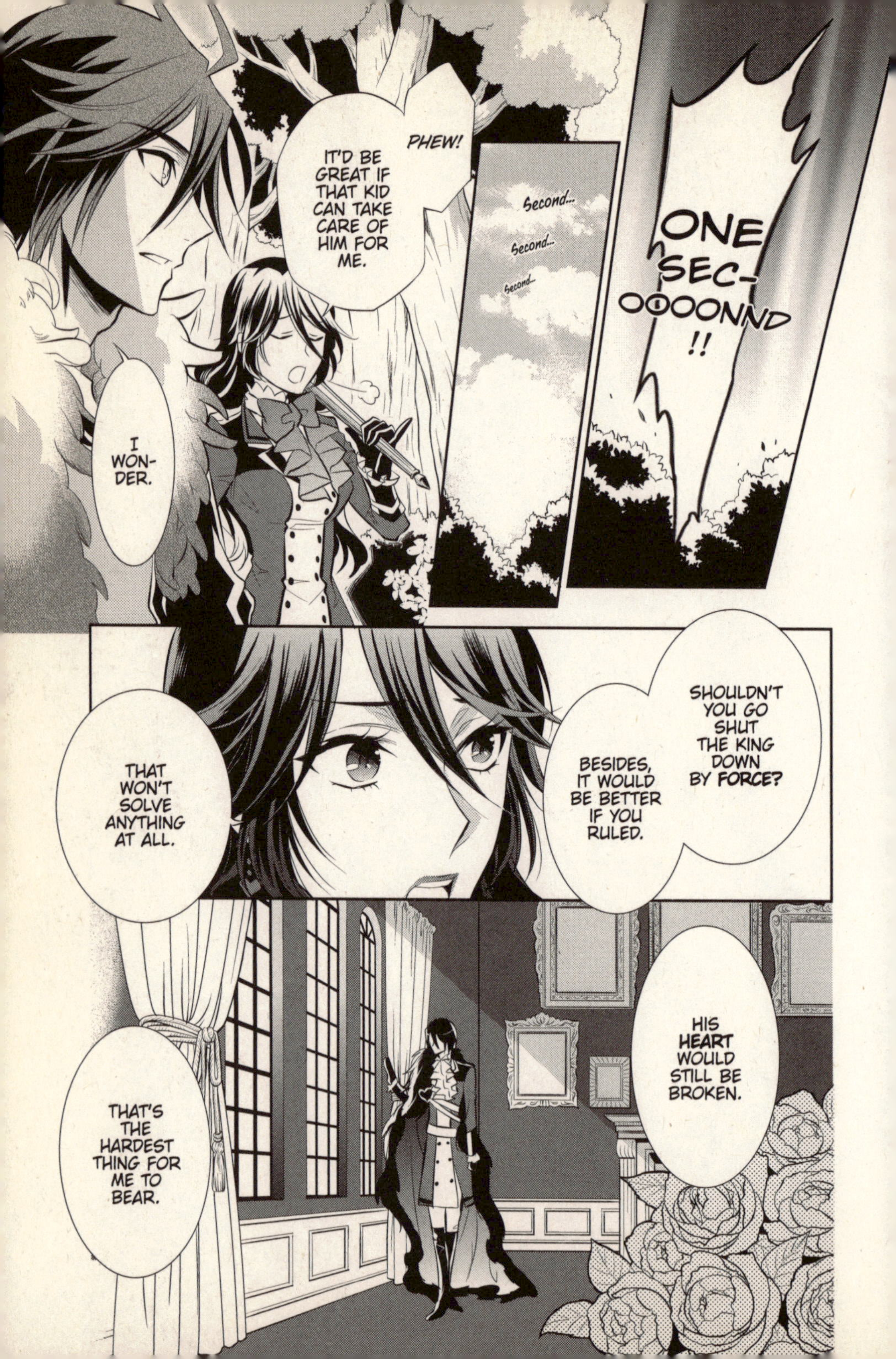
ONE SEC-OOOONND!!
Second...
Second...
Second...
PHEW!
IT'D BE GREAT IF THAT KID CAN TAKE CARE OF HIM FOR ME.
I WONDER.
SHOULDN'T YOU GO SHUT THE KING DOWN BY **FORCE**?
BESIDES, IT WOULD BE BETTER IF YOU RULED.
THAT WON'T SOLVE ANYTHING AT ALL.
HIS **HEART** WOULD STILL BE BROKEN.
THAT'S THE HARDEST THING FOR ME TO BEAR.

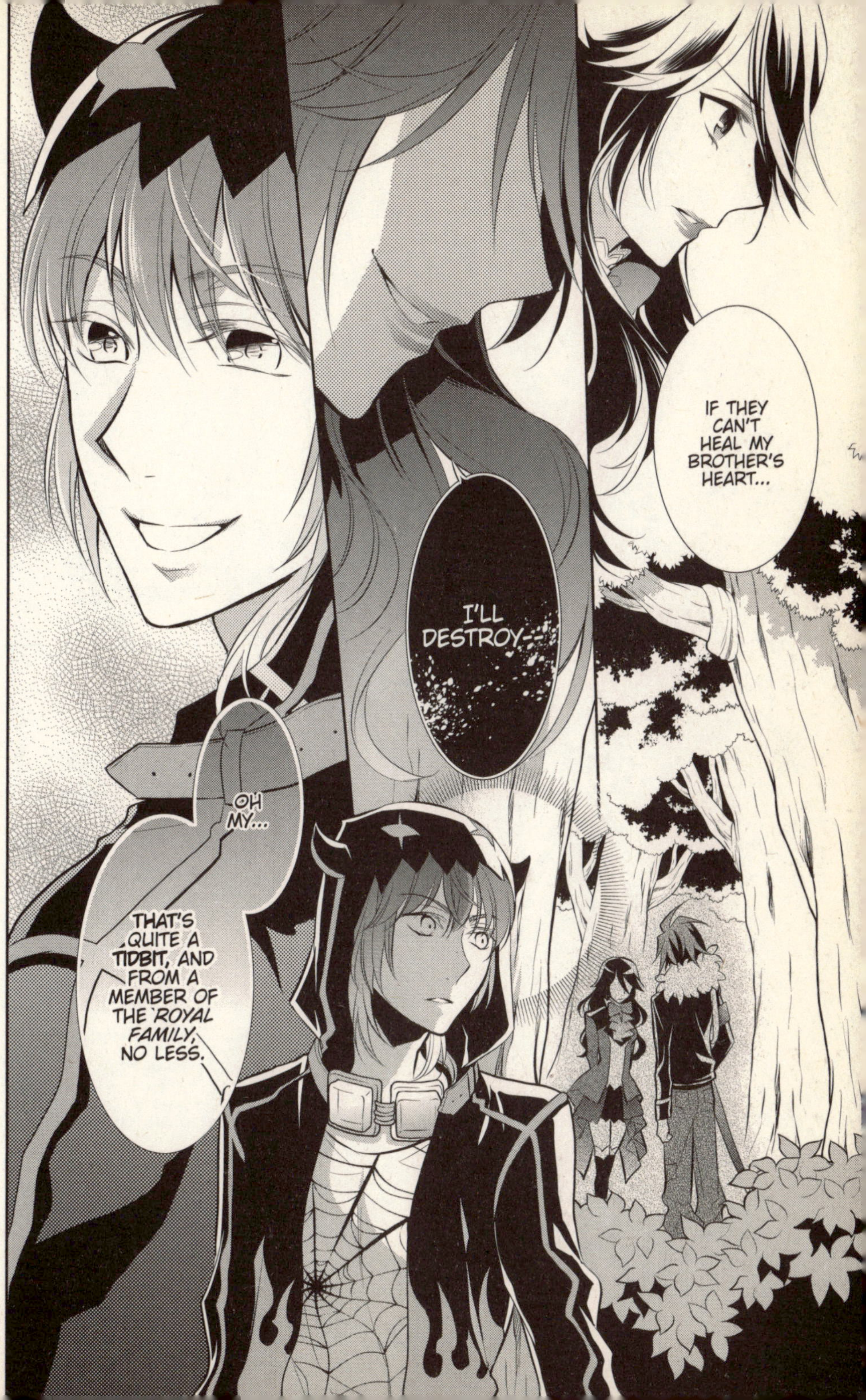
IF THEY CAN'T HEAL MY BROTHER'S HEART...
I'LL DESTROY--
OH MY...
THAT'S QUITE A TIDBIT, AND FROM A MEMBER OF THE *ROYAL FAMILY*, NO LESS.

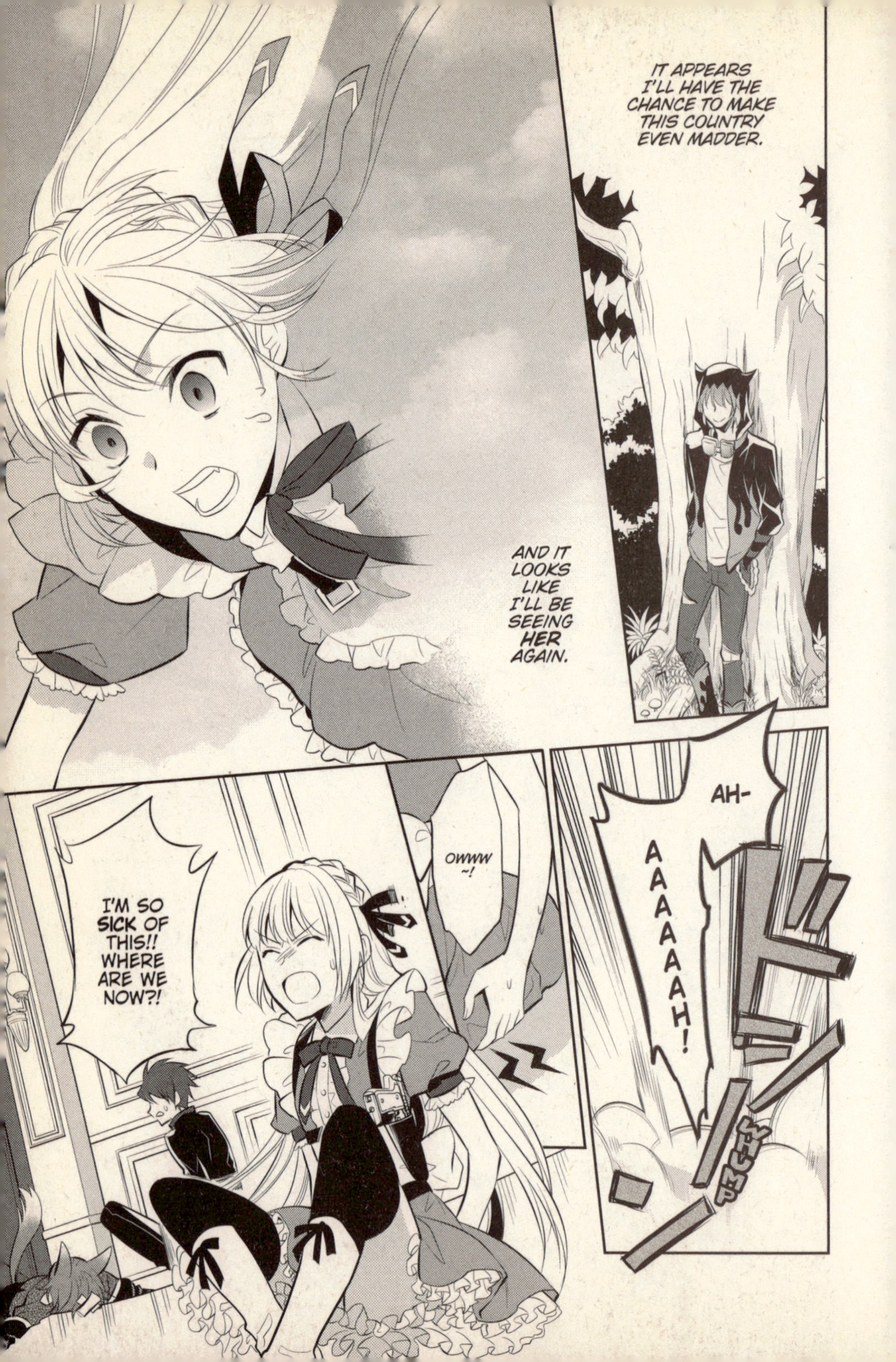
IT APPEARS I'LL HAVE THE CHANCE TO MAKE THIS COUNTRY EVEN MADDER.
AND IT LOOKS LIKE I'LL BE SEEING **HER** AGAIN.
AH-
AAAAAAAH!
WHUMP
OWWW ~!
I'M SO **SICK** OF THIS!! WHERE ARE WE NOW?!

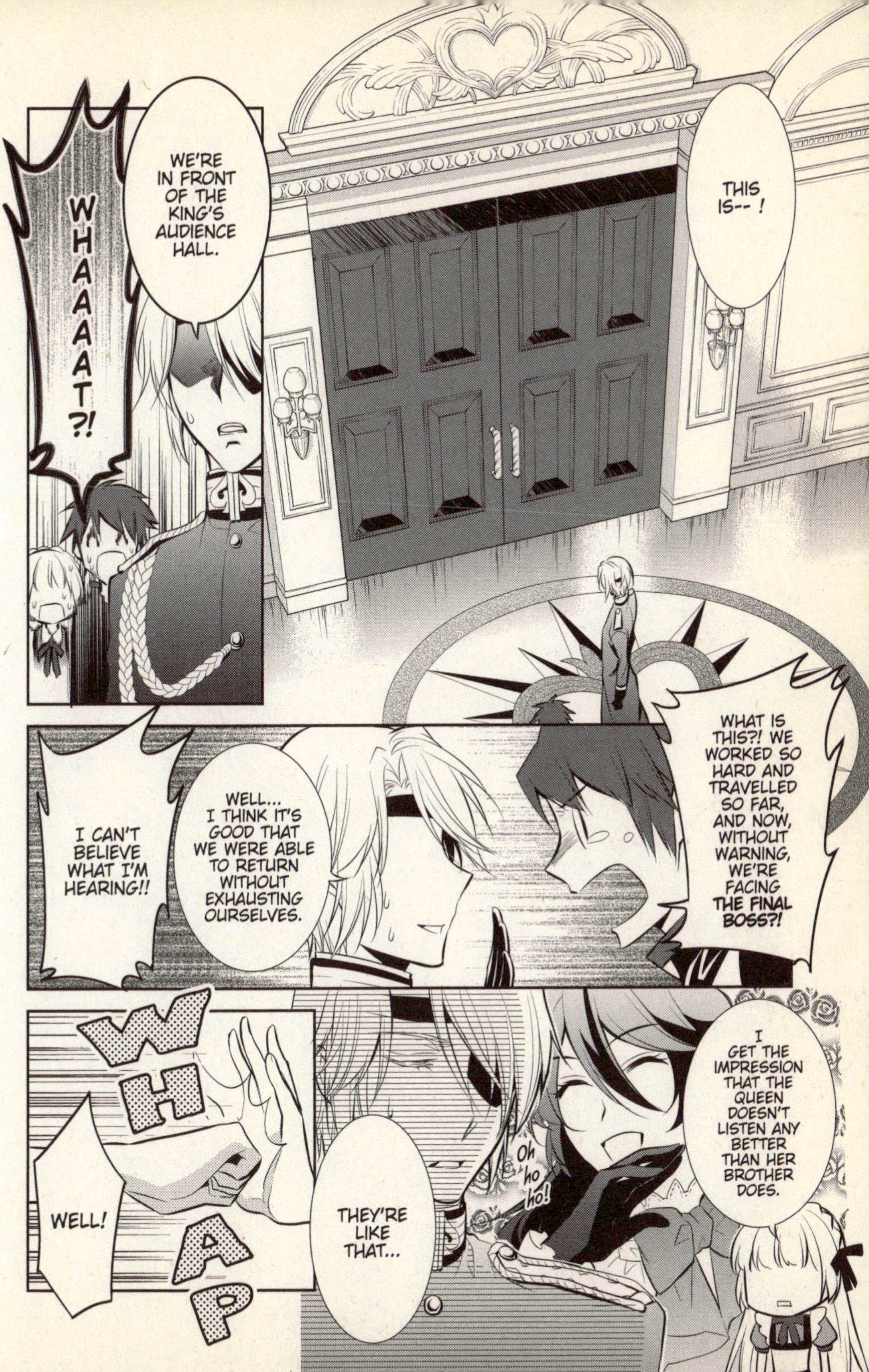
THIS IS-- !
WE'RE IN FRONT OF THE KING'S AUDIENCE HALL.
WHAAAAAT?!
WHAT IS THIS?! WE WORKED SO HARD AND TRAVELLED SO FAR, AND NOW, WITHOUT WARNING, WE'RE FACING **THE FINAL BOSS?!**
WELL... I THINK IT'S GOOD THAT WE WERE ABLE TO RETURN WITHOUT EXHAUSTING OURSELVES.
I CAN'T BELIEVE WHAT I'M HEARING!!
I GET THE IMPRESSION THAT THE QUEEN DOESN'T LISTEN ANY BETTER THAN HER BROTHER DOES.
Oh ho ho!
THEY'RE LIKE THAT...
WHAP
WELL!

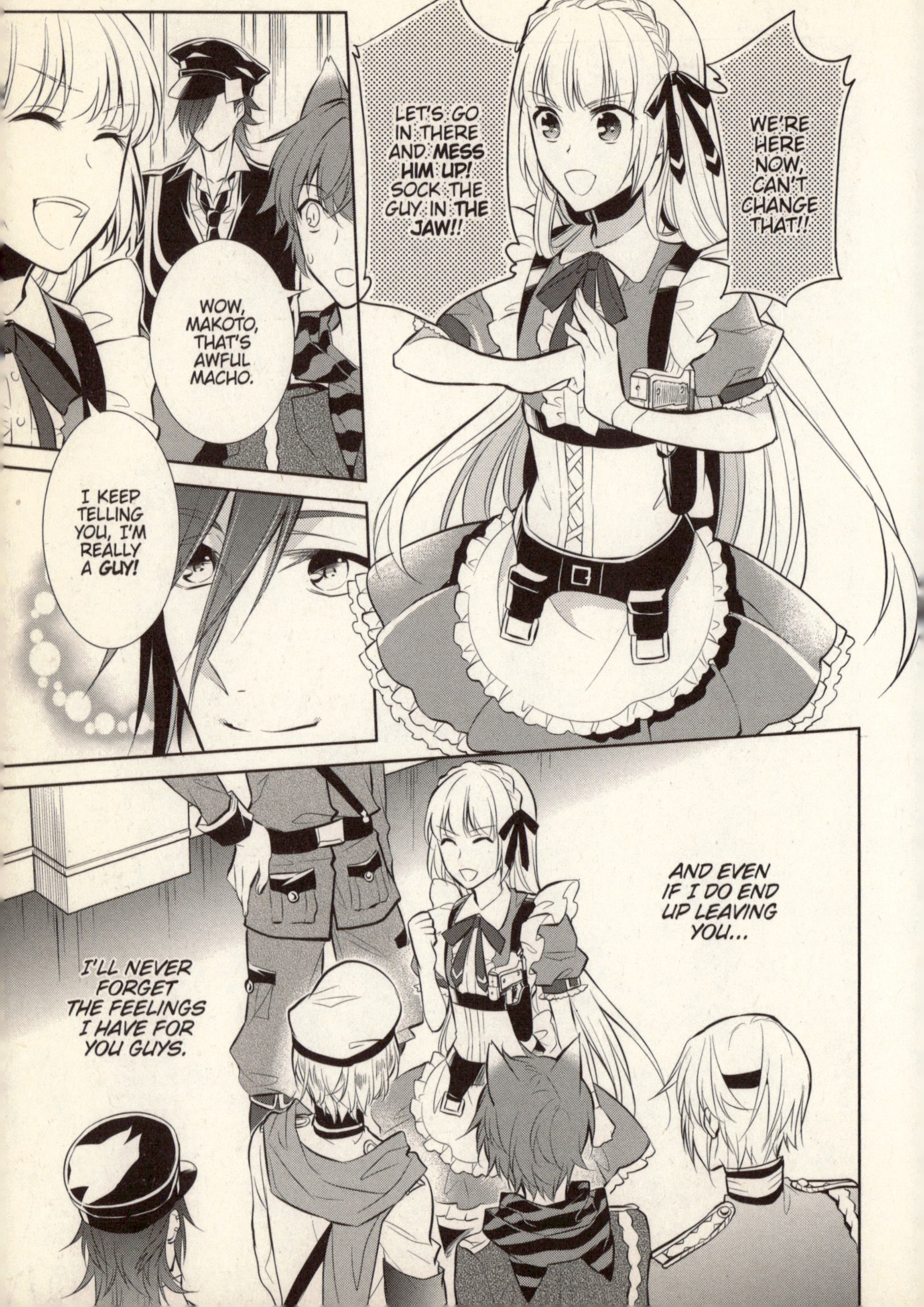
WE'RE HERE NOW, CAN'T CHANGE THAT!!
LET'S GO IN THERE AND MESS HIM UP! SOCK THE GUY IN THE JAW!!
WOW, MAKOTO, THAT'S AWFUL MACHO.
I KEEP TELLING YOU, I'M REALLY A GUY!
AND EVEN IF I DO END UP LEAVING YOU...
I'LL NEVER FORGET THE FEELINGS I HAVE FOR YOU GUYS.

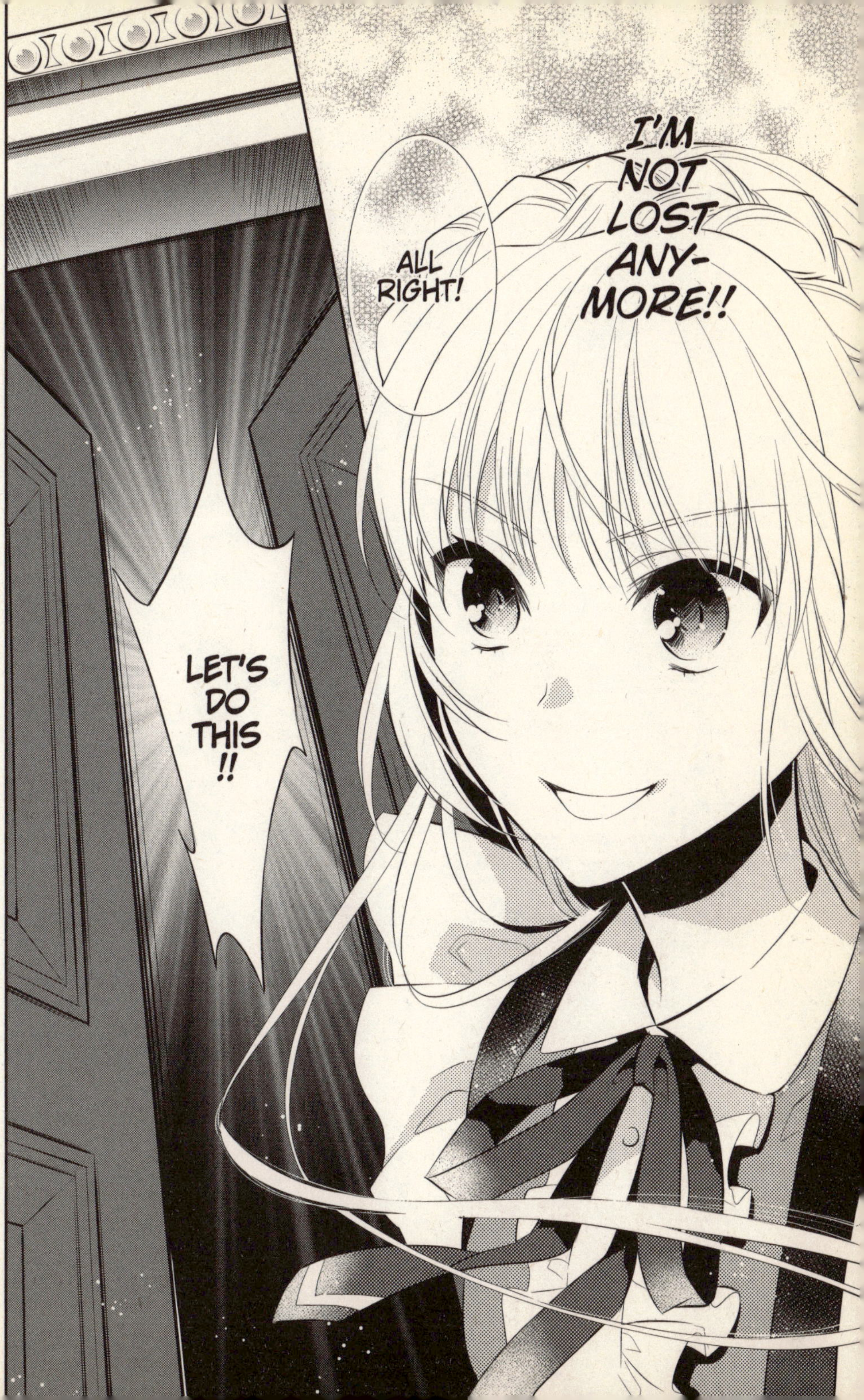
I'M NOT LOST ANY-MORE!!
ALL RIGHT!
LET'S DO THIS!!

I AM ALICE

I AM ALICE

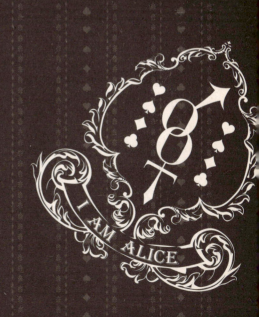

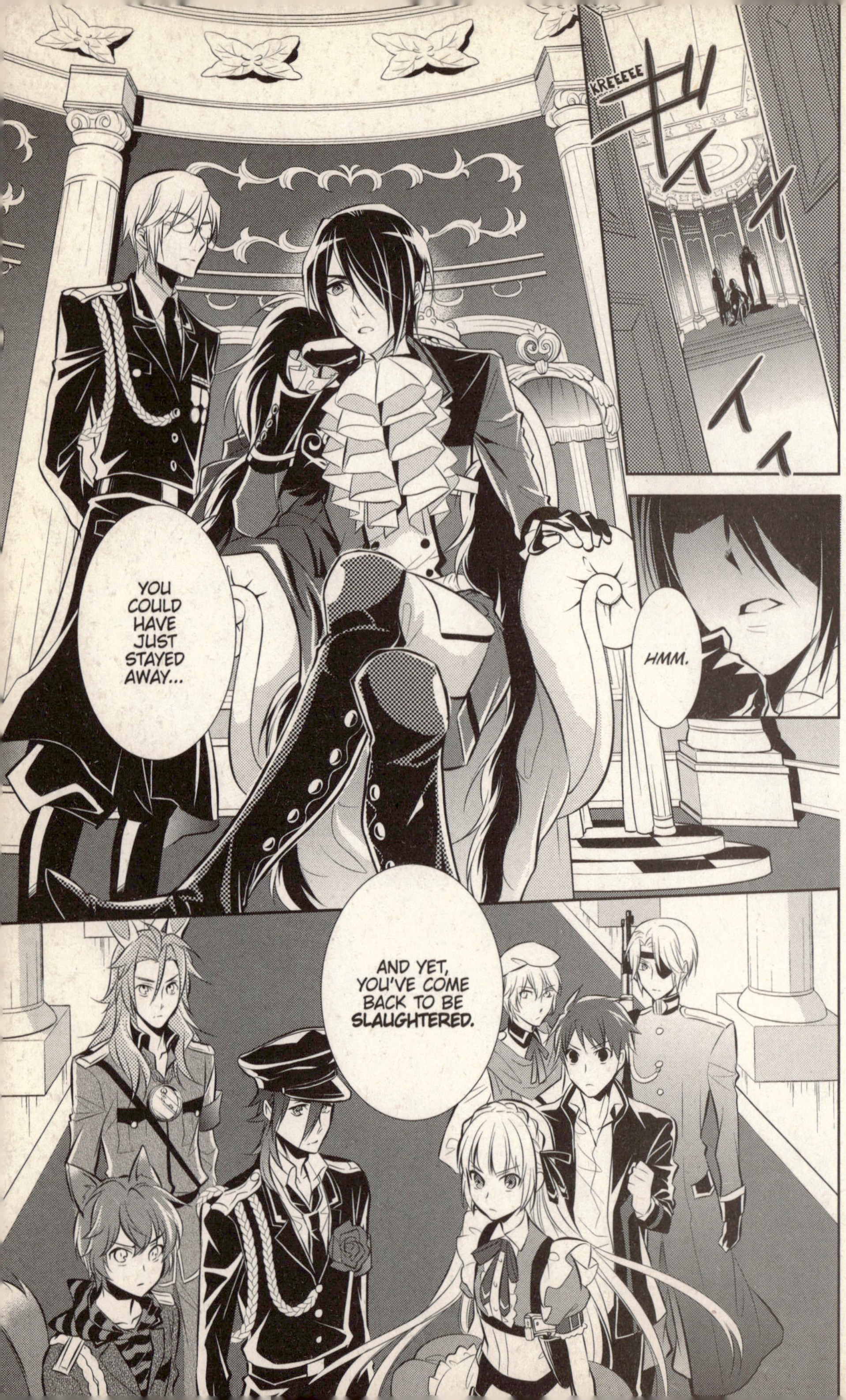
KREEEEE
HMM.
YOU COULD HAVE JUST STAYED AWAY...
AND YET, YOU'VE COME BACK TO BE SLAUGHTERED.

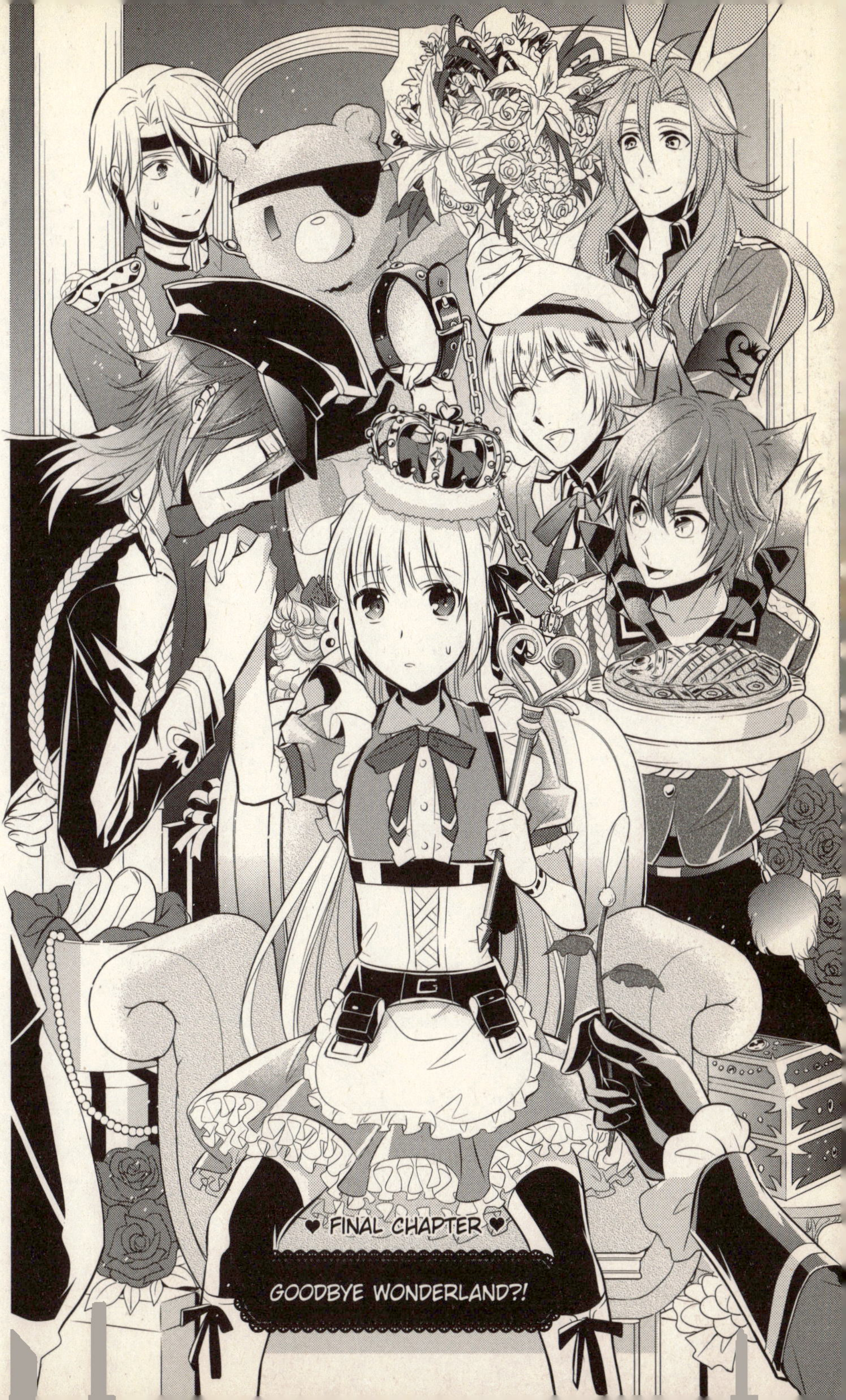
♥ FINAL CHAPTER ♥
GOODBYE WONDERLAND?!

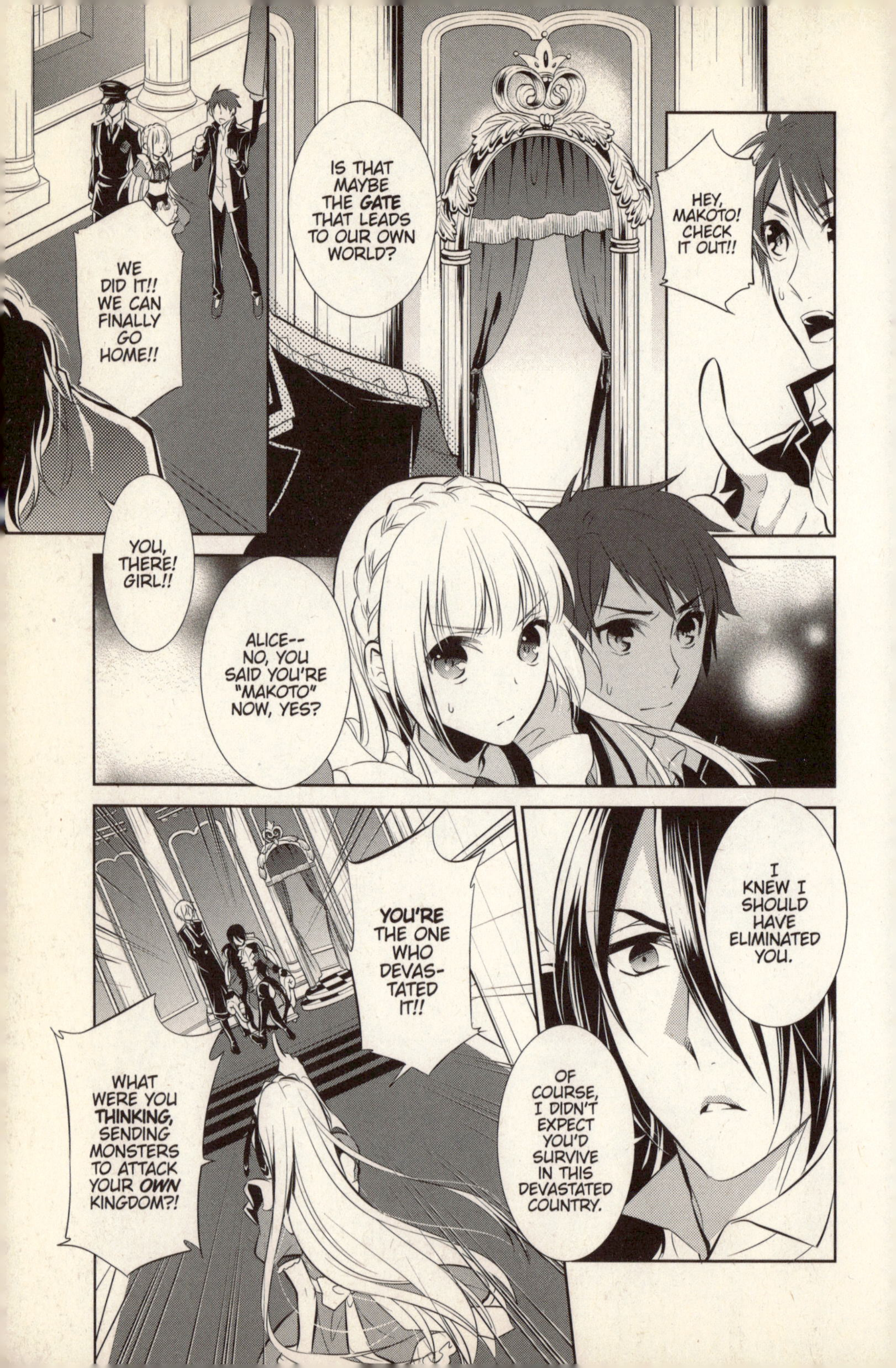
HEY, MAKOTO! CHECK IT OUT!!
IS THAT MAYBE THE **GATE** THAT LEADS TO OUR OWN WORLD?
WE DID IT!! WE CAN FINALLY GO HOME!!
YOU, THERE! GIRL!!
ALICE-- NO, YOU SAID YOU'RE "MAKOTO" NOW, YES?
I KNEW I SHOULD HAVE ELIMINATED YOU.
OF COURSE, I DIDN'T EXPECT YOU'D SURVIVE IN THIS DEVASTATED COUNTRY.
YOU'RE THE ONE WHO DEVASTATED IT!!
WHAT WERE YOU **THINKING**, SENDING MONSTERS TO ATTACK YOUR **OWN** KINGDOM?!

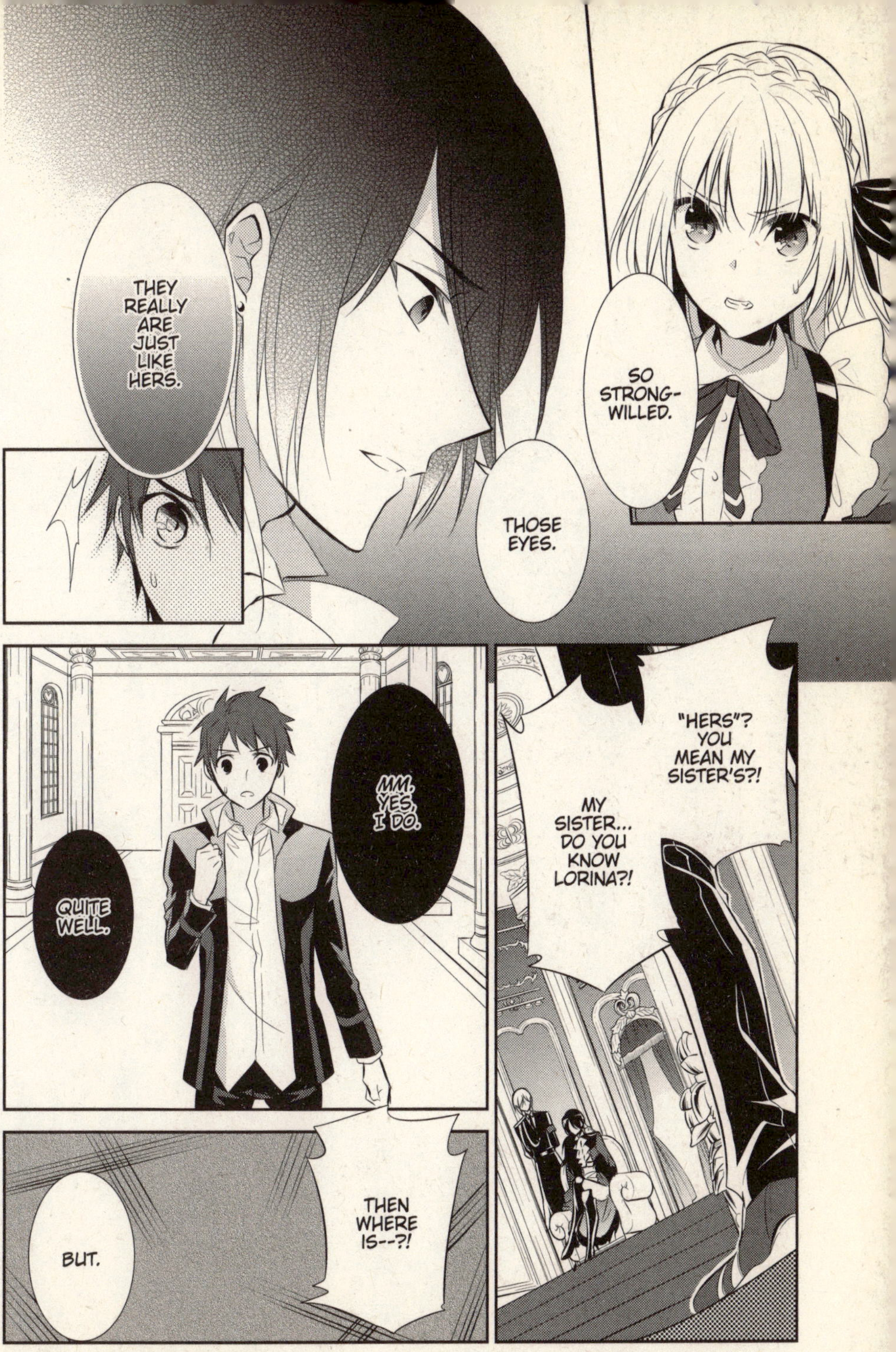
SO STRONG-WILLED.
THOSE EYES.
THEY REALLY ARE JUST LIKE HERS.
"HERS"? YOU MEAN MY SISTER'S?!
MY SISTER... DO YOU KNOW LORINA?!
MM. YES, I DO.
QUITE WELL.
THEN WHERE IS--?!
BUT.

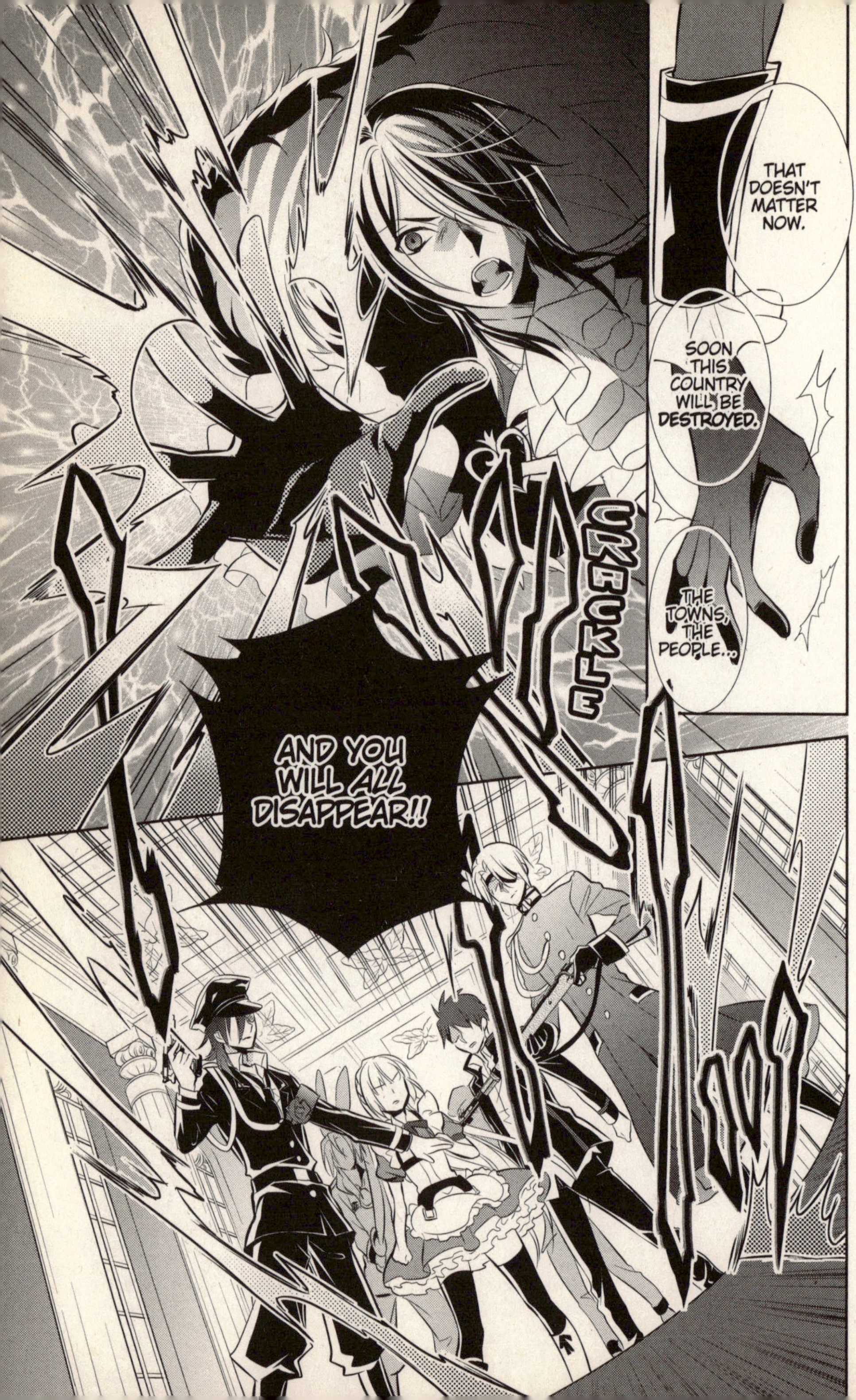
THAT DOESN'T MATTER NOW.
SOON THIS COUNTRY WILL BE DESTROYED.
THE TOWNS, THE PEOPLE...
CRACKLE
AND YOU WILL ALL DISAPPEAR!!

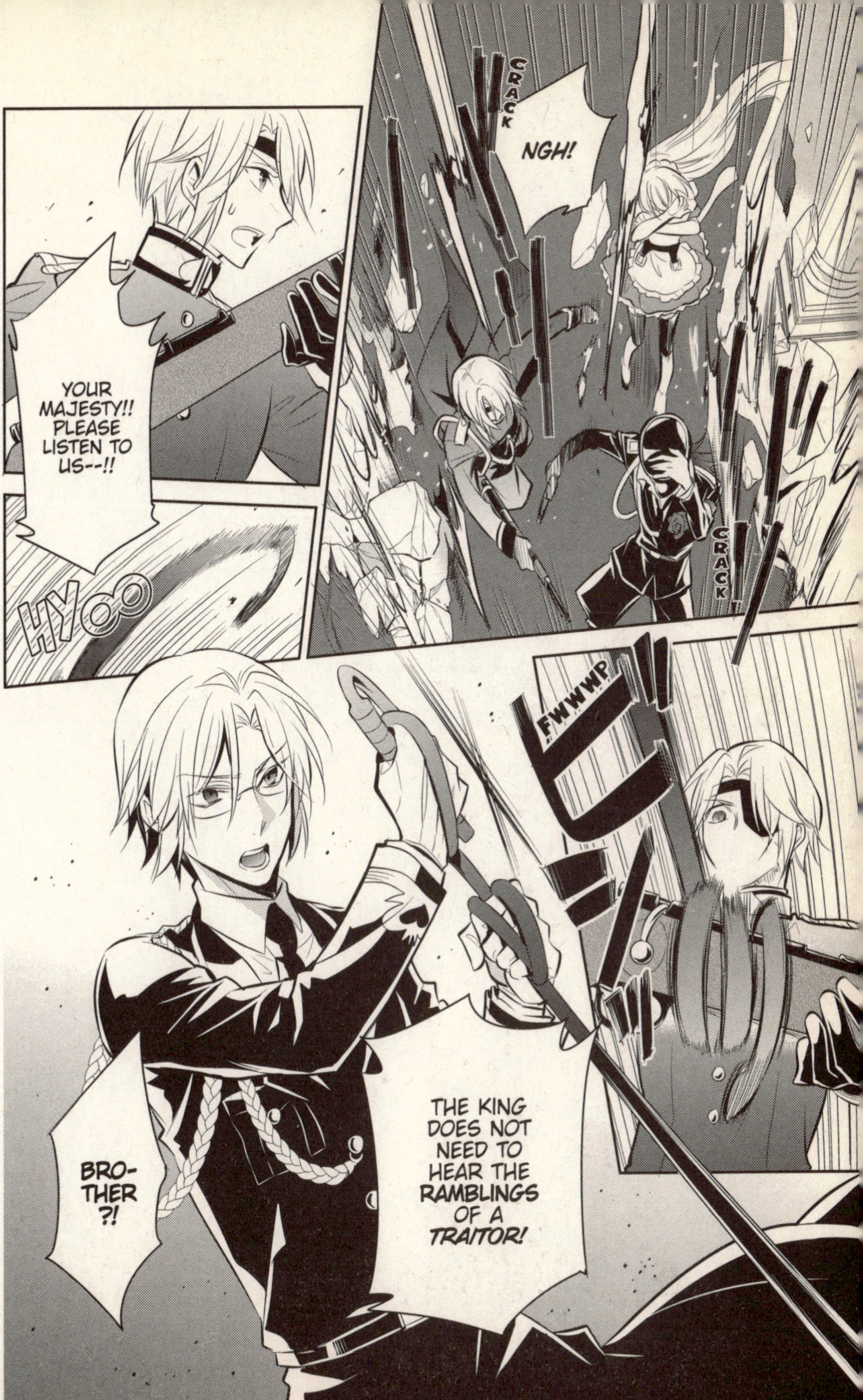
CRACK
NGH!
CRACK
YOUR MAJESTY!! PLEASE LISTEN TO US--!!
HYOO
FWWWP
THE KING DOES NOT NEED TO HEAR THE RAMBLINGS OF A *TRAITOR!*
BRO-THER?!

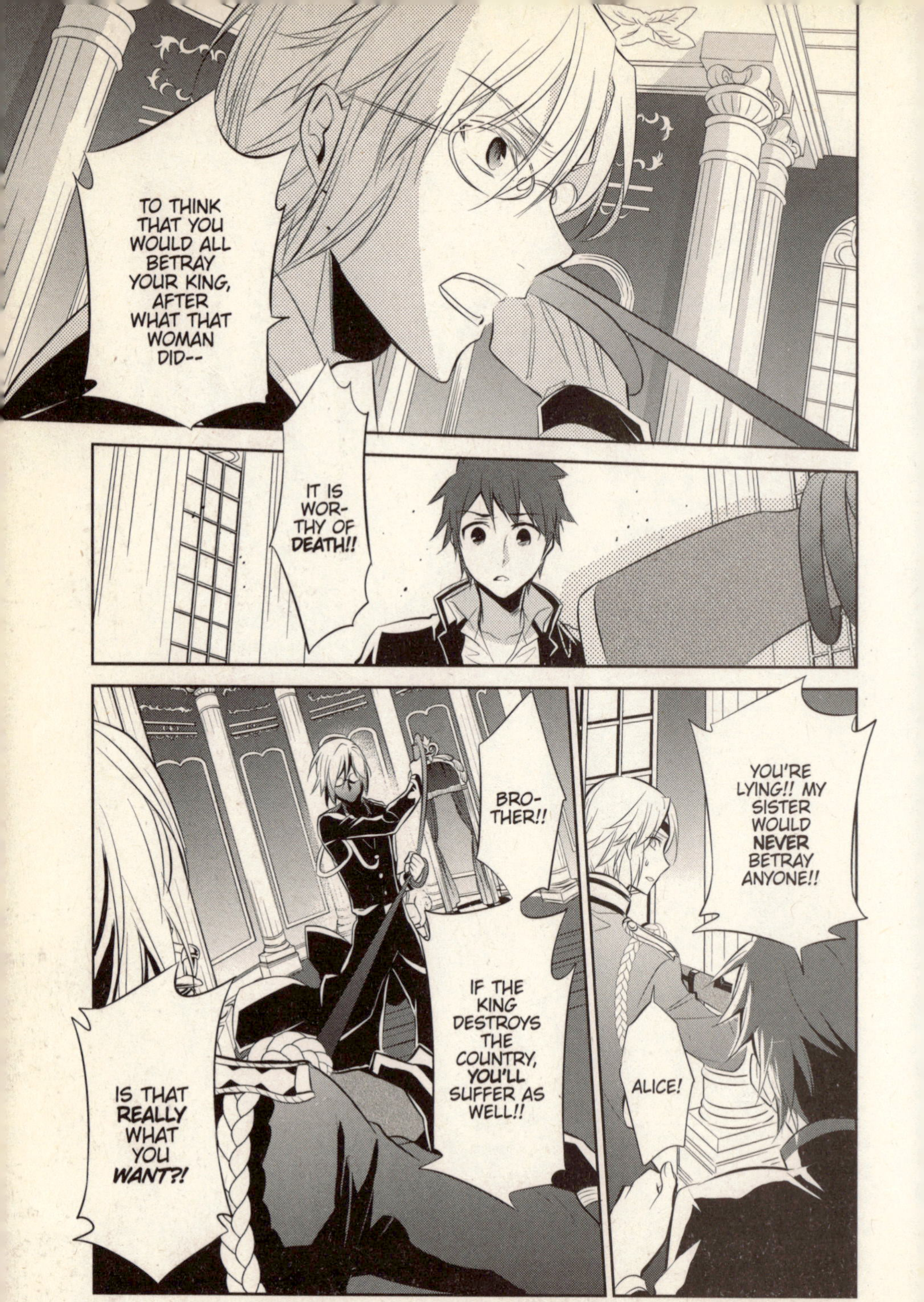
TO THINK THAT YOU WOULD ALL BETRAY YOUR KING, AFTER WHAT THAT WOMAN DID--
IT IS WORTHY OF DEATH!!
YOU'RE LYING!! MY SISTER WOULD NEVER BETRAY ANYONE!!
ALICE!
BROTHER!!
IF THE KING DESTROYS THE COUNTRY, YOU'LL SUFFER AS WELL!!
IS THAT REALLY WHAT YOU WANT?!

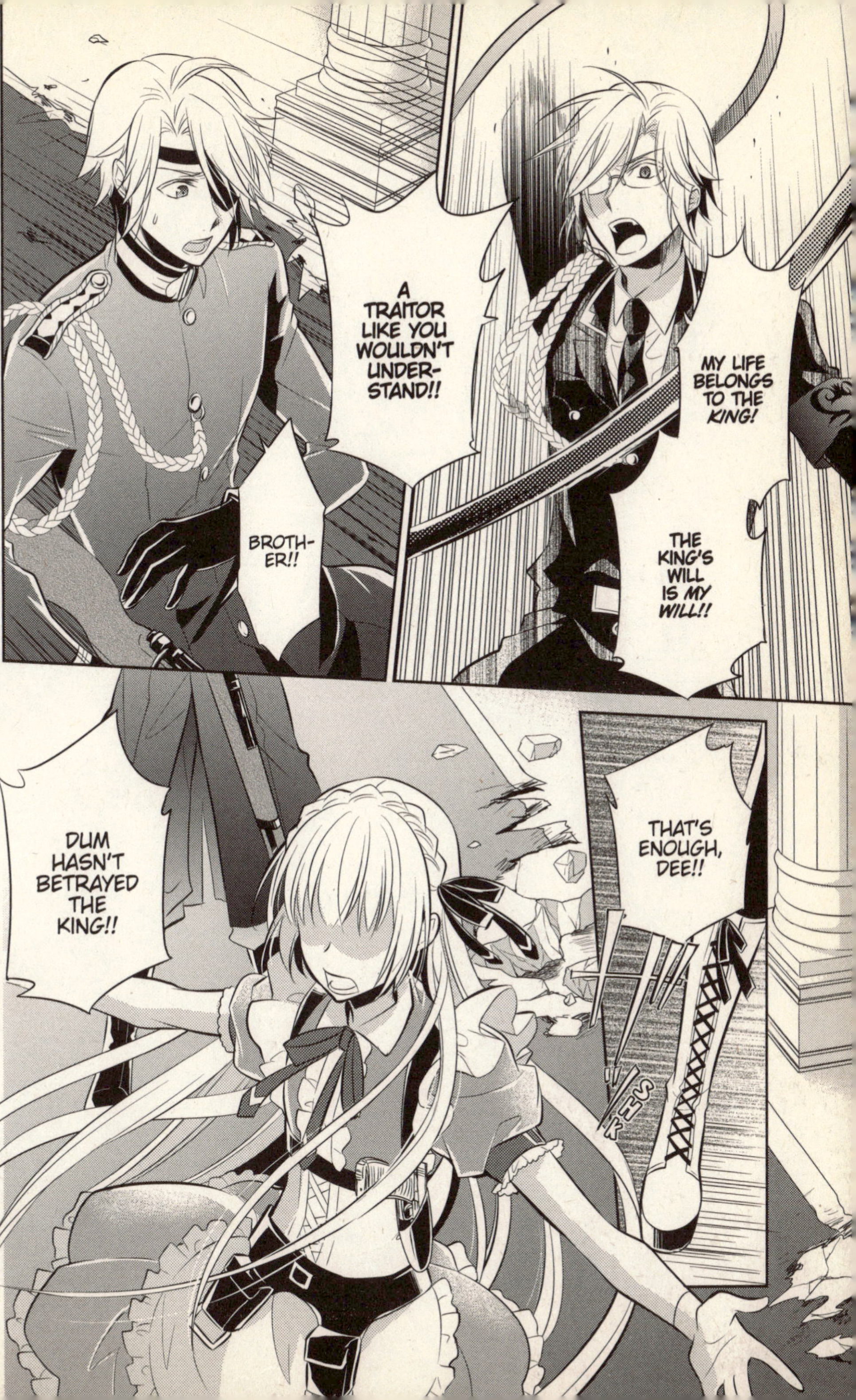
A TRAITOR LIKE YOU WOULDN'T UNDER-STAND!!
MY LIFE BELONGS TO THE *KING!*
THE KING'S WILL IS *MY WILL!!*
BROTH-ER!!
THAT'S ENOUGH, DEE!!
SHK
DUM HASN'T BETRAYED THE KING!!

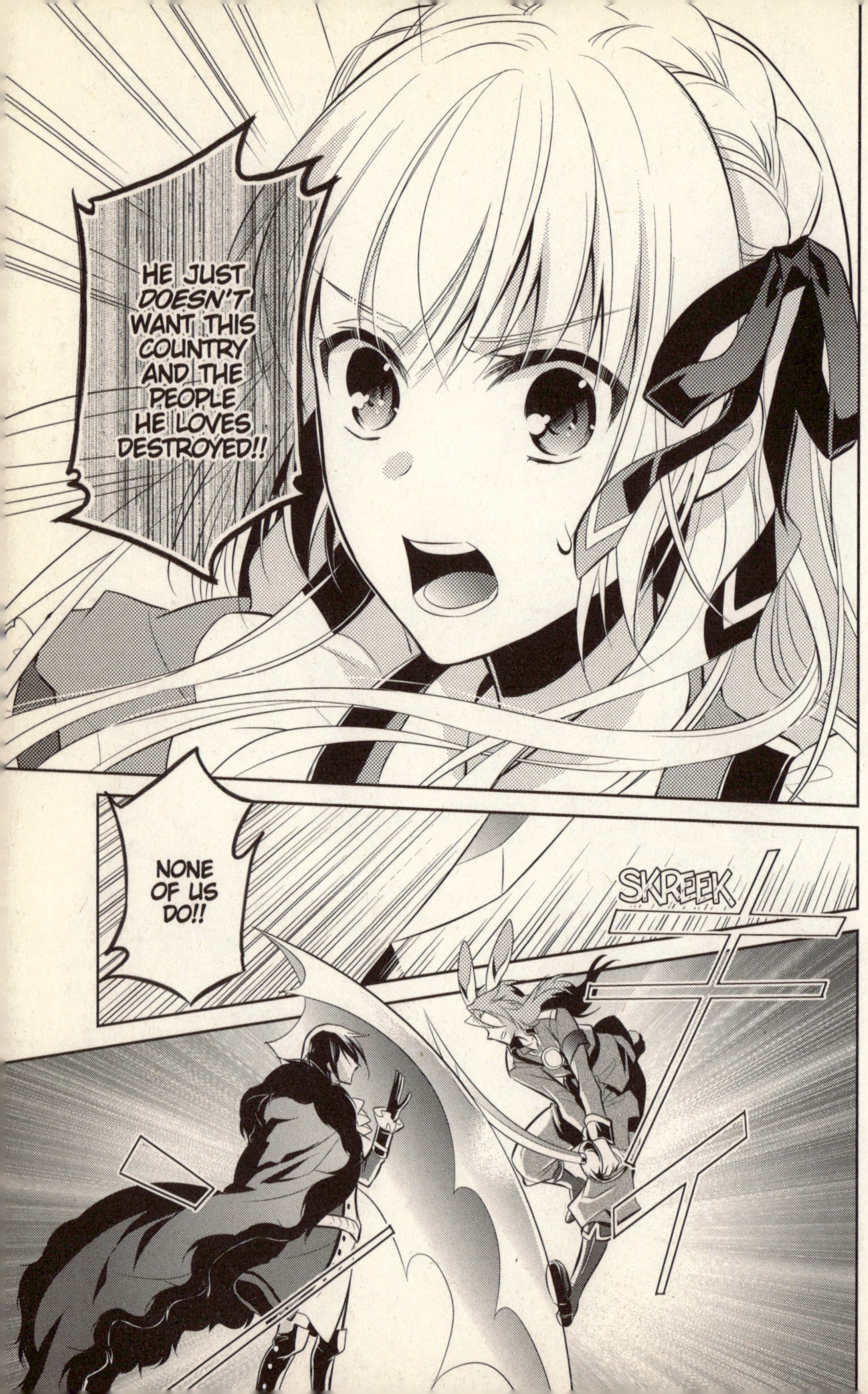
HE JUST DOESN'T WANT THIS COUNTRY AND THE PEOPLE HE LOVES DESTROYED!!
SKREEK
NONE OF US DO!!

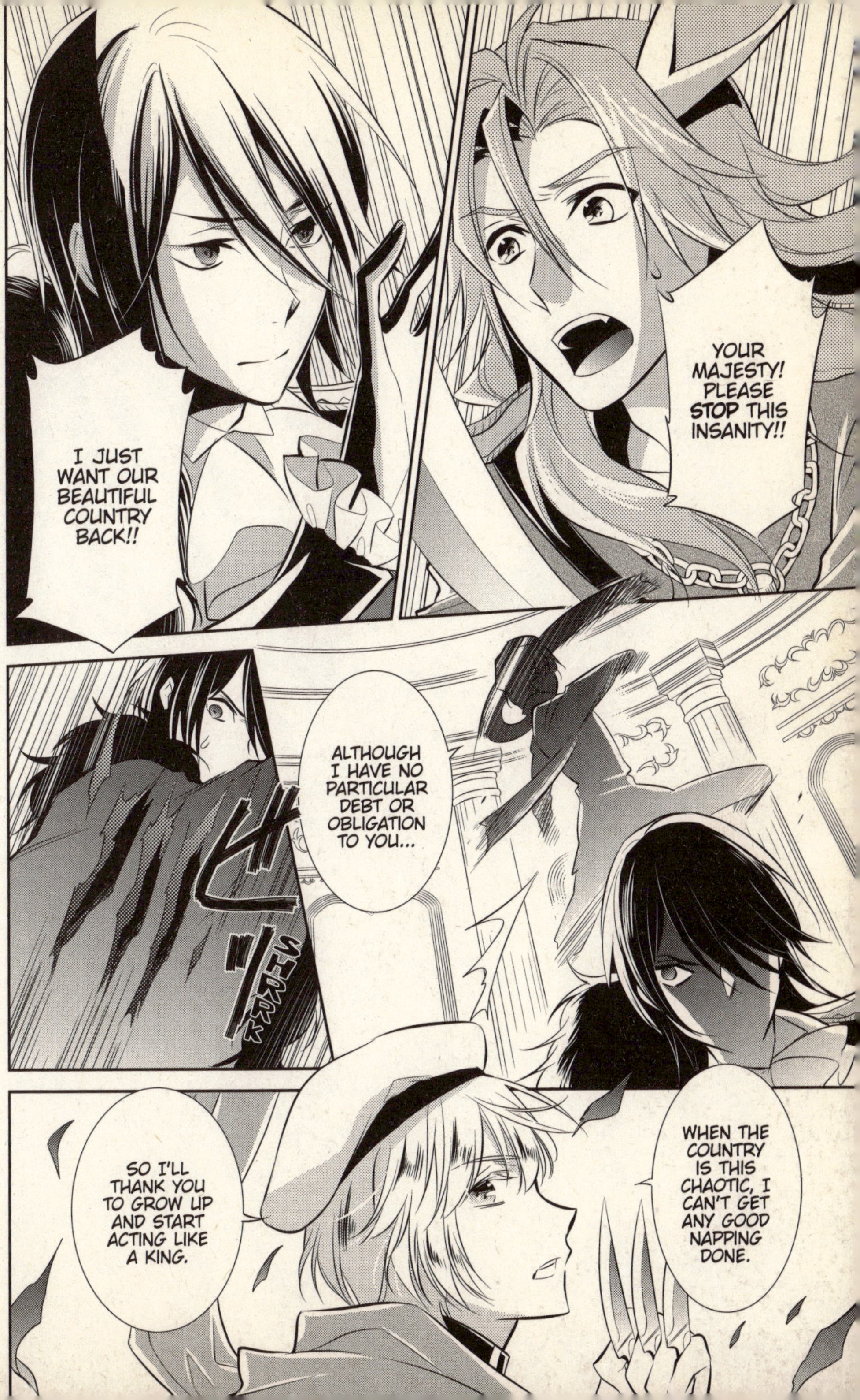
YOUR MAJESTY! PLEASE STOP THIS INSANITY!!
I JUST WANT OUR BEAUTIFUL COUNTRY BACK!!
ALTHOUGH I HAVE NO PARTICULAR DEBT OR OBLIGATION TO YOU...
SHRRK
WHEN THE COUNTRY IS THIS CHAOTIC, I CAN'T GET ANY GOOD NAPPING DONE.
SO I'LL THANK YOU TO GROW UP AND START ACTING LIKE A KING.

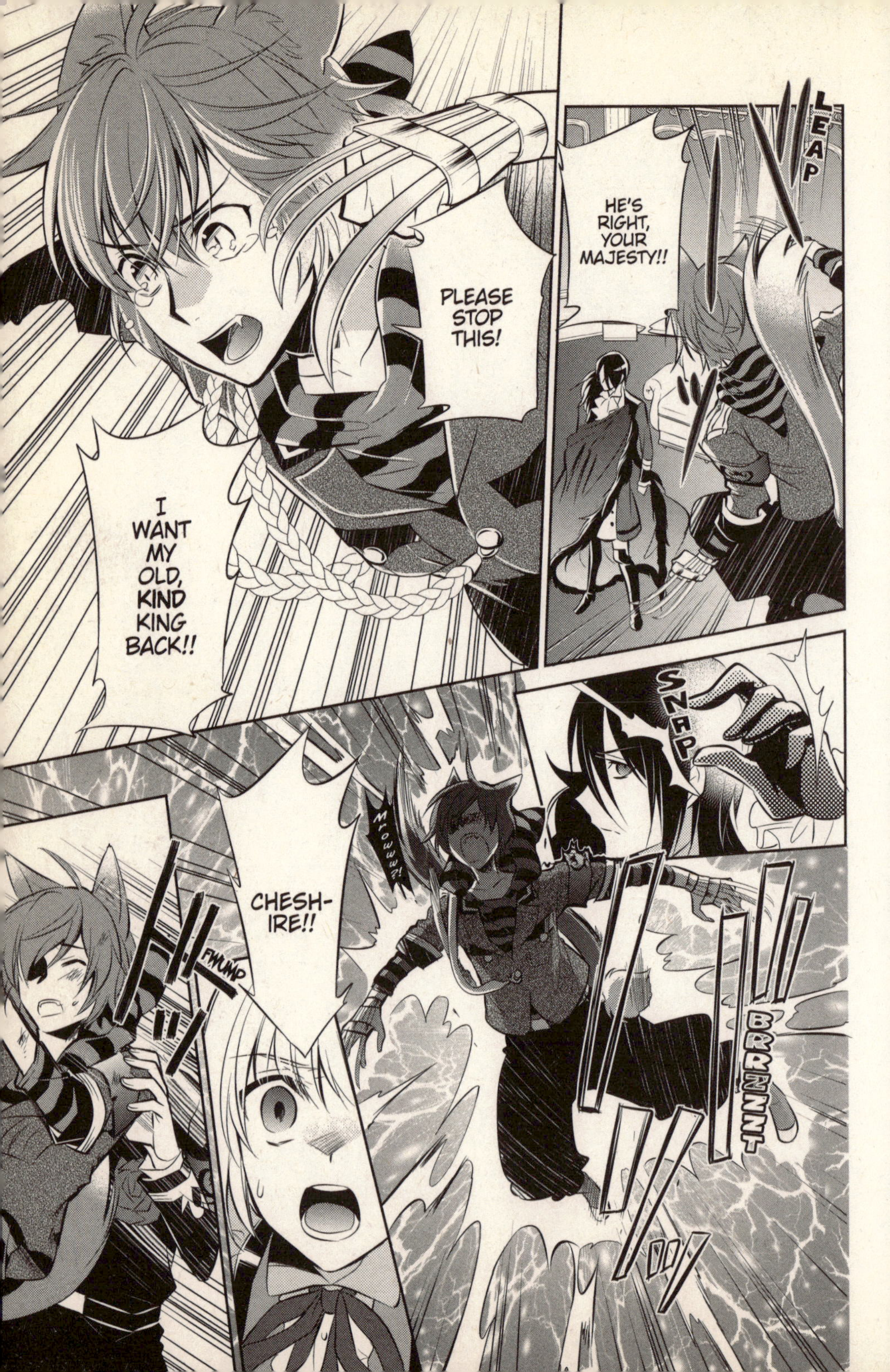
LEAP
HE'S RIGHT, YOUR MAJESTY!!
PLEASE STOP THIS!
I WANT MY OLD, KIND KING BACK!!
SNAP
MROWWW?!
BRRZZNT
CHESHIRE!!
FWUMP

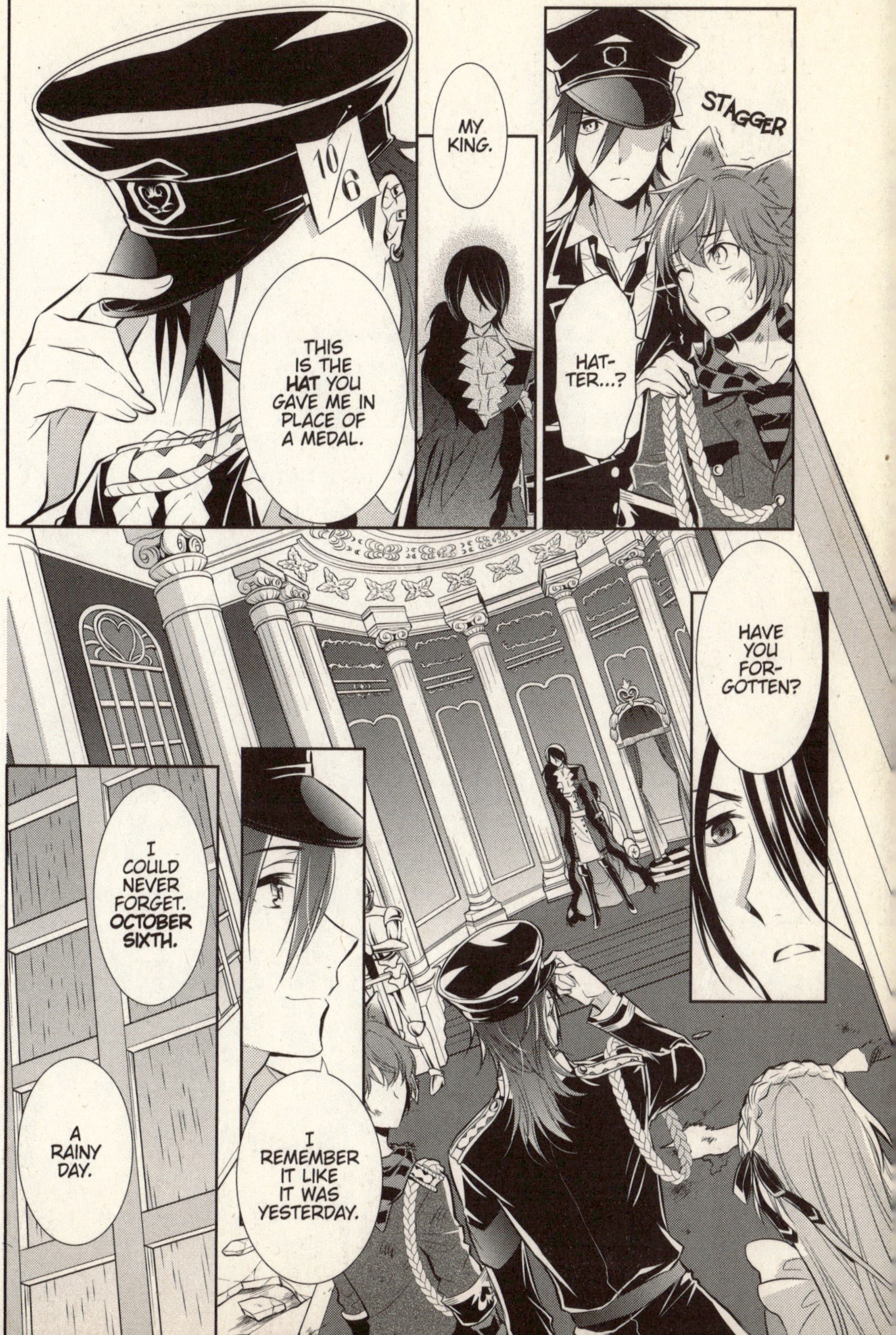
STAGGER
HAT-TER...?
MY KING.
10/6
THIS IS THE HAT YOU GAVE ME IN PLACE OF A MEDAL.
HAVE YOU FOR-GOTTEN?
I COULD NEVER FORGET. OCTOBER SIXTH.
I REMEMBER IT LIKE IT WAS YESTERDAY.
A RAINY DAY.

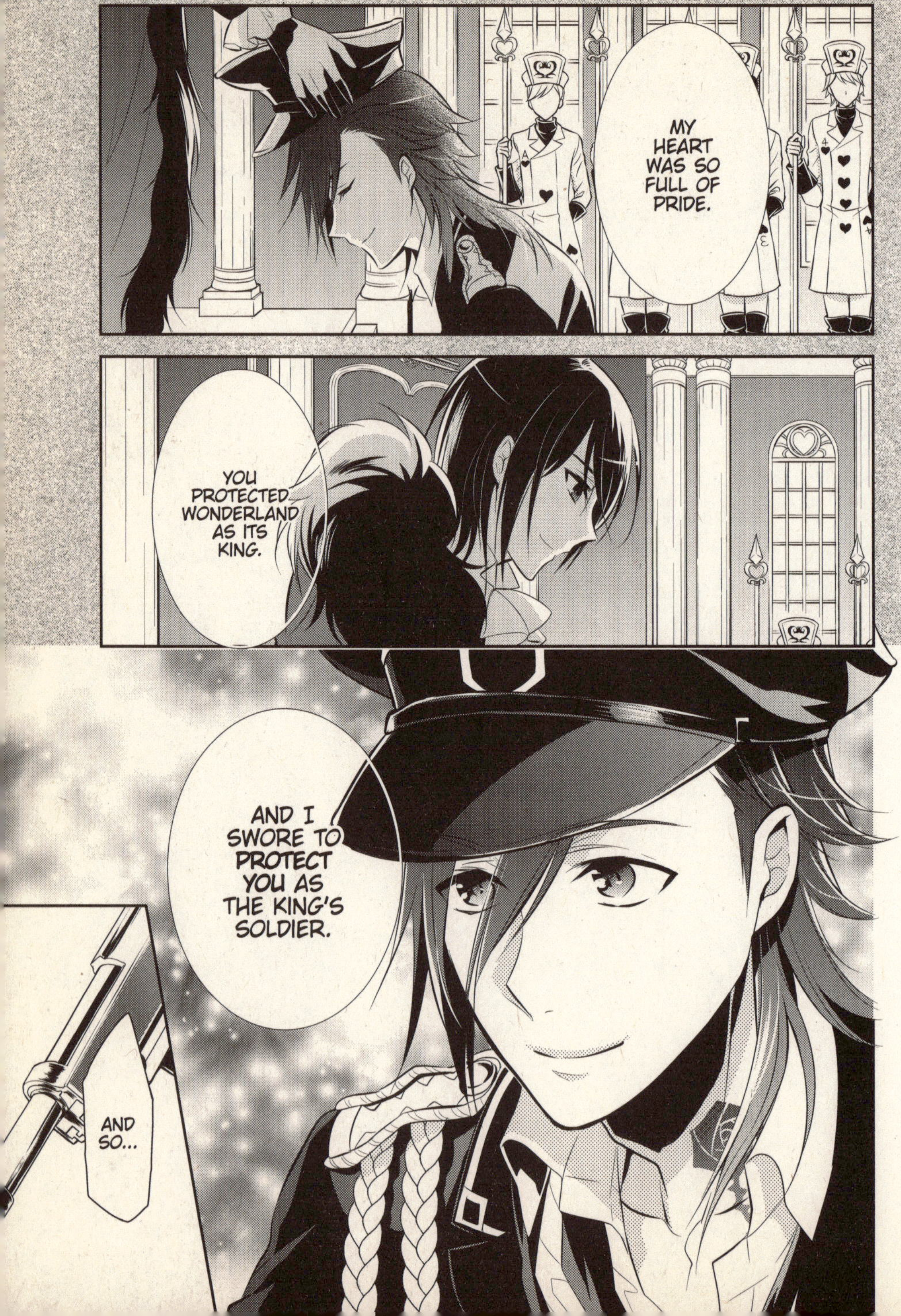
MY HEART WAS SO FULL OF PRIDE.
YOU PROTECTED WONDERLAND AS ITS KING.
AND I SWORE TO PROTECT YOU AS THE KING'S SOLDIER.
AND SO...

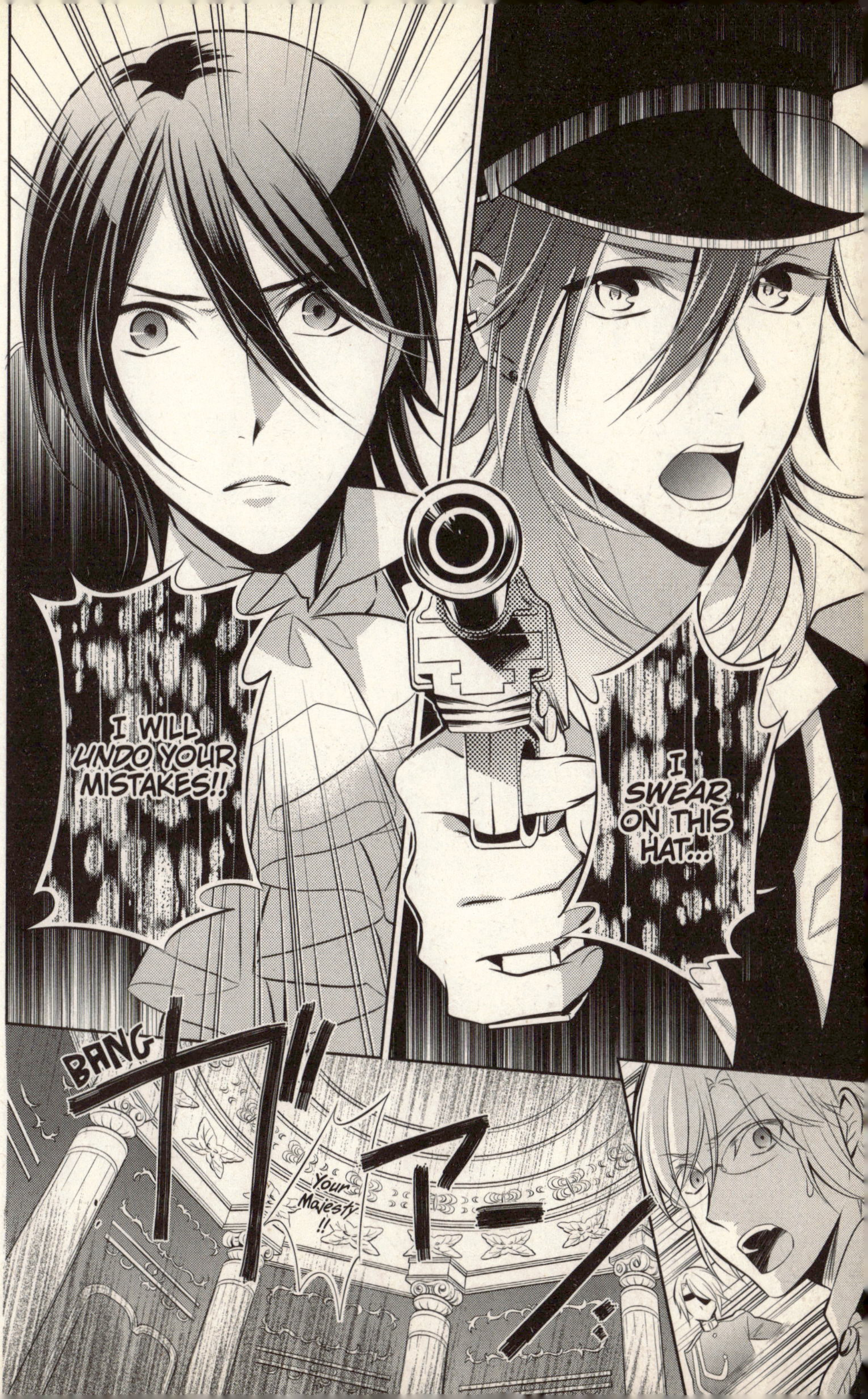
I SWEAR ON THIS HAT...
I WILL UNDO YOUR MISTAKES!!
BANG
Your Majesty!!

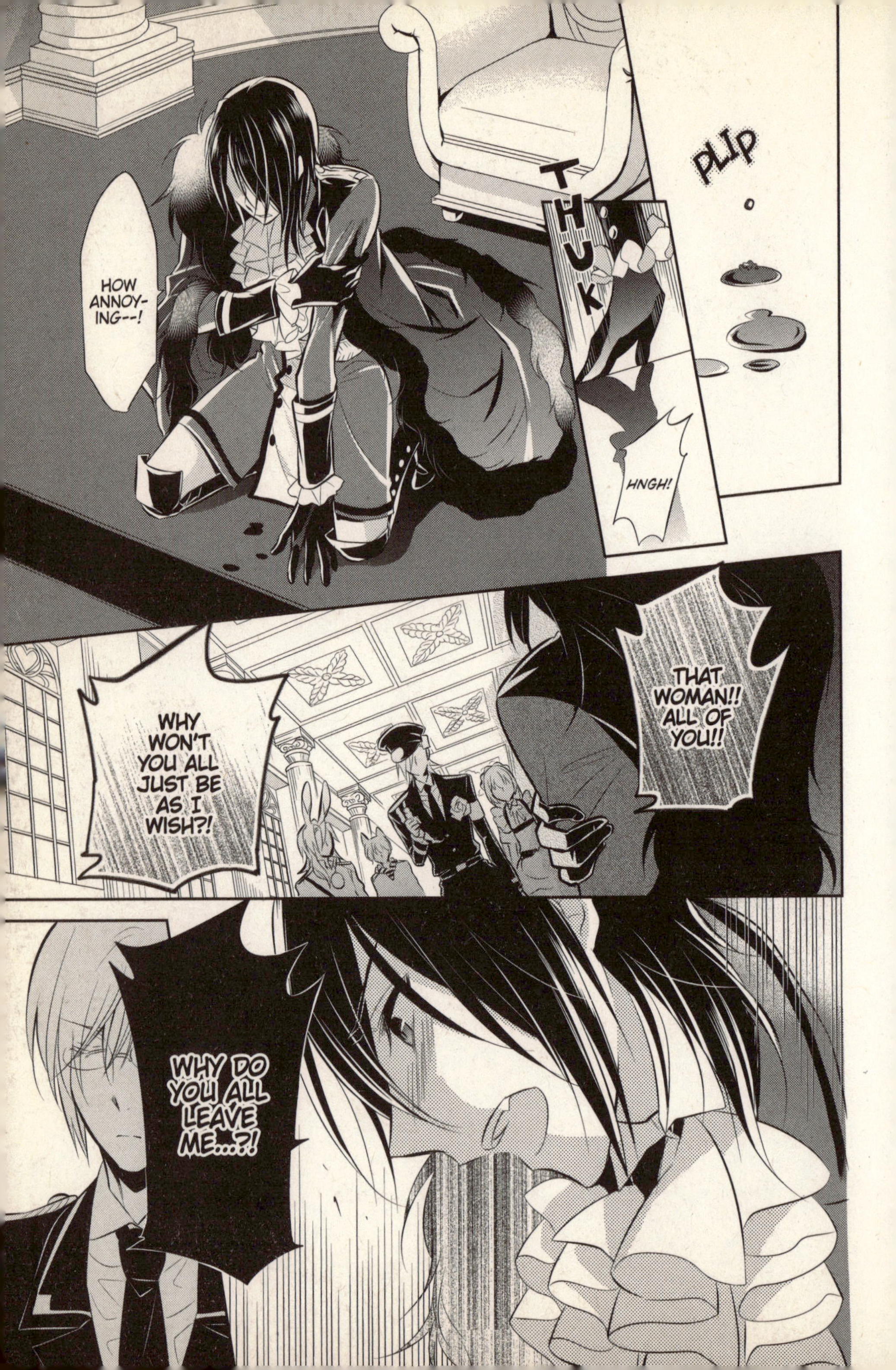
PLIP
THUK
HNGH!
HOW ANNOYING--!
THAT WOMAN!! ALL OF YOU!!
WHY WON'T YOU ALL JUST BE AS I WISH?!
WHY DO YOU ALL LEAVE ME...?!

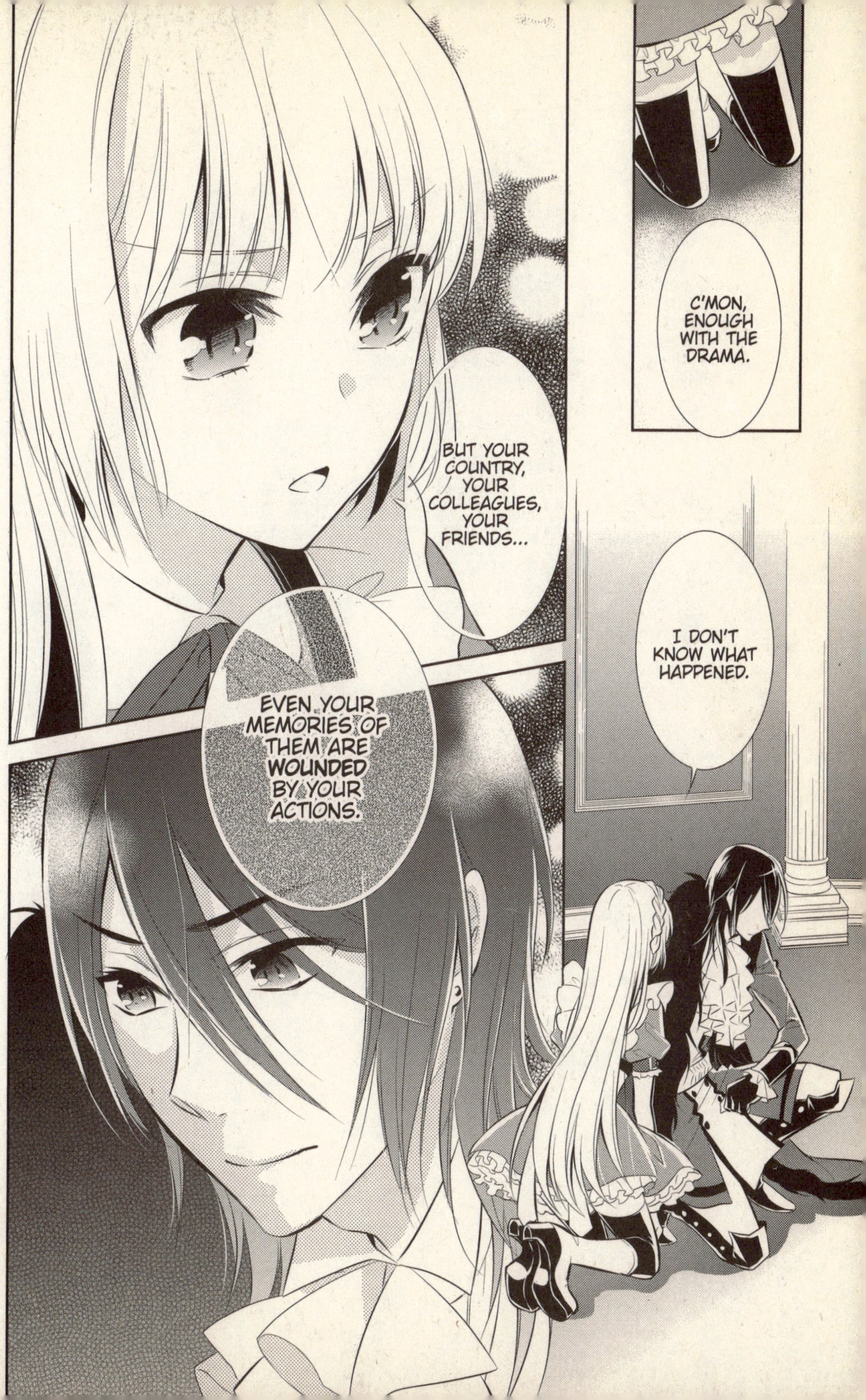
C'MON, ENOUGH WITH THE DRAMA.
I DON'T KNOW WHAT HAPPENED.
BUT YOUR COUNTRY, YOUR COLLEAGUES, YOUR FRIENDS...
EVEN YOUR MEMORIES OF THEM ARE WOUNDED BY YOUR ACTIONS.

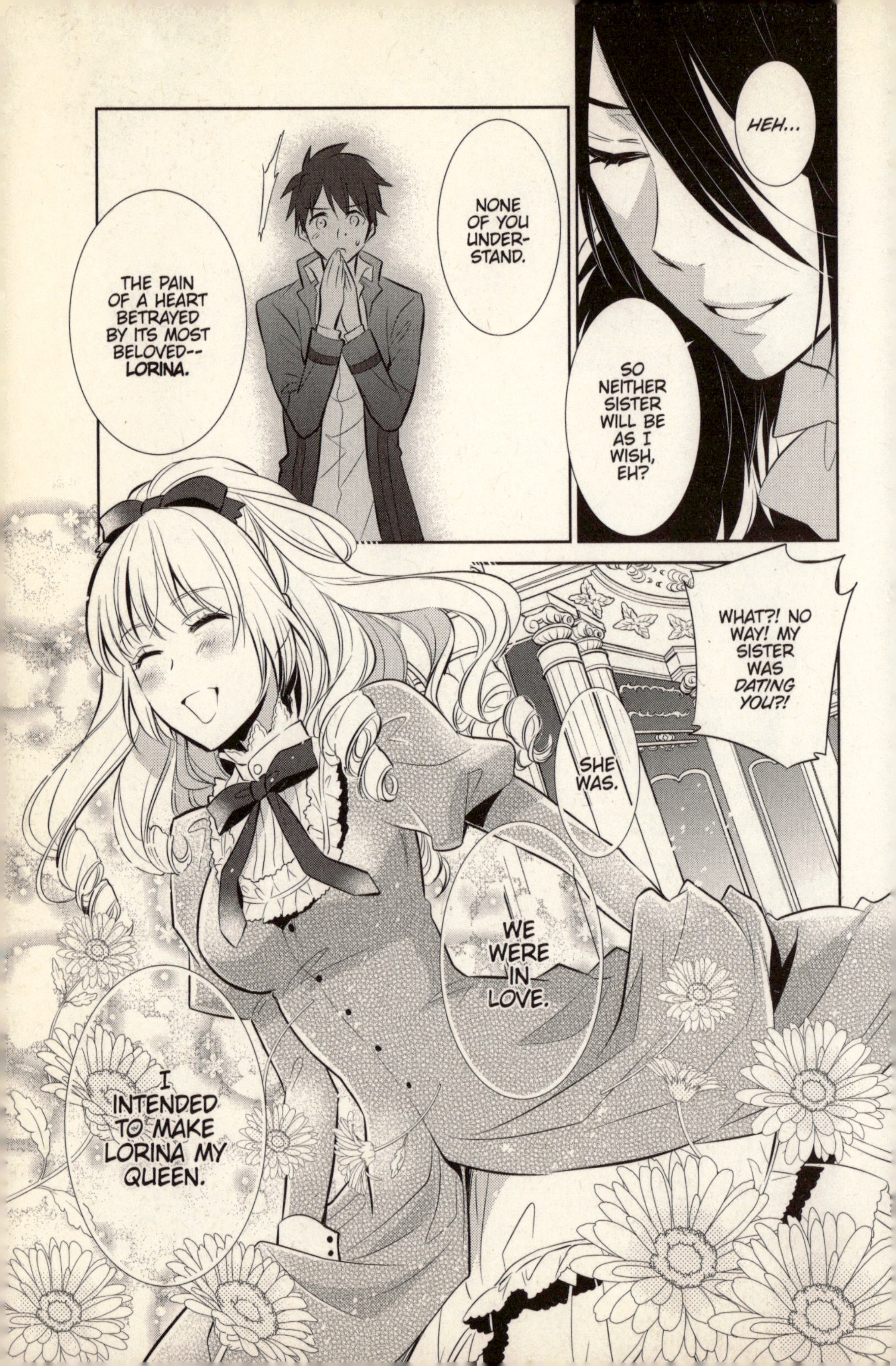
HEH...
SO NEITHER SISTER WILL BE AS I WISH, EH?
NONE OF YOU UNDER-STAND.
THE PAIN OF A HEART BETRAYED BY ITS MOST BELOVED-- LORINA.
WHAT?! NO WAY! MY SISTER WAS DATING YOU?!
SHE WAS.
WE WERE IN LOVE.
I INTENDED TO MAKE LORINA MY QUEEN.

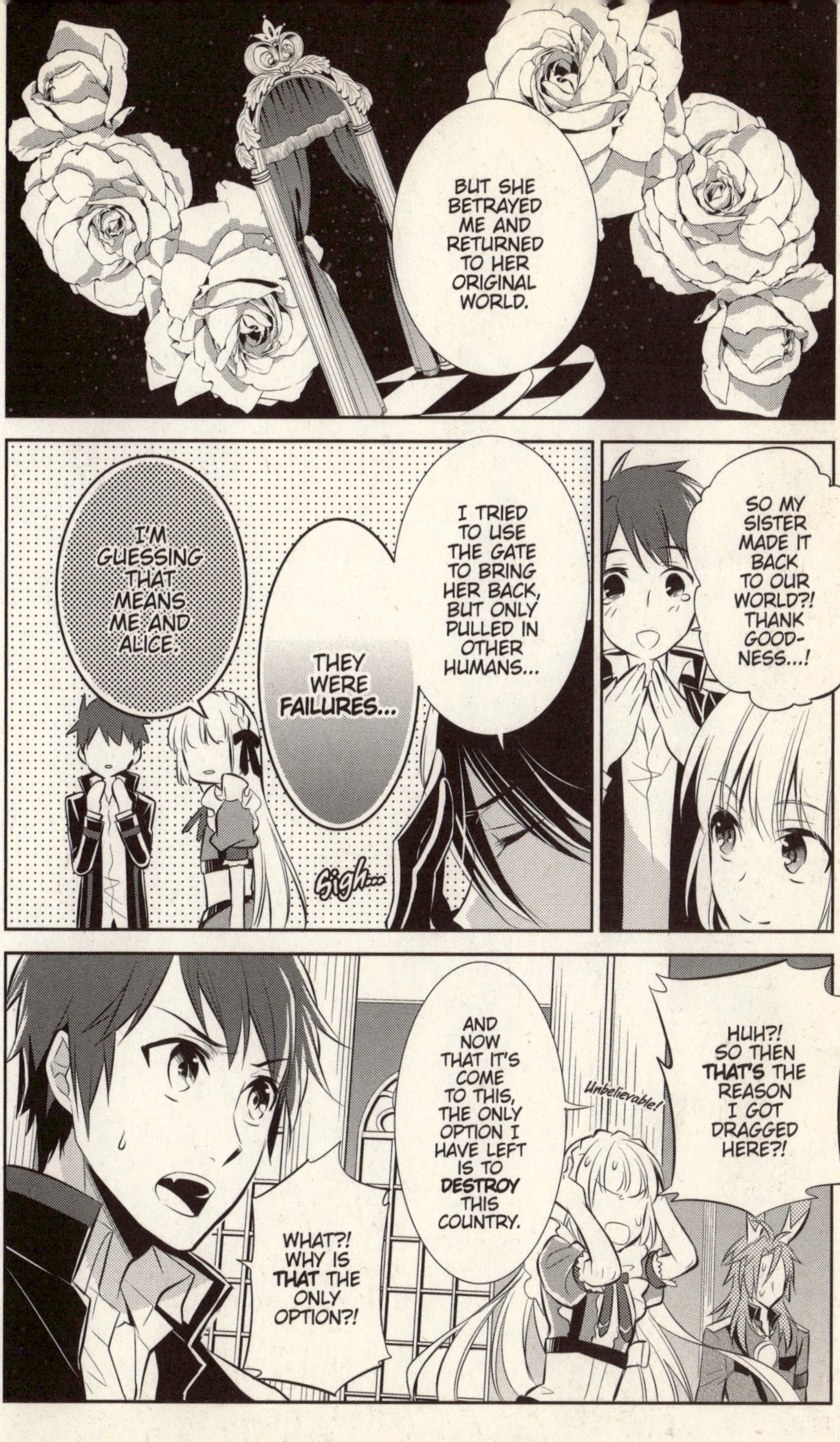
BUT SHE BETRAYED ME AND RETURNED TO HER ORIGINAL WORLD.
SO MY SISTER MADE IT BACK TO OUR WORLD?! THANK GOODNESS...!
I TRIED TO USE THE GATE TO BRING HER BACK, BUT ONLY PULLED IN OTHER HUMANS...
THEY WERE FAILURES...
I'M GUESSING THAT MEANS ME AND ALICE.
Sigh...
HUH?! SO THEN THAT'S THE REASON I GOT DRAGGED HERE?!
Unbelievable!
AND NOW THAT IT'S COME TO THIS, THE ONLY OPTION I HAVE LEFT IS TO DESTROY THIS COUNTRY.
WHAT?! WHY IS THAT THE ONLY OPTION?!

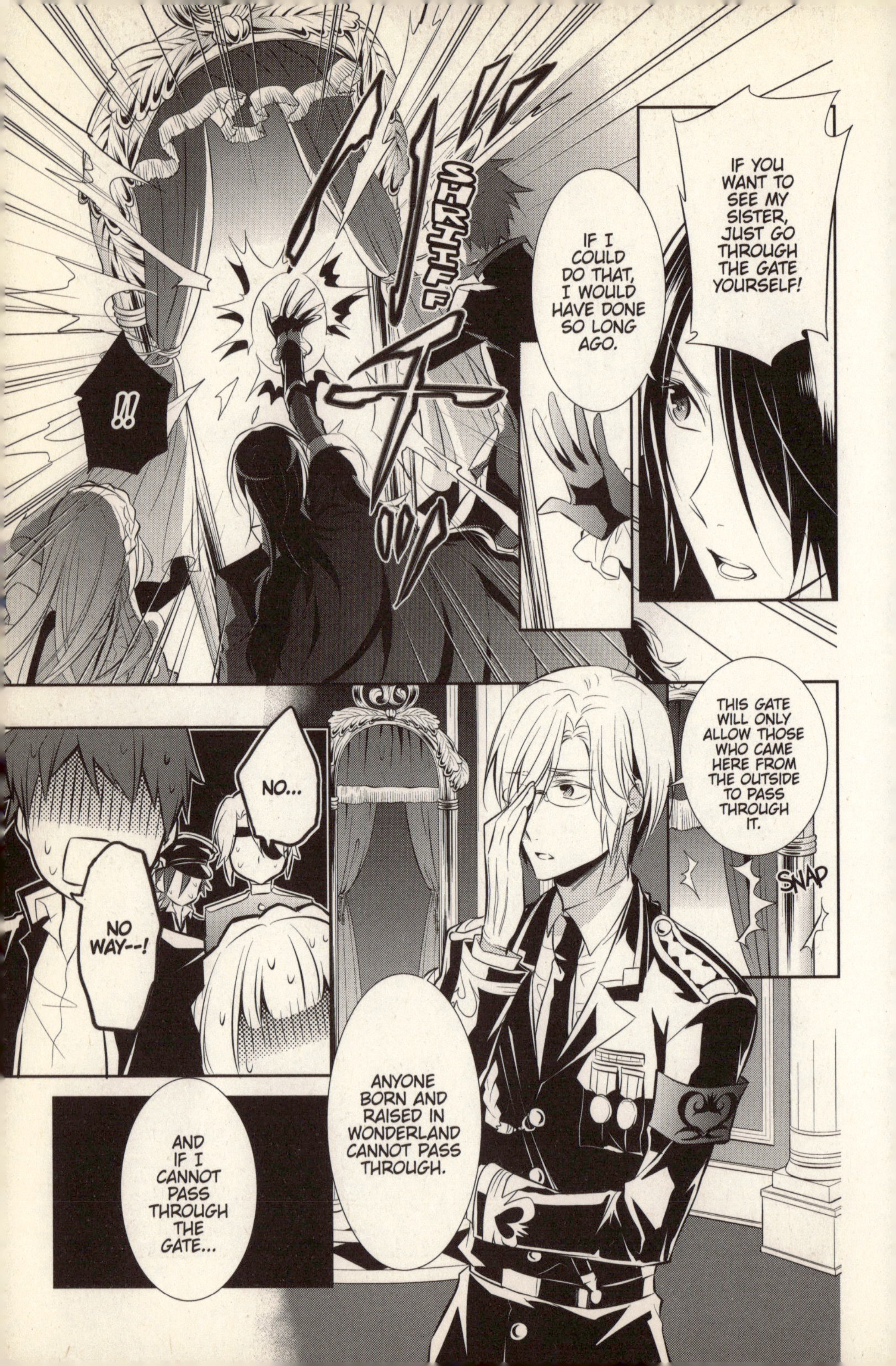
IF YOU WANT TO SEE MY SISTER, JUST GO THROUGH THE GATE YOURSELF!
IF I COULD DO THAT, I WOULD HAVE DONE SO LONG AGO.
SHRIIFF
!!
THIS GATE WILL ONLY ALLOW THOSE WHO CAME HERE FROM THE OUTSIDE TO PASS THROUGH IT.
SNAP
ANYONE BORN AND RAISED IN WONDERLAND CANNOT PASS THROUGH.
NO...
NO WAY--!
AND IF I CANNOT PASS THROUGH THE GATE...

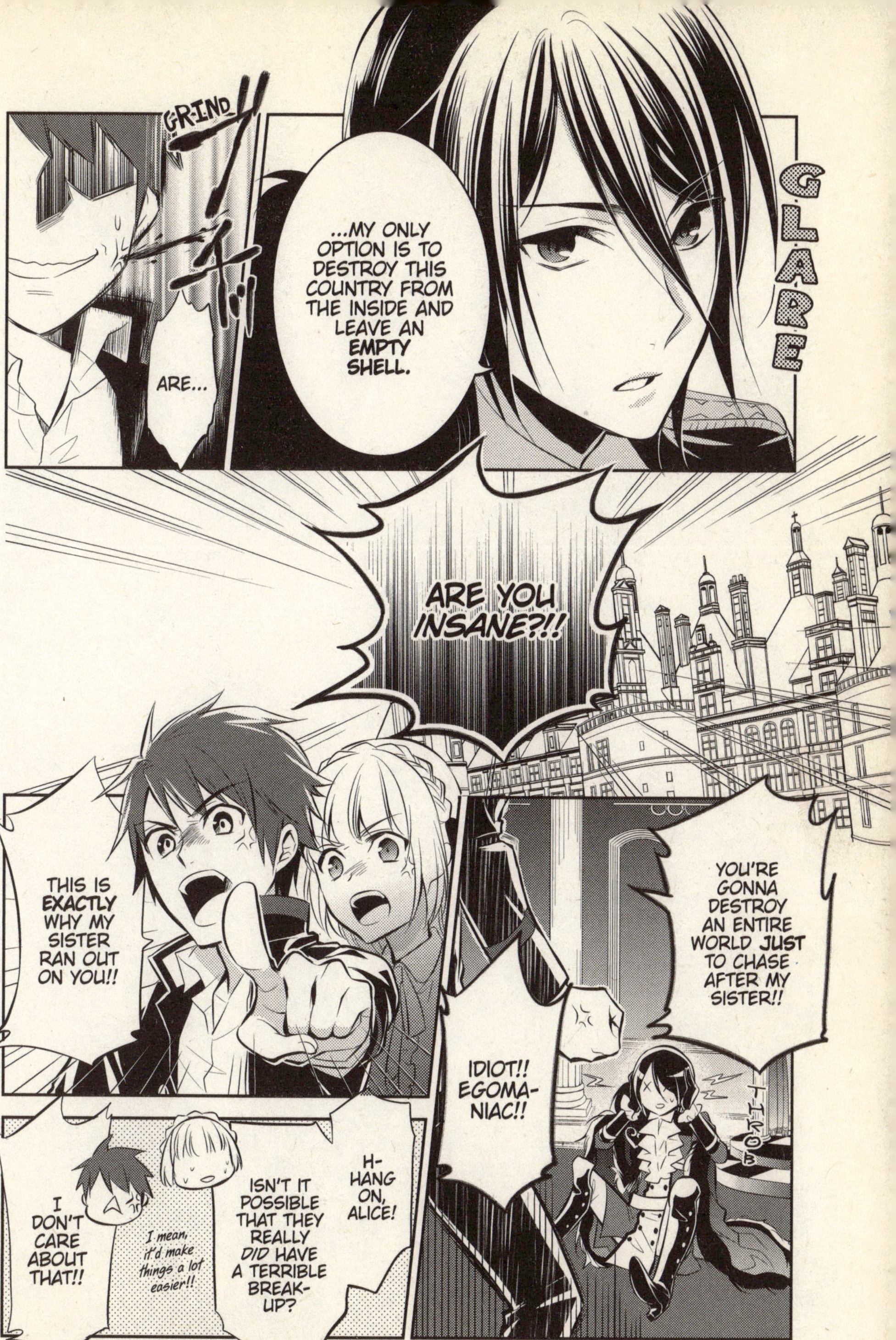
...MY ONLY OPTION IS TO DESTROY THIS COUNTRY FROM THE INSIDE AND LEAVE AN EMPTY SHELL.
GLARE
GRIND
ARE...
ARE YOU INSANE?!!
YOU'RE GONNA DESTROY AN ENTIRE WORLD JUST TO CHASE AFTER MY SISTER!!
IDIOT!! EGOMANIAC!!
THROB
THIS IS EXACTLY WHY MY SISTER RAN OUT ON YOU!!
H-HANG ON, ALICE!
ISN'T IT POSSIBLE THAT THEY REALLY DID HAVE A TERRIBLE BREAK-UP?
I mean, it'd make things a lot easier!!
I DON'T CARE ABOUT THAT!!

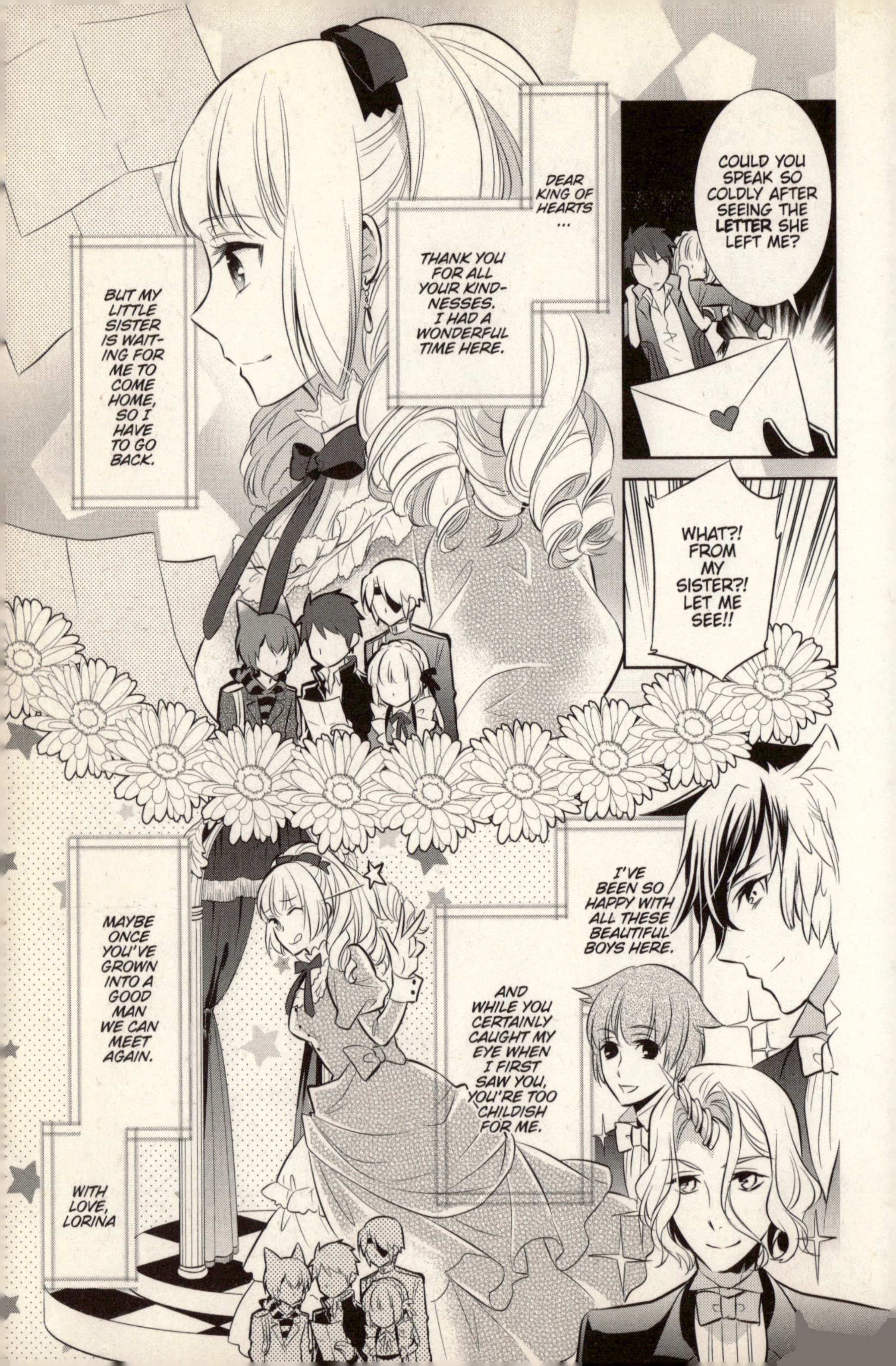
COULD YOU SPEAK SO COLDLY AFTER SEEING THE **LETTER** SHE LEFT ME?
WHAT?! FROM MY SISTER?! LET ME SEE!!
DEAR KING OF HEARTS...
THANK YOU FOR ALL YOUR KINDNESSES. I HAD A WONDERFUL TIME HERE.
BUT MY LITTLE SISTER IS WAITING FOR ME TO COME HOME, SO I HAVE TO GO BACK.
I'VE BEEN SO HAPPY WITH ALL THESE BEAUTIFUL BOYS HERE.
AND WHILE YOU CERTAINLY CAUGHT MY EYE WHEN I FIRST SAW YOU, YOU'RE TOO CHILDISH FOR ME.
MAYBE ONCE YOU'VE GROWN INTO A GOOD MAN WE CAN MEET AGAIN.
WITH LOVE, LORINA

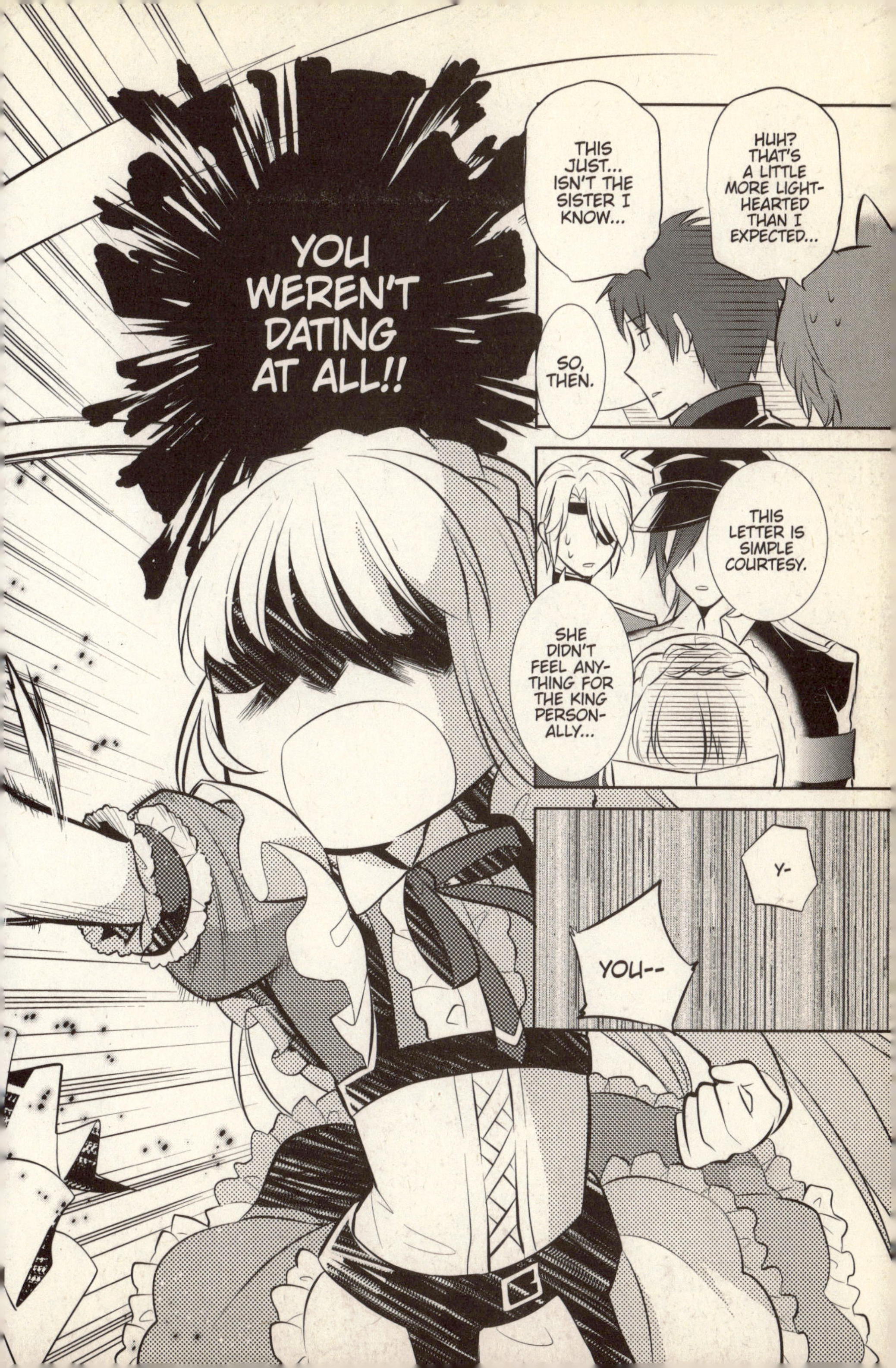
HUH? THAT'S A LITTLE MORE LIGHT-HEARTED THAN I EXPECTED...
THIS JUST... ISN'T THE SISTER I KNOW...
SO, THEN.
THIS LETTER IS SIMPLE COURTESY.
SHE DIDN'T FEEL ANY-THING FOR THE KING PERSON-ALLY...
Y-
YOU--
YOU WEREN'T DATING AT ALL!!

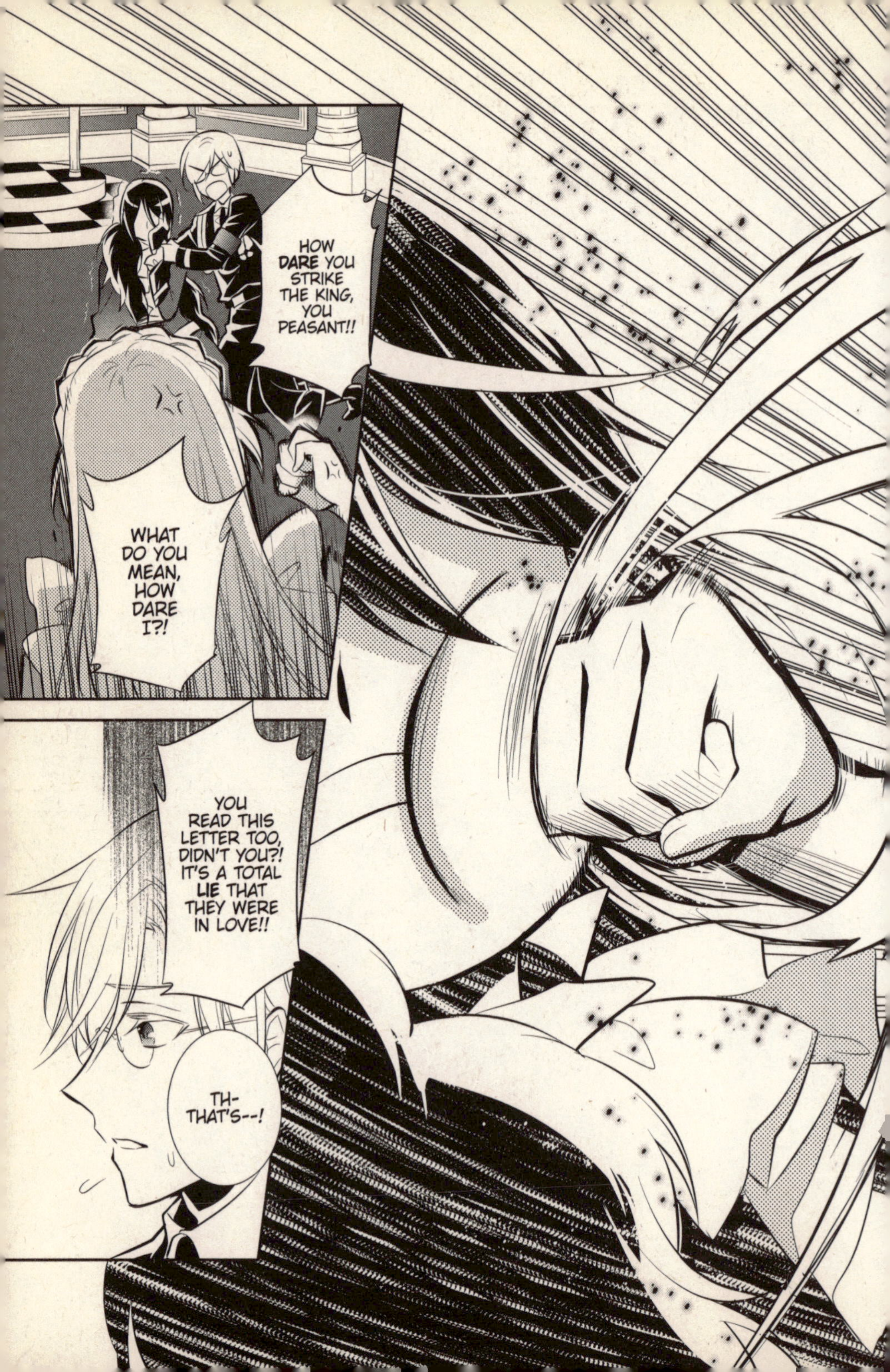
HOW DARE YOU STRIKE THE KING, YOU PEASANT!!
WHAT DO YOU MEAN, HOW DARE I?!
YOU READ THIS LETTER TOO, DIDN'T YOU?! IT'S A TOTAL LIE THAT THEY WERE IN LOVE!!
TH-THAT'S--!

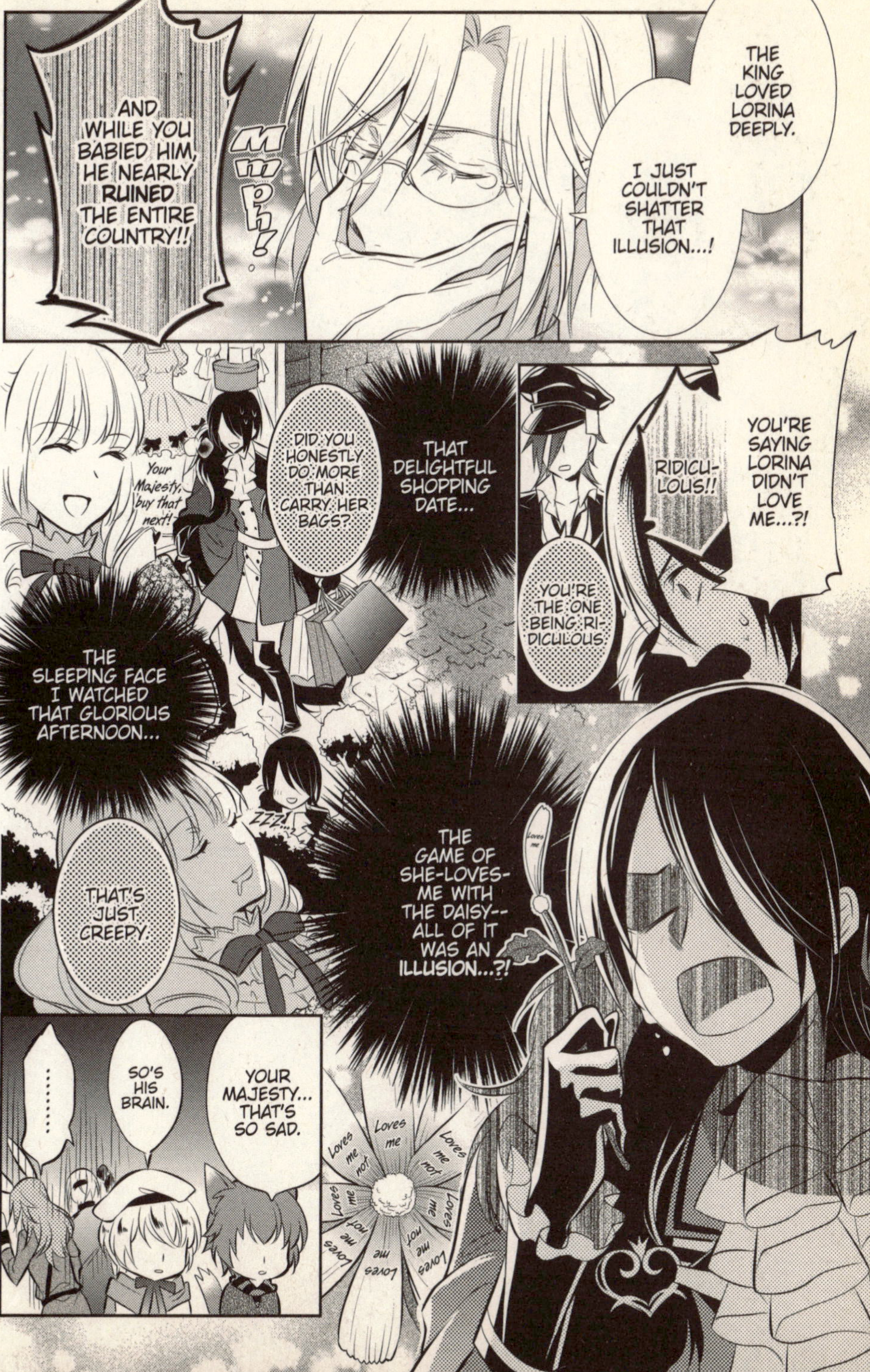
THE KING LOVED LORINA DEEPLY.
I JUST COULDN'T SHATTER THAT ILLUSION...!
Mmph!
AND WHILE YOU BABIED HIM, HE NEARLY RUINED THE ENTIRE COUNTRY!!
YOU'RE SAYING LORINA DIDN'T LOVE ME...?!
RIDICULOUS!!
YOU'RE THE ONE BEING RIDICULOUS.
THAT DELIGHTFUL SHOPPING DATE...
DID YOU HONESTLY DO MORE THAN CARRY HER BAGS?
Your Majesty, buy that next!
THE SLEEPING FACE I WATCHED THAT GLORIOUS AFTERNOON...
ZZZ...
THAT'S JUST CREEPY.
THE GAME OF SHE-LOVES-ME WITH THE DAISY--ALL OF IT WAS AN ILLUSION...?!
Loves me
YOUR MAJESTY... THAT'S SO SAD.
SO'S HIS BRAIN.
......
Loves me
Loves me not

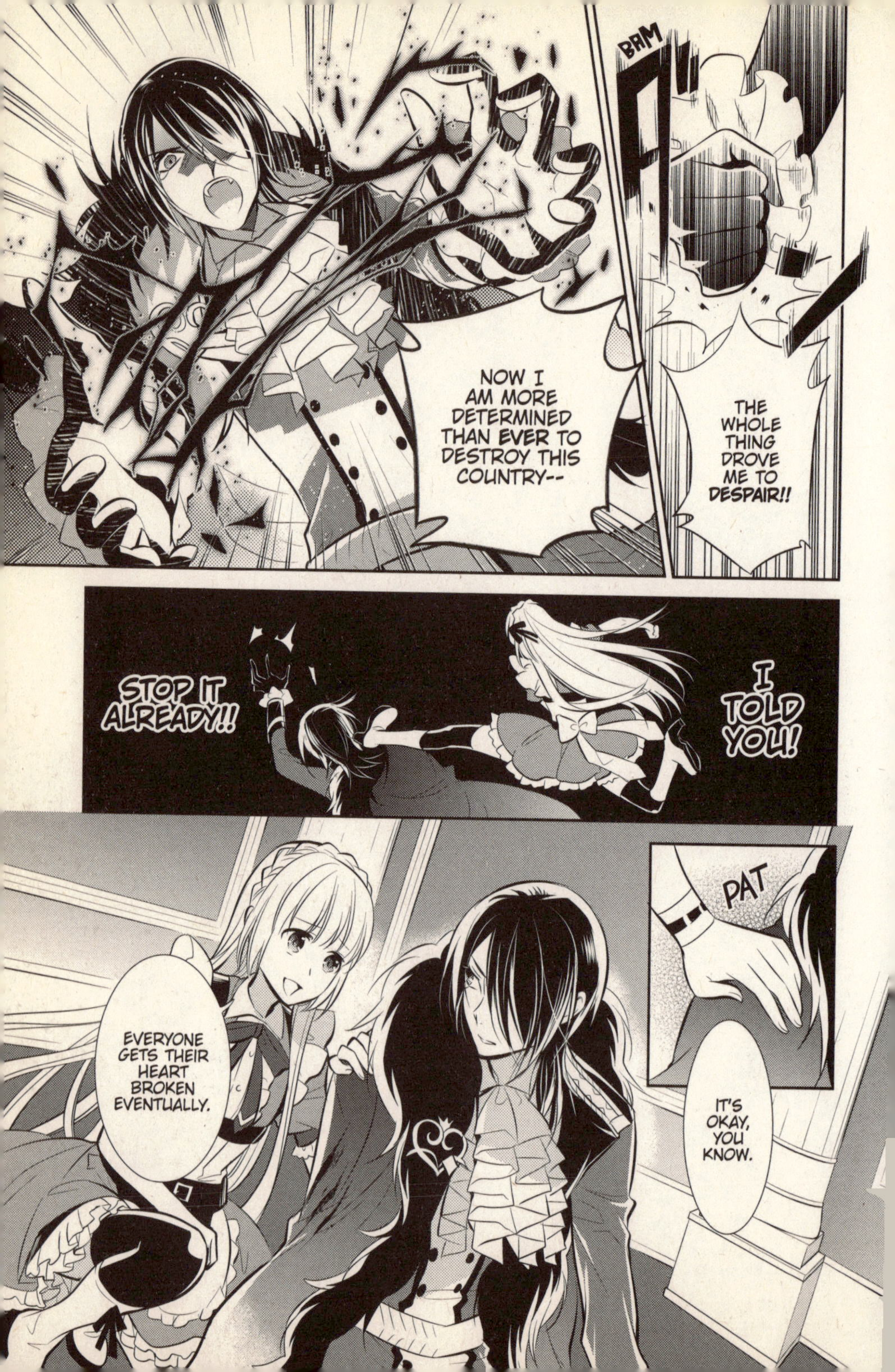
BRM
THE WHOLE THING DROVE ME TO DESPAIR!!
NOW I AM MORE DETERMINED THAN EVER TO DESTROY THIS COUNTRY--
I TOLD YOU!
STOP IT ALREADY!!
PAT
IT'S OKAY, YOU KNOW.
EVERYONE GETS THEIR HEART BROKEN EVENTUALLY.

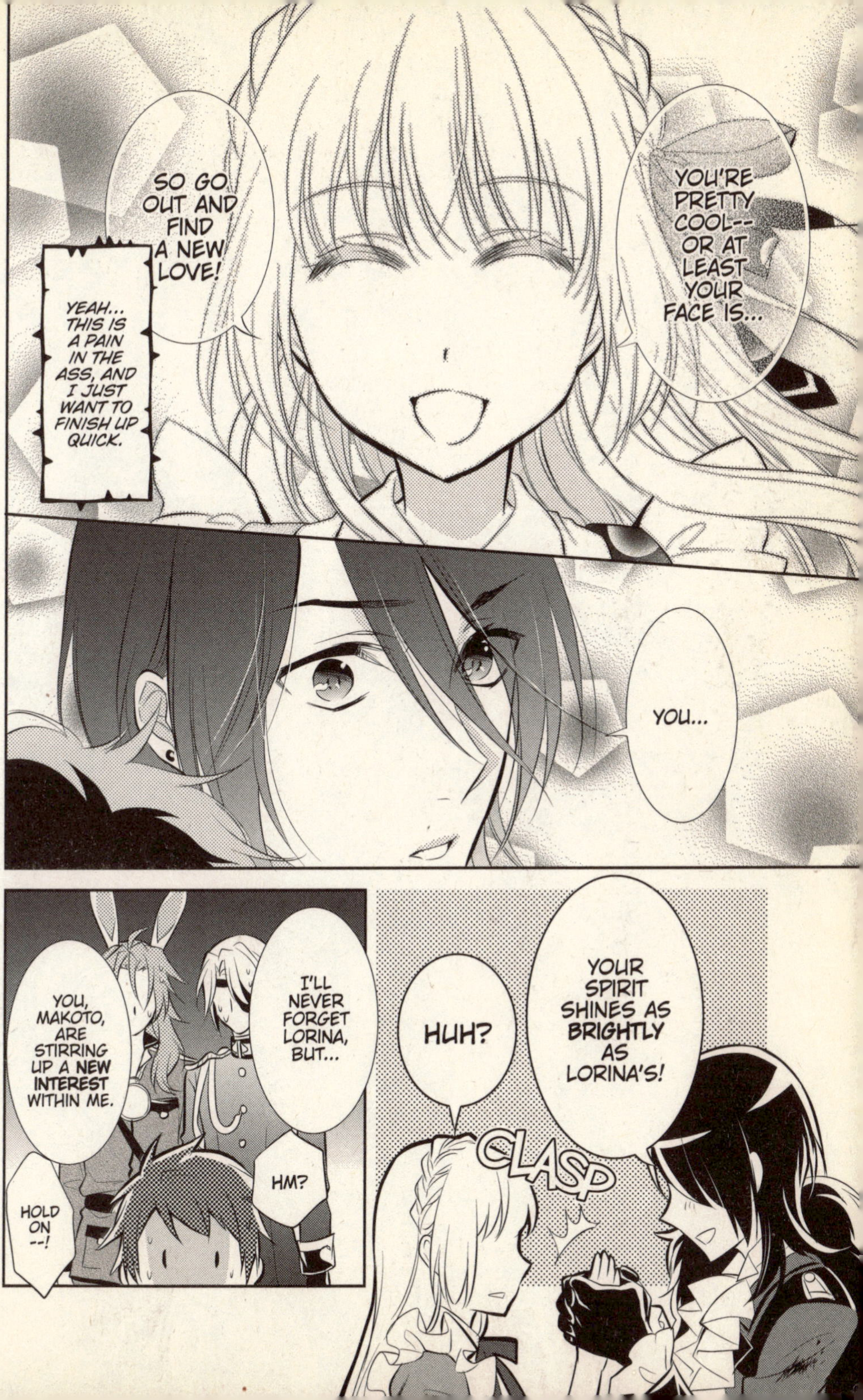
YOU'RE PRETTY COOL-- OR AT LEAST YOUR FACE IS...
SO GO OUT AND FIND A NEW LOVE!
YEAH... THIS IS A PAIN IN THE ASS, AND I JUST WANT TO FINISH UP QUICK.
YOU...
YOUR SPIRIT SHINES AS BRIGHTLY AS LORINA'S!
HUH?
CLASP
I'LL NEVER FORGET LORINA, BUT...
YOU, MAKOTO, ARE STIRRING UP A NEW INTEREST WITHIN ME.
HM?
HOLD ON --!

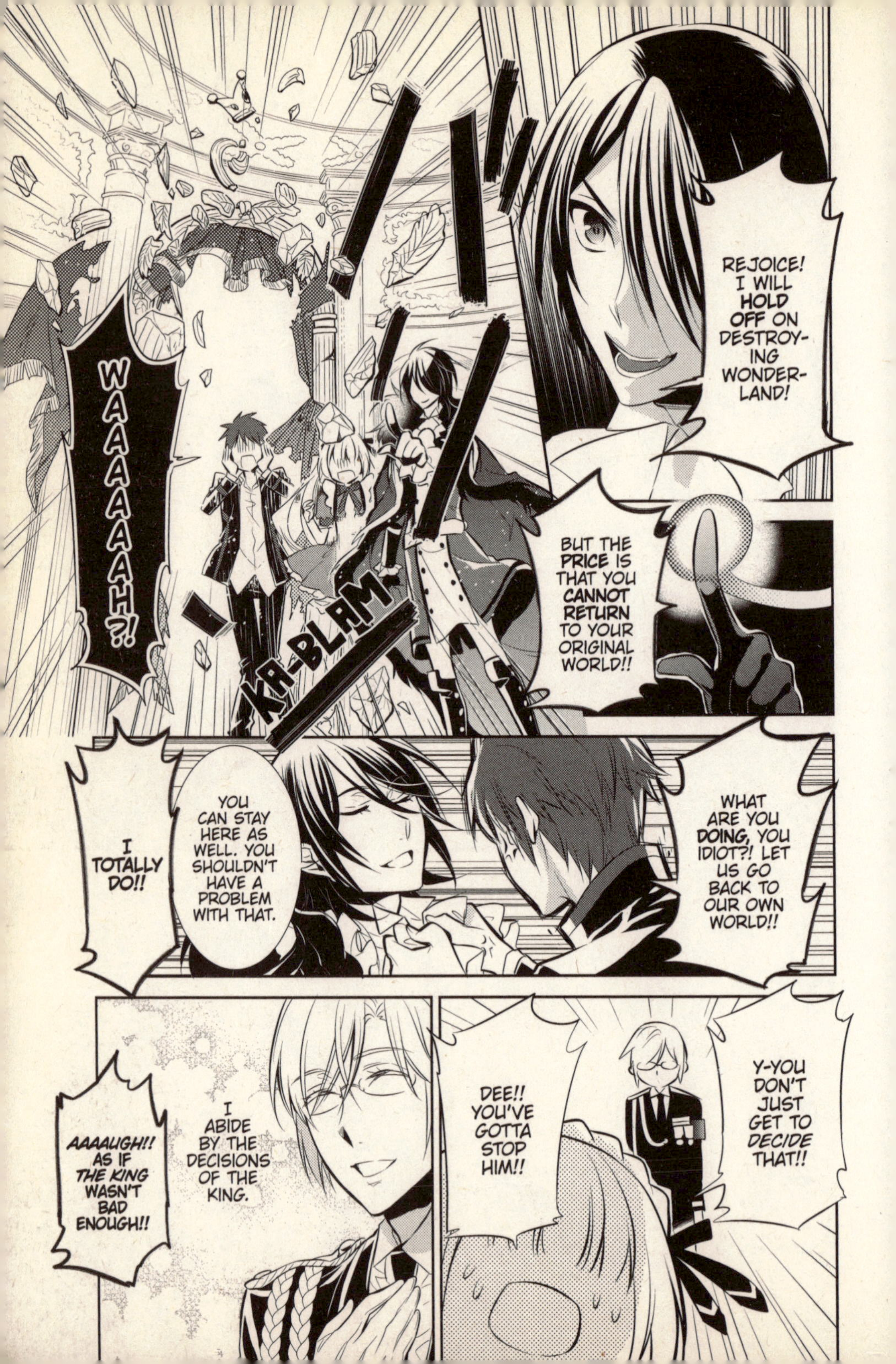
REJOICE! I WILL **HOLD OFF** ON DESTROYING WONDERLAND!
BUT THE **PRICE** IS THAT YOU **CANNOT RETURN** TO YOUR ORIGINAL WORLD!!
WAAAAAAAAH?!
KA-BLAM
WHAT ARE YOU **DOING,** YOU IDIOT?! LET US GO BACK TO OUR OWN WORLD!!
YOU CAN STAY HERE AS WELL. YOU SHOULDN'T HAVE A PROBLEM WITH THAT.
I TOTALLY DO!!
Y-YOU DON'T JUST GET TO *DECIDE* THAT!!
DEE!! YOU'VE GOTTA STOP HIM!!
I ABIDE BY THE DECISIONS OF THE KING.
AAAAUGH!! AS IF *THE KING* WASN'T BAD ENOUGH!!

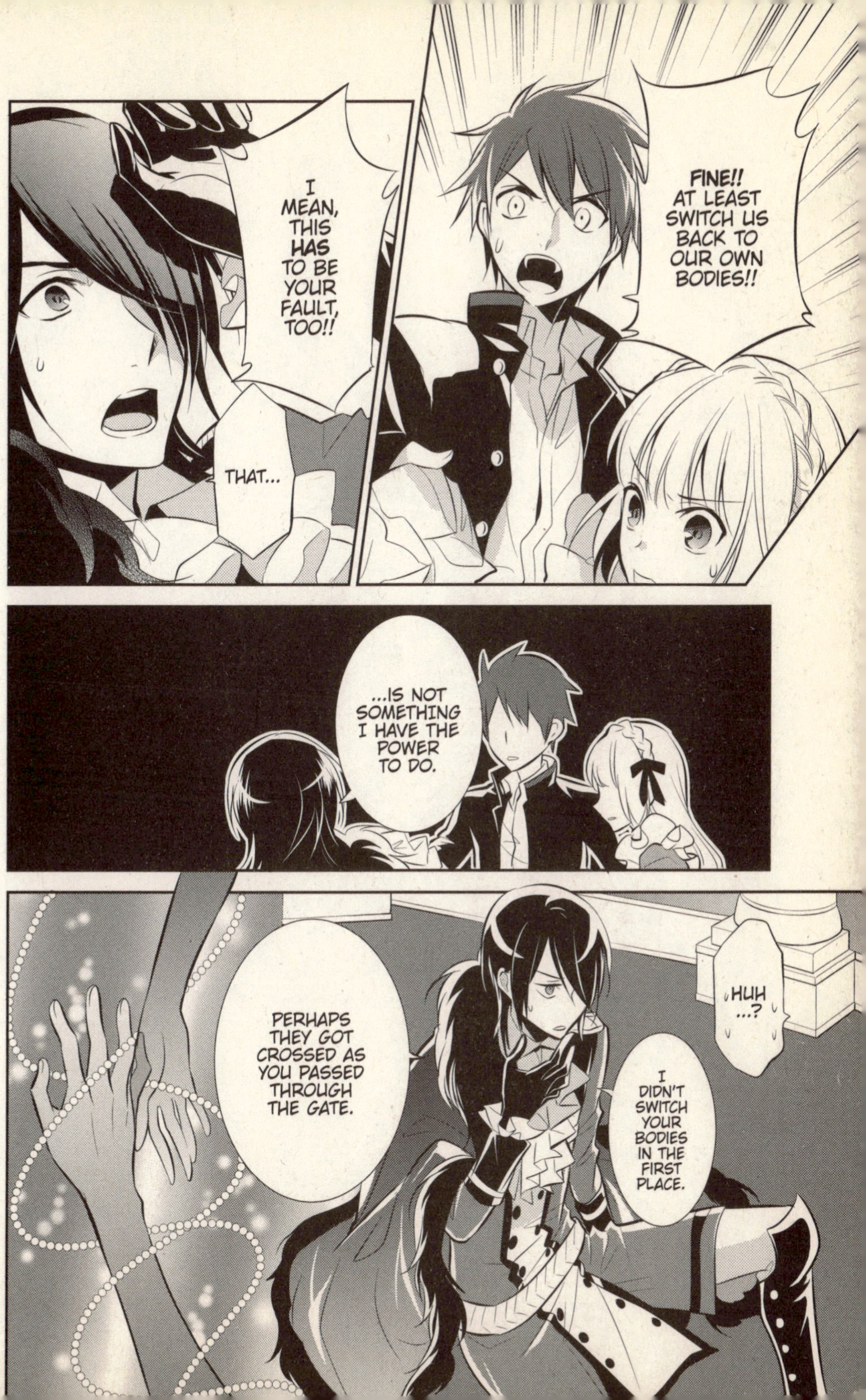
FINE!! AT LEAST SWITCH US BACK TO OUR OWN BODIES!!
I MEAN, THIS HAS TO BE YOUR FAULT, TOO!!
THAT...
...IS NOT SOMETHING I HAVE THE POWER TO DO.
HUH ...?
I DIDN'T SWITCH YOUR BODIES IN THE FIRST PLACE.
PERHAPS THEY GOT CROSSED AS YOU PASSED THROUGH THE GATE.

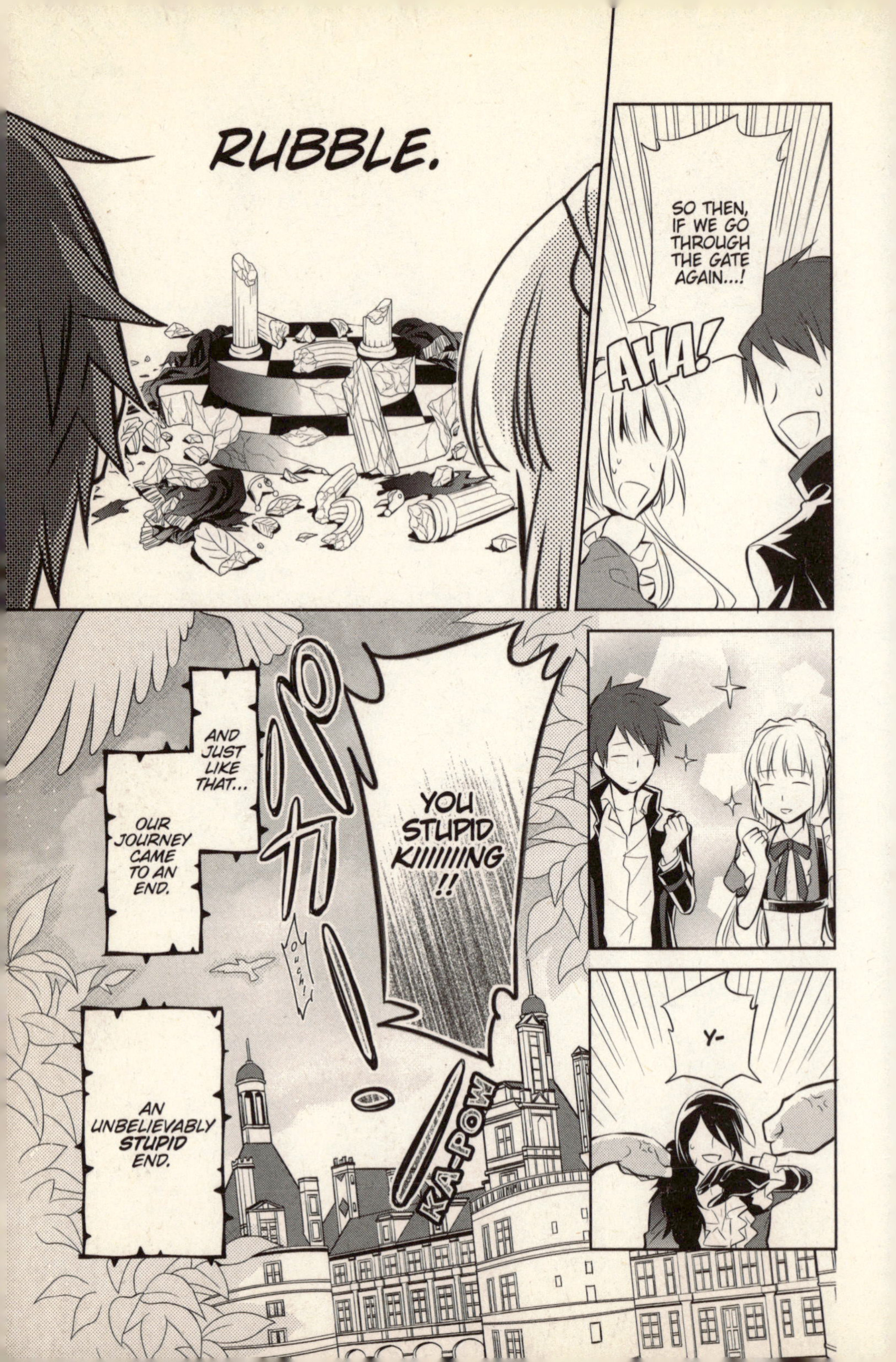
SO THEN, IF WE GO THROUGH THE GATE AGAIN...!
AHA!
RUBBLE.
Y-
YOU STUPID KIIIIIIING!!
KA-POW
Ouch!
AND JUST LIKE THAT...
OUR JOURNEY CAME TO AN END.
AN UNBELIEVABLY STUPID END.

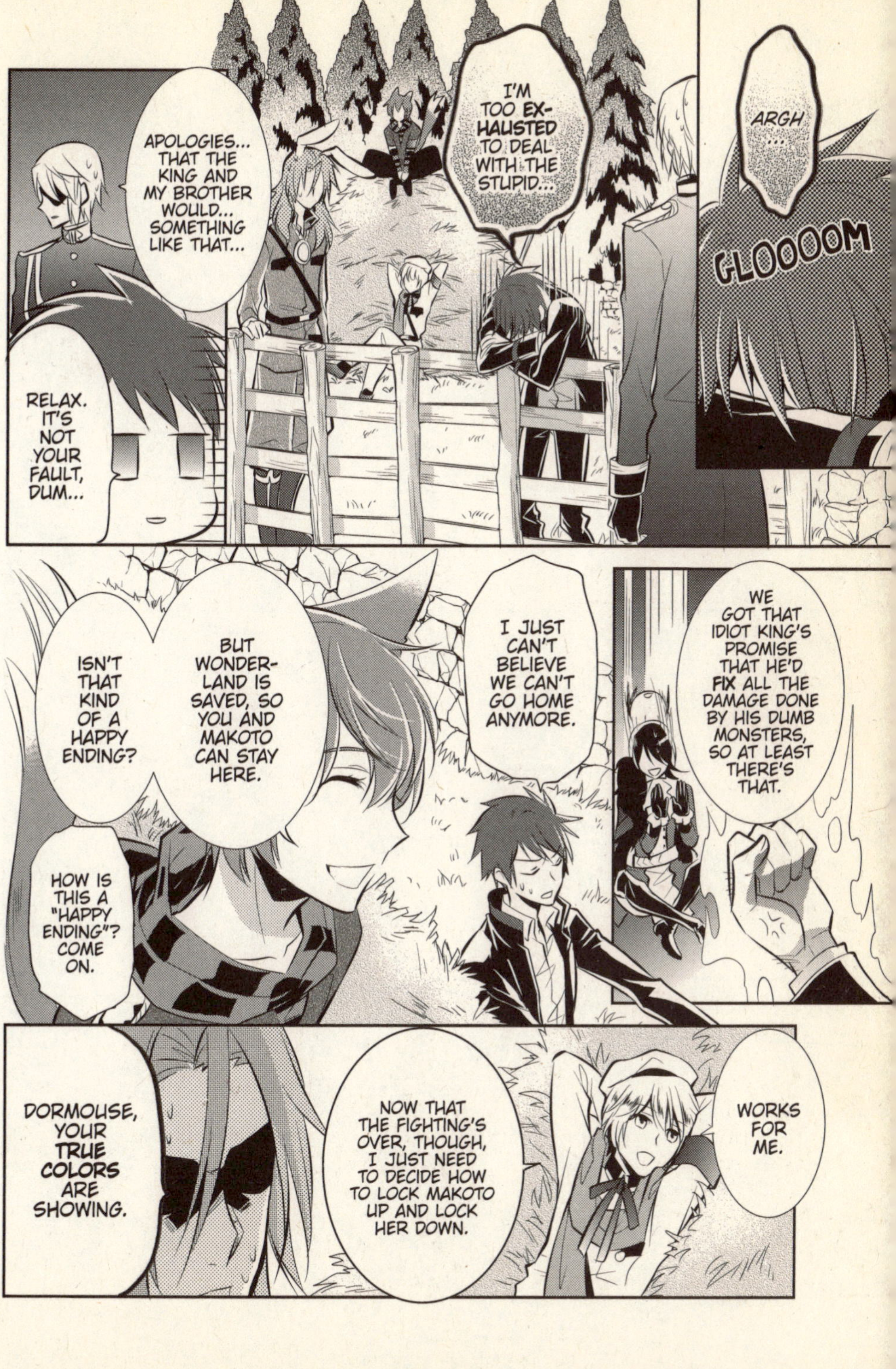
ARGH...
GLOOOOM
I'M TOO EXHAUSTED TO DEAL WITH THE STUPID...
APOLOGIES... THAT THE KING AND MY BROTHER WOULD... SOMETHING LIKE THAT...
RELAX. IT'S NOT YOUR FAULT, DUM...
WE GOT THAT IDIOT KING'S PROMISE THAT HE'D FIX ALL THE DAMAGE DONE BY HIS DUMB MONSTERS, SO AT LEAST THERE'S THAT.
I JUST CAN'T BELIEVE WE CAN'T GO HOME ANYMORE.
BUT WONDERLAND IS SAVED, SO YOU AND MAKOTO CAN STAY HERE.
ISN'T THAT KIND OF A HAPPY ENDING?
HOW IS THIS A "HAPPY ENDING"? COME ON.
WORKS FOR ME.
NOW THAT THE FIGHTING'S OVER, THOUGH, I JUST NEED TO DECIDE HOW TO LOCK MAKOTO UP AND LOCK HER DOWN.
DORMOUSE, YOUR TRUE COLORS ARE SHOWING.

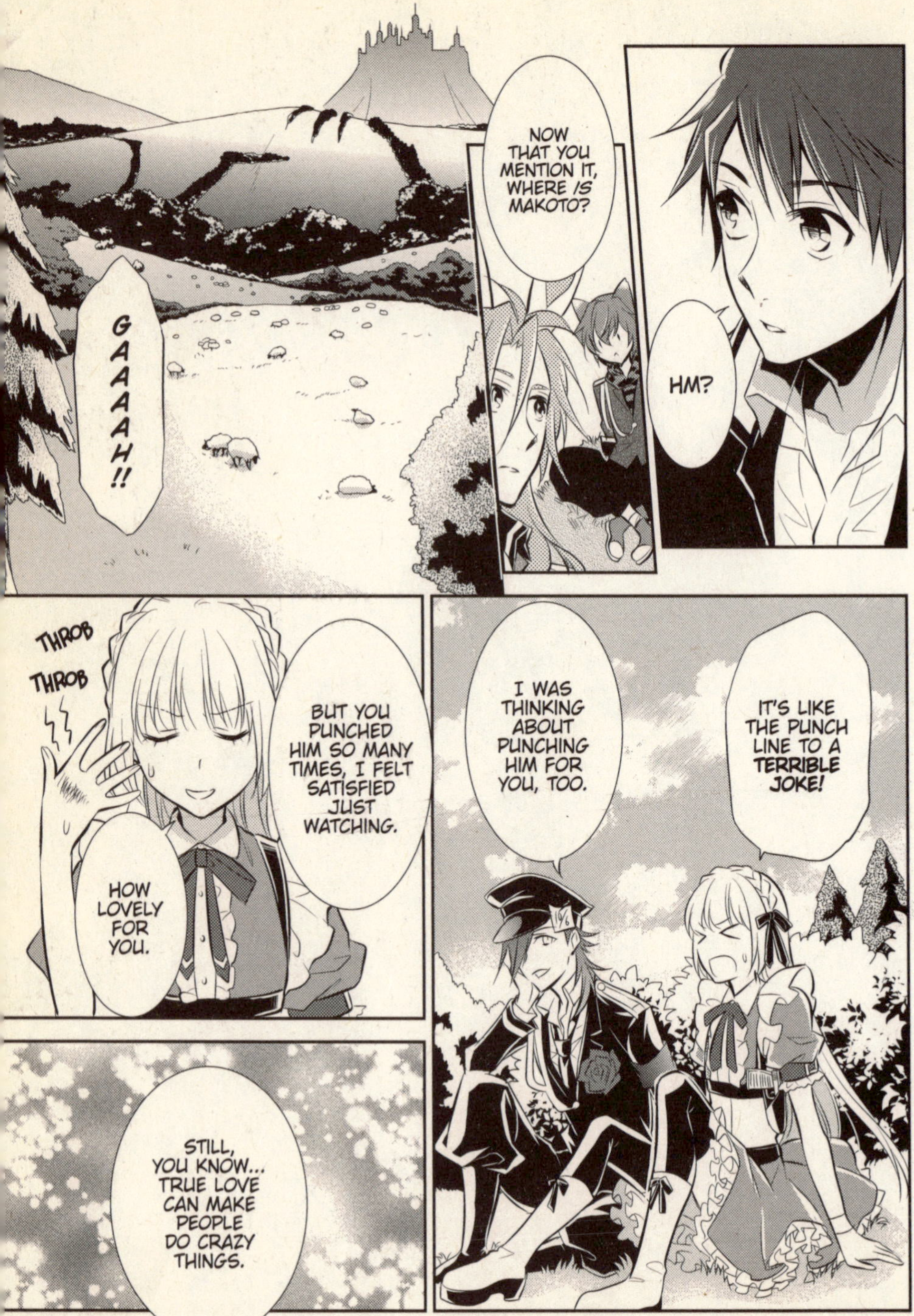
HM?
NOW THAT YOU MENTION IT, WHERE *IS* MAKOTO?
GAAAAAH!!
IT'S LIKE THE PUNCH LINE TO A **TERRIBLE JOKE!**
I WAS THINKING ABOUT PUNCHING HIM FOR YOU, TOO.
THROB THROB
BUT YOU PUNCHED HIM SO MANY TIMES, I FELT SATISFIED JUST WATCHING.
HOW LOVELY FOR YOU.
STILL, YOU KNOW... TRUE LOVE CAN MAKE PEOPLE DO CRAZY THINGS.

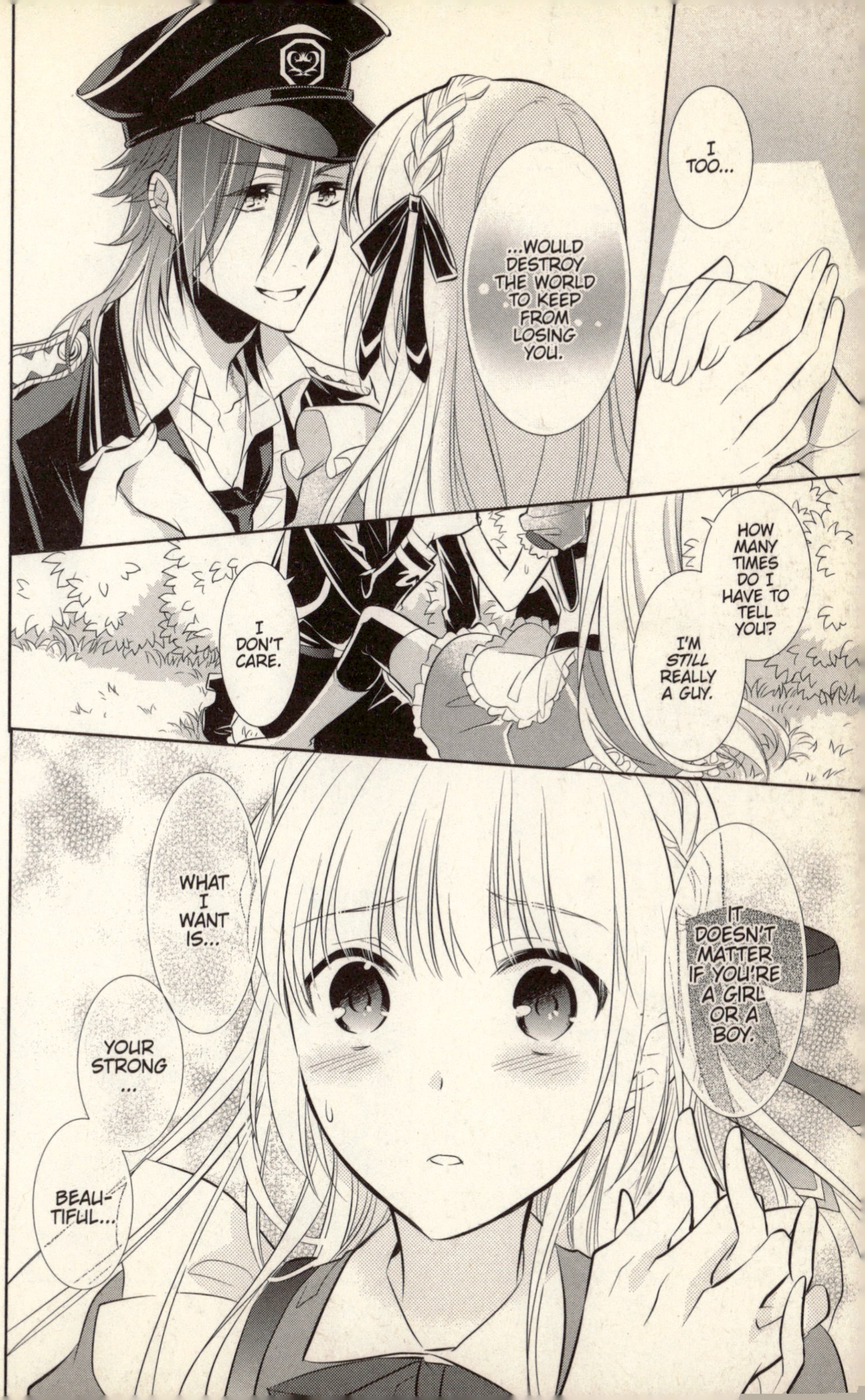
I TOO...
...WOULD DESTROY THE WORLD TO KEEP FROM LOSING YOU.
HOW MANY TIMES DO I HAVE TO TELL YOU?
I'M *STILL* REALLY A GUY.
I DON'T CARE.
IT DOESN'T MATTER IF YOU'RE A GIRL OR A BOY.
WHAT I WANT IS...
YOUR STRONG ...
BEAU-TIFUL...

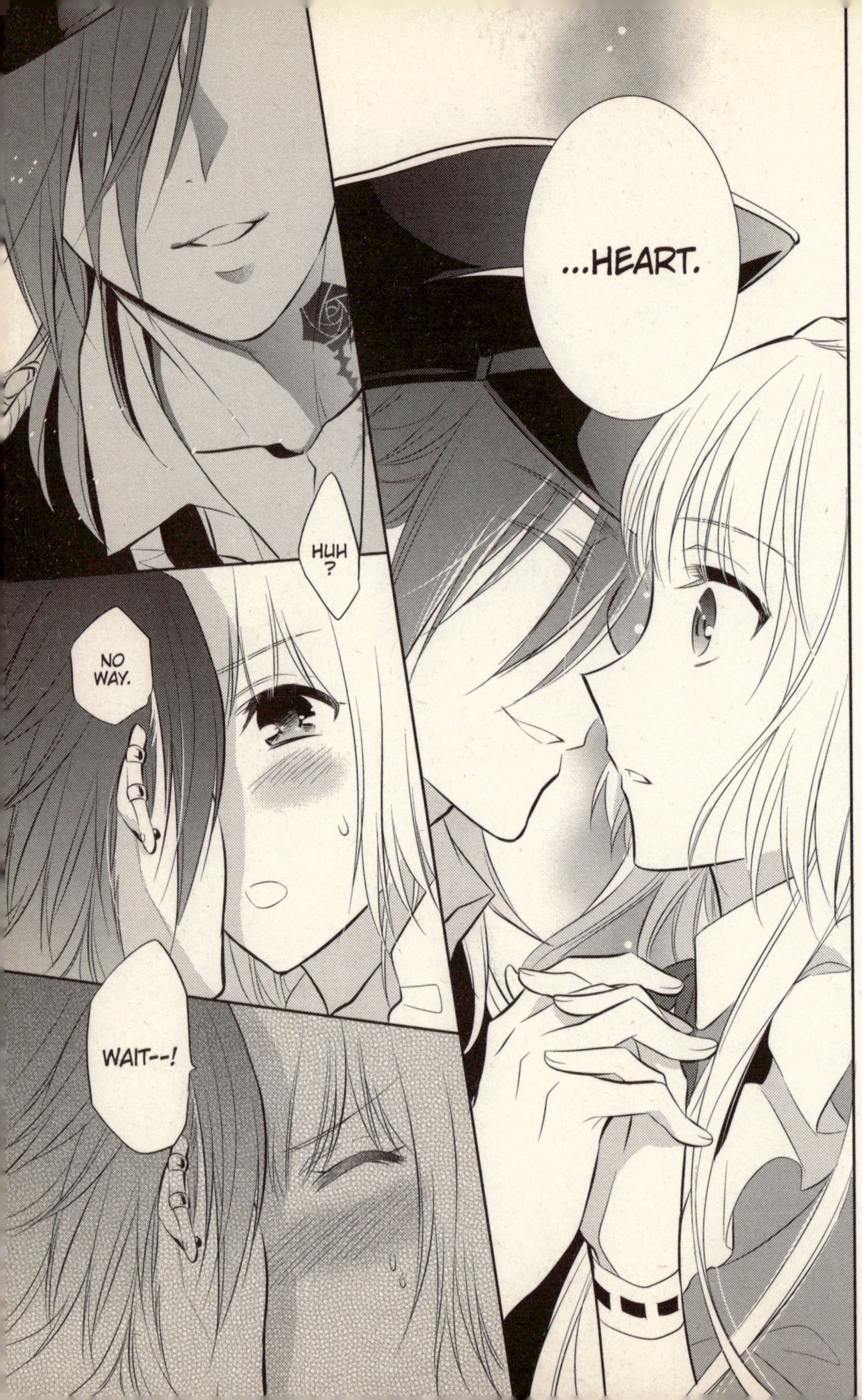
...HEART.
HUH?
NO WAY.
WAIT--!

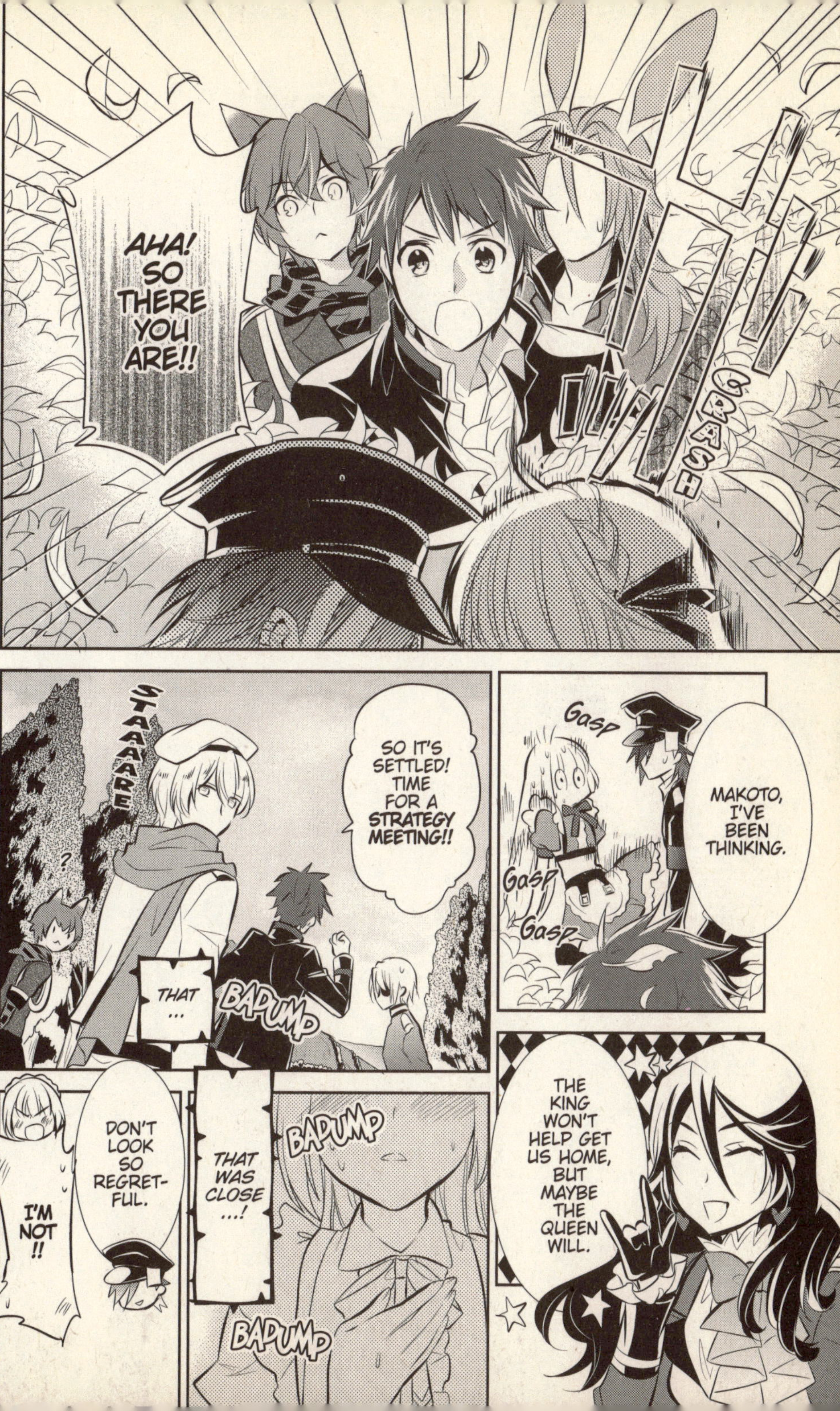
AHA! SO THERE YOU ARE!!
CRASH
Gasp
MAKOTO, I'VE BEEN THINKING.
Gasp
Gasp
SO IT'S SETTLED! TIME FOR A STRATEGY MEETING!!
STAAAARE
?
THAT ...
BADUMP
THE KING WON'T HELP GET US HOME, BUT MAYBE THE QUEEN WILL.
BADUMP
THAT WAS CLOSE ...!
BADUMP
DON'T LOOK SO REGRET-FUL.
I'M NOT!!

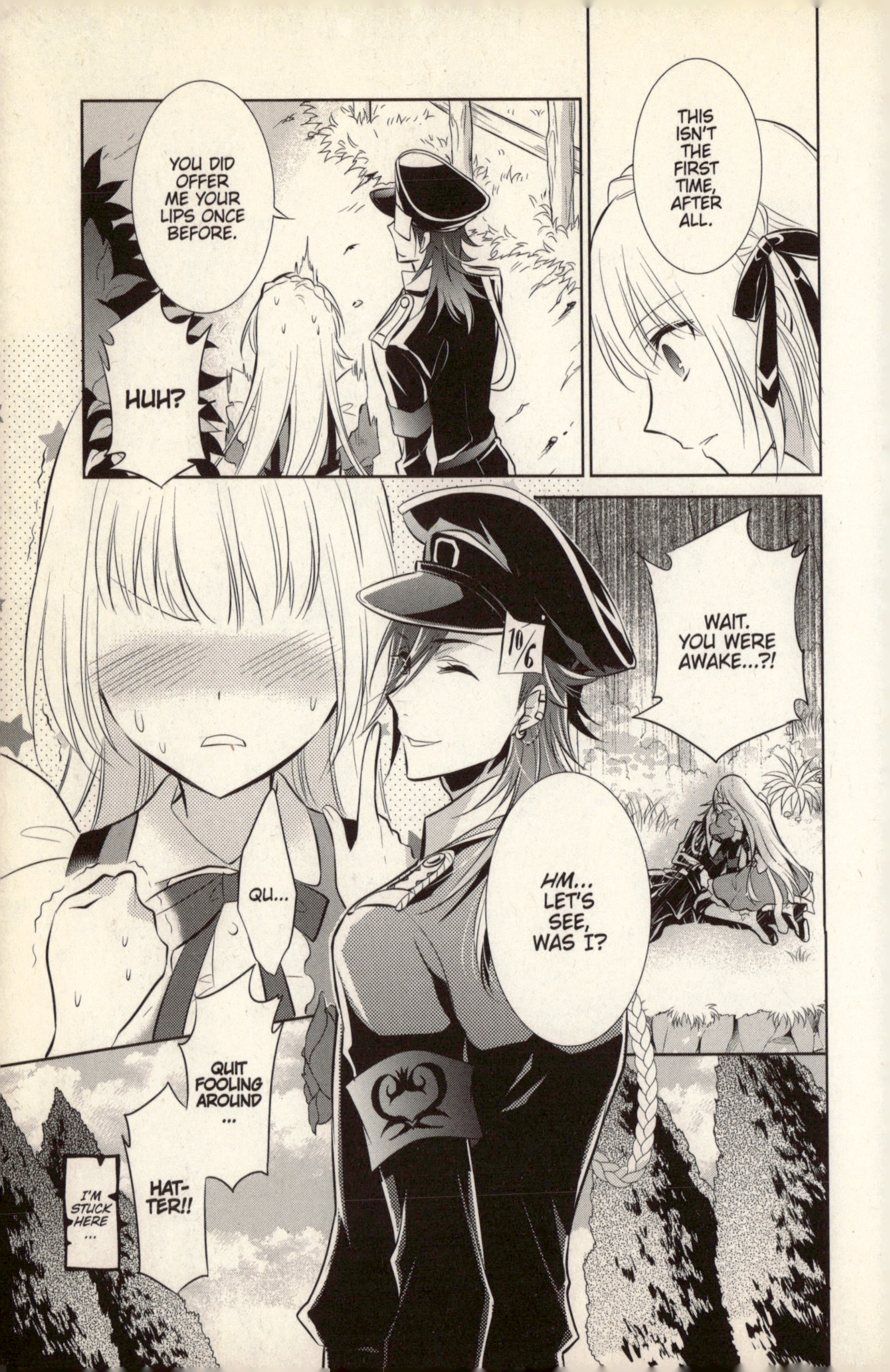
THIS ISN'T THE FIRST TIME, AFTER ALL.
YOU DID OFFER ME YOUR LIPS ONCE BEFORE.
HUH?
WAIT. YOU WERE AWAKE...?!
HM... LET'S SEE, WAS I?
QU...
QUIT FOOLING AROUND ...
HAT-TER!!
I'M STUCK HERE ...

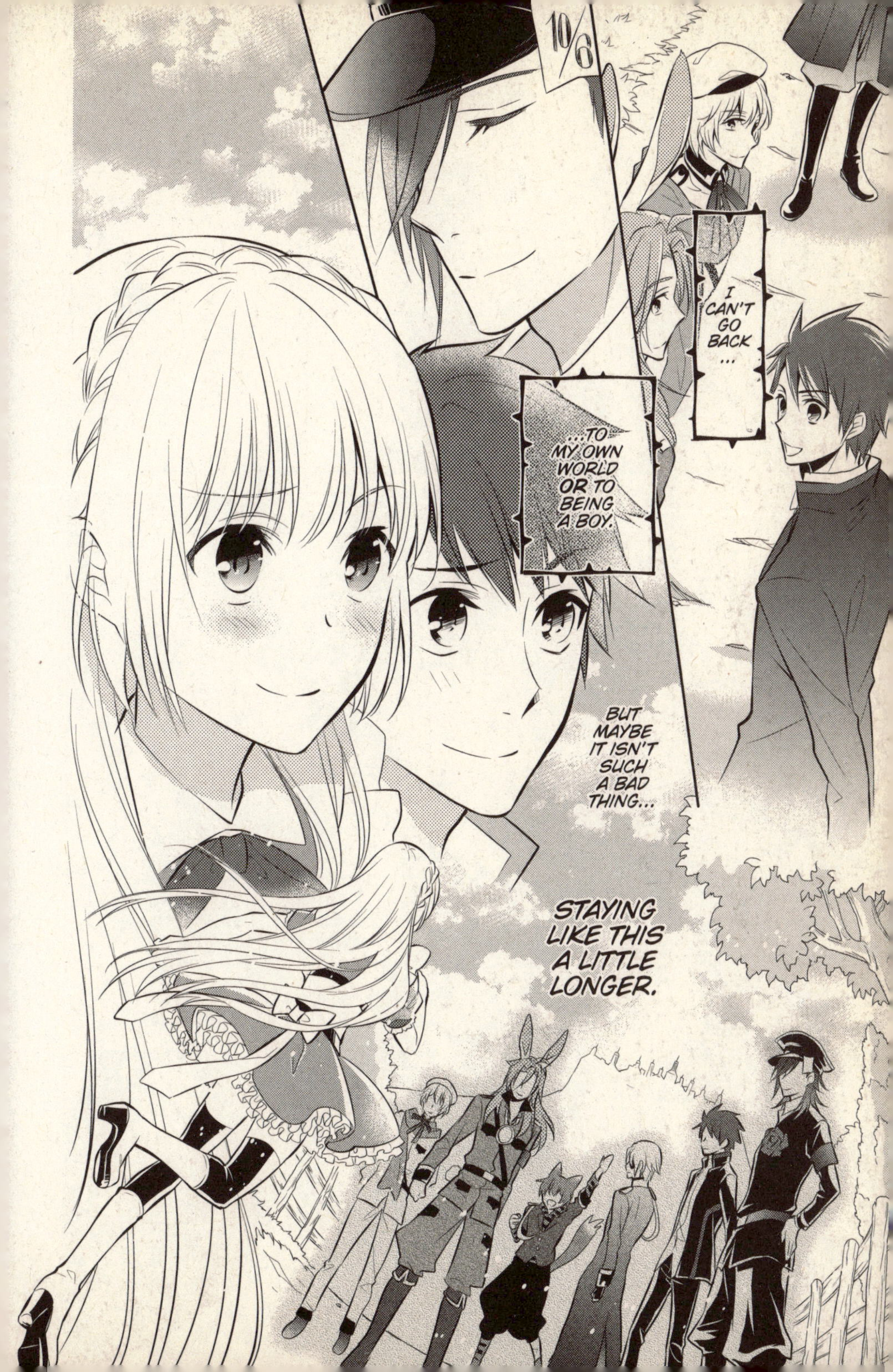
10/6
I CAN'T GO BACK...
...TO MY OWN WORLD OR TO BEING A BOY.
BUT MAYBE IT ISN'T SUCH A BAD THING...
STAYING LIKE THIS A LITTLE LONGER.

FIN

I Am Alice:
Body Swap in
Wonderland

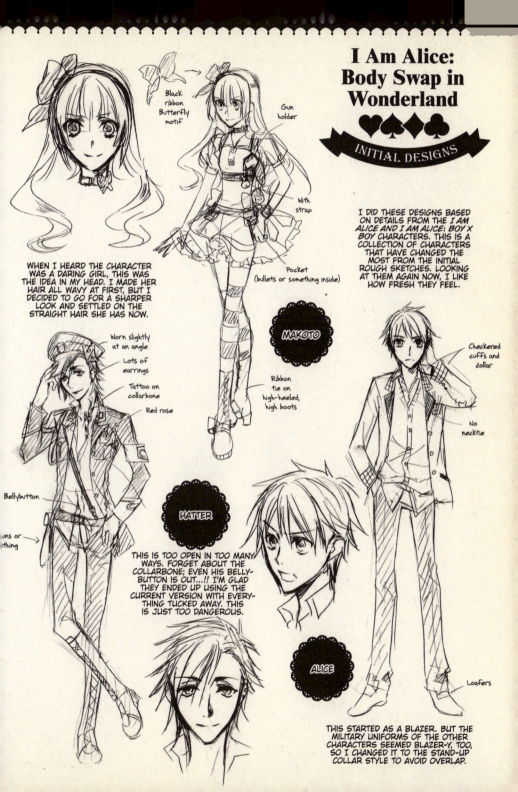

I Am Alice: Body Swap in Wonderland

INITIAL DESIGNS

I DID THESE DESIGNS BASED ON DETAILS FROM THE *I AM ALICE AND I AM ALICE: BOY X BOY* CHARACTERS. THIS IS A COLLECTION OF CHARACTERS THAT HAVE CHANGED THE MOST FROM THE INITIAL ROUGH SKETCHES. LOOKING AT THEM AGAIN NOW, I LIKE HOW FRESH THEY FEEL.

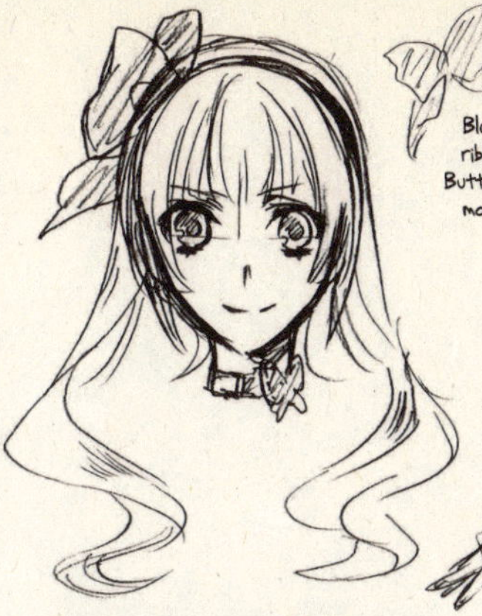

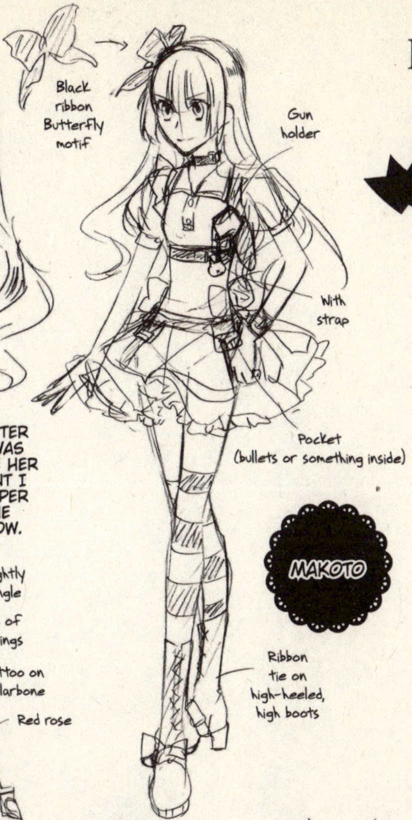
Black ribbon Butterfly motif
Gun holder
With strap
Pocket (bullets or something inside)
Ribbon tie on high-heeled, high boots

MAKOTO

WHEN I HEARD THE CHARACTER WAS A DARING GIRL, THIS WAS THE IDEA IN MY HEAD. I MADE HER HAIR ALL WAVY AT FIRST, BUT I DECIDED TO GO FOR A SHARPER LOOK AND SETTLED ON THE STRAIGHT HAIR SHE HAS NOW.

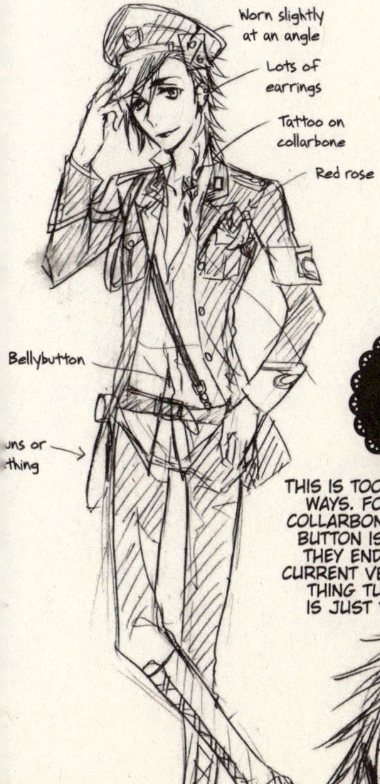
Worn slightly at an angle
Lots of earrings
Tattoo on collarbone
Red rose
Bellybutton

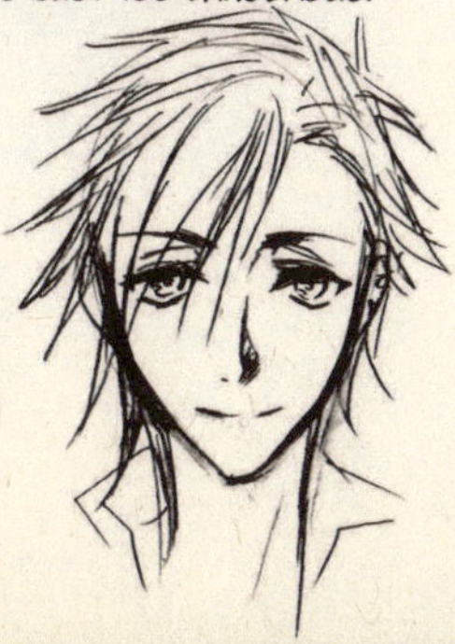

HATTER

THIS IS TOO OPEN IN TOO MANY WAYS. FORGET ABOUT THE COLLARBONE; EVEN HIS BELLY-BUTTON IS OUT...!! I'M GLAD THEY ENDED UP USING THE CURRENT VERSION WITH EVERY-THING TUCKED AWAY. THIS IS JUST TOO DANGEROUS.

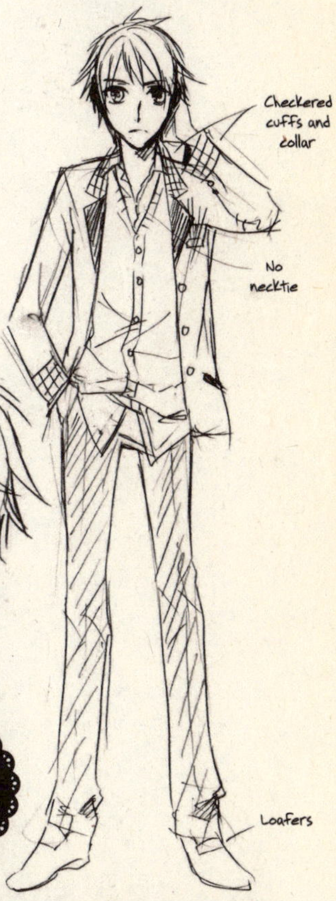
Checkered cuffs and collar
No necktie
Loafers

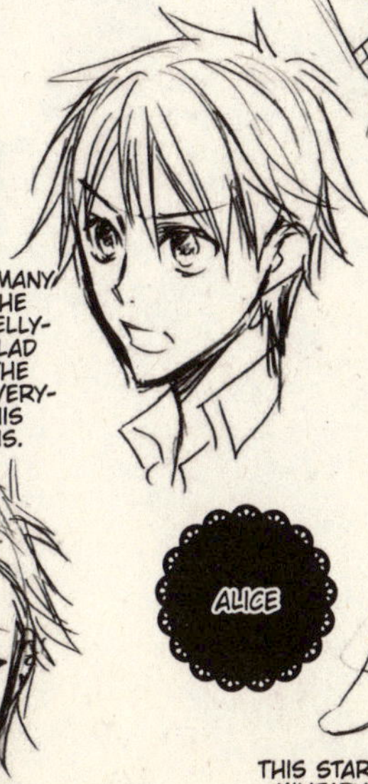

ALICE

THIS STARTED AS A BLAZER. BUT THE MILITARY UNIFORMS OF THE OTHER CHARACTERS SEEMED BLAZER-Y, TOO, SO I CHANGED IT TO THE STAND-UP COLLAR STYLE TO AVOID OVERLAP.

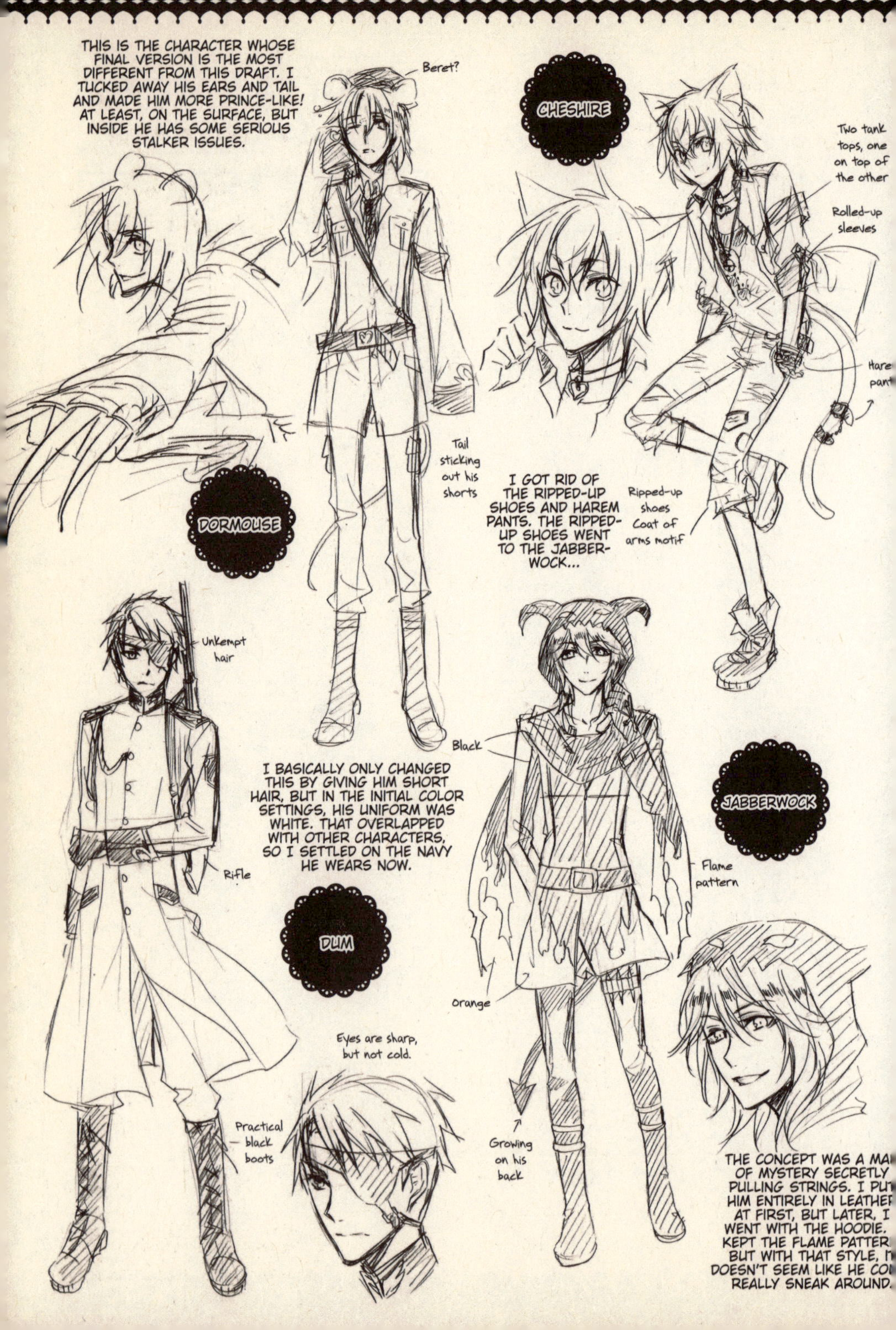
THIS IS THE CHARACTER WHOSE FINAL VERSION IS THE MOST DIFFERENT FROM THIS DRAFT. I TUCKED AWAY HIS EARS AND TAIL AND MADE HIM MORE PRINCE-LIKE! AT LEAST, ON THE SURFACE, BUT INSIDE HE HAS SOME SERIOUS STALKER ISSUES.
Beret?
CHESHIRE
Two tank tops, one on top of the other
Rolled-up sleeves
Hare pant
Tail sticking out his shorts
I GOT RID OF THE RIPPED-UP SHOES AND HAREM PANTS. THE RIPPED-UP SHOES WENT TO THE JABBERWOCK...
Ripped-up shoes
Coat of arms motif
DORMOUSE
Unkempt hair
Black
I BASICALLY ONLY CHANGED THIS BY GIVING HIM SHORT HAIR, BUT IN THE INITIAL COLOR SETTINGS, HIS UNIFORM WAS WHITE. THAT OVERLAPPED WITH OTHER CHARACTERS, SO I SETTLED ON THE NAVY HE WEARS NOW.
JABBERWOCK
Rifle
Flame pattern
DUM
Orange
Eyes are sharp, but not cold.
Practical black boots
Growing on his back
THE CONCEPT WAS A MA OF MYSTERY SECRETLY PULLING STRINGS. I PU HIM ENTIRELY IN LEATHE AT FIRST, BUT LATER, I WENT WITH THE HOODIE. KEPT THE FLAME PATTER BUT WITH THAT STYLE, I DOESN'T SEEM LIKE HE CO REALLY SNEAK AROUND.

Hi there. Nice to see you here. This is Kanou Ayumi. This is the final curtain for the manga version of *I Am Alice: Body Swap in Wonderland* that I've sent out to you in the last three volumes.

"So will Makoto get back to being a boy in the end?! And what is the true intention of the Queen of Hearts?! All mysteries will be revealed!" The story continues in *I Am Alice: Boy x Boy*, available now to rave reviews!!

In other words, please go and check out the game now. This is not stealth marketing; it is blatant marketing!!

Although... it wouldn't be good to end with me shilling for the game, so here are some secrets about the production of the manga!

I think it was at the beginning of 2011 that I was approached about doing the character designs for *I Am Alice*, and around summer of 2012 that the decision was made to start the manga version. I didn't expect at all to be drawing the manga, so I was totally surprised and found myself saying, "Who put them in these complicated clothes?" Especially Makoto, who I had to draw the most... (Frills everywhere...!) He's the protagonist, and he took the most time to draw. And all the hot guys everywhere... I'm not good at drawing hot guys, so I got confused about what a hot guy was, and started to get hot guy fevers. Hot guys = Gestalt destruction.

And that's that. I guess there's no secrets after all...! I don't know when I'll get to see all of you next, but I'll work hard so that we can meet again at the bookstore. Thank you so much for following *I Am Alice: Body Swap in Wonderland* right up to the end!

Autumn 2013 Kanou Ayumi

Special Thanks
Visual Works
MF Gene Editorial Dept.
My supervisor, Y-san
Designer Morohashi-sama
Yukina-san, K-yama-san, my family
All my readers!

WANT TO GO HOME, CAN'T GO HOME
SO WE SPOKE WITH THE QUEEN.
I SEE. YOU WANT TO GO BACK TO YOUR ORIGINAL WORLD.
HMMM. I WAS JUST THINKING OF HOLDING A REALLY FABULOUS FESTIVAL~!
FESTI-VAL?
NOW THAT YOU MENTION IT, IT SEEMED LIKE YOU WERE PLANNING SOMETHING, BUT WHAT?
So did Jabberwock...
HEH HEH HEH! WELL, YOU SEE...
I Am Alice 3
YOU'LL HAVE TO CHECK OUT THE GAME FOR THE REST!
I Am Alice: Boy x Boy Available Now Rave-Reviews!!
CRAP! LOOKS LIKE WE WON'T BE GETTING HOME THAT EASY.

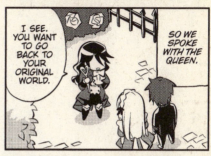

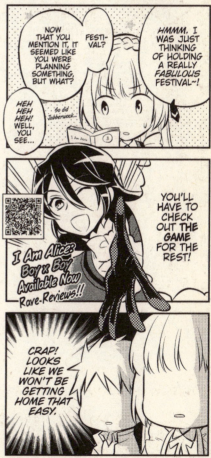

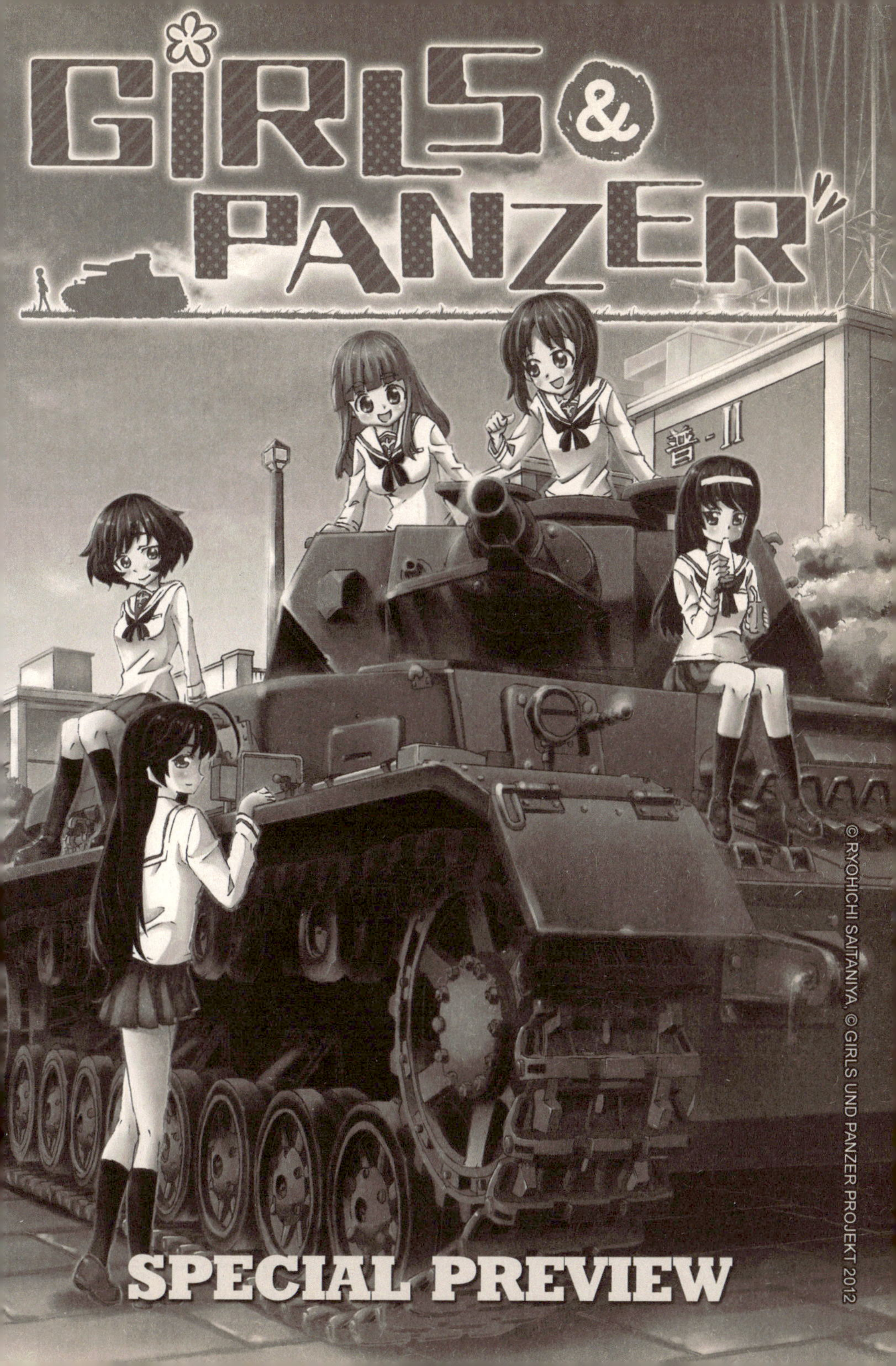
GIRLS &
PANZER
普-II
SPECIAL PREVIEW

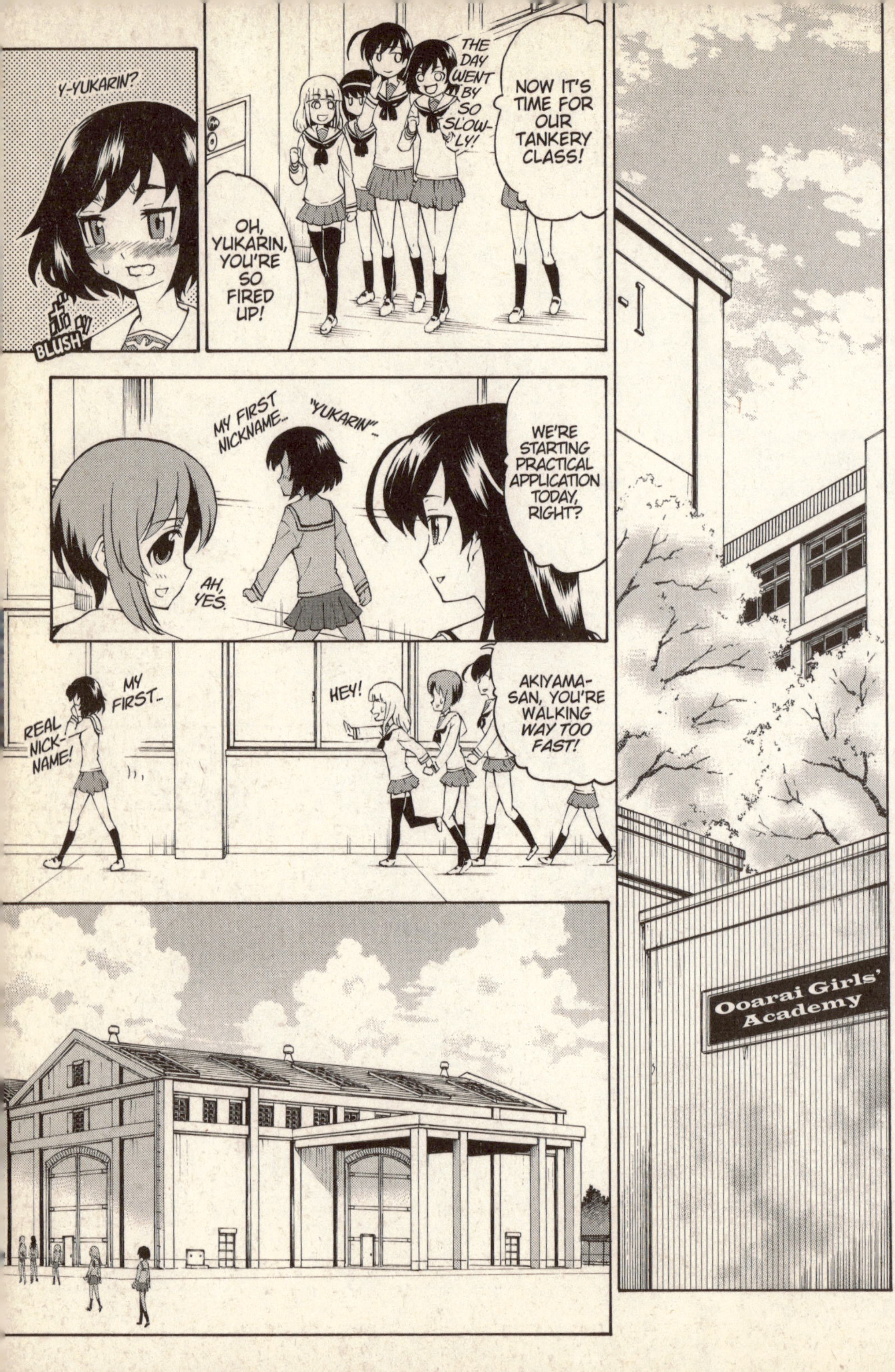
Ooarai Girls' Academy
NOW IT'S TIME FOR OUR TANKERY CLASS!
THE DAY WENT BY SO SLOWLY!
OH, YUKARIN, YOU'RE SO FIRED UP!
Y-YUKARIN?
BLUSH
WE'RE STARTING PRACTICAL APPLICATION TODAY, RIGHT?
"YUKARIN"...
MY FIRST NICKNAME...
AH, YES.
AKIYAMA-SAN, YOU'RE WALKING WAY TOO FAST!
HEY!
MY FIRST...
REAL NICK-NAME!

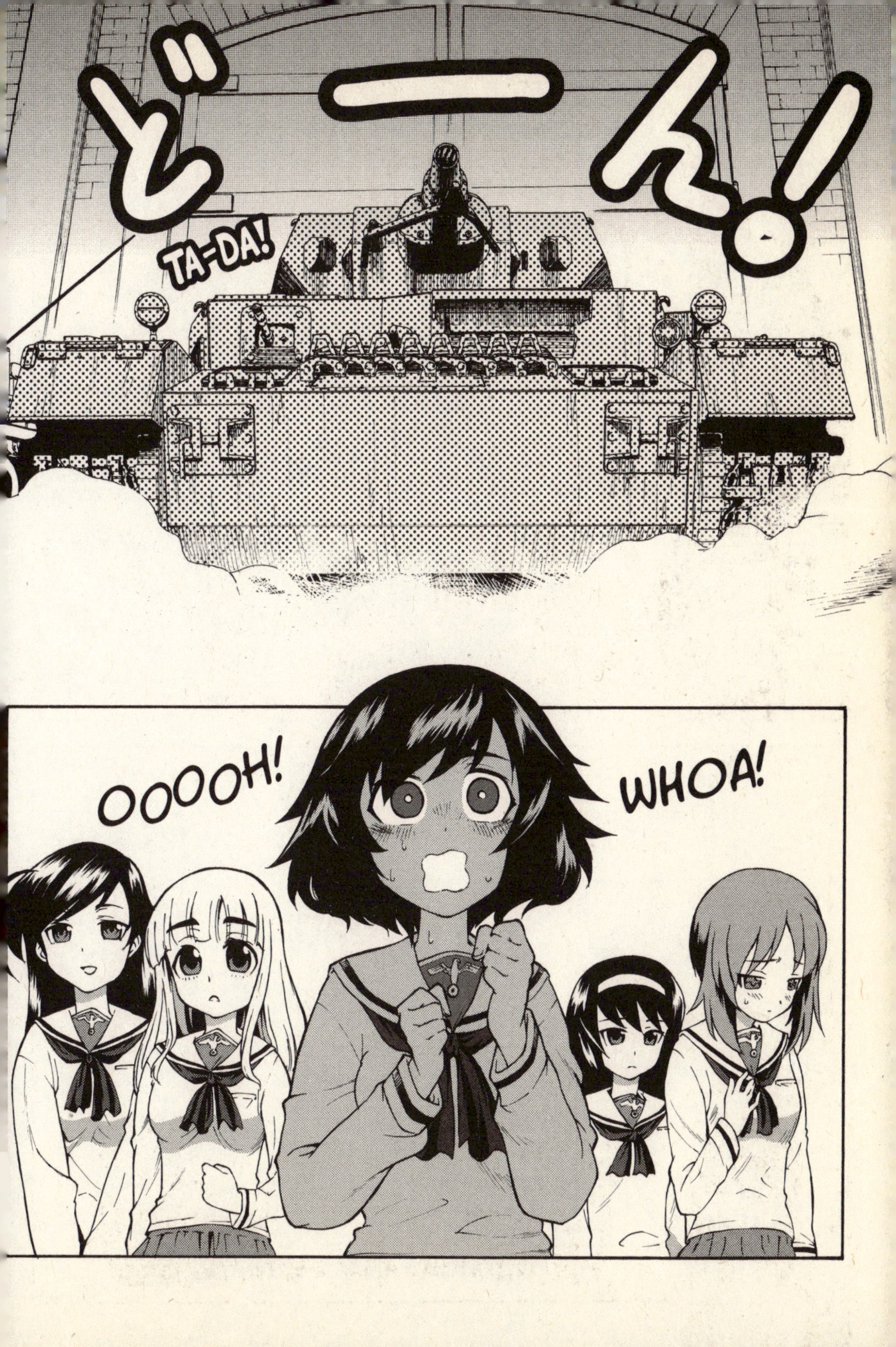
どーん!
TA-DA!
WHOA!
OOOOH!

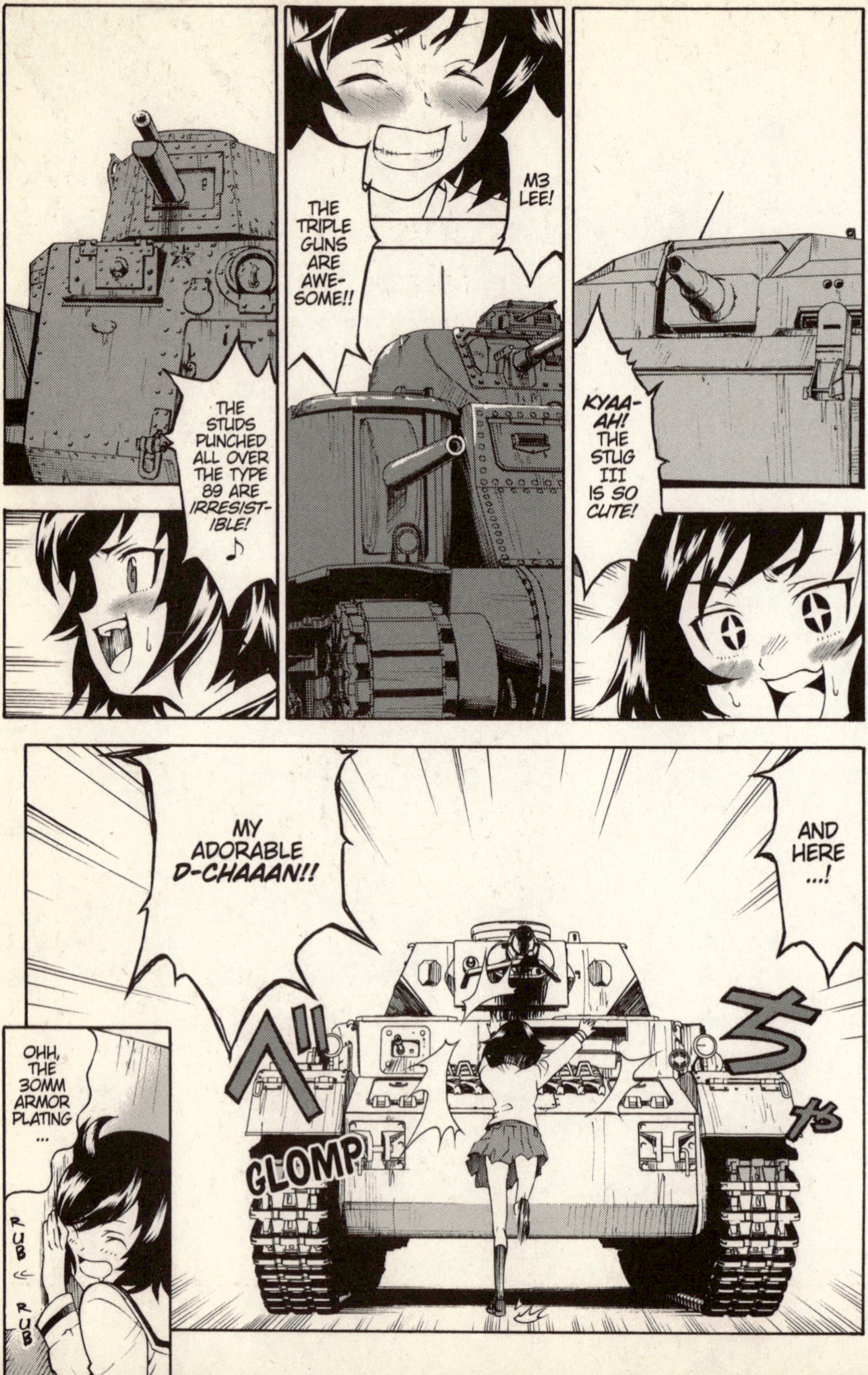
KYAA-AH! THE STUG III IS SO CUTE!
M3 LEE!
THE TRIPLE GUNS ARE AWESOME!!
THE STUDS PUNCHED ALL OVER THE TYPE 89 ARE IRRESISTIBLE! ♪
AND HERE ...!
MY ADORABLE D-CHAAAN!!
べちゃ
GLOMP
OHH, THE 30MM ARMOR PLATING ...
RUB RUB

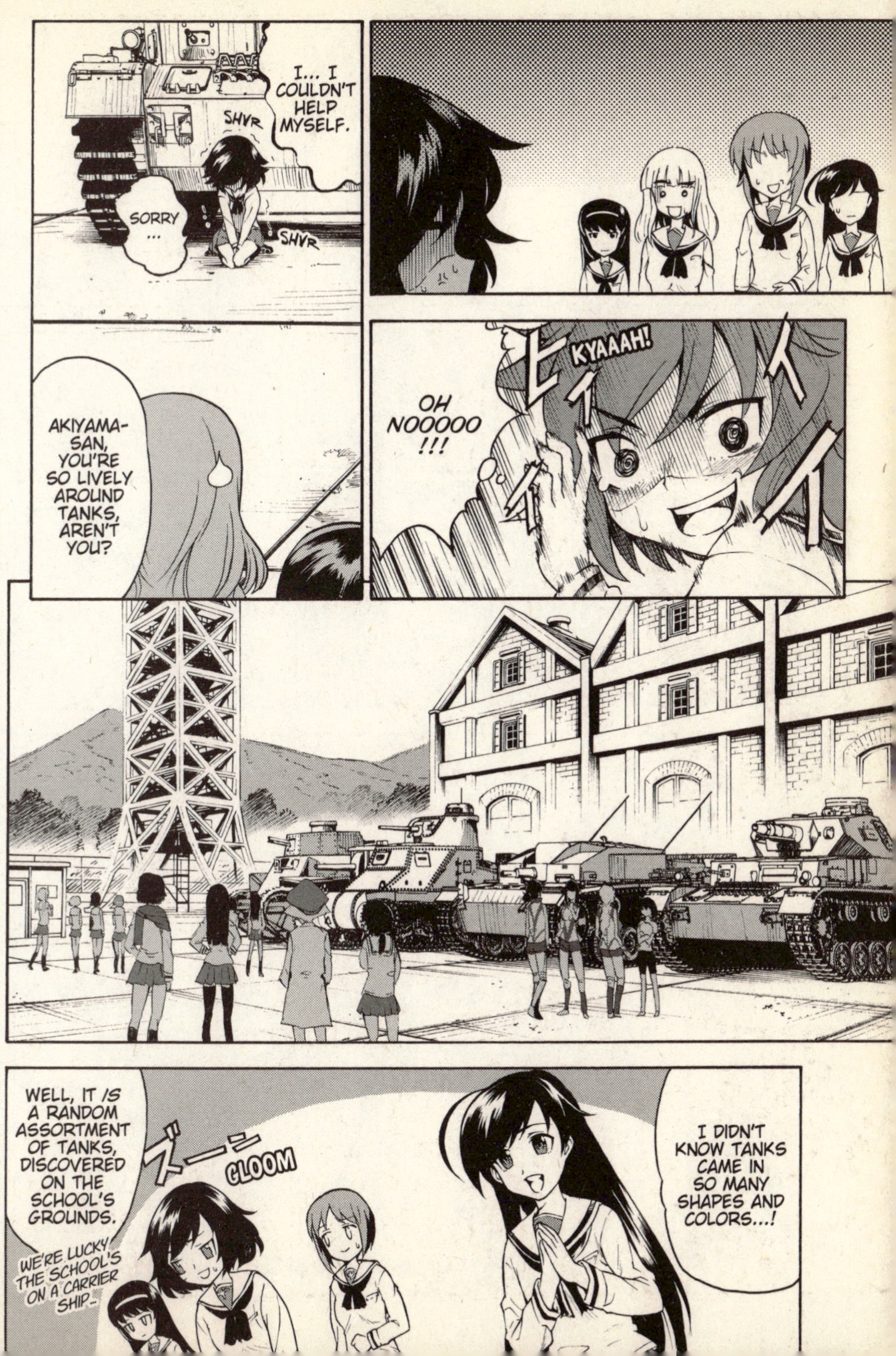
I... I COULDN'T HELP MYSELF.
SHVR
SORRY ...
SHVR
KYAAAH!
OH NOOOOO !!!
AKIYAMA-SAN, YOU'RE SO LIVELY AROUND TANKS, AREN'T YOU?
I DIDN'T KNOW TANKS CAME IN SO MANY SHAPES AND COLORS...!
GLOOM
WELL, IT IS A RANDOM ASSORTMENT OF TANKS, DISCOVERED ON THE SCHOOL'S GROUNDS.
WE'RE LUCKY THE SCHOOL'S ON A CARRIER SHIP...

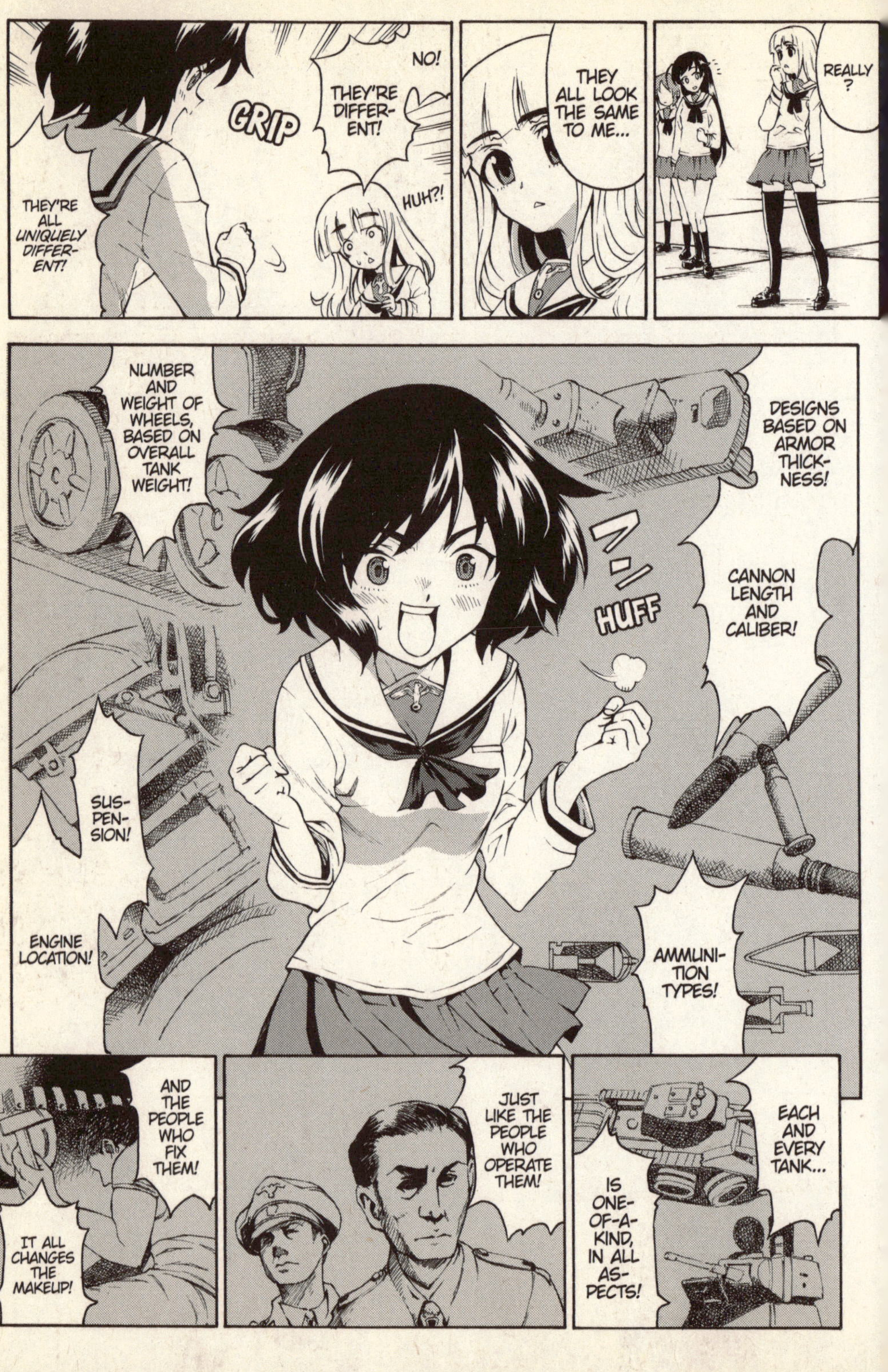
REALLY?
THEY ALL LOOK THE SAME TO ME...
NO!
THEY'RE DIFFERENT!
GRIP
HUH?!
THEY'RE ALL UNIQUELY DIFFERENT!
DESIGNS BASED ON ARMOR THICKNESS!
NUMBER AND WEIGHT OF WHEELS, BASED ON OVERALL TANK WEIGHT!
CANNON LENGTH AND CALIBER!
フン!
HUFF
SUSPENSION!
AMMUNITION TYPES!
ENGINE LOCATION!
EACH AND EVERY TANK...
IS ONE-OF-A-KIND, IN ALL ASPECTS!
JUST LIKE THE PEOPLE WHO OPERATE THEM!
AND THE PEOPLE WHO FIX THEM!
IT ALL CHANGES THE MAKEUP!

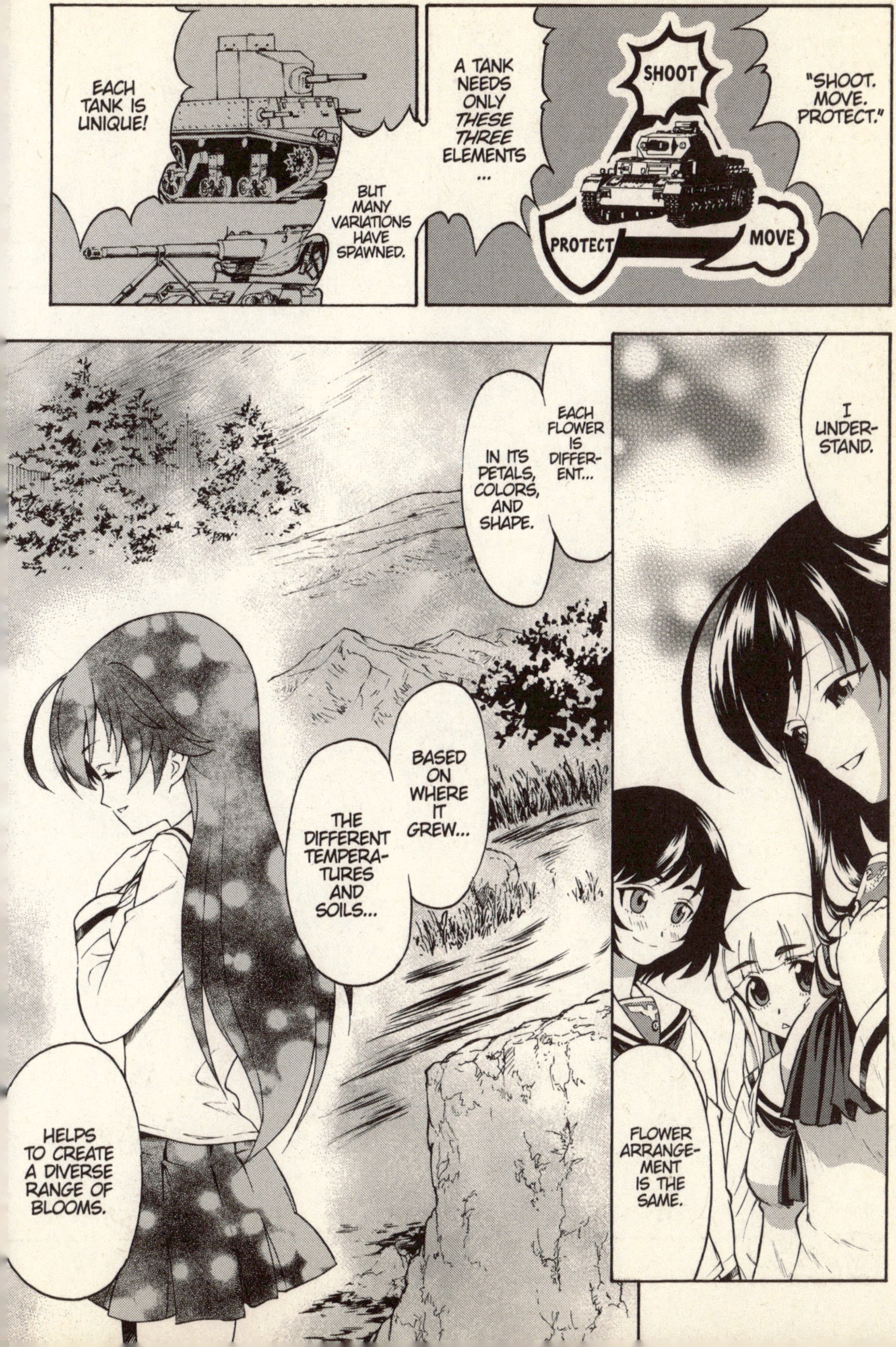
"SHOOT. MOVE. PROTECT."
SHOOT
A TANK NEEDS ONLY THESE THREE ELEMENTS...
MOVE
PROTECT
BUT MANY VARIATIONS HAVE SPAWNED.
EACH TANK IS UNIQUE!
I UNDER-STAND.
FLOWER ARRANGE-MENT IS THE SAME.
EACH FLOWER IS DIFFER-ENT...
IN ITS PETALS, COLORS, AND SHAPE.
BASED ON WHERE IT GREW...
THE DIFFERENT TEMPERA-TURES AND SOILS...
HELPS TO CREATE A DIVERSE RANGE OF BLOOMS.

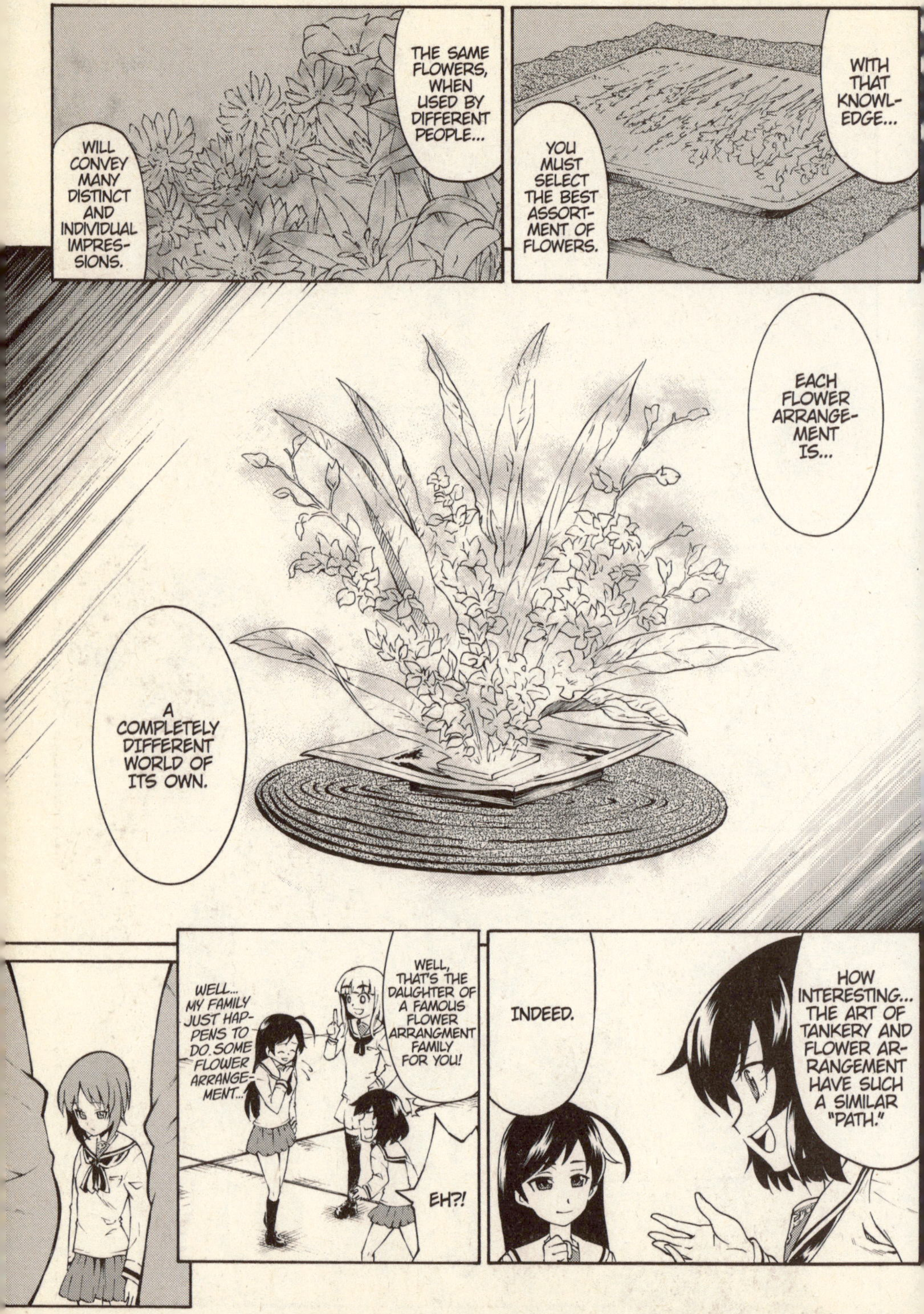
WITH THAT KNOWLEDGE...
YOU MUST SELECT THE BEST ASSORTMENT OF FLOWERS.
THE SAME FLOWERS, WHEN USED BY DIFFERENT PEOPLE...
WILL CONVEY MANY DISTINCT AND INDIVIDUAL IMPRESSIONS.
EACH FLOWER ARRANGEMENT IS...
A COMPLETELY DIFFERENT WORLD OF ITS OWN.
HOW INTERESTING... THE ART OF TANKERY AND FLOWER ARRANGEMENT HAVE SUCH A SIMILAR "PATH."
INDEED.
WELL, THAT'S THE DAUGHTER OF A FAMOUS FLOWER ARRANGMENT FAMILY FOR YOU!
WELL... MY FAMILY JUST HAPPENS TO DO SOME FLOWER ARRANGEMENT...
EH?!

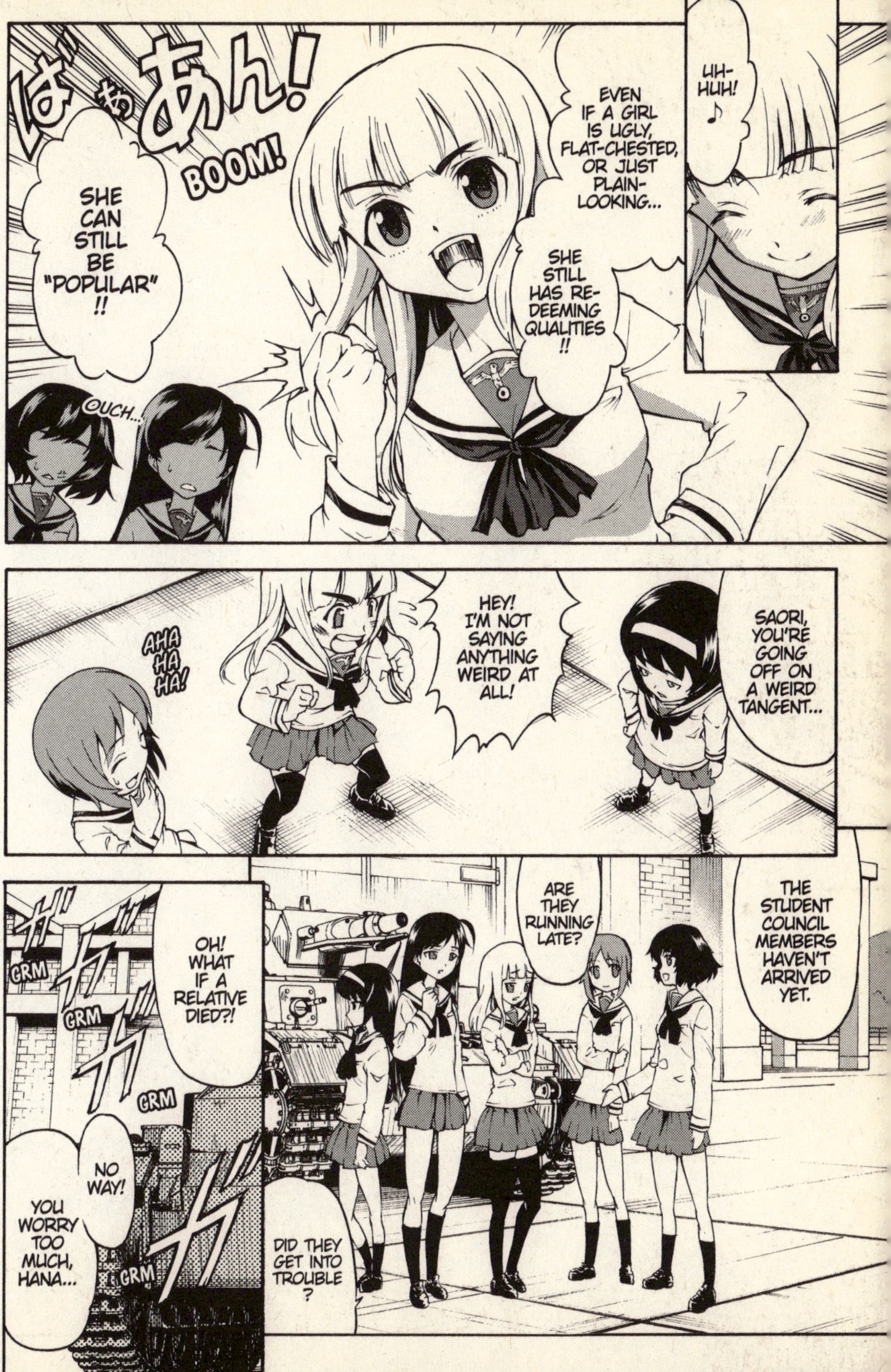
UH-HUH! ♪
EVEN IF A GIRL IS UGLY, FLAT-CHESTED, OR JUST PLAIN-LOOKING...
SHE STILL HAS RE-DEEMING QUALITIES!!
ばあん!
BOOM!
SHE CAN STILL BE "POPULAR"!!
OUCH...
SAORI, YOU'RE GOING OFF ON A WEIRD TANGENT...
HEY! I'M NOT SAYING ANYTHING WEIRD AT ALL!
AHA HA HA!
THE STUDENT COUNCIL MEMBERS HAVEN'T ARRIVED YET.
ARE THEY RUNNING LATE?
OH! WHAT IF A RELATIVE DIED?!
DID THEY GET INTO TROUBLE?
NO WAY!
YOU WORRY TOO MUCH, HANA...
GRM
GRM
GRM
GRM

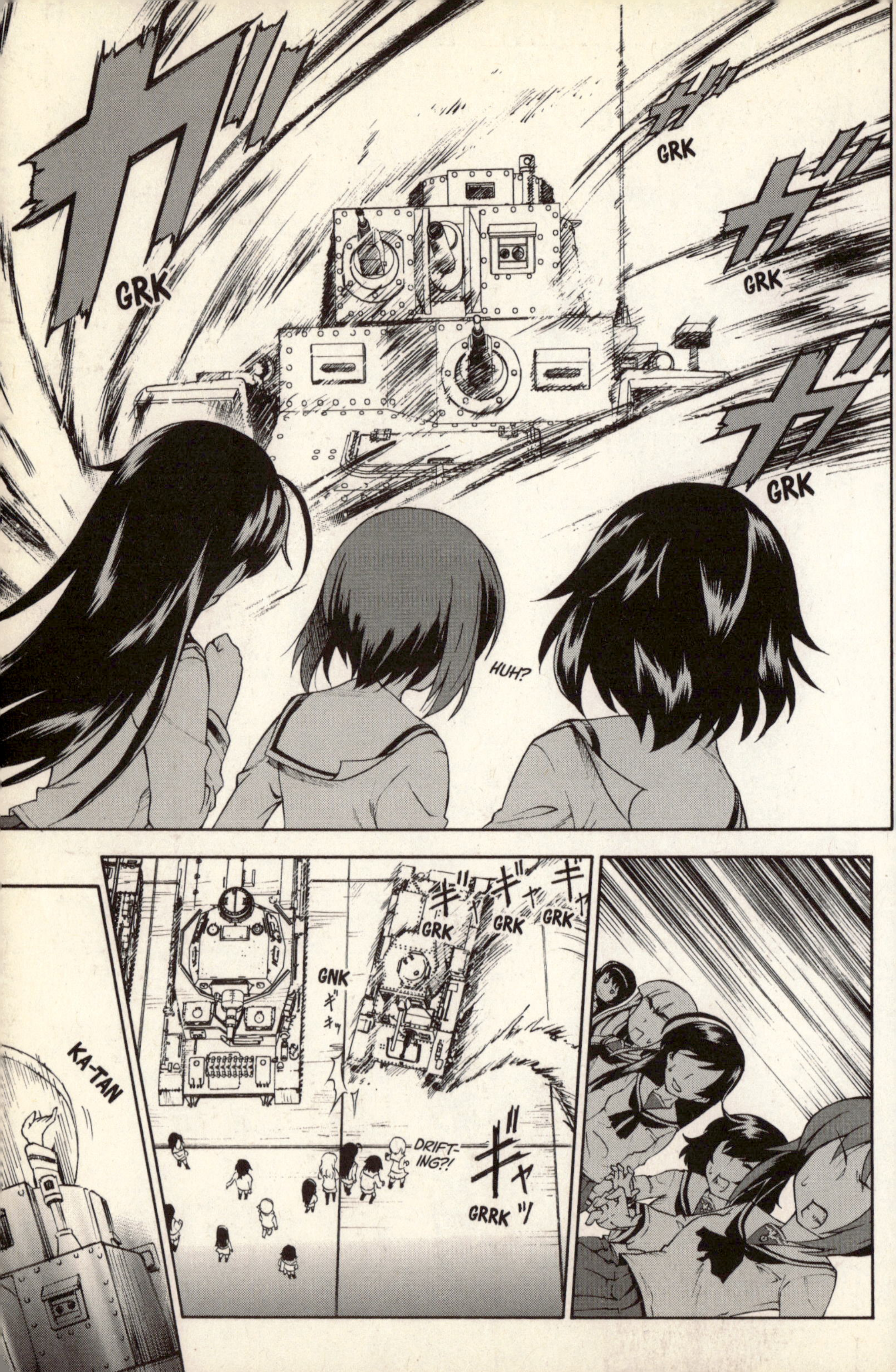
GRK
GRK
GRK
GRK
HUH?
GRK
GRK
GRK
GNK
DRIFTING?!
GRRK
KA-TAN

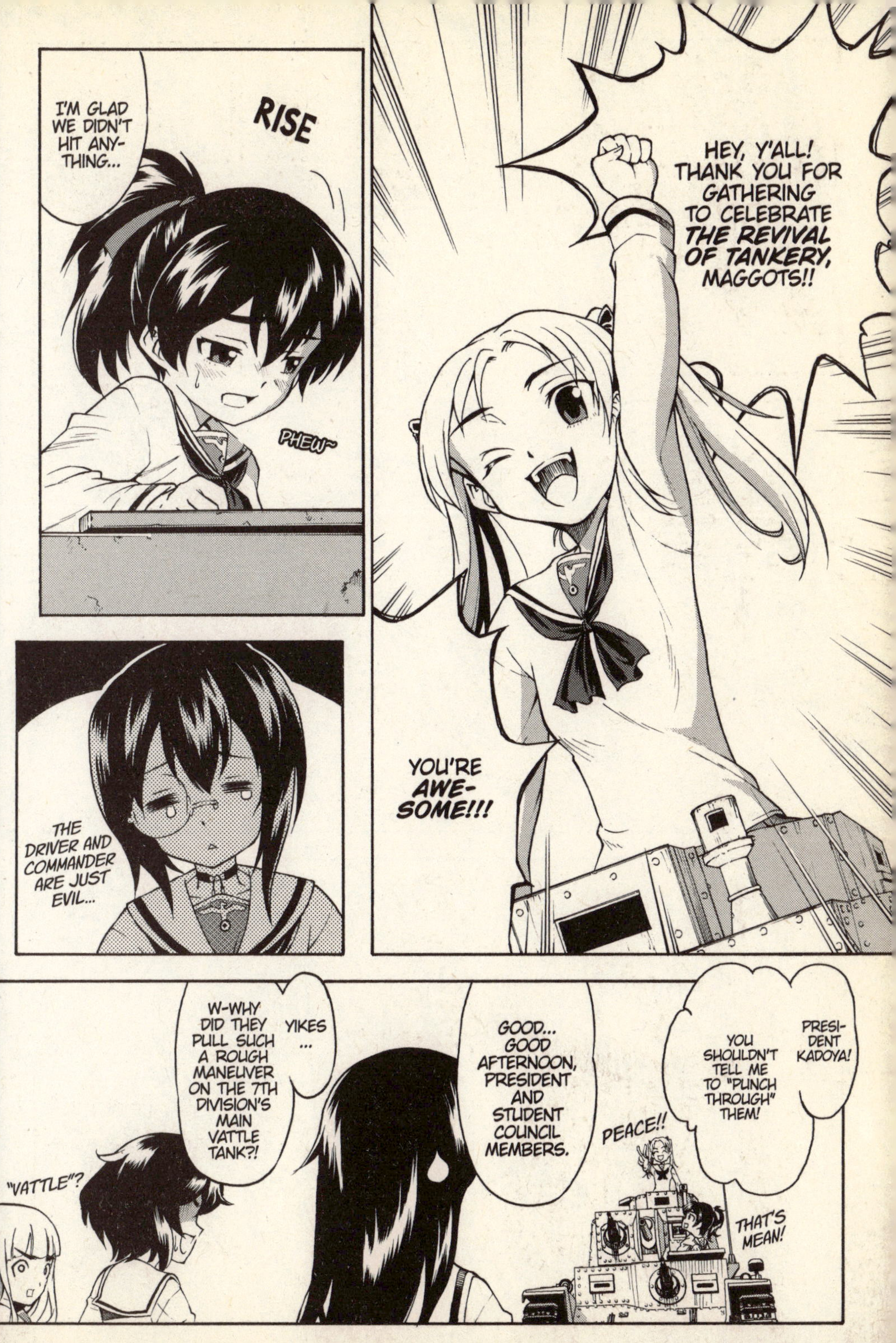
HEY, Y'ALL! THANK YOU FOR GATHERING TO CELEBRATE THE REVIVAL OF TANKERY, MAGGOTS!!
YOU'RE AWESOME!!!
I'M GLAD WE DIDN'T HIT ANYTHING...
RISE
PHEW~
THE DRIVER AND COMMANDER ARE JUST EVIL...
PRESIDENT KADOYA!
YOU SHOULDN'T TELL ME TO "PUNCH THROUGH" THEM!
PEACE!!
THAT'S MEAN!
GOOD... GOOD AFTERNOON, PRESIDENT AND STUDENT COUNCIL MEMBERS.
YIKES...
W-WHY DID THEY PULL SUCH A ROUGH MANEUVER ON THE 7TH DIVISION'S MAIN VATTLE TANK?!
"VATTLE"?

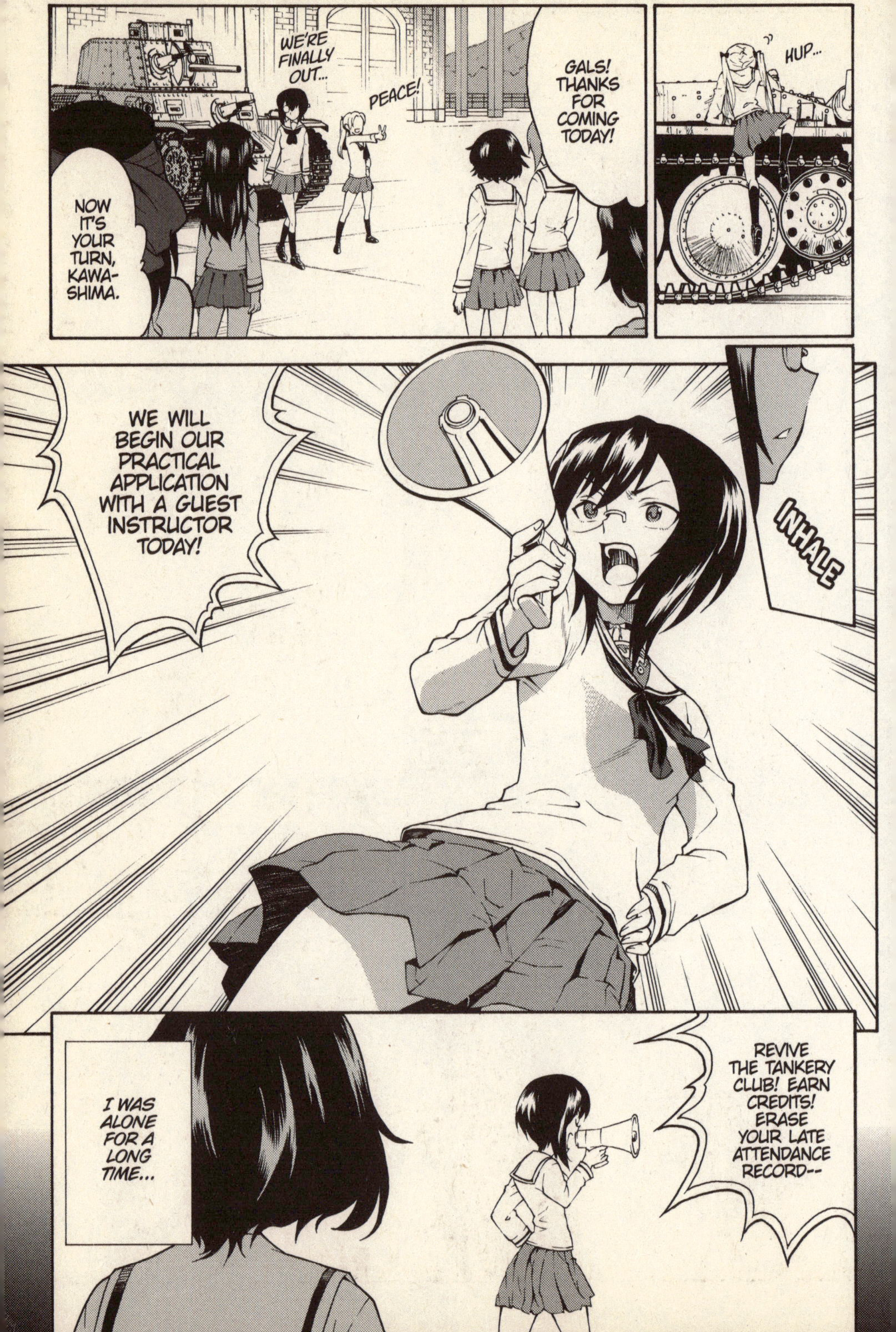
HUP...
GALS! THANKS FOR COMING TODAY!
PEACE!
WE'RE FINALLY OUT...
NOW IT'S YOUR TURN, KAWA-SHIMA.
INHALE
WE WILL BEGIN OUR PRACTICAL APPLICATION WITH A GUEST INSTRUCTOR TODAY!
REVIVE THE TANKERY CLUB! EARN CREDITS! ERASE YOUR LATE ATTENDANCE RECORD--
I WAS ALONE FOR A LONG TIME...

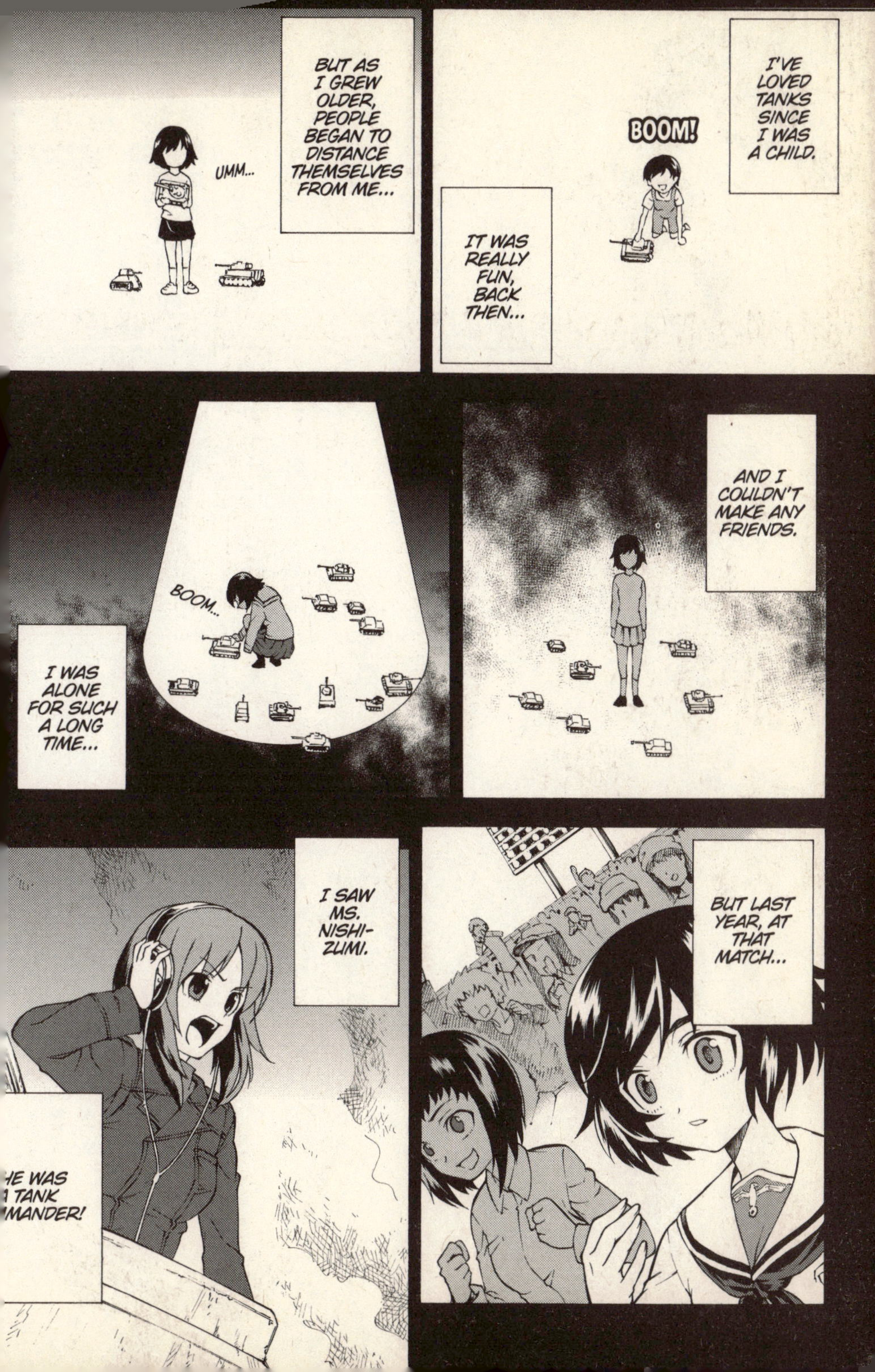
I'VE LOVED TANKS SINCE I WAS A CHILD.
BOOM!
IT WAS REALLY FUN, BACK THEN...
BUT AS I GREW OLDER, PEOPLE BEGAN TO DISTANCE THEMSELVES FROM ME...
UMM...
AND I COULDN'T MAKE ANY FRIENDS.
BOOM...
I WAS ALONE FOR SUCH A LONG TIME...
BUT LAST YEAR, AT THAT MATCH...
I SAW MS. NISHIZUMI.
HE WAS A TANK MANDER!

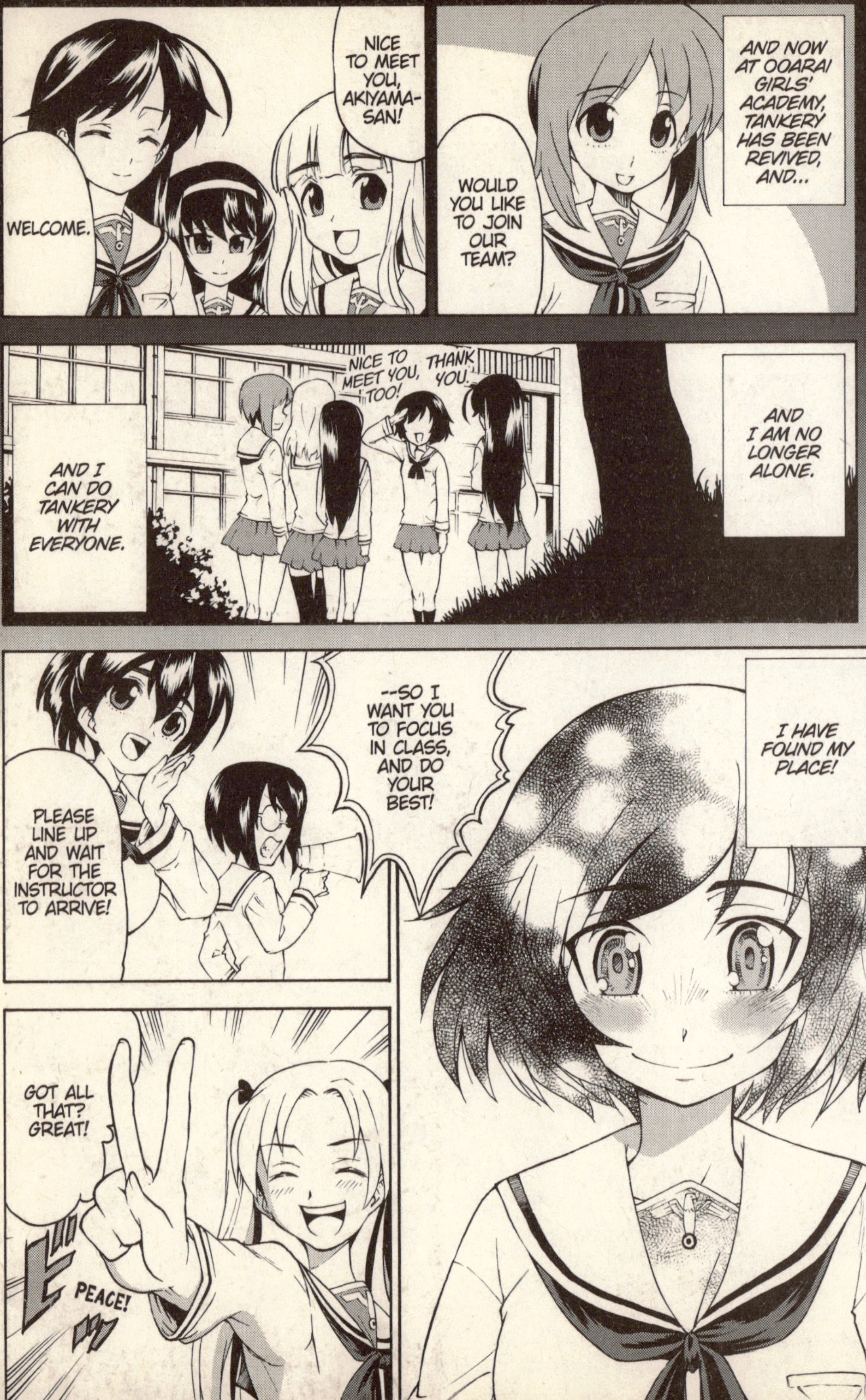
AND NOW AT OOARAI GIRLS' ACADEMY, TANKERY HAS BEEN REVIVED, AND...
WOULD YOU LIKE TO JOIN OUR TEAM?
NICE TO MEET YOU, AKIYAMA-SAN!
WELCOME.
AND I AM NO LONGER ALONE.
THANK YOU.
NICE TO MEET YOU, TOO!
AND I CAN DO TANKERY WITH EVERYONE.
I HAVE FOUND MY PLACE!
--SO I WANT YOU TO FOCUS IN CLASS, AND DO YOUR BEST!
PLEASE LINE UP AND WAIT FOR THE INSTRUCTOR TO ARRIVE!
GOT ALL THAT? GREAT!
PEACE!

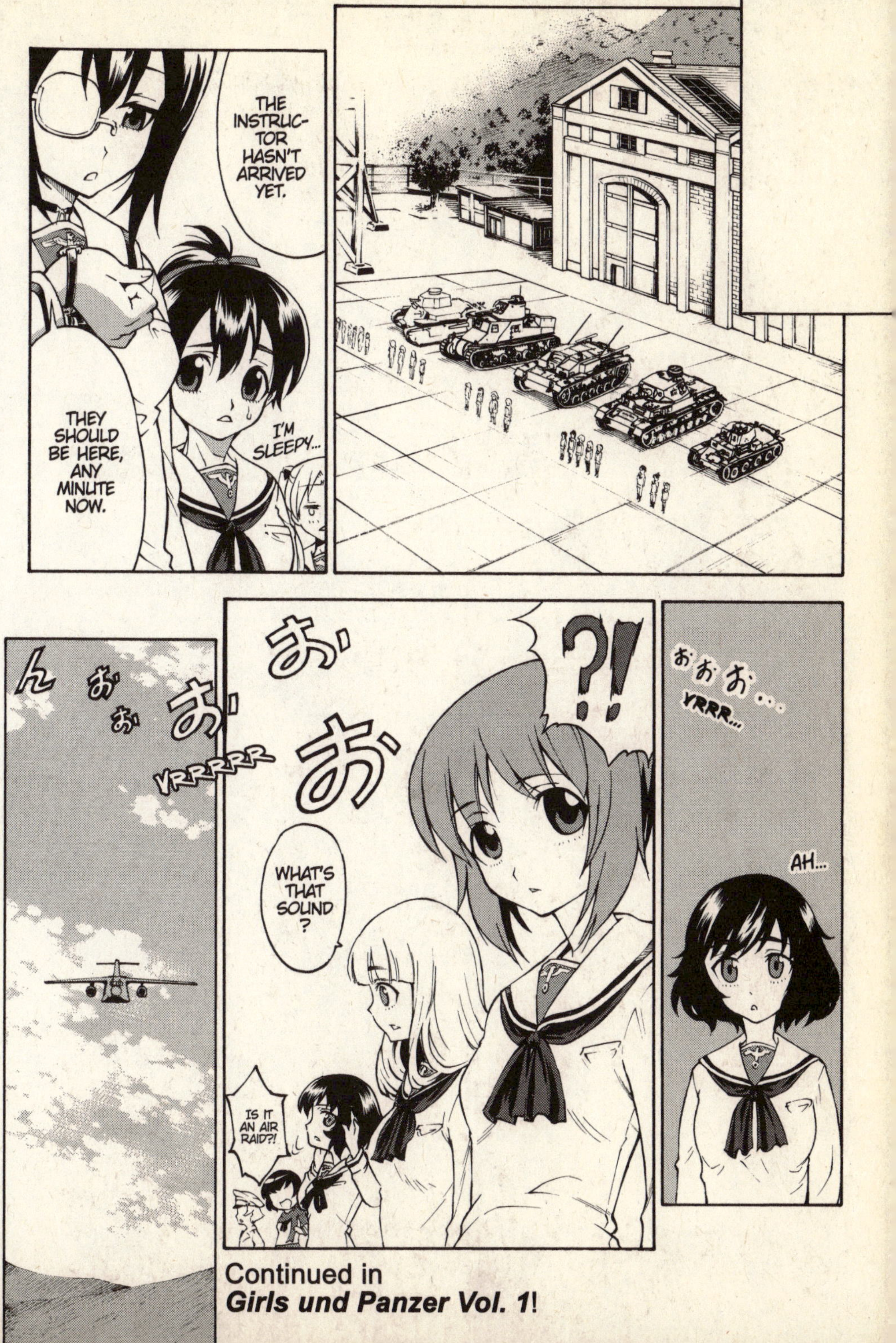

THE INSTRUCTOR HASN'T ARRIVED YET.
I'M SLEEPY...
THEY SHOULD BE HERE, ANY MINUTE NOW.
おおお…
YRRR...
AH...
?!
おお
WHAT'S THAT SOUND?
IS IT AN AIR RAID?!
んおおお
YRRRRR

Continued in
***Girls und Panzer Vol. 1*!**

P9-DNO-080

MAY 1 2 2015

BODY SWAP IN WONDERLAND

art by **KANOU AYUMI** / story by **VISUALWORKS**   **VOLUME 3**

TRANSLATION
Jocelyne Allen

ADAPTATION
Shanti Whitesides

LETTERING AND LAYOUT
Jennifer Skarupa

LOGO DESIGN
Phil Balsman

COVER DESIGN
Nicky Lim

PROOFREADER
Katherine Bell

MANAGING EDITOR
Adam Arnold

PUBLISHER
Jason DeAngelis

I AM ALICE: BODY SWAP IN WONDERLAND VOL. 3
© Kanou Ayumi 2013, © Visualworks 2013
Edited by MEDIA FACTORY.
First published in Japan in 2013 by KADOKAWA CORPORATION, Tokyo.
English translation rights reserved by Seven Seas Entertainment, LLC.
Under the license from KADOKAWA CORPORATION, Tokyo.

Seven Seas books may be purchased in bulk for educational, business, or
promotional use. For information on bulk purchases, please contact Macmillan
Corporate & Premium Sales Department at 1-800-221-7945 (ext 5442)
or write specialmarkets@macmillan.com.

Seven Seas and the Seven Seas logo are trademarks of
Seven Seas Entertainment, LLC. All rights reserved.

ISBN: 978-1-626921-14-6

Printed in Canada

First Printing: February 2015

10 9 8 7 6 5 4 3 2 1

FOLLOW US ONLINE: **www.gomanga.com**

READING DIRECTIONS

This book reads from *right to left*, Japanese style. If
this is your first time reading manga, you start
reading from the top right panel on each page and
take it from there. If you get lost, just follow the
numbered diagram here. It may seem backwards at
first, but you□ll get the hang of it! Have fun!!

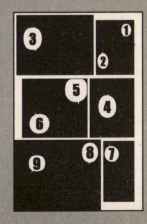